AF553955

Ravigupta's Āryākoṣa

Studia Indo-Buddhica 2

Ravigupta's Āryākoṣa

A Contribution to the Early History of Indian Nīti Literature

By
Michael Hahn

Edited by
Lata Mahesh Deokar
and
Johannes Schneider

Deshana, Pune
&
Aditya Prakashan, New Delhi

First published: 2019

ISBN 978-81-940850-6-5

Published by Deshana, Pune and Aditya Prakashan, 2/18 Ansari Road, New Delhi 110 002.

Email: contact@adityaprakashan.com
Website: www.adityaprakashan.com

Printed at Replika Press, Pvt. Ltd.

Preface

It is our pleasure to present an edition of Ravigupta's *Āryākoṣa*. Prof. Hahn started work on this text as early as 1981 but did not publish it since there were many problems that remained unsettled. This situation changed with the discovery of Ravigupta's other *nīti* text, the *Lokasaṃvyavahārapravṛtti*, wherein he found Sanskrit parallels of all but one verse of the *Āryākoṣa*. It seems that Hahn arrived at the decision to publish the text only after getting access to the Indian editions of the *Lokasaṃvyavahārapravṛtti* by N. Śāha (1986) and V. Śāstrī (2012).

In his last years he expressed on several occasions his intention to bring out Indian editions of all the texts he had edited. He wanted them to be accessible especially for his Indian colleagues. It was a rewarding task for us to fulfil his wish by publishing Jñānaśrīmitra's *Vṛttamālāstuti* in 2016 and now Ravigupta's *Āryākoṣa* in the Devanāgarī and Tibetan scripts, as he had desired.

The editors

Notes to the Reader

The Tibetan text of the *Āryākoṣa* (also known as *Gāthākoṣa*) is preserved in five editions of the *Bstan 'gyur*, section *Thun moṅ ba lugs kyi bstan bcos* or "The science of general prudent conduct in worldly affairs" (HAHN 2007: 303), as follows:

siglum	edition	volume and folios	
C	Co ne	ṅo	112b2–117b4
D	Sde dge	ṅo	116b5–122a3
G	Dga' ldan	go	245b8–253b2
N	Snar thaṅ	go	180b4–186b1
Q	Beijing	go	161a4–167b3

Michael Hahn had prepared a complete collation of all editions. We have tacitly corrected any minor inconsistencies of variant readings in his report.

With the help of Dragomir Dimitrov, Hahn had provided glossaries of the Sanskrit and the Tibetan texts. Because of space constraints in this volume, we have re-arranged them slightly. Whenever a Sanskrit word is rendered several times with identical Tibetan equivalents, we have brought the references together, whereas Hahn had chosen to keep them as separate items.

The Sanskrit versions of the *śloka*s are taken from Ravigupta's *Lokasaṃvyavahārapravṛtti* (LSP). Hahn had studied it on the basis of ŚĀHA's edition (1986), but finally published his own edition of the LSP in the Japanese journal *Minami Ajia Kotengaku* 2–3 (2007–08). We took this publication as the reference edition of the Sanskrit LSP. In these articles Hahn already discussed the readings of ŚĀHA. Hence we decided not to present rejected variants from the previous Śāha edition and instead to indicate all changes, corrections and new emendations against Hahn's "Japanese" edition.

For the convenience of our readers, we give in the Appendix those *śloka*s from the *Lokasaṃvyavahārapravṛtti* and elsewhere that are attributed to Ravigupta but were not included in the *Āryākoṣa*. However, textual criticism of these additional *śloka*s will not be detailed here for a second time and any readers interested in this matter should consult Hahn's Japanese edition.

When Hahn finalised his edition of the Āryākoṣa, his disease was already in its advanced stages. For that reason there were minor inaccuracies, such as spelling errors, typos etc., which he

When Hahn finalised his edition of the *Āryākoṣa*, his disease was already in its advanced stages. For that reason there were minor inaccuracies, such as spelling errors, typos etc., which he did not have the time to eliminate; we have corrected these with discretion. He was ultimately unable to prepare a bibliography and we therefore took it upon ourselves to collect the necessary bibliographical references. Based on the information given in Hahn's other publications we have further compiled a list of abbreviations.

Acknowledgements

We are grateful to Jamyang Dolma, Maheshwar Sing Negi, Narender Bodh, Thubten Gyaltsen, and Vijay Lata for checking the five Tanjur editions and Hahn's critical apparatusses so diligently.

Many thanks to our colleague Dragomir Dimitrov and Kishor Patil for sharing with us their new "Schlegel Nāgari" font.

Contents

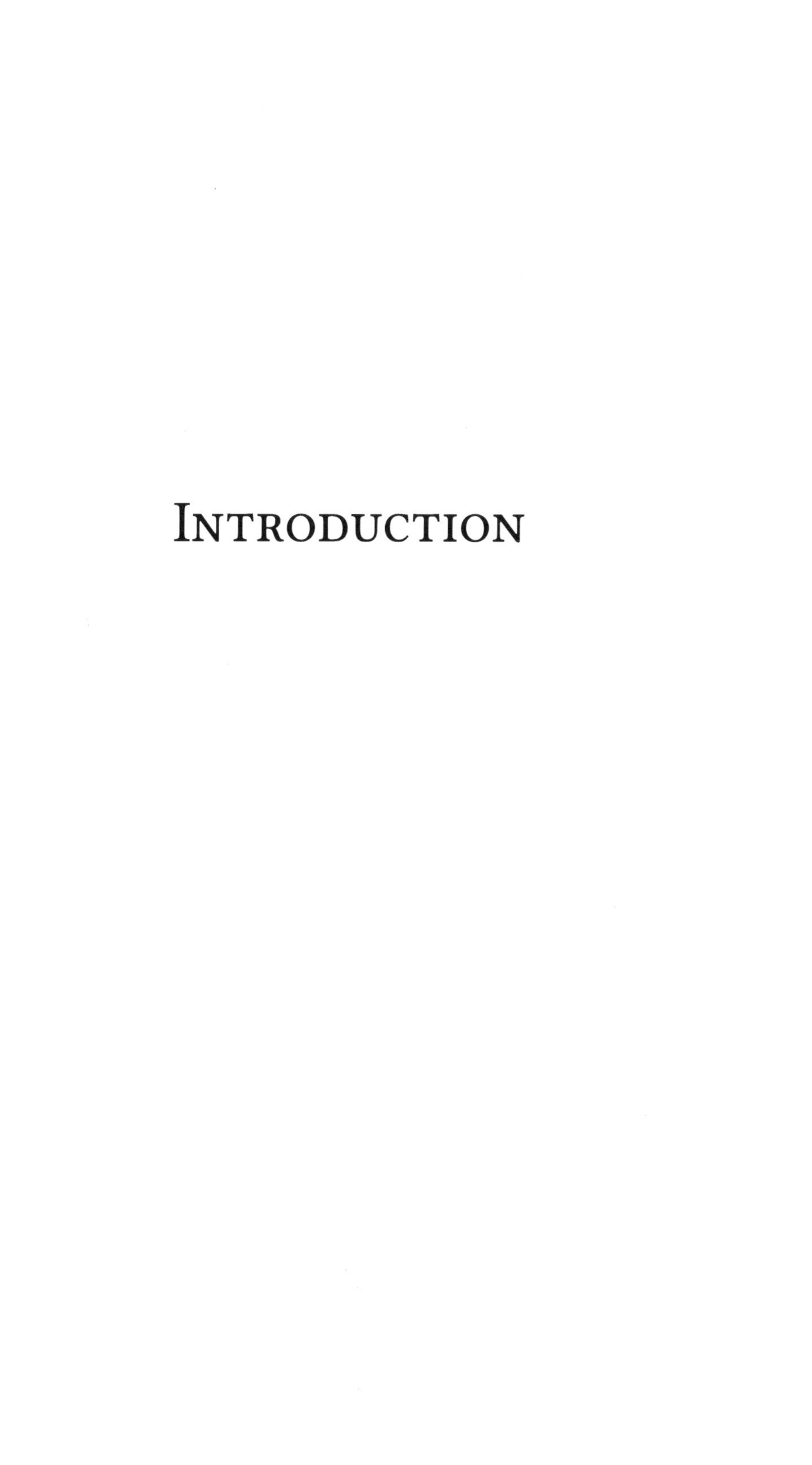

Introduction

1. The Indian *nīti* literature

Indian literature is particularly rich in verses on worldly wisdom. They can be found as stray verses in many literaturary genres, such as the great epics of India, later narrative works, plays, philosophical or scientific writings. From the days of Hāla onwards there exist also shorter and longer collections of stanzas. The best-known medieval anthologies are Vidyākara's *Subhāṣitaratnakoṣa*, Śrīdharadāsa's *Saduktikarṇāmṛta*, Jalhaṇa's *Sūktimuktāvalī*, Vallabhadeva's *Subhāṣitāvalī*, and Śārṅgadhara's *Paddhati*. In modern times, Otto BÖHTLINGK collected almost 8000 stanzas, which he published with precise locations, variant readings and German translations in the three volumes of his *Indische Sprüche* [*Indian Gnomic Sayings*] between 1870 and 1873. Here the stanzas are alphabetically arranged. The modern Indian anthology *Subhāṣitaratnabhāṇḍāgāra* counts more than 13,000 stanzas in its latest edition. As in the great medieval anthologies, the stanzas are arranged subject-wise. Unfortunately, the critical apparatus is very scarce and there are no translations. In 1974, the late Ludwik STERNBACH began to publish his magnificent *Mahāsubhāṣitasaṃgraha*. According to the original plan, this work will consist of 20 volumes and contain approximately 40,000 stanzas. The *Mahāsubhaṣitasaṃgraha* follows the model of BÖHTLINGK, however, it is much richer not only in the material it offers, but also in its extremely detailed documentation.

2. *Nīti* stanzas attributed to Ravigupta

Apart from his *opus magnum*, the *Mahāsubhāṣitasaṃgraha*, STERNBACH has benefitted lovers and students of Sanskrit literature by numerous other important books and papers. In one of them, entitled "Ravigupta and his gnomic verses" (*Annals of the Bhandarkar Oriental Research Institute*, 47/48, 1968, pp. 137–160) he has collected from various anthologies 69 stanzas that are attributed to a certain Ravigupta. The most striking feature of these stanzas is their metrical uniformity; all but seven are composed in the *āryā* metre. When I read this paper, I remembered that the Tibetan Tanjur, the huge collection of approximately 4,500 so-called commentarial writings on the word of the

Buddha translated from Indian languages, contains a small *nīti* work entitled *Āryākoṣa* and consisting of 145 stanzas. Among the verses collected by STERNBACH I could identify 35 which also occur in the *Āryākoṣa.* Later I found 8 more Sanskrit originals in other anthologies such as Sundarapāṇḍya's *Nītidviṣaṣṭikā.* Although I had prepared a new edition of the Tibetan text of the *Āryākoṣa* and the first draft of a translation in 1982, when I was a fellow of the then Reiyukai Library (now: International College for Advanced Buddhist Studies), Tokyo, I never dared to publish it because of the great number of unclear passages and obvious corruptions. However, in three papers, two in German (1984 and 1985) and one in English (1993), I gave a first description and assessment of this remarkable composition and the influence it has exercised on a very influential Tibetan work.

3. Ravigupta's *Lokasaṃvyavahārapravṛtti*

It was only in 1996 that through the good offices of the late Prof. Harivallabh BHAYANI (Ahmedabad) I received a copy of Prof. Nīlāṃjanā ŚĀHA's most valuable booklet *Ācārya-Ravigupta-viracita-Lokasaṃvyavahāra-pravṛttiḥ* (Ahmedabad 1986). Reading her edition was like a revelation for me because I immediately discovered 142 stanzas of the *Āryākoṣa* among the 268 stanzas of the *Lokasaṃvyavahārapravṛtti.* Since I had found one more stanza of the *Āryākoṣa* in another source, all but two of its verses are now available in their original shape. This enabled me to thoroughly revise and improve my edition of the Tibetan *Āryākoṣa*, whose critical edition, translation, linguistic and literary analysis had always been my main objective.

The discovery of the *Lokasaṃvyavahārapravṛtti* by Nīlāṃjanā ŚĀHA compelled me to modify my publication plans for the *Āryākoṣa.* In order to use and to refer to the new text and its content, it became imperative to make it generally accessible because Dr. ŚĀHA's booklet had been printed and circulated only privately and locally. Therefore, I decided to publish a slightly revised edition of the *Lokasaṃvyavahārapravṛtti* together with an English translation that could serve as a reference text. This edition appeared in two parts in a Japanese journal in 2007 and 2008: "Ravigupta and his Nīti Stanzas (I)", *Minami Ajia Kotengaku* (= *South Asian Classical Studies*) 2 (2007), pp. 303–

355, and "Ravigupta and his Nīti Stanzas (II)", *Minami Ajia Kotengaku* (= *South Asian Classical Studies*) 3 (2008), pp. 1–38. Due to many other commitments I could spend only a few weeks on this task and I was well aware that I could not solve all the textual problems of the work. In most cases I indicated my doubts or qualms by question marks or discussions in the footnotes.

Only two years ago, in 2012, a new and again improved edition of the Sanskrit text (together with a Hindi translation) has been published by Vijayapal Shastri: *Lokasaṃvyavahārapravṛttiḥ, Saṃskṛta mūlapātha va Hindī anuvāda*, Rāṣṭriyasaṃskṛtasaṃsthānam: Balāhara (Himācala Pradeśa) 2013 (Vedavyāsa-parisara Granthamālā 1).

4. The author of the *Lokasaṃvyavahārapravṛtti*

Very little can be said about the author of the *Lokasaṃvyavahārapravṛtti*. His name, Ravigupta, seems beyond doubt because it is attested in the manuscript itself, in the Tibetan translation (where it occurs as Ñi mas sbas pa, "protected by the sun"), and in several anthologies. As for Ravigupta's date, it is certain that he must have lived quite some time before 800 CE because the Tibetan translation was done around this time. Below I will argue that the *Āryākoṣa* is the younger work. Therefore, some time must have elapsed between the composition of the original work, the *Lokasaṃvyavahārapravṛtti*, its reduction to the *Āryākoṣa*, its migration to Tibet, and finally its translation into Tibetan.

There are two literary figures by the name of Ravigupta whose lifetime is not so far from this date. One is Ravigupta, author of the medical treatise *Siddhasāra*. R. E. Emmerick, the editor of the Sanskrit text and its Tibetan translation, places him around 650 CE, between Vāgbhaṭa and Mādhava. He also suggests that this Ravigupta "may have been the same as the Ravigupta who is said to have founded a cult of Tārā in Kashmir." The details about this Ravigupta can be found in the Tibetan doxographical work *Blue Annals*; pp. 1050–1051 in Roerich's English translation. The main problem is to establish a connection between the medical author and the composer of the *nīti* stanzas. There is one stanza (LSP 176 = ĀK 96) that might betray the author's familiarity with medicine:

अम्लमपि साधुवचनं दाहविबन्धघ्नमारनालमिव ।
शठवाक्यं तु बदरवन्मधुरमपि जनं विभेदयति ॥

The word of the good, even if it is acid,
destroys burning and constipation,
like vinegar made of rice.
The word of evil persons, however, even if it is sweet,
splits people, like the Badara fruit.

The other Ravigupta is the author of the *Pramāṇavārttikavṛtti*, a commentary on chapters II and III of Dharmakīrti's *Pramāṇavārttika*. This Ravigupta was a student of Prajñākaragupta (around 800 CE) and is said to have lived in the first half of the ninth century. This is actually a little too late, but not entirely impossible if the *Lokasaṃvyavahārapravṛtti* was one of his earliest works. The commentary has not yet been edited and studied, so that we do not know whether it contains anything that connects its author with the *nīti* work. Therefore the question must remain open.

5. The content of the *Lokasaṃvyavahārapravṛtti*

As for the content of *Lokasaṃvyavahārapravṛtti*, there are good reasons to assume that it is the work of an individual author and not an anthology, not even partly. The information given by the author himself is very scarce. The first stanza is a very general *namaskāra*, which discloses nothing about the author's religious affiliation. The second stanza is unfortunately heavily mutilated and not preserved in the Tibetan *Āryākoṣa*. From what is extant it does not seem to contain information about the nature and purpose of the work. The concluding section consists of four stanzas, 265–268, which are separated from the preceding section by the change of metre, *vaṃśastha*, *āryā*, *puṣpitāgrā*, and finally *mālinī*:

That speech which is not read by good people,
which is not followed, not considered,
and not recited in an assembly,

is regarded only a speech by name;
like the charm of poor people, it does not shine much.

'May it be that (at least) somebody
glances through this poetry
and then, having become familiar (with its content),
follows the path of the great!' Thinking this,
I have taken the trouble (to compose) this prate.

Therefore one should accumulate fame in this world,
in which the fire of manifold vices
has destroyed the seeds of goodness,
from which the sprouts of virtues come forth,
as long as the God of Death,
who is eager to devour the Three Worlds,
has not let fallen down his thunderbolt(-like club).

"Who has applied collyrium to the eyes of does?
Who makes the tails of peacocks so charming?
Who assembles, so attractively, the petals of lilies?
Who makes men of noble families possessed of modesty?"
(A. A. R. in MSS 11363)

In my opinion, stanzas 265 to 267 are very suitable for the conclusion of the work because they inform us about the author's motive to compose his poem. Moreover, they contain some general moral reflections. The last stanza, consisting of four rhetorical questions, is very strange and I would not be surprised if it could be shown to be the later addition of a scribe. The stanza can only be found in some modern anthologies (see STERNBACH, MSS 11363). I am even suspicious about stanza 265. The two concluding stanzas of the *Āryākoṣa* (144 and 145) are stanzas 266 and 267 of the *Lokasaṃvyavahārapravṛtti*. This makes more sense because they are sufficient for a conclusion and we would have only one change of metre, from *āryā* to *puṣpitāgrā*, which then clearly marks the final stanza.

The main part of the work is characterized by the dominating principle of *arthāntaranyāsa*. In most cases, the first half of the stanza contains a general statement, which is then illustrated in its second half by a concrete example taken from everybody's experience including well-known "facts" from mythology. The topics vary from stanza to stanza, only rarely two of them belong together, and there seems to be no deliberate principle of arrangement. The statements and observations follow each other like single "pearls or jewels on a chain"; cf. the many titles of anthologies ending in *°muktāvalī* or *°ratnamālā*. The most remarkable feature of the work is the simple, yet very elegant language and the charm of the clear ideas and illustrations expressed in its stanzas. This makes it one of the finest compositions of *nīti* verses, and the many quotations in the great anthologies bear ample testimony of how much Ravigupta's stanzas were appreciated by connoisseurs.

6. The relationship between the LSP and the ĀK

With the existence of both the *Āryākoṣa* and the *Lokasaṃvyavahārapravṛtti*, several questions with regard to their relationship automatically arise. Is the *Āryākoṣa* an extract of the longer work, or is the *Lokasaṃvyavahārapravṛtti* an amplification of the shorter work? Was the shortening or the expansion done by the author himself or by someone else? What could have been the reason for composing two so closely related works? For the time being only a provisional answer can be given. A comparison of the arrangement of stanzas in both works shows their close relationship. Three sets of LSP correspond to three sets of ĀK. LSP 1–66 contains ĀK 1–55 in exactly the same order, the only difference being the omission of 11 stanzas of LSP. The next section is LSP 67–92, where we find ĀK 33–43, again in the same order. The third section is LSP 93–267, where we find ĀK 56–145. This section contains two deviations from the order of verses in LSP: stanzas 233 and 234 occur as ĀK 123 and 122, and stanza 208 occurs as ĀK 142, thus interrupting the sequence of ĀK 105 (= LSP 206) and ĀK 106 (= LSP 213). This important change will be discussed below. Moreover, stanzas 93 and 94 of LSP became the single stanza 56 of ĀK by the omission of LSP 93cd and 94ab.[1]

1. As one can easily see, only the LSP version is meaningful. For this reason, it is more likely that this mistake goes back, not to the compiler of ĀK but rather to a copyist or even to the inner-Tibetan transmission of ĀK. Note that both stanzas of LSP illustrate the general statement of the first half by the spider's web in the latter half. This might have caused the error.

Viewed from the *Āryākoṣa*, it looks as if, after stanza ĀK 33, its compiler had jumped forward to a later section of LSP (stanzas 67–92), from which he culled the next 11 stanzas for the ĀK (ĀK 33–43). Thereafter, from LSP 93 onwards, the normal order was restored. Since this single deviation from the order of verses in LSP cannot be explained by the content of the verses, the reason might have been a mechanical one: most likely, one or two folios had been misplaced and this was overlooked by the compiler of ĀK. This explanation would work also the other way round: if the model had been the *Āryākoṣa*, which was later expanded to the *Lokasaṃvyavahārapravṛtti*, we have to assume that one folio of the *Āryākoṣa* had been misplaced. However, in both cases the compiler of the new work cannot have been Ravigupta himself, because he would inevitably have noticed the misplacement.

Consequently, we are left with a formal criterion, the language of both works. If the *Lokasaṃvyavahārapravṛtti* were an expansion of the shorter and if this had been done, not by Ravigupta, but by someone else, as suggested above, then one would necessarily expect a change in the quality and style of the stanzas. Since such a change cannot be observed in the *Lokasaṃvyavahārapravṛtti*, which is of a very uniform character, it is more likely that this was the original composition. There are two other points which seem to support this assumption. The first is the titles of the two works. *Lokasaṃvyavahārapravṛtti*, on the one hand, is a specific title that aptly characterizes the purpose and content of the work. *Āryākoṣa*, on the other hand, is a very general and featureless title, which discloses nothing about the content of the work and can be chosen for any collection of *āryā* stanzas. Again, it is more likely that the original author, whose talent can be seen in his work, chose the more specific title and that the anonymous redactor who prepared the extract from the larger work opted for a more general title. The second point is that there are the traces of editorial work in the *Āryākoṣa*. The *Lokasaṃvyavahārapravṛtti* shows no specific religious affiliation, except for some general Buddhist terms, e. g. *dāna* (181, 262), *kleśa* (207, 208), *anuśaya* (208), *prajñā* (208, 258), *samādhi* (208). However, none of them is used in an unambiguous Buddhist sense. The most noteworthy case is perhaps stanza 208, where we find four terms in one stanza:

प्रज्ञाग्नौ संतप्तः क्लेशानुशयोपलः समाधिजले ।
क्षिप्तो गतश्च शतधा सुधोपल इवाम्बुनिक्षिप्तः ॥

When the stone «propensity» (*anuśaya*)
towards «defilements» (*kleśa*)
has been heated in the fire «wisdom» (*prajñā*)
and is then thrown into the water «meditation» (*samādhi*),
it splits into a hundred pieces—
like a (heated) brick thrown into water.

The reason for this shift is, as we shall see below, that this stanza has been used for the concluding section of the *Āryākoṣa.*

In stanza 259, the «Victorious One» (*jina*) is mentioned. Again, it is not clear whether the Buddha, Mahāvīra, or only any sage teaching the way to liberation is meant. An interesting variation can be found in stanza 200, where the *Lokasaṃvyavahārapravṛtti* has the word *śākinī* "a kind of female demon attendant on Durgā," whereas the *Āryākoṣa* reads *ḍākinī* "a female imp attending Kālī (feeding on human flesh)." The *ḍākinī*s play a very important role in later Buddhist literature. This looks like a deliberate change rather than like a scribal error. The most important change, however, is the concluding section of the *Āryākoṣa*, stanzas 141–145. Important terms are marked in bold face.

दानादेव विभूतिं प्राप्य पुनर्यो ददाति नार्थिभ्यः ।
एष कृतघ्न इति न तं रुषेव भूयो भजन्त्यर्थाः ॥ १४१ ॥ LSP 262

If someone, having obtained wealth
only because of the **charity** (of others)
does not (readily) give to supplicants,
then material goods will never come to him again,
as if they were angry about his ingratitude.

།ཇི་སྲིད་དམ་པ་མི་བརྩོན་པ། །དེ་སྲིད་ཉེས་པ་སྟོབས་ལྡན་འགྱུར།
།བརྩོན་པས་ཉོན་མོངས་སྐྲར་མ་ལ། །བློ་ལྡན་སྐྲག་པར་མི་བྱ་སྟེ། ༡༤༢ །

As long as a good person does not show **energy**,
(his moral) **faults** will become stronger and stronger.
By (the application of) **energy** the wise one
should not be terrified with regard
to cowardly **defilements**.

प्रज्ञाग्नौ संतप्तः क्लेशानुशयोपलः समाधिजले ।
क्षिप्तो गतश्च शतधा सुधोपल इवाम्बुनिक्षिप्तः ॥ १४३ ॥ LSP 208

When the stone «propensity» (*anuśaya*)
towards «defilements» (*kleśa*)
has been heated in the fire «wisdom» (*prajñā*)
and is then thrown into the water «meditation» (*samādhi*),
it splits into a hundred pieces—
like a (heated) brick thrown into water.

།བདག་ཉིད་ཆེན་པོས་བསྟེན་པའི་ལམ། །གཞན་དག་གོམས་པར་བྱེད་པ་ཡིས།
།ཅི་ནས་འདི་ལ་དགའ་ལྟའི་ཕྱིར། །འདི་ནི་བསྒོམས་ནས་སྨྲས་པ་ཡིན། ༡༥༥ །

The path which is followed by the magnanimous ones
is also practised by others.
(I) have first reflected upon it and then spoken about it,
so that one may somehow rejoice in it.[2]

इति जगति विचित्रदोषवह्निदग्धशुभबीजगुणाङ्कुरप्रसूतौ ।
उपचिनुत यशांसि नैति यावत्त्रिभुवनघस्मरमृत्युवज्रपातः ॥ १४५ ॥ LSP 267

145. Therefore one should accumulate fame in this world,
in which the fire of manifold vices
has destroyed the seeds of goodness
from which the sprouts of virtues come forth,
as long as the God of Death,
who is eager to devour the Three Worlds,
lets not fall down his thunderbolt(-like club).

For a Buddhist reader there can be little doubt that these stanzas were composed by a Buddhist because they mention several key terms of Buddhist lay ethics. The allusion to the six moral perfections (*pāramitā*)—donation (*dāna*),

2. This stanza shows greater deviations from the corresponding LSP stanza 266. Therefore we present the Tibetan text.

morality (*śīla*), forbearance (*kṣānti*), energy (*vīrya*), meditation (*dhyāna*), and wisdom (*prajñā*)—is obvious. Therefore, it seems that an anonymous compiler took Ravigupta's *Lokasaṃvyavahārapravṛtti*, selected about half of its stanzas, and gave them a Buddhist varnish by adding a rather uniform concluding section. In order to achieve this, stanza 208 of LSP had to change its place to ĀK 143 and one more stanza (ĀK 142) was inserted before it. All this must have taken place before the beginning of the 9th century CE, when the now lost Sanskrit text of the *Āryākoṣa* was translated into Tibetan.

7. The *Āryākoṣa* and its influence upon Sa skya Paṇḍita's "Ocean of Well-Formulated Sayings"

As I have shown elsewhere, the Tibetan *Āryākoṣa* was taken as model when the great Tibetan scholar Kun dga' rgyal mtshan (1181–1252), also called Sa skya Paṇḍita "The great scholar of the Sa skya monastery," compiled his *Legs par bshad pa Rin po che'i gter* or *Subhāṣitaratnanidhi*, the "Ocean of well-formulated sayings." His work became extremely popular, not only in Tibet, but also in Mongolia, and has recently been translated into several modern languages. Sa skya Paṇḍita adopted the general structure of the work and at least 30 stanzas of his work are clearly influenced by stanzas from the *Āryākoṣa*. Sometimes Sa skya Paṇḍita adopted the general statement, sometimes the illustration, sometimes both. Here are three examples.

1) This is the original stanza, LSP 160:

> अतिकुपिता अपि सुजना योगेन मृदूभवन्ति न क्लीबाः ।
> हेम्नः कठिनस्यापि द्रवणोपायो ऽस्ति न तृणानाम्॥ १६० ॥

> Good persons, even if they are extremely angry,
> will become mellow by a suitable means,
> but not weak-minded and low persons.
> There is a means to melt even hard gold,
> but not (to melt) grass.

This is the Tibetan version of *Āryākoṣa* 87:

། སྐྱེ་བོ་དམ་པ་རབ་ཁྲོས་ཀྱང་། ། ཐབས་ཀྱིས་*མཉེན་འགྱུར་དམུ་རྒོད་མིན།
། ཆབ་རོམ་སྲ་ཡང་གཞུ་བ་ཡི། ། ཐབས་ཡོད་རྩྭ་འཇམ་མ་ཡིན་ནོ། ༨༧ །

A good person, even if he has become very angry,
will become mellow by a suitable means,
but not wild and unmanageable.
There is a means to melt even hard ice,
but not (to melt) soft grass.

This is *Subhāṣitaratnanidhi* 106:

། དམ་པ་ཁྲོས་ཀྱང་བཏུད་ན་ཞི། ། དམན་ལ་བཏུད་ན་ལྷག་པར་རེངས།
། གསེར་དངུལ་སྲ་ཡང་བཞུ་ནུས་ཀྱི། ། ཁྱི་ལུད་བཞུ་ན་དྲི་ངན་འབྱུང་།

Noble people, when angry, are mollified by apology,
But coarse people become even more obstinate.
Solid gold and silver can be melted,
But heating dog turds just creates a foul stench.[3]

2) This is the original stanza, LSP 70:

साधयति यत्प्रयोजनमज्ञस्तत्तस्य काकतालीयम् ।
दैवात्कथमप्यक्षरमुत्किरति घुणो ऽपि काष्ठेषु ॥ ७० ॥

When an ignorant person reaches his purpose,
this happens to him (only) coincidentally.
By chance even a woodworm
somehow carves a letter into wood.

This is the Tibetan version of *Āryākoṣa* 34:

། བླུན་*པོས་དོན་*སྒྲུབ་གང་ཡིན་པ། ། དེ་ནི་བྱ་རོག་ཏ་ལར་མཚུངས།
། སྲིན་བུས་ཤིན་དག་བྲོས་པའི་རྗེས། ། སྐྱེས་དབང་ཡི་གེར་འབྱུང་བ་བཞིན། ༣༤ །

3. The translations are quoted from *Ordinary Wisdom. Sakya Pandita's Treasury of Good Advice.* Trsl. by John T. Davenport. Boston: Wisdom Publications 2000.

When an aim has been reached by a fool,
then this is (due only to) coincidence—
like the trace gnawed into wood by an insect,
which by chance can assume the shape of a letter.

This is *Subhāṣitaratnanidhi* 61:

།བླུན་པོའི་བྱ་བ་ལེགས་གྲུབ་ཀྱང་། །སྐྱེས་དབང་ཡིན་གྱི་བསྒྲུབས་པས་མིན།
།སྲིན་བུའི་ཁ་ཆུ་དར་སྐུད་དུ། །འགྲོ་བ་མཁས་ནས་བྱུག་པ་མིན།

Although a fool may do something good
It's a lucky coincidence, not deliberate.
The silk thread from a silk worm's saliva
Does not come about through skill.

And this is another variation, *Subhāṣitaratnanidhi* 85:

།མ་དཔྱད་པ་ལས་དོན་གྲུབ་པ། །བྱུང་ཡང་མཛངས་པར་སུ་ཞིག་སྟེ།
།སྲིན་བུ་དག་གིས་ཟོས་པའི་རྗེས། །ཡི་གེར་བྱུང་ཡང་ཡིག་མཁན་མིན།

Things may be achieved without investigation,
But who would consider that a wise procedure?
Insects leave tracks that look like letters,
But they themselves are not literate.

3) This is the original stanza, LSP 136:

प्राप्तानपि न लभन्ते भोगान्भोक्तुं स्वकर्मभिः कृपणाः ।
मुखपाकः किल भवति द्राक्षापाके बलिभुजां हि ॥ १३६ ॥

Because of their own (former) deeds
misers cannot enjoy enjoyments,
even if they are at hand.
As it is known, the crows develop an abscess
on their beaks when the grapes are ripe.

This is the Tibetan text of *Āryākoṣa* 72:

།ལོངས་སྤྱོད་བདོག་ཀྱང་འཇུངས་པ་དག། །རང་གི་ལས་ཀྱིས་སྤྱོད་དབང་མེད།
།རྒྱུན་གྱི་འབྲས་བུ་སྨིན་པའི་ཚེ། །ཁྭ་ལ་མཆུ་ནད་འོང་ཞེས་གྲགས། ༧༢ །

Because of his own (former) deeds
the miser cannot freely relish enjoyments,
even if they are at hand.
It is said that the crows develop a disease of the beak
when the grapes are ripe.

Cf. *Subhāṣitaratnanidhi* 92:

།ལོངས་སྤྱོད་ཡོད་ཀྱང་ལས་ངན་གྱིས། །འཇུངས་*པ་སྤྱོད་པའི་རང་དབང་མེད།
།རྒྱུན་འབྲུམ་སྨིན་པ་ཟ་བའི་ཚེ། །ཁྭ་ལ་མཆུ་ནད་རྒྱུན་དུ་འབྱུང་།

Though greedy people may have wealth,
Their bad karma renders them powerless to enjoy it.
In the season when grapes are ripe for eating,
The didi bird's mouth is always sore.

By their direct and undeniable influence upon Sa skya Paṇḍita's "Ocean of well-formulated sayings," many of Ravigupta's stanzas have travelled as far as Tibet, Mongolia, Russia, Japan, the USA, and Europe, where they can now be read and enjoyed by many people.

8. The edition and restoration of the *Āryākoṣa*

The following critical edition and translation of the Tibetan *Āryākoṣa* and the restoration of its underlying Sanskrit text follows the model of my previous editions of Pseudo-Nāgārjuna's *Prajñādaṇḍa* or "Staff of Wisdom"[4] and

4. See Michael HAHN, "The Tibetan Shes rab sdong bu and its Indian Sources (I)," *Minami Ajia Kotengaku (= South Asian Classical Studies)* 4 (2009), pp. 1–78; "The Tibetan Shes rab sdong bu and its Indian Sources (II)," *Minami Ajia Kotengaku (= South Asian Classical Studies)* 5 (2010), pp. 1–50; "The Tibetan Shes rab sdong bu and its Indian Sources (III)," *Minami Ajia Kotengaku (= South Asian Classical Studies)* 6 (2011), pp. 1–71.

the *Gāthāśataka* attributed to a certain Vararuci.[5] The stanzas are presented individually. The Tibetan text is given first, because it is here regarded the primary text; it is followed by the Sanskrit text as extracted from the published *Lokasaṃvyavahārapravṛtti*. No Sanskrit manuscript of the *Āryākoṣa* is so far known to exist. The two texts are rendered into English and accompanied by detailed philological discussions. The wording of the Tibetan text is not the archetype of the five known editions of the Tibetan Tanjur, which would represent the state of the text at the beginning of the 14th century when the first edition of the Tanjur was compiled. Instead, an attempt is made at getting far behind it, i. e., as close as possible to what the two translators Jñānaśānti and Dpal gyi lhun po'i sde wrote. Our main guide is the wording of the stanzas in the *Lokasaṃvyavahārapravṛtti* and the tacit assumption that, apart from a few exceptions, this is what the translators had before them and what they tried to render into Tibetan. There are countless cases where the existing Sanskrit text allows a quick and safe decision about which of the variant readings is genuine. A single illustration might suffice here. These are the restored texts of ĀK 3 and LSP 4:

།འགྲོ་བ་མི་སྲུན་དུས་ཀུན་ཏུ། །སྐྱེ་བོའི་ཡོན་ཏན་*འཆར་བར་བྱེད།
།རིགས་བཟང་པོ་ཡི་རིན་ཆེན་དག། །ཀུར་བྱིན་ད་ཡིས་སྤ་བར་བྱེད། ༣ །

a *bsrun du* N, *srun du* GQ. **b** *'chub par* GQ, *'tshub par* N, *'chab par* CD. — **d** *kun gyi don du* CD [!]; *spa ba byed* CD.

At all times evil beings
make the (good) qualities of men shine ('rise').
Jewels of fine quality
are made brilliant by a ruby.

प्रायः खलसांनिध्ये याति विशेषो जनस्य साफल्यम् ।
कुरुविन्द एव रत्नं जातिविशुद्धं द्युतिं लभते ॥ ४ ॥

Mostly in the presence of an evil being
the (specific) quality of a man reaches fulfilment.

5. See Michael Hahn, "Vararuci's *Gāthāśataka*," *Minami Ajia Kotengaku* (= *South Asian Classical Studies*), vol. 7 (2012) pp. 367–458.

> Only in the presence of a ruby a jewel
> of the purest quality becomes brilliant.

While three of the Tibetan witnesses (GNQ) correctly represent the Sanskrit term *kuruvinda* "ruby" in Tibetan transliteration, the editors of the Derge Tanjur did not understand it and "Tibetanized" it by changing it into *kun gyi don du* "for the benefit of everybody", which produces a different meaning: "Jewels of fine quality create an ornament for the benefit of everybody." This is also meaningful, but it is not what the Sanskrit text says. As a consequence, the correct verb compound *spa bar byed* was changed into *spa ba byed* "make an ornament." The first half of the Tibetan stanza is more difficult to explain. At first sight it seems as if it was not properly understood or rendered extremely freely. For the verb at the end of the second line we have three variant readings: *'chub par* GQ, *'tshub par* N, *'chab par* CD. None of them corresponds to Sanskrit *yāti sāphalyam* "becomes fruitful, effective." *'chab pa* means "to hide, to conceal, to suppress," while *'chub pa* seems to be a mere carving error for *'tshub pa* "to toss about, to swirl, to entwine; to be choked, suffocated." I suspect that the Sanskrit expression was understood correctly and rendered, if somewhat freely, by **'char bar byed* "rises, appears in all its splendour." At a certain stage this became corrupted into *'chab par byed* (D), which was replaced by the synonym *'tshub par byed* in GNQ.

The example illustrates three things:

1. The readings of the available Tanjur editions cannot be taken at face value.

2. The range of variant readings is greater than in many other cases. At many places, the editors of the Tibetan text did not understand the text they had before them and tried to improve upon it by making bold changes.

3. Without the Sanskrit text there is no objective criterion for the selection of the correct, i. e. original, reading or for an emendation.

In my opinion the main reason for this situation is the unfortunate decision of the translators to render the original *āryā* stanzas by the Tibetan blank verse of four times seven syllables. The comparison of other *āryā* stanzas with their Tibetan renderings shows that this is too brief. As a rule, *āryā* stanzas are rendered by verses consisting of at least nine syllables per line.[6] As a consequence, the stanzas of the Tibetan *Āryākoṣa* became extremely terse and more than once some Sanskrit words had to be omitted. In combination with the use of rare words this made the translation obscure or even unintelligible at many places for a Tibetan reader. Therefore it is no surprise that in attempt to make the text meaningful, many changes were introduced in the course of its transmission from the ninth to the eighteenth century.

What is indeed surprising is the fact that another Sanskrit work, the *Praṇidhānasaptati* (attributed to Aśvaghoṣa, Āryaśūra, Mātṛceṭa, or *Parahitaghoṣa by various authors), which was also translated in collaboration with Dpal gyi lhun po'i sde is written in a completely lucid style that offers no difficulties at all. Maybe this is due to the influence of the Indian co-translator Dharmaśrīprabha.[7]

The main purpose of this publication is to present the Tibetan version of the *Āryākoṣa* in a restored form that is much closer to its original shape than the modern Tanjur editions. At the same time it restores the Sanskrit text, which was not published before in this form. Since all but two stanzas are now easily accessible in the three modern editions of the *Lokasaṃvyavahārapravṛtti*, the main focus is the Tibetan text and its reconstruction. It once again illustrates how much an original text could become altered and distorted in the course of its transmission and how cautious one has to be with the wording of the modern Tanjur editions. In addition to that, the relationship between the *Āryākoṣa* and Sa skya Paṇḍita's *Subhāṣitaratnanidhi* can be studied on a much safer basis. While the edition of the Tibetan text heavily relies on the availability of the *Lokasaṃvyavahārapravṛtti*, the Sanskrit text has also profited more than once from the Tibetan translation in those places

6. See, e. g., Michael HAHN, *Jñānaśrīmitras Vṛttamālāstuti. Ein Beispielsammlung zur altindischen Metrik.* Nach dem tibetischen Tanjur zusammen mit der mongolischen Version herausgegeben, übersetzt und erläutert. Wiesbaden 1971. (*Asiatische Forschungen.* 33.), pp. 53 and 75–79.

7. *Āryaśhūra's Aspiration, with Commentary by Gendun Gyatso, the 2nd Dalai Lama, and A Meditation on Compassion, from a Discourse by His Holiness the 14th Dalai Lama together with a Sādhana of Avalokiteśhvara with Original Tibetan Texts,* tr. and ed., Brian C. BERESFORD, L. T. Doboom TULKU, Gonsar TULKU, Sherpa TULKU, Library of Tibetan Works and Archives (Dharamsala 1979), and Christian LINDTNER, Mātṛceta's Praṇidhānasaptati, *Asiatische Studien,* vol. 38 (1984), pp. 100–128.

where the Sanskrit manuscript has a wrong or corrupted reading.

The two glossaries at the end of the book were prepared by my former student, now colleague, Dr. Dragomir Dimitrov while he was a research assistant at the Department of Indian and Tibetan Studies at the Philipps University Marburg.

Edition, Translation, Commentary

།།ཚིགས་སུ་བཅད་པའི་མཛོད་ཅེས་བྱ་བ་བཞུགས།། N180b4

།རྒྱ་གར་སྐད་དུ། ཨཱ་ཐཱ་ཀོ་ཥ་ནཱ་མ། C112b3 D116b5 G245b6 Q161a4

བོད་སྐད་དུ། ཚིགས་སུ་བཅད་པའི་མཛོད་ཅེས་བྱ་བ།

Pretitle in small letters, omitted by CDGN; *gā thā ko ṣa* CD; *tshigsu* N

།འཇམ་དཔལ་གཞོན་ནུར་གྱུར་པ་ལ་ཕྱག་འཚལ་ལོ།

—1—

།གང་ཞིག་རྣམ་པ་ཐམས་ཅད་དུ། །ཡོན་ཏན་ཀུན་ལྡན་སྐྱོན་སྤངས་ཤིང་།
།ས་ཀུན་སྐྱོང་བ་གང་ཡིན་*པ། །དེ་ལ་རྟག་ཏུ་ཕྱག་འཚལ་ལོ། ༡ ། G246a

c *sa gaṅ skyoṅ ba gaṅ lags pa'i* GNQ, *sa kun skyoṅ ba gaṅ yin la* CD

I always bow before him
who is the protector of the whole world,
endowed in every respect with all (kinds of) virtues
and free from (all) faults.

[सर्वत्र गुणैः सर्वैर्दोषैश्च य अन्वि]ता विमुक्ताश्च
पान्ति भुवनं समन्ताद्ये केऽपि नमः सदा तेभ्यः ॥ १ ॥ LSP 1

Homage to all those beings
whosoever protect the world,
endowed in every respect with all (kinds of) virtues
and free from (all) faults.

In line c) I have adopted the reading of CD although GNQ would also be possible if we understand *gaṅ* in the sense of "full, whole". Both the readings suffer from grammatical defects: CD repeat the dative particle *la*, whereas

GNQ have a genitive before the personal pronoun *de* which is unusual but not impossible. The latter phenomenon can be observed in the Tibetan translation of Haribhaṭṭa's *Jātakamālā*; cf. HAHN, *Lehrbuch*, p. *246. Perhaps one should simply emend *gaṅ yin la* as *gaṅ yin pa*.

—2—

།ཡོན་ཏན་སྐྱོན་དག་གློ་བུར་*འབབ། །འདི་ཉིད་འཇིག་རྟེན་གོམས་པ་སྟེ།
།ངང་གིས་བྱ་རྒོད་དུར་ཁྲོད་དང་། །ངང་པ་མཚོར་འབབ་ཇི་བཞིན་ནོ། ༢ །

a *mñam* CDGNQ **d** *dad pa* C; *bźino* N

'Virtues and vices occur accidentally'—
just this is the practice of the world.
In the same manner the vulture by its very nature
rushes down upon the cemetery
and the goose into the lake.

गुणदोषयोरकस्मात्पतति यथाभ्यासमेव लोकोऽयम् ।
निपतन्ति गृध्रहंसाः श्म[शानसरसोः प्रकृत्येव] ॥ २ ॥ LSP 3

It is only through habituation
that men unexpectedly turn to virtue or vice.
By their own nature vulture and geese
rush down upon cemeteries or lakes.

In the Tibetan translation the original position of *eva* and *ayam* is distorted in such a manner that the resulting sentence is to be construed differently. Moreover the predicate *patati* has been replaced by *mñam* "even" which is very difficult to account for. I suspect that *mñam* is a corruption of an original *'*bab* (cf. line d) or *'jug*; cf. *Subhāṣitaratnanidhi* 139:

།དམ་པ་དང་ནི་དམན་པ་ཡི། །སྤྱོད་པ་གཉིས་ཀ་གོམས་པའི་ཤུགས།
།བྱུང་བ་མི་རྟོག་ཚོལ་བ་དང་། །ངང་པ་ཆུར་འཇུག་བསླབ་མི་དགོས།

"The deportment of both the excellent and the base
(comes) by the power of practice.
The bee does not have to learn to seek the flower,
nor the goose to enter the water." (Bosson)

—3—

།འགྲོ་བ་མི་སྲུན་དུས་ཀུན་ཏུ། །སྐྱེ་བོའི་ཡོན་ཏན་འཆར་བར་བྱེད།
།རིགས་བཟང་པོ་ཡི་རིན་ཆེན་དག །ཀུར་བྱིན་ད་ཡིས་སྤ་བར་བྱེད། ༣ །

a *bsrun du* N, *srun du* GQ **b** *'chub par* G, *'tshub par* NQ, *'chab par* CD **d** *kun gyi don du* CD [!]; *spa ba byed* CD

At all times evil beings
make the (good) qualities of men shine ('rise').
Jewels of fine quality
are made brilliant by a ruby.

[प्रायः खलसान्निध्ये या]ति विशेषो जनस्य साफल्यम् ।
कुरुविन्द एव रत्नं जातिविशुद्धं द्युतिं लभते ॥ ३ ॥ LSP 4

[Mostly in the presence of an evil being]
the (specific) quality of a man reaches fulfilment.
Only in the presence of the *kuruvinda* ruby a jewel
of the purest quality becomes brilliant.

The predicate in line b) of the Tibetan version, *'chab par byed* "hides, conceals, suppresses", cannot be correct since is does not render the predicate of the corresponding Sanskrit: *[yā]ti … sāphalyam* "reaches fulfilment". The graphically easiest way to solve the problem is to emend *'chab par byed* as *'char bar byed* "makes rise".

As for the predicate of the second half of the Tibetan stanza the verb *spa ba(r) byed* is obviously but a variant (or cognate) of *spra ba* "to adorn, decorate". Cf. the entry *spa ba* in ZHD (pp. 1648b–1649a) where its meaning is given as *brgyan pa daṅ spras pa* and *mdzes pa daṅ byin chags pa. spa bar byed* is certainly a suitable rendering of *dyutiṃ labhate* "becomes resplendent, brilliant".

—4—

།*ཡོན་ཏན་*སྐྱོན་དང་འདྲེས་ན་ཡང་། །ཡོན་ཏན་ལྡན་པས་ཡོན་ཏན་བླང་།
།ཆུ་ལས་འོ་མ་འབྱེད་པ་ཡང་། །ངང་པ་ལས་གཞན་སུ་ཡིས་ཤེས། ༤ །

a *sems can* CDGNQ **c** *laṅ* N

Even if *virtues are mixed with vices,
the virtuous one should (always) take the virtues.
To separate the milk from water—
who else than the goose knows how to do it?

व्यामिश्रानपि दो[षैः ⏑⏑ ⏑⏑ ⏑⏑ ⏑⏑ ⏑ — ⏑ ⏑⏑ ⏑⏑ ⏑ |
क्षीरं विवेक्तुमु]दकात्कोऽन्यो जानाति हंसेभ्यः ॥ ४ ॥ LSP 5

Even if virtues are mixed up
[with vices (only) the virtuous ones are able
to take out the virtues.
To separate milk] from water—
who else than geese know how to do it?

Cf. *Subhāṣitaratnanidhi* 20:

།ཡོན་ཏན་སྐྱོན་གཉིས་སུས་ཀྱང་གསལ། །འདྲེས་པ་འབྱེད་ཤེས་མཁས་པ་ཡིན།
།ཆུ་ལས་འོ་མ་ངང་པས་ཕྱེད། །བ་ལས་འོ་མ་ཀུན་གྱིས་ལེན་ལོངས།

d *loṅs*: v. l. *len*

"Everyone is clear about (what is) virtue and misdeed,
but he who knows how to separate a mixture (of them)
is a wise man,
The goose separated milk from water;
anyone can get milk from a cow." (Bosson)

—5—

།མི་སྡུན་འགྲོ་ལ་འཚེ་བ་དང་། །སྐྱེས་མཆོག་ཕན་འདོགས་ངོམས་པ་མེད།
།ཉུན་པས་ས་སྟེངས་སྣང་བ་མིན། །ཉི་མས་རྟག་ཏུ་གསལ་བར་བྱེད། ༥ །

a *yaṅ* G **c** *steṅ* CD; *ba med* GNQ

While the evil one finds no end to do harm to others
the excellent one finds no end to help others.
While darkness darkens the earth
the sun always illuminates it.

[जगतो ऽपकृत्यु]पकृतौ खलसत्पुरुषौ न तृप्तिमायातः ।
ग्रसते हि तमो भुवनं सवितापि सदा प्रकाशयति ।। ५ ।। LSP 7

Evil beings and good beings—
in doing harm to others and helping them
they find no contentment.
For darkness devours the earth,
but the sun always illuminates it.

—6—

།མི་སྡུན་གཞན་ལ་གནད་གཅོད་*སྒོགས། །འཕན་མཁས་དེ་ནི་རིགས་མ་ཡིན། D117a N181a
།འདི་ལྟར་དུག་ནི་གནོད་ནུས་ཀྱི། །དེ་ནི་ཕན་པར་བྱེད་མི་ནུས། ༦ ། Q161b

a *gnad gcod tshig* CD, *gdams la sogs* GNQ **b** *'phen* GNQ; *rigs smra min* QCD **d** *der ni* GNQ

The skill an evil person has in hurting
the weak spots of others and similar things,
is not (the skill he has with regard to doing)
what is appropriate.
While poison can do harm in such a (high degree),
it cannot render help (in a similar degree).

परमर्मघट्टनादिषु खलस्य यत्कौशलं न तत्कृत्ये ।
यत्सामर्थ्यमुपहृतौ विषस्य तन्नोपकाराय ॥ ६ ॥ LSP 8

The skill which an evil person shows
with regard to hurting the weak points of others etc.
is not (shown) with regard to what is appropriate.
Poison has a much greater power to do harm than to help.

The original Tibetan translation seems to have suffered both from corruption and contamination of readings. In line a) CD have equivalents of *marman-* (*gnad*) and *ghaṭṭana-* (*gcod*), but not of *ādi-*. Its standard equivalent *la sogs* can be found only in GNQ. However, we may assume a development which began with **stsogs*, a more ancient rendering of *ādi-* which first changed to **tshogs* and later, under the influence of another corruption in line b) (*smra*) became *tshig* and then *tshigs*.

'phan mkhas seems to be a hitherto unattested equivalent of *kauśalam*.

de ni rigs ma yin (GN) is the metrical contraction of *de ni rigs pa la ma yin*. Because this was too brief to be understood even for a Tibetan it first became *rigs smra yin* in D and later *rigs smra min* in the futile attempt to establish an meaningful text.

—7—

།སྐྱེ་བོ་དམ་པ་རབ་བསྒྲིམས་ཏེ། །གཞན་གྱི་སྐྱོན་*སྡུད་སྨད་རིགས་མཚུངས།
།འོན་ཀྱང་འདི་གཉིས་ཁྱད་ཡོད་དེ། །སྐྱེས་མཆོག་སྦེད་ཀྱི་སྨད་རིགས་སྒྲ། ༧ །

b *sbed* CDGNQ; *dmaṅs rigs* GNQ **d** *sbed skye* GNQ, *sbad kyi* C; *dmaṅs rigs* NQ

In *collecting (or: hiding) with great zeal
the faults of others
noble beings are similar to mean beings.
However, there is a difference between the two:
while noble beings hide them, mean beings disclose them.

आगमयत्यतियत्नात्परदोषान्सज्जनो ऽपि नीच इव ।
किं तु विशेषणामनयोः पातुं सुजनः खलो वक्तुम् ॥ ७ ॥ LSP 9

Just like a mean being a good person
ascertains the faults of others with utmost zeal.
However, there is a difference between the two of them:
the good person (does it) with the aim of hiding (them),
the mean person with the aim of disclosing (them).

In line b) all the four blockprints have *sbed* "hides, conceals" as the equivalent of *āgamayati* "ascertains". I suspect that this is the corruption of an original *sdud* "collects" which was altered under the influence of *sbed kyi* in line d).

The stanza is also quoted in Prajñāvarman's *Udānavargavivaraṇa.* It can be found in Balk's edition on p. 735.23–26. In line b) CDQ read: *gźan gyi skyon sbed smad rim bźin,* not confirming our emendation **sdud. smad rim bźin,* a good alternative translation of *nīca iva* confirms at least *smad* the reading of CD. In line c) Q read *'di ñid,* CD *'di gñis.* Again the text of CD is confirmed. Line d) has the following wording: *dam pa sruṅ gi smad rim smra. skycs mchog* looks like a more literal (hence original) translation of *sujanaḥ* than *dam pa* which is, of course, also correct. *sruṅ gi* might be a deliberate variation of expression because *sbed* occurs already in line b). This again points to the work of a redactor. *smad rim* confirms the text of CD for *smad.*

Stanza No. 68 of Sternbach's list which is also attributed to Ravigupta has a somewhat similar content:

स्वगुणानिव परदोषान्वक्तुं न सतो ऽपि शक्नुवन्ति बुधाः ।
स्वगुणानिव परदोषानसतो ऽपि खलास्तु कथयन्ति ॥

References: JS 59.22 attributed to Ravigupta; VS 410 attributed (?) to Ravigupta; SR 58.184 attributed to VS, SSR 321.191; Āryā metre, no variants.

"The wise ones are able to tell neither their own virtues
nor the faults of others, even if they exist (beyond doubt).
The evil ones, however, speak of their own virtues
and of the faults of others, even if they do not exist.

—8—

།གཡོ་སྒྱུད་སྐྱེ་བོས་རབ་གཙེས་ན། །ལྷག་པར་དེས་པ་དྲན་པར་འགྱུར།
།འཇིག་རྟེན་ཉི་མས་རབ་གདུངས་ན། །ལྷག་པར་ཟླ་བ་མངོན་པར་འདོད། ༨ །

b *ṅes pa* N

When one is heavily tormented by cunning people
one remembers even more those
who are friendly and polite.
When people are heavily tormented
by (the heat of) the sun
they long even more for the (coolness of the) moon.

शठचरितैरेव जनैर्भृशमुपतप्ताः स्मरन्ति साधूनाम् ।
अभिलषति शशाङ्कमधिकं [!] दिनकरतापितो लोकः ॥ ८ ॥ LSP 10

a *janair*: *janā* H

They who are heavily tormented by people
whose conduct is mean remember the good ones.
People who are tormented by the (heat of the) sun
long even more for the moon.

—9—

།ངན་པ་ཕ་རོལ་འབྱེད་བརྩོན་ལྟར། །སྐྱེ་བོ་དམ་པ་སྡུམ་དེ་བཞིན།
།ཁབ་ཀྱིས་རིམ་གྱིས་ཕུག་པ་ཡི། །བུ་ག་སྐུད་པས་དགོད་པར་བྱེད། ༩ །

b *sdums* GNQ **c** *rims kyis* GNQ **d** *dgoṅ* Q, *dgog* CD

In the same way as the evil one attempts to divide others
the noble one (attempts to) unite (them).
A hole which has gradually been pierced by a needle
is sewn together by a thread.

उद्युक्तः परभेदे यथा खलः सज्जनस्तथा संधौ ।
छिद्रं करोति सूची सपदि पिधत्ते तदनु तन्तुः ॥ ९ ॥ LSP 11

In the same way as the evil one is intent on dividing others
the good person (is intent) on uniting (them).
The needle makes a hole
and immediately thereafter the thread sews it together.

A stanza with a very similar content can be found in IS² 3480:

अनुकुरुतः खलसुजनावग्रिमपाश्चात्यभागयोः सूच्याः ।
विदधाति रन्ध्रमेको गुणवानन्यस्त्वपिदधाति ॥

Variant readings: **a** *khalu* i. o. *khala* **b** *āgrima, pāścātyabhāgo yo sūcyāḥ, sūnyāḥ* i. o. *sūcyāḥ* **d** *tvadhāhati; ekaḥ kurute chidram anyaś ca pidadhāti*

References: Cf. MSS 1425

"Der Bösewicht und der Gute machen es wie die Spitze und das Oehr einer Nadel; der Eine macht das Loch, der Andere aber, der Tugendhafte (mit einem Faden Versehene), schließt es."
(BÖHTLINGK).

—10—

།ཕ་རོལ་གཙེས་མཐོང་ངན་པ་དག །དགའ་བར་འགྱུར་གྱི་སྟོད་རིགས་མིན།
།ལྕགས་ལས་བྱས་པའི་མཚོན་ཆ་དག །ཕལ་ཆེར་གཡུལ་ངོར་སྤ་བ་བཞིན། ༡༠ ། C113a

a *brtses* GNQ **b** *bstod rim* GNQ **d** *spyod pa* CD, *dpa' ba bźin* CDGNQ; *dpa' ba* < **spa ba* = *sphur*, cf. ĀKtib 3d

On seeing that somebody is tormented by others
only the mean one rejoices, not the noble one.
In a battle generally (only) those weapons shine
which are made of iron.

दृष्ट्वा परस्य पीडां प्रीतः खल एव भवति न कुलीनः ।
प्रायः स्फुरन्ति समरे लोहमयान्येव शस्त्राणि ॥ १० ॥ LSP 13

Seeing somebody else's pain
only the mean one is pleased, not the noble one.
In a battle generally only those weapons shine
which are made of iron.

Stanza No. 6 of Sternbach's list has a somewhat similar content:

अप्यात्मनो विनाशं गणयति न खलः परव्यसनहृष्टः ।
प्रायः सहस्रनाशे समरमुखे नृत्यति कबन्धः ॥

Variants: **a** *naivātmano* ŚP, SR, SSR **b** *na gaṇayati* SRh, *piśunaḥ* (for *khalaḥ*), SP, SR, SSR **c** *prāyo mastakanāśe* Pts, PtsK, SRK, *prāpya sahasravināśaṃ* SP, SR, SSR **d** *samare nṛtyati* (*nṛtyati mudā* SR; contra metrum / *kabandha iva (°ndhaś ca)* ŚP, SR, SSR: *naṭati* PtsK (wrong, contra metrum)

References: JS 59,21 attributed to Ravigupta; SRh 44.54 attributed to Caphaladeva. Also Pts 1.395, PtsK 1.443, SR 56.115 attributed to Pañcatantra (1.443), SSR 318.317, ŚP 374 (SR, SSR follows ŚP and not P), SRK 24.23 (follows P), IS[2] 456 Āryā metre.

"A wicked person gloating over the misfortunes of others
minds not his own destruction (downfall).
Generally in the thick of battle the headless trunk dances
though it has its head cut off." (A. A. R. ad MSS 2139)

With the reading *sahasranāśe* one would have to translate:

"Generally in the thick of a battle which causes the death of thousands,
the Kabandha dances."

Cf. also *Upadeśaśataka* 2b:

"A Kabandha che continuava a vivere
pur essendo stato privato della testa
da un colpo di fulmine Indra fornì una bocca
in [mezzo al] petto perchè potesse mangiare:
chi si trova nei gnaì va aiutato,
anche [se si tratta di] un nemico." [Oscar Botto in JRSO 27]

For the first half of the stanza STERNBACH (No. 14) reports the following variant:

आस्वाप्यात्मविनाशं गणयति न खलः परस्य संकष्टम् ।

References: VS 412 attributed (?) to Ravigupta. Āryā metre. Not found in other sources. No variants.

—11—

།སྐྱེ་བོ་ངན་པས་སྨད་པར་ཤེས། །སྐྱེ་བོ་དམ་པས་ལེགས་བསྔགས་ཤེས།
།དགུན་གྱི་དུས་ནི་སྐེམས་པར་བྱེད། །དཔྱིད་ཉིད་ནགས་ཚལ་ཁ་ཡང་འབུ། ༡༡ །

a *pa śes* GNQ **c** *rgun* GNQ; *dus na skam* CD; *skyems* GNQ **d** *spyid ñid* GNQ

(While) a bad person knows (how) to criticize,
a good person knows (how) to praise in a proper manner.
(While) winter dries (it) up
spring makes the forest blossom again.

निन्दितुमेव खलजनः साधूञ्जानाति सज्जनः स्तोतुम् ।
शोषयति शिशिरसमयः कुसुमयति वसन्त एव वनम् ॥ ११ ॥ LSP 14

(While) a bad person is an expert only in criticizing the good
a good person (is an expert) in praising (others).
(While) the cool season dries the forest up
it is spring that makes (it) blossom.

—12—

།གནོད་དང་ལྷག་པར་གདུག་པ་ཡང་། །འཚེ་ཁེངས་རྩུབ་པའི་རང་བཞིན་གྱི།
།དུས་ན་བདག་ཉིད་ཆེན་པོ་བས། །སྒྲི་རྫོལ་ཅན་དག་ཕལ་ཆེར་བཀུར། ༡༢ །

a *snod dag* CD; *sdug pa* CD **d** *rdol* Q

At certain times those impudent beings
who are harmful, extremely poisonous
and whose nature is mischievous, stubborn and harsh
are honoured even more than noble-hearted beings.

उपघातिनोऽतितीक्ष्णाः हिंस्रतया स्तब्धदारुणाकृतयः ।
प्रायः कलौ महत्स्वपि निस्त्रिंशा एव युज्यन्ते ॥ १२ ॥ LSP 15

It is a general rule that in the Kali age
even among the great [persons]
only [those] swords (or: cruel people) are used
which (or: who) are suited to kill,
which (or: who) are extremely sharp,
and whose form is, on account of its quality to kill,
unbendable and hard.

In the Tibetan translation the subject of the sentence, *nistriṃśa-*, is rendered only as "merciless, cruel" whereby the intended pun which is caused by its second (and more common) meaning "sword" is lost.

bkur "are honoured" obviously translates **pūjyante* i. o. *yujyante*. This meaning also suits the context. As both forms resemble each other paleographically it is impossible to decide whether the Sanskrit manuscript used by the translators did indeed contain such a variant reading or whether is was simply misread.

dus na "at (certain) times" seems to be a gross mistake: *kalau* "in the Kali age" is obviously confused with *kāle*! The position of *dus na* (between a genitive attribute and the noun it refers to) is also remarkable if we look at the Tibetan version only, but can be explained by the word order of the Sanskrit original.

—13—

།དམ་པ་སྡིག་པ་ཆུང་ཡང་སྦྱོང་། །ངན་པ་རྣམས་ནི་ཆེ་ཡང་མིན།
།མིག་ནི་རྡུལ་ཡང་འཇོམ་པར་བྱེད། །ལག་པ་མི་ལྷེར་རེག་པར་བྱེད། ༡༣ །

c *rdul la* GNQ **d** *mig rtsar* GNQ

A good person avoids even a small misdeed,
a bad person not even a big one.
The eye shirks even a particle of dust,
The hand touches (even) a flame.

उत्सृजत्यण्वपि पापं साधुरसाधुस्तु नो महीयो ऽपि ।
स्पृशति करोऽग्निशिखामपि नयनं तु रजो ऽपि न क्षमते ।। १३ ।। LSP 16

A good person avoids even a small misdeed,
a bad person not even big ones.
The eye does not stand even a particle of dust,
while the hand touches even a flame.

—14—

།སྨད་རིགས་གོ་འཕང་བསྟོད་བྲགས་དང་། །གཞུང་ངན་ཕན་བཏགས་མི་སེམས་ཏེ།
།གྱེན་དུ་མི་གཙང་རྫས་གཏོར་ན། །ཐོག་མར་མགོ་ལ་འབབ་པར་འགྱུར། ༡༤ །

a *dmaṅs rigs mgo* GNQ; *grags* GNQ **c** *zas* CD **d** *thog mar raṅ gi mgo la 'bab* GNQ

Even if a low person has been raised
into a very high position
out of his mean character he does not remember
the favours (extended to him).
When one casts impure matters into the air
they will first fall down on one's (own) head.

अतिसत्कारैरग्रं गमितो न हिताय कल्पते नीचः ।
मलिनयति शिरः केवलमशुचिरजो दूरमुत्क्षिप्तम् ।। १४ ।। LSP 18

a *agraṃ*: *agatiṃ* H

A low person will not become beneficial
even when he has been brought to ...

by excessive well-treatment.
Dirty dust that has been thrown away far
will invariably make one's head dirty.

bstod drags "excessively praised; excessively raised". *drags* renders *ati-*; cf. LC[2] p. 924b.

gźuṅ ṅan usually renders *durjana-* or *daurjanya-*, cf. LC[2] p. 1621a. Here it seems to be an addition.

The edition of Śāha reads *agatiṃ* which makes no sense to me. What we expect here is the equivalent of *go 'phaṅ bstod.*

Sa skya Paṇḍita has twice used this stanza for his own collection. In *Subhāṣitaratnanidhi* 208 only the general idea can be found:

།རྒྱལ་པོས་གོ་འཕང་བསྟོད་དྲགས་ན། །དེ་ཡི་ཐ་མར་བརླག་པའི་རྒྱུ།
།སྒོ་ང་མཁའ་ལ་འཕངས་གྱུར་ན། །འཆག་པ་ཉིད་ལས་གཞན་ཅི་འབྱུང་།

"If somebody has been promoted by the king
in too high a position,
it will in the end cause that man's destruction.
If an egg is thrown up into the air,
what happens but that it breaks?"

(Bosson, slightly modified; I have chosen the variant reading *drags* i. o. *grags*, in accordance with *Āryākoṣa* 14.)

The first line in its wording clearly points to *Āryākoṣa* 14 as the model. Sa skya Paṇḍita has only replaced the simile by a related one. In *Subhāṣitaratnanidhi* 393 the agreement is much greater:

།དམན་པའི་སྐྱེ་བོ་བསྟོད་དྲགས་ན། །ཕྱི་ནས་དེ་ཉིད་ཁྱད་དུ་གསོད།
།མཁའ་ལ་མི་གཙང་གཏོར་གྱུར་ན། །འཐོར་བ་པོ་ཡི་སྤྱི་བོར་འབབ།

"If a low person has been promoted in too high a rank,
in the future (he) will despise the very person
(who has promoted him).
If dirt is thrown skywards,
it will fall on the head of the thrower."

(As above, I have slightly modified BOSSON's text and translation.)

Āryākoṣa 82 repeats the same idea in a slightly varied diction. The underlying idea can already be found in the oldest layer of the Indian Buddhist literature; cf., e. g., *Udānavarga* 28.9 which has parallels in *Dhammapada* 125, *Saṃyuttanikāya* I, p. 13, 164, *Suttanipāta* 662 and *Jātaka* III, p. 203 (367.5):

यो ह्यप्रदुष्टस्यानरस्य दुष्यते शुद्धस्य नित्यं विगताङ्गणस्य ।
तमेव बालं प्रतियाति पापं क्षिप्तं रजः प्रतिवातं यथैव ॥

—15—

།རིགས་ཤིང་འོས་པའི་འགྲོ་བ་ལ། །དཔྱད་ཐག་བཅད་པ་འབྱུང་འགྱུར་གྱི།
།ཐང་སྐྱེད་བཟང་པོ་མ་ཡིན་ཏེ། །མི་སྲུན་པ་ཡི་སྐྲ་སེན་བཞིན། ༡༥ །

a *ris śiṅ 'os par 'gro ba las* GNQ; *'gron po la* CD **b** *dpyad thad dpyad pa* GNQ, *dpyad thag bced (?) pa* C, *dpyaṅ thag bcad pa* D **c** *bskyed* GNQ **d** *bsrun* GNQ; *dgra* GNQ

While by suitable and adequate reasoning
about the world certainty will arise,
it is not good to produce something (too) excessive,
like hairs and nails of the enemies.

युक्त्या जनयति जगतः कल्पनमनुरूपमेव परभागम् ।
अतिवृद्धिस्तु न राजति केशनखानामिव खलानाम् ॥ १५ ॥ LSP 20

Only when men create something in a reasonable
and appropriate manner
then this will produce an excellent (result).
Excessive growth, however, does not shine,
neither in the case of hair and nails
nor in the case of rogues.

The Tibetan text with its numerous variants is extremely difficult to understand. If, however, we accept the basic presupposition that it reflects an attempt to understand and translate the Sanskrit text quoted above then it becomes possible to determine the Sanskrit equivalents of the Tibetan text: *rigs śiṅ* ~ *yuktyā*, *'os pa'i* ~ *anurūpam*, *'gro ba la* ~ *jagataḥ*, *dpyad* ~ *kalpanam*, *thag bcad pa* ~ *parabhāgam*, *gyi tu*, *thaṅ skyed* ~ *ativṛddhis*, *bzaṅ po ma yin te* ~ *na rājati*, *mi bsrun pa yi* ~ *khalānām*, *skra sen* ~ *keśanakhānām*, *bźin* ~ *iva*. Apart from the whole construction only two pairs are really difficult: *thag bcad pa* ~ *parabhāgam*, and *thaṅ skyed* ~ *ativṛddhis*. In the first case one could establish a relationship by the equivalents *niyata-* or *niyama-* which are given for *thag bcad pa* by LC (p. 1014b, < SCD!). That which is "determined" or "firmly established" (*nītārtha-*) is the absolute truth, *paramārtha-*. It seems as if *parabhāgam* was understood in this sense.

thaṅ (b)skyed seems to go back to the adjective *thaṅ po* "enduring, able to stand fatigue; able and hardy, strong, tense; tight, firm". Without claiming to fully understand the intentions of the translators my own rendering of the Tibetan aims at reconciling it as much as possible with the Sanskrit text.

—16—

།མཆོག་ལས་མཆོག་དག་སྐྱེ་བ་དང་། ། ངན་ལས་ངན་སྐྱེ་དེ་རིགས་ཏེ།
།ཕུག་ལ་*མུན་པ་བརྟེན་པ་དང་། ། ཐང་ལ་ཟླ་ཟེར་འབབ་པར་བྱེད། ༡༦ །

a *skya* (< *skye*?) *ba* C, *bskyed* DGNQ **b** *dman las dman skyed* CD **c** *phug las* GNQ, *brten nas mun pa* CDGNQ

Excellence is produced from excellence,
inferiority from inferiority—this is appropriate.
Adhering on caves darkness (occurs),
while the rays of the moon fall down
upon the (open) plane.

उच्चैरुदात्तमुदयति नीचैरनुदात्तमित्युचितमेतत् ।
ज्योत्स्ना स्थलीषु निपतति विवराणि तमः समाश्रयते ।। १६ ।। LSP 21

What is (already) high produces highness,

what is low lowness—this is customary.
The splendour (of the moon) falls down
upon the (open) plane,
while darkness adheres to vacuities.

Apart from the strange position of *brten nas* before *mun pa* the Tibetan translation correctly renders the Sanskrit original.

As already hinted at by Nīlāṃjanā Śāha the first half of the stanza alludes to Pāṇini 1.2.29 and 30: *uccair udāttaḥ* "(The terminus technicus) *udātta* 'high-pitched' denotes [a vowel] with rising tone (*uccaiḥ*)" and *nīcair anudāttaḥ* "(The terminus technicus) *anudātta* 'low-pitched' denotes [a vowel] with falling tone (*nīcaiḥ*)."

—17—

།ངན་པ་ཇི་ལྟར་འཕང་མཐོ་ཡང་། །རིགས་ལྡན་རྒུད་པས་ཟིལ་གྱིས་གནོན། Q162a
།རིགས་ལྡན་ནོར་བུ་ཉམས་མདུན་དུ། །བཅོས་མའི་ནོར་བུས་གཟི་མི་འབྱིན། ༡༧ །

a *mthos kyaṅ* GNQ **b** *non gnon* C **c** *bdun du* CN **d** *bcos pa'i nor bu* GNQ; *mi phyin* GNQ; *ma byin* CD

However high the position of a bad person may be—
a noble-born one, (even) if he is in trouble, will defeat him.
In the presence of a jewel of good quality,
(even) if it is damaged,
an artificial (semi-precious) stone will not shine.

अत्युच्छ्रितानपि खलानभिभवति कुलोच्छ्रितः शतहतो ऽपि ।
न विज्ञातयश्चकास्ति सुरुचो ऽपि पुरोऽभिज्ञातमणेः ।। १७ ।। LSP 22

A person of noble descent,
even if defeated a hundred times,
surpasses mean persons,
even if raised to the highest ranks.

Jewels lacking genuine quality,
even if they shine brightly,
do not shine in the presence of a jewel of fine quality.

In the Tibetan translation *suruco 'pi* was wrongly taken as attribute of *abhijātamaṇeḥ*, not of *vijātayaḥ*. This possibly led to the strange interpretation as *ñams* with the omission of *api*.

—18—

།ཡོན་ཏན་ལྡན་པའི་གྲགས་པ་དག །ཕྱོགས་བཅུར་གྲགས་པས་དགྲ་གྲགས་འཚུབ།
།གཡའ་དང་ལྡན་པའི་མེ་ལོང་*ན། །གཟུགས་བརྙན་འབྱུང་ལ་དགའ་བ་མེད། ༡༨ ། N181b

b *grags pa dgra yi 'tshub* G, *grags pa dgra yi 'tshug* N, *grags pa dgra yis 'tshub* Q, *grags pas sgra sgrags tshul* CD **c** *loṅ gis* CD, *loṅ ni* GNQ **d** *'byuṅ bar dgra bo med* GNQ, *byuṅ bar dgra bo med* CD

The fame of a virtuous one, spreading in the ten directions
of the compass, suppresses the fame of the enemy.
The mirror image reflected in a rusty mirror
is not pleasant.

गुणावत एव दश दिशः स्फुरति यशो रिपुयशांसि रुन्धानम् ।
न विरूपस्यादर्शे प्रतिबिम्बमुदेति रमणीयम् ।। १८ ।। LSP 23

The fame of a virtuous one radiates into the ten directions
of the compass and suppresses the fame of (his) enemy.
The mirror image of an ugly person
will never look pleasant (in a mirror).

g.ya' daṅ ldan pa'i "covered with rust" is an unsuitable translation of *virūpasya*. Moreover it is difficult to realize that this was meant as the genitive attribute of *gzugs brñan*, Skr. *pratibimbam*. Did the translators read (or emend) **virūpe hy ādarśe*, with **virūpe śyāmike*? Or did the original translation contain a correct translation of *virūpasya*, e.g. *byad gzugs ṅan pa'i or cha byad ṅan pa'i*?

—19—

།ཉི་མ་རྒྱ་མཚོར་ནུབ་པ་དང་། །ཟླ་བ་བྲི་ཡང་གཞན་མི་འགྱུར།
།ཡོན་ཏན་ལྡན་པ་རྒུད་གྱུར་ཀྱང་། །ནམ་དུའང་ཆེ་བ་ཉིད་མི་ཉམས། ༡༩ ། D117b

d *nam yaṅ* GNQ

Even when the sun has set in the ocean
and even when the moon has waned—
neither of them has altered.
A virtuous one, even when in distress,
will never loose his greatness.

सलिलनिधेरपसृतयः पूष्णोऽस्तमितिः क्षयः शशाङ्कस्य ।
विनिपाताश्च गुणवतां न जातु वृद्धिं व्यभिचरन्ति ।। १९ ।। LSP 24

When the ocean retreats, when the sun sets,
when the moon disappears
and when the virtuous ones fall down,
they do not do any harm
to their (former and future) growth.

The Tibetan translators have treated both the content and construction of the stanza rather freely (*apasṛtayaḥ* is entirely omitted), however without spoiling its general idea.

—20—

།ཚེ་དང་ལང་ཚོ་དག་དང་ནི། །མེ་ལྕེ་རྩེ་དང་ཆུ་རྒྱུན་ནི།
།འདས་པའི་ཕྱིར་ན་ཕྱིར་ལྡོག་མེད། །མི་སྲུན་གོ་འཕང་དེ་བཞིན་ནོ། ༢༠ །

b *lce'i* CD; *rgyun gyi* CD, *rgyun mi* GNQ **c** *'das pa phyir ni ldog pa med* CD; read *phyin chad* instead of *phyir na*? **d** *sruṅ* GQ; *bźino* N

One's life, one's youth, the tip of a flame,
and a torrent of water—
when they have disappeared, they will not return.
It is similar with the high rank of a bad person.

आयूंषि यौवनानि ज्वालाः शिखिनो रयाः स्रवन्तीनाम् ।
उच्छ्रायाश्च खलानां गता न भूयो निवर्तन्ते ॥ २० ॥ LSP 25

One's life, one's youth,
the flames of a fire, the torrents of a river,
and also the high ranks of bad persons—
once they are gone they will not return.

—21—

།མི་རིགས་ཞེན་པའི་མི་སྲུན་དག །རིགས་པའི་གཞི་ལ་གནས་པ་མེད།
།རུལ་པའི་རོ་ལ་ཟ་བས་ཀྱང་། །ཙན་དན་སྡོང་པོ་སྤོང་བར་བྱེད། ༢༡ །

a *źes pa'i* GNQ; *bsrun* GNQ **c** *rus pa'i* GNQ **d** *tsandan* N

Bad persons who are longing for what is inappropriate
do not live on a foundation which is appropriate.
Although the [bluebottle fly] feeds on rotten corpses
it abandons the stump of sandal-wood.

अनुचितगुणरागितया शुचिनि पदे न स्थितिं खलो लभते ।
चन्दनमपास्य सरघा मृतकुणपेष्वेव लीयन्ते ॥ २१ ॥ LSP 26

On account of his longing for inappropriate qualities
a bad person does not live in a pure place.
The bees abandon the sandal-wood [on a funeral pyre]
and stay only with the corpses of the deceased.

—22—

།ངན་པ་དག་བསྟོད་རང་བཞིན་གྱིས། ། ལྷན་ཅིག་སྐྱེས་པ་འདོར་མི་སྲིད།
།ཟླ་བ་ཚེས་པ་ངེས་པར་ནི། ། དབང་ཕྱུག་ཆེན་པོའི་སྤྱི་བོར་ཐོགས། ༢༢ །

a *ṅan g.yo can bstod* GNQ; *gyi* CD **c** *tshes na* CD (?); *ṅas* (< *ṅes*) C **d** *spyi la* GNQ

Bad people, (even) if they are extolled,
do not abandon their inborn nature.
The waxing (and therefore still crooked) moon
is necessarily fixed on the Head of the Great Lord, Śiva.

अतिसत्कृता अपि शठाः सहभुवमुज्झन्ति जातु न प्रकृतिम् ।
शिरसा महेश्वरेणापि [!] ननु धृतो वक्र एव शशी ॥ २२ ॥ LSP 27

Bad people, (even) if they are excessively honoured,
do not abandon at all their inborn nature.
Is not the moon still crooked
(even) when carried on the head of the Great Lord, Śiva?

In the beginning of line a) one would rather expect *ṅan pa bstod kyaṅ*.
raṅ bźin gyis: Either an original *raṅ bźin *ni* became corrupted as *raṅ bźin gyis* or the translator freely interpreted *prakṛtim* as *prakṛtyā*.

—23—

། ཕལ་པ་དག་ནི་རླུང་བཞིན་དུ། ། གཞན་གྱི་དྲི་ཡི་རྗེས་སུ་འབྲང་།
། སྐྱེས་བུ་དམ་པ་ཉི་ཟེར་བཞིན། ། སྐྱོན་གྱིས་རྟག་ཏུ་གོས་པ་མེད། ༢༣ །

b *rjes su 'byuṅ* Q; *rjesu 'byuṅ* GN

Like the wind ordinary people
carry ('follow') the smell of others.
Like the sun noble persons
are never stained by faults.

वायुरिव खलजनोऽयं प्रायः पररूपमेति संपर्कात् ।
सन्तस्तु रविकरा इव सदसद्योगेऽप्यसंश्लिष्टाः ॥ २३ ॥ LSP 29

Like the wind, the bad person generally adopts
somebody else's form by way of contact.
Like the sun, good beings, however, remain uninfluenced
by the contact with good or bad people.

gźan gyi dri yi rjes su 'braṅ "follow the smell of others" is a free but still acceptable rendering of *prāyaḥ* (not translated) *pararūpam eti saṃparkāt* (not translated).

skyon gyis renders *asadyoge*. *rtag tu* obviously reflects **sadā* i. o. *sad*. For metrical reasons the hypothetical underlying reading **sadāsadyoge 'py* cannot be correct.

—24—

།ཁྲིམས་ལྡན་གཞན་ལ་གནོད་སྤངས་པ། །རྣམ་ཤེས་སྤངས་ཀྱང་དགའ་བར་བྱེད། C113b
།རྒྱུད་དང་འབྲལ་བ་དབང་པོའི་གཞུ། །ས་དང་ནམ་མཁའི་རྒྱན་དུ་འགྱུར། ༢༤ །

a *gnad* N; *spoṅs* GNQ **b** *rnam shis* D **c** *rgyu* GNQ; *bral ba* Q, bral ba'i CD (!) **d** *namkha'i* NQ

A lawful person who has abandoned doing harm to others
is pleasant, even if lacking discriminative knowledge.
(Even) lacking the string Indra's bow, the rainbow,
becomes an ornament of both heaven and earth.

विरतः परोपघाताद्विज्ञानमृते ऽपि रमयति सुशीलः ।
गुणरहितमपीन्द्रधनुर्द्यावापृथिव्योरलंकृतये ॥ २४ ॥ LSP 30

A moral person who abstains from doing harm to others
is pleasant, even if lacking discriminative knowledge.
Even lacking the string Indra's bow, the rainbow,
adorns both heaven and earth.

It is remarkable that only C has the grammatically correct reading *'bral ba'i.* From the point of view of normative grammar this is certainly preferable to *'bral ba,* however it is clear that *'bral ba,* the *lectio difficilior,* is to be presupposed for the archetype of D and GNQ.

—25—

།མི་སྲུན་གང་ཞིག་ཆེ་བདག་གང་། །རིགས་ལྡན་ངེས་གང་རྒུད་པ་གང་།
།འབྱོར་པ་མི་འདྲ་བྱེད་པ་འདི། །རང་བཞིན་སླུན་པོས་ཅིས་མི་གདུང་། ༢༥ །

a *bsrun* GNQ; *bdag pa* (< *bdagaṅ*?) GNQ **b** *ṅes* (?) C; *rgyud* GNQ **d** *blun po* CD

What is a bad person on the one hand
and what is (his) greatness on the other hand?
What is noble-born and chaste person on the one hand
and what is (his) misfortune (on the other hand)?
How is it possible not to be feeling pain about this one
who in his stupidity creates (such) unfitting combinations?

क्व खलजनः क्व महत्त्वं क्व कुलीनाः साधवः क्व च विपत्तिः ।
सदृशवियोगे जडता धातुरियं कं न तापयति ॥ २५ ॥ LSP 31

What contrast between a wicked person and (his) success,
between good people of noble descent
and (their) misfortune!
Who is not tormented by this lack of ability of the creator
in joining those (who belong together)
on account of their equality?

The interpretation of the Tibetan stanza is based on the assumption that the translators correctly understood the meaning of the Sanskrit stanza. I am not sure whether the construction ... *gaṅ (źig)* ... *gaṅ (źig)* "what (is) ... (and) what (is) ..." will automatically be understood by a Tibetan reader in the same way as the Sanskrit construction *kva* ... *kva* ... "What a difference (or constrast) between ... and ...!"

The fourth line is given in a metrically incorrect form by Śāha: *sadṛśaviniyoge jaḍatā*. There are two possible ways to establish a metrically correct and meaningful text: a) *sadṛśaviniyogajaḍatā*, b) *sadṛśaviyoge jaḍatā*. I have chosen the second one because it requires only a minor change. The Tibetan renders the compound freely as "unfitting combinations".

'byor pa "wealth, possessions" is not a correct equivalent of *(vini)yoga-*; it creates an entirely different meaning. *sbyor ba* would have been a more appropriate translation. Perhaps *'byor pa* is only a corruption of an original **sbyor ba* which occurred in the course of transmission. If one restores **sbyor ba* one would have to translate: "How is it possible not to feel pain about the creator whose nature is stupid because (he) is (so) odd in his junctions?" This is indeed much more likely because it is difficult to conceive why *(vini)yoga-* should have been translated in the sense of *vibhava-*.

Note that the Tibetan translates **kiṃ*, not *kaṃ*.

—26—

།བདག་ཉིད་ཆེན་པོས་སྨད་རིགས་དག །ཡོངས་བཟུང་ཤིན་ཏུ་སྐྱིད་ཀྱང་འབྱུང་།
།བཟོ་བོ་མཁས་པས་ཤེལ་སྦྲམ་ཡང་། །ཚོན་གྱིས་བསྒྱུར་ན་ནོར་བུར་སྣང་། ༢༦ །

a *dmaṅs rigs kyaṅ* GNQ **b** *bskyed* GNQ **c** *bzo bo dag gis* GNQ

When they are accepted by noble-hearted beings
(even) people of low descent appear to be high-bred (?).
Even a piece of crystal looks (like) a ruby
when it is changed by a skilful craftsman
by (the application of) colour.

नीचो ऽपि परिगृह्लीतो मह्लात्मभिः परमुपैति मह्लिमानम् ।
स्फटिकोपलो ऽपि रक्तः कुशलैर्माणिक्यमुपयाति ।। २६ ।। LSP 32

When he is accepted by noble-hearted beings
even a low person attains the highest greatness.

Even a crystal looks (like) a ruby
when it has been reddened by a skilful person.

(b)skyed (kyaṅ) "producing" is a rather unusual translation for *mahimānam*. In ĀK 85d it is translated by *phan pa*. *mahattva-* is rendered by *che bdag* in ĀK 25a, by *bdag ñid* in ĀK 80d, by *ṅaṅ che* in 95b and by *bdag ñid chen po* [!] in ĀK 95d. Is *skyed* a corruption of *che*?

śel sbram "genuine, natural (?) crystal" seems to be a free rendering of *sphaṭikopala-* "stone (consisting of) crystal". For *sbram* cf. *sa le sbram* "unwrought gold", Skt. *cāmīkara* and *jātarūpa* (LC[2], p. 1996b).

—27—

།ཁ་ཅིག་སྨྲ་བ་ལྷུར་ལེན་ཏེ། །ཁ་ཅིག་མི་སྨྲ་དོན་ཡང་སྒྲུབ།
།འདམ་བུའི་མེ་ཏོག་འབྲས་བུ་མེད། །སྟར་ཀའི་འབྲས་བུ་མེ་ཏོག་མེད། ༢༧ །

b *grub* GNQ **d** *star ga'i* GNQ

Some are eager (only) to speak,
other realize their aim without talking.
A flower (which blossoms) in the mud has no fruits,
the fruit of the walnut has no blossoms.

वक्ति न करोति कश्चित्कश्चिदनुक्तो ऽपि साधयति कार्यम् ।
पुष्पत्यफलो ऽपि शरः क्षीरी तु फलत्यपुष्पापि ।। २७ ।। LSP 34

d *apuṣpāpi*: *apuṣpo 'pi* H

Some speak but do not act,
others fulfill their task unasked.
Although it has no fruits, the *śara* grass blossoms,
the *kṣīrī* plant bears fruit, although it does not blossom.

Kṣīrī: "N[ame] of several plants containing a milky sap" (Apte, p. 626b). This stanza can also be found as *Prajñādaṇḍa* 167.

—28—

། ཡོན་ཏན་དྲང་བས་མི་ཆོག་སྟེ། ། སྐྱེ་བོའི་གྱ་གྱུ་སྐྱོན་མིན་ནོ།
། མདའ་དྲང་བ་ཡིས་གསོད་པར་བྱེད། ། ཕུབ་ནི་འཁྱོགས་ཏེ་ལུས་ཀྱང་སྲུང་། ༢༨ ། Q162b

b *skye bo gya sgyu* GNQ **c** *driṅ ba* N, *draṅ bas ni* CD **d** *'khyog ste* CD; *bsruṅ* GNQ

Straightness is not sufficient to be a virtue
and the crookedness of a person is not (always) a fault.
A straight arrow kills,
whereas a shield is crooked, but protects the body.

गुणा एव नालमृजुता कौटिल्यं दोष एव न च जन्तोः ।
ऋजुरपि मारयति शरो वक्रो ऽपि फलस्तनुं पाति ॥ २८ ॥ LSP 35

Neither is straightness by itself a virtue
nor is crookedness of a person by itself a fault.
Although straight, the arrow kills;
although crooked, the shield protects the body.

It is noteworthy that the *Lokasaṃvyavahārapravṛtti* reads *phalas* "shield" as does ĀKtib (*phub*). The two Indian anthologies which quote this stanza read *vakram api dhanus* (VS 2853) and *vakro 'pi* [!] *dhanus* (Srh 199.141) "a crooked bow".

The *Subhāṣitaratnanidhi* 66 has two variations of this thought:

། བློ་ངན་དྲང་པོ་ལ་ལས་རང་། ། ལྷག་འགྱུར་ལ་ལས་གཞན་ལ་གནོད།
། ནགས་ཀྱི་ཤིང་དྲང་རྩད་ནས་གཅོད། ། མདའ་ཡི་དྲང་པོས་ཕ་རོལ་གསོད། ༦༦ །

"Some honest, simple-minded persons
destroy themselves, and some harm others.
A straight tree of the forest is cut from the root,
(but) the straightest arrow kills the enemy." (Bosson, modified)

and

།དྲང་པོར་སྨྲ་བའི་སྐྱོན་བཅས་དང་།   །འཁྱོག་སྨྲ་ཡོན་ཏན་ལྡན་པ་སྲིད།
།ལམ་དྲང་འགའ་ཞིག་ནོར་འཇིག་ལ།   །དུང་དཀར་གཡས་འཁྱིལ་བཀྲ་ཤིས་བྱེད།། ༡༨༥ །

a read *smra ba skyon bcas*! **b** v.l. *'khyog sgra*

"It is possible that what is spoken sincerely
('in an upright manner') may become harmful,
and that a crooked speech may have an excellent quality.
Some straight paths can devastate one's possessions,
(but) a white conch shell winding to the right causes fortune."

—29—

།ཤིན་ཏུ་གཏུམ་ཡང་དྲང་བ་*དམ།   །ངན་གཡོ་ཕུབ་མི་རྩུས་གཡོགས་མིན།
།སོ་གའི་སྤྲིན་མེད་ཉི་མ་བས།   །སྤྲིན་མེས་མི་གསལ་ཤིན་ཏུ་སྲེག ༢༨ །

a *draṅ po* GNQ; *bdam* CDGNQ **b** *rtsus* C, *rtswas* D; *g.yog* GNQ **c** *sos ka* GNQ
d *sprin gyis* CD; *bsreg* GNQ

Even if he is extremely fierce, a straight one is good,
not a bad and cunning person,
who is (like) a chaff-fire, covered by grass.
Much more intensely than the cloudless sun
of the hot season
does the heat of a cloud, (although) invisible, burn.

अतितीक्ष्णो ऽपि वरमृजुर्न तु शाठ्यतृणावृतो मृदुतुषाग्निः ।
ग्रीष्मविघनातपादप्यधिकं बालातपः पचति ।। २९ ।। LSP 36

Although extremely sharp,
a straight (fire) is better than the soft fire of chaff,
which is covered by the grass of wickedness.
Much more than even the heat of the cloudless (sun)
of the hot season
burns the heat of the newly risen (sun).

Note that *tṛṇa-* "(dry) grass" was translated by *phub* "chaff" (for which cf. LC[2], p. 1185b) and *tuṣa-* "chaff" by *rtswa* "grass".

In the Tibetan translation there is no equivalent of *mṛdu* and the rendering of *bālātapaḥ* is difficult to explain. Why was *ātapa-* "heat" expanded to *sprin mes* "heat of the clouds" and why was *bāla-* "young; newly risen (of the sun)" translated by *mi gsal* "not bright, not clear, invisible"?

—30—

།དཔལ་འགོན་ནི་བླུན་པོ་ཡང་། །ཤེས་རིག་གསལ་བའི་སྐྱེས་བུར་འགྱུར།
།ལང་*ཚོའི་རྒྱགས་པའི་འདོད་ལྡན་དག །འཛེ་བ་སྒེག་པ་སྟོན་པར་བྱེད། ༣༠ །

a *mgon* N **b** *śes ñen* GNQ; *spyod pa 'byuṅ* GNQ **c** *laṅ tsho* GNQ, *laṅ tshos* CD; *rgyags pa'i spyod pa yaṅ* GNQ

When he is touched by good fortune
even a fool turns into a person of clear knowledge.
Women in love who are filled with pride of their youth
display charm (and) coquettishness.

श्रीपरिचयाज्जडा अपि भवन्त्यभिज्ञा विदग्धचरितानाम् ।
उपदिशति कामिनीनां यौवनमद् एव ललितानि ॥ ३० ॥ LSP 37

By the accumulation of good fortune
even fools become experts in the ways of shrewd conduct.
It is only the hilarity of youth
which teaches coquettishness to the young women in love.

It seems as if the translators did not recognize *abhijñā* as predicate noun of *bhavanti* but took it as the first member of a compound. In that case the compound should have ended in the nominative, **abhijñāvidagdha caritāḥ* "(people) whose conduct is shrewd on account of (clear) knowledge". None of the two variant readings in line b) corresponds exactly to the Sanskrit text. *spyod pa* (GNQ) is closer to *caritānām* than *skyes bu* (CD), but *'gyur* (CD) suits *bhavanti* better than *'byuṅ* (GNQ). Is *skyes bu* (CD) perhaps only a later corruption of an original *spyod pa*?

In line c) only a minor change is required to establish perfect agreement with the Sanskrit text: we only have to alter *laṅ tsho rgyags pa'i* into *laṅ tsho'i rgyags pas.* Perhaps *laṅ tshos* (CD) is still a reflection of the original genitive.

—31—

།ཞི་བ་ཡི་ནི་ལུས་ཅན་ལས། །འཇིགས་པ་མི་འབྱུང་ངེས་མེད་དེ།
།མར་མེའི་རྩེ་མོ་དཀར་བ་ལས། །དུད་པ་ནག་པོ་ཅིས་མི་འབྱུང་། ༣༡ །

a *can la* GNQ **c** *dkar po* GNQ **d** *'byuṅ ba bźin* GNQ

It is (by no means) certain that danger does not arise from
him who has a peaceful appearance ('body').
Is it not so that black smoke
arises from the white tip of a flame?

शान्तवपुरेष नास्माद्भयमुद्भवतीति नायमेकान्तः ।
शुक्लाः कज्जलमसितं दीपशिखाः किं न जनयन्ति ।। ३१ ।। LSP 39

'His appearance is peaceful,
therefore no danger will arise from him'—
this is not a necessary conclusion.
Is it not so that the white flames of a lamp
produce dark lampblack?

The stanza was also quoted by Prajñāvarman in his *Udānavargavivaraṇa* ad *Udānavarga* 701. The Tibetan text can be found in Michael BALK's transcript (*Prajñāvarman's Udānavargavivaraṇa. Transliteration of its Tibetan version.* By Michael Balk. Bonn 1984) on p. 810.1–4. This translation has *gzugs can* i. o. *lus can* and *nag po'aṅ* i. o. *nag po.* Otherwise it follows exactly the wording of CD which we have adopted above.

—32—

| ···· ···· ···· ···· ···· ···· ···· | །འཇིགས་འབྱུང་གཅིག་ཏུ་མ་ངེས་ཏེ།
།འཇིགས་བྱེད་ཆེན་པོ་ཞི་བའི་གཟུགས། །ཞི་བའི་ཆེད་དུ་ཅིས་མི་འགྱུར། ༣༢ | N182a

a is omitted in CDGNQ **b** is omitted in GNQ **c** *'jigs̱* N; *źig pa'i* CD **d** *mi 'byuṅ* GNQ

It is by no means certain that danger will arise
[from him who is frightful by his appearance].
Is it not so that something very frightening,
Śiva's body, is suited to create (mental) peace?

आकारदारुणोऽयं भयमस्मादित्यनिश्चयोऽयमपि ।
भवति महाभैरवमपि शिवस्य रूपं शिवायैव ॥ ३२ ॥ LSP 40

'He is frightening by his appearance,
danger (might) arise from him'—
this is also not a necessary conclusion.
Śiva's body, although extremely frightening,
is suited to create nothing but (mental) peace.

—33—

།ཡོན་ཏན་ཆུ་ཡིས་མི་མཛའ་བའི། །འགྲོ་བའི་མེ་འཇིལ་སྐྱོན་ཕུབ་མིན།
།སྣང་བ་ཁོ་ནས་མུན་པ་ནི། །སེལ་འགྱུར་མིན་ནམ་མུན་པས་མིན། ༣༣ | D118a

b *'bar ba'i skyon 'jil* GN; *bus min* GNQ **d** om. GNQ

Only by the water of virtues the fire of unfriendly beings
can be extinguished, not by the chaff of faults.
Is it not so that darkness is removed
only by light, not by darkness?

गुणसलिलेनैव शमं व्रजन्त्यमित्राग्नयो न दोषतृणैः ।
आलोक एव तमसां निषिद्धये नैव जातु तमः ॥ ३३ ॥ LSP 67

The fire of enmity is extinguished
only by the water of virtues,
not by the (dry) grass of faults.
Only the light is able to remove darkness,
but not at all darkness.

'gro ba'i me: Did the translators understand *vrajanty* as **vrajanto*, as attribute of *amitrāgnayo*. Or did they have the wrong (and unmetrical) reading **vrajanto 'mitrāgnayo* in their manuscript? Then, of course, the verb required by *śamaṃ* would be missing. The variant reading *'bar ba'i me* (NQ) is certainly an attempt at improving the meaning of the passage.

skyon phub: Did the translators read **doṣatuṣaiḥ* (via **doṣatuśaiḥ*, *na* and *śa* being very similar in the Bengali script)? Cf. stanza 29b.

—34—

།བླུན་*པོས་དོན་*བསྒྲུབ་གང་ཡིན་པ། །དེ་ནི་བྱ་རོག་ཏ་ལར་མཚུངས།
།སྲིན་བུས་ཤིང་དག་ཟོས་པའི་རྗེས། །སྐྱེས་དབང་ཡི་གེར་འགྱུར་བ་བཞིན། ༣༤ །

a *blun pas* CD, *blun po* GNQ; *'grub* CD, *grub* GNQ; *yin la* GNQ **b** *de yi* GNQ **c** *srun bus* Q; *mtshuṅs pa'i rjes* GNQ **d** *ge snaṅ* D, *ge (...)* C. – For the emendation in line a) cf. *Subhāṣitaratnanidhi* 61.

When an aim has been reached by a fool
then this is (due only to) coincidence
– like the trace which has been gnawed into wood
by an insect which by chance
can assume the shape of a letter.

साधयति यत्प्रयोजनमज्ञस्तत्तस्य काकतालीयम् ।
दैवात्कथमप्यक्षरमुत्किरति घुणो ऽपि काष्ठेषु ॥ ३४ ॥ LSP 70

When an ignorant person reaches his aim
then this happens to him (only) coincidentally.
By chance even a woodworm
somehow carves a letter into wood.

Sa skya Paṇḍita in his *Subhāṣitaratnanidhi* has exploited this stanza twice:

།མ་དཔྱད་པ་ལས་དོན་གྲུབ་པ། །བྱུང་ཡང་འཛངས་པར་སུ་ཞིག་རྩི།
།སྲིན་བུ་དག་གིས་ཟོས་པའི་རྗེས། །ཡི་གེར་བྱུང་ཡང་ཡིག་མཁན་མིན། ༨༥ །

"One who has not considered (and yet) attains his aim,
although it turns out (well): who will consider him wise?
Although the tracks of the eating of worms have turned out
as letters, they (the worms) are not literate."

།བླུན་པོས་བྱ་བ་ལེགས་གྲུབ་ཀྱང་། །སྐལ་དབང་ཡིན་གྱི་བསྒྲུབས་པས་མིན།
། སྲིན་བུའི་ཁ་ཆུ་དར་སྐུད་དུ། །འགྲོ་བ་མཁས་ནས་བྱུང་བ་མིན། ༦༧ །

a read *sgrub*

"Even if a fool accomplishes a deed well,
it is by good fortune and not his accomplishment.
The saliva of a worm (converting) to silk floss
is not something that has come forth from a skilled person."

—35—

།སྐྱེ་བོ་ཡོན་ཏན་ལྡན་པ་དག །མཁོ་བའི་སྒོ་ནས་ཕལ་ཆེར་ཉམས།
།ནེ་ཙོ་ཚིག་གསལ་སྨྲ་བ་ཡང་། །གཞེབ་ཀྱི་སྐྱིལ་བུས་སྲུང་བར་འགྱུར། ༣༥ །

a *pa la* GNQ **c** *smra mkhas pa* GNQ **d** *bsruṅs par snaṅ* GNQ

People endowed with (useful) qualities
generally suffer from their being useful.
The parrot, although it utters distinct words,
is kept in ('protected by') a bird-cage.

योग्यतयैव विनाशं प्रायो ऽनार्येषु यान्ति गुणवन्तः
स्फुटवचना एव शुकाः पञ्जरबन्धे निबध्यन्ते ॥ ३५ ॥ LSP 72

Just on account of their usefulness
talented people generally perish among the ignoble.
Only the parrots that are endowed with a clear voice
are incarcerated in the prison of a cage.

It is noteworthy that the translators omitted *anāryeṣu* although it would have been easy to include it in the first line by omitting the superfluous *skye bo.* Did they regard it as not so important for the idea expressed in the stanza?

In line d) the Tibetan renders *pañjarabandh**e** ni**badhyante***, the reading of the *Lokasaṃvyavahārapravṛtti,* not *pañjarabandh**aṃ** ni**ṣevante***, the reading of the anthologies (VS 239, Srg 48.140).

Sa skya paṇḍita has used this stanza as a model for *Subhāṣitaratnanidhi* 228:

།སྨྲ་མང་ཉེས་པ་འཛིན་པའི་རྒྱུ། །མི་སྨྲ་ཉེས་པ་སྤོང་བའི་གཞི།
།ནེ་ཙོ་སྨྲ་བས་གཞེབ་ཏུ་བཅུག །འདབ་ཆགས་ལྐུགས་པ་བདེ་བར་རྒྱུ།

"Much talking is the cause of grasping harmfulness.
No talking is the cause of rejecting harmfulness.
The parrot has been put into a cage because it speaks.
The mute winged creatures roam about happily." (Bosson).

—36—

།གདུལ་བར་སླ་བའི་དགྲ་དག་ཀྱང་། །སེམས་ཅན་ཆེ་བསྟེན་གདུལ་བར་དཀའ།
།ཆུ་ཐིགས་མཚོ་ནང་བཞག་པ་དག །ཉི་མས་སྐེམས་པར་མི་ནུས་སོ། ༣༦ །

a *bla ba'i* CD **b** *chos bsten* CD **c** *lhuṅ ba dag* CD **d** *skams* GNQ; *nuso* N

Even an enemy who is (usually) easy to tame
is hard to tame when he adheres to a noble-hearted being.
The sun is not able to dry up a drop of water
that has been placed in the ocean.

भवन्ति सुसाध्यो ऽपि रिपुर्दुःसाध्यः संश्रितो महासत्त्वम् ।
न क्षपयितुमलमर्कोऽप्युदबिन्दुमुदन्वति निषिक्तम् ॥ ३६ ॥ LSP 73

Even an enemy who is (usually) easy to defeat
is hard to defeat when he adheres to a noble-hearted being.
Not even the sun is able to make disappear
a drop of water that has been placed in the ocean.

Cf. *Subhāṣitaratnanidhi* 311:

།ཉམས་སྟོབས་ཆུང་བའི་སྐྱེ་བོ་ཡང་། །ཆེན་པོ་གཞན་ལ་བརྟེན་ན་འགྲུབ།
།ཆུ་ཡི་ཐིགས་པ་ཉམས་ཆུང་ཡང་། །མཚོ་དང་འདྲེས་ན་སྐམ་མི་ནུས།

"Even persons with little strength,
if they rely on other great (persons), will succeed.
Although the water-drop is weak, if it mixes with the sea,
it cannot dry up." (Bosson)

—37—

།བདག་ཉིད་*ཆེན་པོ་མཐར་ཕྱིན་པའམ། །ཡང་ན་*མི་བརྩམ་རྩོམ་མི་བྱེད།
།གང་དུ་ཐོག་བབས་འཇོམས་བྱེད་ཅིང་། །ཡང་ན་འབབས་པར་མི་བྱེད་དོ། ༣༧ །

a *bdag ñid brtsams pa* CD, *bdag ñid brtsam pa* GNQ; *phyin pa'aṅ* CD **b** *ma* CDGNQ; *brtsams* CD **c** *thogs* N; *gnod pa med* (for *'joms byed ciṅ* GNQ **d** *'bab par mi byed de* CD; *thog babs mi byed do* GN (*byedo* N)

A noble-hearted being either accomplishes
(what he has begun) or he does not (even) begin
with what cannot be accomplished.
The lightning destroys where it strikes upon
or it does not strike (at all).

पर्यन्तं वा गच्छति नारभते वा महाननारभ्यम् ।
दारयति यत्र निपतति महाशनिर्नैव वा पतति ।। ३७ ।। LSP 74

A noble-hearted being either reaches the (very) end
or does not set out for what should not be undertaken.
The thunderbolt splits where it strikes upon
or it does not strike (at all).

*bdag ñid *chen po*: Although the transmitted text (*bdag ñid brtsam(s) pa*) is also meaningful—"Either oneself brings (?) to an end what one has begun (or: what is to be accomplished) or one does not (even) begin what cannot be accomplished"—*mahān* would then have no Tibetan equivalent and *bdag ñid brtsam(s) pa* no Sanskrit equivalent. On the other hand we have numerous instances in the *Āryākoṣa* where *mahant-*, *mahātman-* or *mahattva-* are translated into Tibetan by the combination of *bdag (ñid)* and *che* or *chen po*. This is the complete list: ***bdag ñid chen po*** = *mahant-* 12c, 66a, 94b, 127a, 144c; = *mahātman-* 26b; = *mahattva-* 95b; ***bdag ñid che*** = *mahant-* 49a, 122a; = *balavant-* 48a; ***che bdag*** = *mahant-* 106b, 107b, 120a, 123b; = *mahattva-* 25a. The figures always refer to the position of the Sanskrit word.

—38—

།རྟོགས་པར་སླ་བའང་བླུན་པོས་ནི། །ཡོན་ཏན་སྐྱོན་དག་འབྱེད་མི་ནུས།
།སྐྱེ་བོ་མིག་ནི་ལོང་བ་ལ། །སྣང་བ་དང་ནི་མུན་*པ་མཚུངས། ༣༨ །

a *bla yaṅ* CD **b** *skyon yaṅ* GNQ **d** *mun par* CDGNQ

Even when they are easy to recognize,
the fool is not able to discriminate
between virtues and vices.
For a blind person light and darkness are the same.

नालं विवेक्तुमज्ञो गुणदोषाणां सुबोधमपि भेदम् ।
मुषितनयनस्य जन्तोः प्रकाशतमसी समे भवतः ।। ३८ ।। LSP 75

An ignorant person is not able to recognize the difference
between virtues and vices even if it is very easy to see.
For a person who has lost his eyesight
light and darkness are the same.

—39—

།འགྲོ་བ་སྣོད་ལ་སྟོད་སྨད་དེ། །རྟག་ཏུ་རོ་གཅིག་འབབ་པའི་ཆར། C114a
།སྤྲུལ་ཁར་བབ་ན་དུག་ཏུ་འགྱུར། །ཉ་ཕྱིས་ཁར་བབ་མུ་ཏིག་གྱུར། ༣༩ །

a *gnod las snod* CD; *bstod* DN **d** *steṅ bab* N; *'gyur* N

According to the vessel (in which they are placed) men
become (either) laudable (or) despicable.
The rain which has always one taste when it falls down
becomes poison when it falls into the mouth of a snake
and a pearl when it falls into the orifice of a shell.

स्तुतिनिन्दाभाजनतां व्रजति समं वस्तु सदसतोः पतितम्।
विषमह्मिमुखेऽम्बु साध्वपि शुक्तौ मुक्ताफलं भवति ॥ ३९ ॥ LSP 79

The same thing can become the object of praise or blame,
depending on whether it has fallen
into a good or bad (receptacle).
Water, even of good quality,
becomes poison in the mouth of a snake
but a pearl in a shell.

This stanza was rendered unusually freely by the translators without, however, spoiling the main idea. Therefore it is difficult to decide whether this was done deliberately, whether their Sanskrit manuscript was corrupt or whether they did not understand it fully. There are two hints that there might have been a problem of understanding. It is not impossible that *'gro ba* goes back to *vrajati* (which would be a gross mistake as far as syntax is concerned) and *rtag tu* seems to render a misread or miswritten **sadā* in *sadasatoḥ*. The same mistake occurred already in stanza 23. *char* "rain" points to a misread or miswritten *vastu* (> **varṣaḥ*), and *ro gcig* "of one taste (only)" could be a free (but in this context meaningful) rendering of *samaṃ*. Even line a) can be interpreted as a kind of misunderstanding if we read it as *stutinindā* (= *stod smad*) *bhājane* (= *snod la*) *tāṃ* (= *de*). This would have been a very clumsy interlinear version, and it is surprising that it still allows a meaningful interpretation by translating *'gro ba* as "the world; men" and by taking *de* as the connective particle (*te, ste, de*), not the demonstrative pronoun. The same idea is expressed in several other stanzas. Cf. MSS 8778 (= IS^2 1544; < ŚP 477):

करोति निर्मलाधारं तुच्छस्यापि महार्घताम् ।
अम्बुनो बिन्दुरल्पो ऽपि शुक्तौ मुक्ताफलं भवेत् ॥

"A flawless container might make invaluable
even a worthless thing.
Lo! even a small drop of water
becomes a pearl in a shell."

See also MSS 9802 (= IS^2 1689; = Kusumadeva's *Dṛṣṭāntaśataka* 99):

कालक्रमेण परिणामवशादनव्या भावा भवन्ति खलु पूर्वमतीव तुच्छाः ।
मुक्तामणिर्जलदतोयकणोऽप्यणीयान्संपद्यते च चिरकीचकरन्ध्रमध्ये ॥

a *anavyā* v. l. *anarghyā*

"Things that were formerly insignificant
do indeed become priceless in the course of time;
a drop of water, though very minute,
becomes a pearl by remaining for long inside a bamboo."

And IS^2 4029 (= Kālidāsa's *Mālavikāgnimitra* 9):

पात्रविशेषे न्यस्तं गुणान्तरं व्रजति शिल्पमाधातुः ।
जलमिव समुद्रशुक्तौ मुक्ताफलतां पयोदस्य ॥

"The skill of a teacher,
when communicated to a worthy object,
attains greater excellence, as the water of a cloud,
when dropped into a sea-shell, acquires the nature of a pearl."
(TAWNEY)

Note that Kālidāsa also uses the Āryā metre.

—40—

།བླུན་པོ་ཕལ་ཆེར་ཐུབ་ཚོད་བྱེད། །མཁས་པ་དེ་ལྟ་མ་ཡིན་ནོ།
།ཆུ་ནང་ཟླ་བའི་གཟུགས་བརྙན་ནི། །བྱིས་པ་ལས་གཞན་སུ་ཞིག་འཛིན། ༤༠ །

a *thub gsod* GN, *thab gsod* Q **b** *mkhas la* C; *yino* N **c** *zas kyi gzugs* GNQ; *brñen* C

A fool generally commits inappropriate deeds,
while a wise acts in a different manner.
Who else but a child (seeks to) grasp
the mirror-image of the moon in the water?

अस्थानाभिनिवेशी प्रायो जड एव भवति नो विद्वान्।
बालादन्यः कोऽम्भसि जिघृक्षतीन्दोः स्फुरद्बिम्बम्॥ ४० ॥ LSP 83

"Only fools and not the wise
love what they cannot have.
Who but a child seeks to grasp
the moon as it shines in water?" (D. H. H. INGALLS)

thub chod (CD) is a word belonging to the old 'language'. ZHD (p. 1174a) paraphrases it as *mi 'os pa'i bya ba* "an inappropriate deed" which is exactly the meaning which is required here.

—41—

།ཆུང་ཟད་མི་མཐུན་བྱས་པའི་རྒྱུས། །ཡང་བའི་སེམས་ཅན་ལྷག་པར་ཁྲོ། Q163a
།རླུང་གིས་བདས་པའི་རྡུལ་ཕྲ་ཡང་། །ཤིན་ཏུ་ཐག་རིང་འཕྱུལ་བར་བྱེད། ༤༡ །

b *sems yaṅ ba dag* CD **c** *phran* GN

Because a minor inappropriateness has been committed
persons of weak character become extremely angry.
Even the smallest particles of dust are carried away
by the wind and spread to very far places.

अल्पेऽप्यपकृतिहेतौ विकारमत्यर्थमेति लघुसत्त्वः ।
वाति मृदावपि पवने रज एव सुदूरमुन्नमति ॥ ४१ ॥ LSP 85

On account of even the smallest offence
persons of weak character become extremely set up.
Even when [only] a mild breeze blows
dust raises very high.

In line a) GNQ seem to have preserved the better reading because *sems can yaṅ ba* literally translates *laghusattvāḥ* whereas *sems yaṅ ba dag* rather corresponds to *alpabuddhayaḥ* or *alpamatayaḥ*. *mṛdau* has not been translated.

The first line reminds of *Mahābhārata* 5.39.13cd and 14 (= MSS 3211):

अल्पेप्यपकृते मोहान्न शान्तिमुपगच्छति ।
तादृशैः संगतं नीचैः नृशंसैरकृतात्मभिः ।
निशाम्य निपुणं बुद्ध्या विद्वान्दूराद्विवर्जयेत् ।

—42—

།ཡོན་ཏན་ཅན་ལ་མི་སྲུན་དག །ཐིབས་ནོན་བརྙས་ཐབས་སྣ་ཚོགས་བྱེད།
།རྩྭ་ཤིང་ཆུ་བོའི་སྟེང་ན་འཕྱོ། །རིན་པོ་ཆེ་དག་མ་ཡིན་ནོ། ༤༢ །

a *bsrun* GNQ **b** *thabs non* Q; *sna tshogs byed* CD *byed par 'gyur* GNQ **c** *chu śiṅ* Q; *rtsa śiṅ* GNQ *chu yi* GNQ **d** *yino* N

Bad persons attack the virtuous
and humiliate them in various ways.
While grass (and) wood float on a river,
this is not the case with jewels (i. e., they sink down).

प्रखला एव गुणवतामाक्रम्य धुरं पुरः प्रकर्षन्ति ।
काष्ठतृणमेव जलधेरुपरि प्लवते न रत्नानि ।। ४२ ।। LSP 86

Only very bad persons attack (?)
the leading position of the virtuous
and place themselves in front [of them].
While grass (and) wood float on a water-receptacle,
this is not the case with jewels (i. e., they sink down).

thibs non translates *ākramya*. I know of only one other occurrence of this compound, the one given by LC[1], p. 1030a, where *thibs kyis non pa* is quoted from the Tibetan *Abhisamayālaṃkāra* 2.27 as the equivalent of *adhiṣṭhāna-* "magic or supernatural power" (here of Māra). The *Brda dkrol* explains *thib non* as *rdib kyis non pa*. The meaning of this paraphrase is also not clear. According to SCD *rdib pa* is an intransitive verb meaning "to crumble, to fall to pieces, collapse, cave in". In Bodhic 6.93 *rdib gyur* translates *bhinna* and in AKBh 237a *rdib pa* renders Skt. *pāta* which both confirm this meaning. By its formation *rdib kyis non pa* seems to be comparable with *zil gyis non pa* which would make *rdib* a noun.

brñas thabs sna tshogs byed (CD) translates *dhuraṃ puraḥ prakarṣanti* "bear the yoke in front (of him), i. e., exceed, excel (him)". The relationship between the Sanskrit and the Tibetan remains unclear to me. It would be mere speculation to assume that *prakarṣanti* was miswritten, misread or misinterpreted as **prakurvanti* or *apakurvanti*. *brñas thabs* occurs again in stanza 65 where it translates *paribhava-* "humiliation".

The idea of the stanza occurs also in *Subhāṣitaratnanidhi* 103:

།བླུན་པོའི་ཡོན་ཏན་ཁར་འབྱིན་ཏེ། །མཁས་པའི་ཡོན་ཏན་ཁོང་དུ་སྦེད།
།སོག་མ་ཆུ་ཡི་སྟེང་ན་འཕྱོ། །ནོར་བུ་སྟེང་དུ་བཞག་ཀྱང་འབྱིང་།

"The fool lets his attainments proceed into his mouth.
The sage hides his virtue inside.
A straw floats on top of the water;
if one places a jewel on top (of the water), it sinks."

—43—

།བློ་དང་ལྡན་པས་རྒུད་པ་ལས། །བསླང་བར་ནུས་ཀྱི་ཕལ་པས་མིན།
།ཤ་ར་བྷ་ཡིས་དབུགས་རྔུབས་པས། །ཁྲོན་པའི་ཆུ་ནི་འཐུང་བར་བྱེད། ༤༣ །

a *gduṅ ba las* GNQ **b** *nus kyis* Q **c** *śa ra bla yi* GNQ; *brṅubs* GNQ

While an intelligent person is able
to raise himself from a calamity
this is not the case with an ordinary person.
The *śarabha* deer drinks the water
of a well by inhaling it.

व्यसनेभ्यः संयन्तुं धीमन्तः शक्नुवन्ति नाल्पबलाः ।
शरभा एवोच्छ्वासैः कूपादभ्युद्धरन्ति जलम् ॥ ४३ ॥ LSP 92

The wise are able to guard themselves against calamities,
not people of little strength.
Only the *śarabha* deers take the water
out of a well by inhaling (it).

The ability of the *śarabha* deer to drink water from a well without using its tongue is already mentioned in *Ṛtusaṃhāra* 1.23d: *śarabhakulam ajihvaṃ proddharaty ambu kūpāt*. There is a variant reading *ajihmaṃ* (thus also Amarakīrti and Maṇirāma who explain it as *akuṭilam*; Kale who has the same reading explains *ajihmaṃ* as *niralasaṃ*!) which is, however, certainly not correct. Is there a relationship between these two passages? The *śarabha* is either a kind of deer or a mythological eight-legged animal.

—44—

།ཡུན་རིང་འདྲིས་པའི་ཡོན་ཏན་ལ། །སེམས་ཅན་དག་ནི་སྐྱོ་བ་བསྐྱེད།
།ཤིན་ཏུ་སྐོམ་པས་ཆུ་འཐུང་ན། །དེ་ཉིད་ཡོངས་སུ་སྤོང་བར་བྱེད། ༤༤ །

a *riṅs* GNQ **b** *lus can* CD; *skyo ba skye* CD **c** *śin tu ṅoms par chu 'thuṅs nas* CD **d** *yoṅsu* N

One (usually) develops surfeit of those qualities
one is accustomed to for a long time.
After one has drunken water with the greatest thirst
one completely avoids the same (water).

चिरपरिचयाद्गुणा अपि वैमुख्यं कल्पयन्ति सत्वानाम् ।
अतितृषिता अपि सलिलं पिबन्त एवापरज्यन्ते ।। ४४ ।। LSP 42

Even (good) qualities can create aversion in beings
when they are accustomed to them for a long time.
Even though they are extremely thirsty people
become disinterested in water as soon as they drink it.

At least in two cases the readings of GNQ suit the Sanskrit text better than those of CD: *sems can* (GNQ) is the usual translation of *sattva-*, not *lus can* (CD), and likewise *śin tu skom pas* (GNQ) is the precise equivalent of *atitṛṣitā*, not *śin tu ṅoms par* (CD) "until they are satiated".

A very closely related stanza is VS 2894 (= MSS 574; = IS^2 139 < Subh 295; cf. also Dvi App. 27):

अतिपरिचयादवज्ञा भवति विशिष्टे ऽपि वस्तुनि प्रायः ।
[लोकः प्रयागवासी कूपस्नानं सदाचरति] ।।

"Excessive familiarity breeds contempt,
even of something excellent;
the inhabitants of the holy place where the Gaṅgā
joins the Yamunā, perform their ablutions in a well."

In the first half of the stanza there is a variant reading *saṃtatagamanād anādaro bhavati*, and in the second half *kūpe snānaṃ saṃcarati*.

—45—

།ཐབས་དང་བྲལ་བར་བྱེད་པ་ན། །དམ་པས་ཀྱང་ནི་དོན་མི་འགྲུབ།
།གཞུ་ནི་ལོག་པར་འགོངས་པའི་མིས། །མདའ་དྲང་འཕེམ་ལ་ཕོག་མི་འགྱུར། ༤༥ ། N182b

a *thabs daṅ śas bral bar* G **c** read *'god pa'i?* **d** *'phen la* GN

If he acts without having the right means
then even the good man will not accomplish his purpose.
A man who fastens his bow in a wrong manner
will not hit his target (even) with a straight arrow.

अनुपायेन नियुक्ताः सन्तो ऽपि न साधयन्ति कार्याणि ।
ऋजवो ऽपि शरा लक्ष्यं न यान्ति विपरीतसंधानात् ॥ ४५ ॥ LSP 43

When they are commissioned without (appropriate) means
then even good people will not accomplish their tasks.
Even straight arrows will not reach their targets
when they are placed (on the bow) in a wrong manner.

—46—

།མི་དག་གོ་འཕང་མཆོག་སྙེད་ན། །ཕལ་ཆེར་དེ་ལ་རྨོངས་པར་འགྱུར།
།རི་རྩེ་མཐོ་ལ་འདུག་པས་ཀྱང་། །གཞོང་ཡང་ཐང་དང་འདྲ་བར་མཐོང་། ༤༦ །

a *mtho* CD **b** *de na* CD **d** *thad* CD

When men reach a high rank
they usually become confused about that fact.
He, too, who stays on the high tip of a mountain
looks at deep valleys as if they were plains.

उच्चैःपदमधितिष्ठंल्लोकस्तत्त्वेषु मुह्यति प्रायः ।
विषममपि पश्यति समं पर्वतशिखराग्रमारूढः ॥ ४६ ॥ LSP 44

When occupying an elevated position,
people generally are confused
with regard to the true nature of things;
he who has climbed to the top of a mountain
regards as even (agreeable)
what is [in fact] uneven (dangerous).

This is the translation of the MSS 333:

"When occupying an elevated position,
the people generally are confused in seeing things truthfully;
they see rugged places as though they are even,
as persons who have climbed to the top of a mountain." (A. A. R.)

de la "about that" corresponds to *tattveṣu* "about the true nature (of things)". Did the translators read **tat teṣu*?

—47—

།ཁ་ཅིག་ཡོན་ཏན་མེད་འཁོར་ནའང་། །དམ་པ་འཁོར་བ་སྤོང་མི་བྱེད།
།ཟླ་དཀྱིལ་ལ་བརྟེན་ར་རི་ཡི། །ལྷན་ཅིག་སྐྱེ་ཞིང་འགྲིབ་པ་བཞིན། ༤༧ ། D118b

a *mes 'khor na* GNQ **c** om. GNQ **d** *skyes śiṅ* G

If even some people without quality are around him
the good never abandon their retinue.
They are like the dark spots on the disk of the moon
which arise together with (it)
and disappear together with (it).

निर्गुणमप्यनुरक्तं प्रायो न समाश्रितं जहति सन्तः ।
सहवृद्धिक्षयभाजं वहति शशाङ्कः कलङ्कमपि ॥ ४७ ॥ LSP 49

The good generally do not abandon the one
who relies on them even if he is without qualities,
if he is (only) devoted.
The moon carries even the dark spots on him
that share together with him waxing and waning.

prāyo "generally" was not translated in the usual manner by *phal cher* "generally" but by *kha cig* "some".

The third line is preserved only by CD!

—48—

།བདག་ཉིད་ཆེ་ལ་རྒྱུད་དུས་སུའང་། །ལྷག་པར་མཐུ་གསལ་ཐ་མལ་མིན།
།ཨ་ག་རུ་ནི་མེར་བསྲེགས་ན། །དྲི་ཞིམ་ཐ་མལ་དེ་ལྟ་མིན། ༤༨ །

a *chen po* GNQ; *dus su* GNQ **b** *mthu rtsal* CD; *tha mar* GNQ **c** *mes* GNQ **d** *tha ma* GNQ

Particularly in the time of calamities
the power of the noble-hearted shines,
not (of) ordinary beings.
When Aloe wood has been burnt by fire,
it becomes fragrant, not ordinary (wood).

आपत्स्वेव हि महतां शक्तिरभिव्यज्यते न संपत्सु ।
अगुरोस्तथा न गन्धः प्रागस्ति यथाग्निपतितस्य ।। ४८ ।। LSP 50

a *hi mahatāṃ*: *balavatāṃ* H **b** *abhivyajyate*: *alaṃ vyajyate* H; *saṃpatsu*: *saṃpattau* H

Only in the time of calamities the power of the great
becomes clearly visible, not in the time of prosperity.
The fragrance of the Aloe wood is not so intensive
as long as it has not fallen into a fire.

Either the Tibetan translation is intentionally somewhat free or it was slightly modified in the course of transmission. *tha mar* "in the end" (GNQ) cannot be explained as representation whereas *tha mal* (CD) "ordinary (being)" can at least be interpreted as the logical opposite of *bdag ñid che la* which in fact presupposes a slight change of construction, because *saṃpatsu* (whose place is taken by *tha mal*) is, of course, the logical opposite of *āpatsu*.

bdag ñid chen po (GNQ) would yield a more elegant construction, however *bdag ñid che la* (CD) corresponds better with the genitive *mahatāṃ*, and a meaningful construction is still possible.

In line d) *tha mal* (CD) takes the position of *prāg* "earlier", however there is no semantical connection between the two. And *tha ma* (GNQ) "the last; (at) the end" is just the opposite of *prāg*. The reading of CD at least allows for a meaningful interpretation.

—49—

།བདག་ཉིད་ཆེ་ལ་སྐྱོན་ཕྲ་ཡང་། །*གསལ་གྱི་ཕལ་ལ་དེ་ལྟ་མིན།
།ཇི་ལྟར་ཟླ་བ་ཉ་བ་ལ། །ར་རི་མངོན་གྱི་ཚེས་ལ་མིན། ༤༩ །

ab om. GNQ **b** *bsal* CD **c** *ñi ba la* Q **d** *gyis* GNQ; *tshas* G

Even the smallest fault becomes visible
at a noble-hearted one, but not at an ordinary being.
When the moon is full, its dark spots
are clearly visible, but not at the new moon.

महति यथा दृश्यन्ते दोषास्तनवो ऽपि नो तथा *लघुनि ।
लक्ष्यत इन्दौ पूर्णे यथा कलङ्कस्तथा न शिशौ ।। ४९ ।। LSP 52

Even the tiniest faults are visible at a great being,
but at an insignificant person this is not the case.
The dark spots can clearly be seen at the full moon,
but at the young moon this is by no means the case.

bsal (CD) seems to be only a misspelling of **gsal*; cf. 48b where *gsal* renders *abhivyajyate* which can be regarded as synonym of *lakṣyate.*

mahati at the end of line b) can only be a *lapsus calami* for **laghuni* or any synonym which is metrically equivalent.

A loosely related stanza can be found in IS[2] 5113:

यथा दोषो विभात्यस्य जनस्य न तथा गुणाः ।
प्रायः कलङ्क एवेन्दोः प्रस्फुटो न प्रसन्नता ॥

Its source is *Dṛṣṭāntaśataka* 4.

—50—

།མཐུ་ཡིས་ཕོངས་པའི་ཕལ་པ་དག །གཞན་ལ་རྩོལ་ཞིང་འགྲོ་བའི་*འཚེ།
།རང་གཅོད་མི་ནུས་བདར་རྡོས་ཀྱང་། །སྟ་རེ་རྣོན་པོ་བདར་བར་བྱེད། ༥༠ །

a *mthu yi* C; *'phoṅs* GNQ **b** *rgol ciṅ* GNQ; *'gro ba'i tshe* CDGNQ **c** *brdar rdos* GNQ **d** *por* CD; *'dar* GNQ

Ordinary beings who are destitute of power
take great pain for others and do harm to the people.
The whetstone is unable to cut itself
but sharpens an axe which is (already) sharp.

प्रेरयति परमनार्यः शक्तिदरिद्रो ऽपि जगदभिद्रोहे ।
तेजयति खड्गधारां स्वयमसमर्था शिला छेत्तुम् ॥ ५० ॥ LSP 53

An ignoble person, although himself destitute of power,
instigates others to do harm to the people.
A stone which itself is not able to cut
sharpens the blade of a sword.

The Tibetan translation of the second line is not very felicitous because it reverses the order of subordinate and main clause. Moreover *prerayati* "instigates" should have been translated by *skul ba* "to exhort", not by *rtsol ba* "to endeavour".

'gro ba'i tshe (CDGNQ) has to be changed into *'gro ba'i* (or *'gro ba*) *'tshe* in the light of Skr. *jagadabhidrohe*.

The change from *khaḍga-* "sword" to *sta re* "axe, hatchet" does not change the general meaning of the stanza.

—51—

།སྐྱེ་བོ་གཙམ་བུ་ཕ་རོལ་གྱི། །ཐག་རིང་སྐྱོན་ལྟ་རང་གི་མིན།
།མིག་གིས་རང་གི་སྐྱོན་མི་མཐོང་། །ཟླ་བའི་ར་རི་རྟོག་པར་བྱེད། ༥༡ །

a *bcam bu* N, *cam bu* GQ, *gcam pa* D, *gcam ba* C **d** *rtogs* CD

Men who are (very) keen (on them)
see the faults of somebody else
(even when they are) far away, (but) not their own ones.
The eye does not see its own faults,
(but) it investigates the dark spots of the moon.

दूरे ऽपि परस्यागसि पटुर्जनो नात्मनः समीपेनापि ।
स्रवणमक्षि न पश्यति शशिनि कलङ्कं निरूपयति ।। ५१ ।। LSP 54

Men are harsh with the offences of others,
even if they are far away,
but not with their own ones, even if they are near.
The eye does not see its own outflow (discharge),
(but) it examines the dark spot in the moon.

In the Tibetan *Prasādapratibhodbhava* 11 we find *gcam bu* as equivalent of *atilolatā* "excessive greediness" which at least partly suits the meaning of *paṭu-* "keen". The translators did not recognize that *paṭur* functions as noun predicate. They mistook it as an attribute of *jano* and supplemented the predicate from the second half of the stanza.

samīpe 'pi remains untranslated.

The second half of the stanza is also quoted in Prajñāvarman's *Udānavarga-vivaraṇa*. Its Tibetan version can be found in BALK's edition on p. 734.18-19.

In line d) the *Udānavargavivaraṇa* reads *rtog* in accordance with NQ.

—52—

།*སྐྱོ་བ་མེད་ཅིང་རིན་ཆེན་དང་། །*ཟེལ་མེད་བརྟན་ལ་དབྱེ་*དཀའ་དང་།
།ནོར་བུ་འབར་འདྲའི་དམ་པ་དག །འཕྲན་ཚེགས་ཙམ་གྱིས་འགྱུར་བ་མེད། ༥༢ །

a *skye* CDGNQ; *rin che* GN **b** *sel byed bstan* GNQ, *sel med brtan la* CD; *dpye* N; *rga* GNQ, *dga' ba'i* (?) CD **c** *bum pa* GNQ **d** *phran* CD

Good persons who never become weary,
who are precious, who cannot be removed,
who are firm and difficult to split,
thereby resembling a blazing jewel,
cannot be changed by mere trifles.

अविरागिणी महार्घा निश्छिद्रा स्थेयसी मृदुर्भेदे ।
माणिक्यशिखेव सतां स्वल्पापि न संगतिश्चलति ।। ५२ ।। LSP 60

Like the rays of a ruby
which never loose their reddishness,
which are very precious, immaculate,
lasting, yet mild when they are split,
even the smallest association with the good
which is (always) affectionate,
precious, without weak spots, lasting,
yet soft at the time of parting will not sway.

Since *skye* (CDGNQ) *ba med ciṅ* represents *avirāgiṇī* the first syllable seems to be a corruption of *skyo* because *skyo ba* "weariness; grief, sorrow" is semantically at least slightly related to *virāga-* "aversion, dislike, disgust" which is not the case with *skye ba med ciṅ* "without birth".

For *rin chen* = *mahārgha-* cf. *rin po che* as equivalent of *mahārha* in the *Udrāyaṇa-Avadāna*, p. 3.2

sel med "unremovable" is not a suitable rendering of *niśchidra-* "without hole, fault, weak spot". I believe that it goes back to an original **zel med* "without fissures, cleavages". Cf. *Subhāṣitaratnanidhi* 2.23 where *'phan zel* seems to mean "fissures, cleavages".

*dbye *dka'* (*rga* GNQ, *dga'* CD) seems to go back to a wrong separation of words: *mṛdur bhede* was separated and translated as if it were *durbhedā*!

śikhā- "flame" was translated somewhat freely as *'bar* "burning, blazing".

—53—

|གཉུག་ཐུང་རང་བཞིན་ཡང་བ་དང་། |མགུ་དཀའ་ཁྲེལ་མེད་ཁོང་རྩུབ་པའི། C114b
|ངན་པས་མཛའ་བཤེས་ཡིད་གཅོད་བྱེད། |མཁའ་ལ་མེ་ནི་རླུང་གིས་སྦྱོར། ༥༣ । Q163b

a *gñugs* GNQ **c** *gcod de* GNQ

Close friendship with a bad person, who is unsteady,
has a careless nature, is difficult to please,
shameless and coarse torments the heart;
fire is raised into the air by the wind.

क्षणिका स्वभावलघ्वी दुरुपचरा भङ्गिनी प्रकृतिरूक्षा ।
तापयति नीचपरिचितिरग्निशिखेवात्युपचितापि ।। ५३ ।। LSP 61

Familiarity with low persons which is transient,
casual by nature, difficult to attend,
fragile and coarse by nature, even if greatly increased,
torments (the heart) like a flame of fire.

gñug thuṅ (*gñugs* GNQ) is only an orthographic variant of *sñug(s) thuṅ* "of short duration, momentary"; cf. *sñug riṅ (du)* "lengthened or continual" (SCD).

khrel med "shameless" for *bhaṅginī* "fragile" is strange.

In line d) the Tibetan presupposes something like **agniśikhā vātyupaciteva* "(like) the flame of fire which has been raised by the wind". This makes also good sense.

—54—

།ཕན་བྱེད་ས་བོན་དམ་པའི་སར། །བཏབ་འབྲུང་མི་སྲུན་ཚ་སྒོར་མིན།
།ཏིལ་མར་ཐིགས་པ་ཆུང་*ངུས་ཀྱང་། །ཆུ་ལ་སྙོམས་ཀྱི་བྱེ་*མར་མིན། ༥༨ །

b *'khruṅs* CD; *sgo* GNQ **c** *thig* Q; *dus* (?) *kyaṅ* CD, *ṅus ni* GNQ **d** *bye mas* CDGNQ

The seed of a favour shoots if it has been sowed
into the soil 'good person',
not into the barren ground 'bad person'.
Even a small drop of Sesamum oil becomes even (?)
in water, not *in sand.

उपकारबीजमुप्तं सद्भूमौ न तु खलोषर् उदेति ।
स्वल्पो ऽपि तैलबिन्दुर्विकसति सलिले न सिकतासु ॥ ५४ ॥ LSP 64

The seed of a favour shoots if it has been sowed
into the soil 'good person',
not into the barren ground 'bad person'.
Even a tiny drop of Sesamum oil
spreads in water, not in sand.

In the light of the Sanskrit original there can be little doubt that *chuṅ dus* (CDGNQ) goes back to an original *chuṅ ṅus* (= *svalpo*) and *bye mas* (CDGNQ) to *bye mar* (= *sikatāsu*).

sñoms for *vikasati* is strange. I suspect a corrupted text.

For a related content cf. stanza 86 with further parallels.

—55—

།བློ་ལྡན་དགྲ་སྒྲོག་ཉིད་འཇོམས་ཀྱི། །མི་མཁས་པ་ནི་ཡན་ལག་གོ
།སེང་གེ་ཁྲོས་ནས་མི་གསོད་ཀྱི། །ཁྱི་ཁྲོས་ནས་ནི་རྡོ་ལ་སྐྱེགས། ༥༥ །

a *dgra'o* GN; *'joms śiṅ* GNQ **b** *lag ñid la'o* GNQ **c** *khros na* NQ, *'khros na* G **d** *mi khros* NQ, *mi mkhros* G; *la brdeg* GNQ

While an intelligent person destroys the enemy's life itself,
the stupid person (destroys only his) limbs.
While a lion kills a man when it becomes angry,
the dog hastens angrily towards a stone (thrown at it).

मूले निपतन्ति बुधा शत्रूनामनिपुणास्तु शाखासु ।
श्वाभिक्रुध्यति लोष्ठं द्रुह्यति पुरुषाय तु मृगेन्द्रः ॥ ५५ ॥ LSP 66

While clever people attack
the root (i. e., fundament) of their enemies,
dull people (attack only their) twigs
(i. e., their less vital parts).
While the dog gets angry at a lump of clay (thrown at it),
the lion, the lord of the animals,
injures the man (challenging it).

For *abhidruhyati* cf. P. 1.4.38: *krudha-druha-īrṣya-āsūyānām*; for *druhyati* P. 1.4.37: *krudha-druhor upasṛṣṭayoḥ karma*. *abhikrudhyati* was translated freely, but suitably by *sñegs* "hastens towards". Was this translation influenced by the expression *śvaloṣṭānujavanasadṛśa-* (Tib. *khyi rdo la sñegs pa daṅ mtshuṅs pa*) "like a dog chasing after a clod of clay" which occurs twice in the *Kāśyapaparivarta* (pp. 105 and 107)? *brdeg* (GNQ) looks like an attempt at improving the strange meaning of what is to be regarded as a *lectio difficilior*. It is also possible that *abhikrudhyati* was interpreted as a present participle (= *abhikrudhyan*) referring to both *śvā* and *mṛgendraḥ*. This would explain why *khros nas* occurs in lines c) and d). In this case *druhyati* would also have been translated twice, by *gsod* and *sñegs*.

—56—

།འགྲོར་པ་འཕྲུན་ཚོགས་གང་དག་གིས། །སེམས་ཡང་བ་དག་དྲོད་མི་ཐུབ།
།བ་རྒྱུས་སྦྲང་བུ་འཛིན་བྱེད་ཀྱི། །མ་ཏང་ཀ་ཡི་གླང་པོ་མིན། ༥༦ །

a *phan rtse* CD; *'phren* N; *dgu* N **c** *nus kyi* GNQ **d** *ma ta ka'i* GNQ, *ma taṅ kā yis* CD; *pos* GNQ

Insignificant possessions, whatever (they may be),
are [not] able to overcome (entice?) those
whose minds are careless.
While a spider's web (is able to) hold a fly
it is not (able to do this) with a Mātaṅga elephant.

चित्तस्य तल्लघुत्वं यद्विभवाः प्रतनवो ऽपि मदयन्ति ।
बध्नाति मशकमेव ह्नि लूतातन्तुर्न मातङ्गम् ॥ ५६ ॥ LSP 93ab, 94cd

This is the weakness of mind
that it gets intoxicated by even the smallest possessions.
A spider's web is able to hold only a fly,
not an elephant.

Āryākoṣa 56 is composed of the first half of stanza 93 and the second half of stanza 94 of the *Lokasaṃvyavahārapravṛtti*. This is the full text of the two stanzas:

चित्तस्य तल्लघुत्वं यद्विभवाः प्रतनवो ऽपि मदयन्ति ।
लूतानामपि तानान्मक्षिकमशकं निधनमेति ॥ ९३ ॥

विषयगणाः कापुरुषं करोति वशवर्तिनं न सत्पुरुषम् ।
बध्नाति मशकमेव ह्नि लूतातन्तुर्न मातङ्गम् ॥ ९४ ॥

This is the weakness of mind
that it gets intoxicated by even the smallest possessions.
It is because of the web of the spiders
that flies and mosquitos die.

The sense objects govern a bad person,
not a good person.
A spider's web (is able to) hold only a fly,
not a *mātaṅga* elephant.

The sequence of the two stanzas sounds much more logical than *Āryākoṣa* 56. The opposition *maśaka* – *mātaṅga* becomes meaningful only with the preceding opposition *kāpuruṣa* – *satpuruṣa*. It seems as if the twofold occurence of *lūta* has caused the loss of the four lines 93cd and 94ab, either already in the Sanskrit manuscript which formed the basis of the Tibetan translation or in the course of the transmission of the Tibetan text.

drod mi thub formally represents the equivalent of *madayanti* "intoxicate". The usual meaning of *drod* is "warmth, heat", from the qualitative verb *dro ba* "to be warm". Here, however, it obviously has a different meaning. The ZHD (p. 1337) explains it also as *tshod* "size, extent, degree" and quotes the three expressions *ñams drod*, *yon tan gyi drod*, and *drod mi śes pa*. Cf. also the expression *drod mi zin* "cannot be fathomed" (Mongolian *ülü činegdeyü*). It is difficult to understand why *madayanti* was translated by this expression; especially the introduction of the negation *mi* which has no equivalent in Sanskrit is puzzling.

—57—

།མང་པོས་རེག་པར་མི་བཟོད་པའི། །*ཡོན་ཏན་*བཀྲ་ཤིས་ཟླ་བའི་ཡང་།
།སྐྱོན་གྱི་རྡུལ་གཅིག་*བརྗོད་པ་ན། །ཡོན་ཏན་བརྒྱ་*རྣམས་འཚུབ་པར་བྱེད། ༥༧ །

b *zer ldan* CD, *gzer ldan* GNQ; *zla ba* CD, *za ba'i* GNQ **c** *cig* GNQ; *bskyed* CDGNQ; *pas na* GNQ **d** *brgya ldan* CDGNQ; *mtshuṅs* CD

When a single particle of a fault has been *mentioned
of even the auspicious moon
whose *virtues do not tolerate to be touched by many,
this veils its hundred of virtues.

एकमपि वाच्यमानं दोषरजः प्रोर्णुते गुणशतानि ।
लक्ष्म शशिनः प्रमार्ष्टुं बह्वो ऽपि न शक्नुवन्ति गुणाः ।। ५७ ।। LSP 96

A single particle of faults veils hundreds of virtues
when it is made public.
Even many virtues cannot wipe off
the characteristic spot of the moon.

The Tibetan translation deviates considerably from the Sanskrit text. In my opinion this is due to two mistakes of the translators and three further mistakes that crept in in the course of transmission. The translators mistook *lakṣma śaśinaḥ* for a compound and moreover *pramārṣṭuṃ* for *pramarṣṭuṃ* (from *pra-mṛś* "to touch"), unless the manuscript itself did already contain this mistake. *lakṣmaśaśinaḥ* now became a genitive attribute of *guṇaśatāni* so that the rest of the stanza no longer formed an independent sentence but was interpreted as a relative clause with its relative pronoun missing. This relative clause was translated as attribute of *bkra śis zla ba'i* ending in **yon tan*. *yon tan* later corrupted into *zer ldan* in an attempt to create a more intelligible meaning, **brjod pa na* into *bskyed pa na*, perhaps only for graphical reasons, and *yon tan brgya *rnams* into *yon tan brgya ldan*, perhaps under the influence of the wrong *zer ldan*.

—58—

།ངན་པ་འཚོ་བ་ཚུལ་འཆོས་པས། །གླགས་རྙེད་གཞན་ལ་འཚེ་བར་བྱེད།
།ལག་འགྲོ་ཟས་སུ་རླུང་ཟ་ཡང་། །ཕ་རོལ་འཚེ་བ་མི་གཏོང་ངོ་། ༥༨ །

a *ṅaṅ pa mtsho la* GNQ **cd** om. GNQ

A bad person who lives with hypocrisy
does harm to others whenever he finds an opportunity.
The snake, although it feeds on air,
does not abandon doing harm to others.

परिशुद्धामपि वृत्तिं समाश्रितो दुर्जनः परान्व्यथते ।
पवनाशिनोऽपि भुजगाः परोपघातं न मुञ्चन्ति ।। ५८ ।। LSP 102

Even when his conduct is completely pure
the bad person torments others.
The snake, although it feeds on air,
does not abandon doing harm to others.

It is not clear to me why *pariśuddhām* "completely pure" was rendered as *tshul 'chos pa* "full of hypocrisy". This seems to be a deliberate alteration of the translator. Likewise *samāśrito*, here "leading (a completely pure life)" has been translated in a strange manner, by *glags rñed* "(when they) find an opportunity".

—59—

།མི་སྡུན་མི་ཡིས་ངན་པ་དག །སྐྱོན་བཏགས་རབ་ཏུ་*འཚེ་བར་*བྱེད།
།བ་ཡིས་མཁའ་ལ་རྒྱ་བརྩུགས་ནས། །སྦྲང་བུ་བཟུང་ཞིང་གསོད་པར་བྱེད། ༥༩ །

ab om. GNQ **a** *me yis* (?) D **b** *'tsher ba* CD **c** *pa yis* CD

A wicked person accuses (other) bad person of faults
and torments them heavily.
The spider erects its web in the (clear) sky,
catches the fly and kills it.

साधूनामपि दोषं दत्वा लोकान्खलाः प्रबाधन्ते ।
खे ऽपि विरचय्य चक्रं लूता मशकान्विनिघ्नन्ति ।। ५९ ।। LSP 103

Bad persons accuse even the good
of faults and torment people heavily.
The spider erects its web even in the (open) sky
and kills the flies.

The Tibetan translation seems to have suffered in the course of transmission. *ṅan pa dag* takes the place of *sādhūnām*, but I can see no reason why the translators should have translated *sādhu-* "good" by its opposite *ṅan pa* "bad". *mi yi* corresponds to *lokān*, however the change of syntax is hard to account for. If we emend *mi yi* to *mi *rnams* and *ṅan pa dag* to **bzaṅ po dag* (which is to be understood as *bzaṅ po dag la*) then the Tibetan would by and large agree with the Sanskrit. In its actual form it rather represents the following text: *lokānām api doṣaṃ dattvâsādhūn khalāḥ prabādhante.*

The relationship between the two parts of the Sanskrit stanza is not fully clear to me.

'tsher ba could also be a corruption of *'tshir ba*, which is attested as an equivalent of *pīḍayati* Mvy 5342 (= 5354). For other occurrences of the equation *'tshir ba* = *pīḍ* cf. LC[2], p. 1553b. Cf., however, stanza 61b where *'tshe bar byed* translates *prabādhate*.

—60—

།ཡུལ་གྱི་དུག་གིས་གྲོང་བའི་ཡིད། །རང་བཞིན་ངན་*པས་ཅི་*མི་བྱེད།
།ཤ་རུལ་དྲི་མི་ཞིམ་པ་དག ཁྱི་ལྟོགས་རྣམས་ཀྱིས་ཅིས་མི་ལེན། ༦༠ ། N183a

a *yul gyis* Q; *dus gis* D; *draṅs pa'i* GNQ **b** *pa cis* CDGNQ **c** *dri ma źim* N **d** *ltogs kyis de* CD

What will not be done by those who are bad by nature
and whose heart has become stiff
because of the poison 'sense objects'?
Will hungry dogs not takc mcat
which is rotten and stinks?

विषयविषातुरमनसः किं नाम दुरात्मनोऽस्त्यकरणीयम् ।
दुर्गन्धि विरसमस्थ्यपि न लेढि किं श्वा क्षुदुपतप्तः ॥ ६० ॥ LSP 104

What is actually impossible to do for an evil-hearted being
whose mind is sick because of the poison 'sense objects'?
Does a dog, when it is suffering from hunger,
not lick even at a (piece of) bone
which smells and tastes bad?

groṅ ba'i (CD): If this reading is correct (at least it is to be regarded as *lectio difficilior*) it has to be interpreted as a secondary form of *groṅs pa'i* "stiff, dead". This rather drastic meaning for *ātura-* "sick, ill" might have been chosen because of *viṣa-* "poison".

asthi "bone" became *śa* "meat". Did the translators read *durgandhivirasaṃ* **māṃsam*?

—61—

།སྐྱེ་བོ་དམ་པ་གཡོ་མེད་ལ། །ངན་པས་ལྷག་པར་འཚེ་བར་བྱེད།
།པདྨས་གནོད་པ་མ་བྱས་པར། །བ་མོས་རྟག་ཏུ་སྐེམས་པར་བྱེད། ༦༡ །

b *ṅan pa* CD

A bad person torments more than anybody else
the good person who is free of deceit.
Although the lotuses have not done any harm
the hoar-frost always dries them up.

अविकारिणामपि सज्जनमनिशमनार्यः प्रबाधतेऽत्यर्थम् ।
कमलिन्या किमपकृतं हिमस्य यत्तां सदा दहति ॥ ६१ ॥ LSP 108

The ignoble person always torments excessively
the good person even if he has not been hostile (against him).
What kind of offence has the lotus committed against the frost
that it always destroys ('burns') it?

For the meaning of *vikāra-* cf. pw s. v. under No. 10. "Wandlung der Gesinnung, feindliche Gesinnung, Auflehnung, Abfall".

—62—

།མི་སྲུན་པ་དག་མི་སྲུན་པས། །འདུལ་འགྱུར་སྐྱེ་བོ་དམ་པས་མིན། D 119a
།མཛེ་ཡི་ནད་དང་མཐུན་པའི་སྨན། །ཨ་རི་ཏ་ཡི་ཤིང་སྟོན་ནོ། ༦༢ །

a *mi bsrun* N; *bsrun pas* GNQ **c** om. GNQ [!]. **d** *ari te* GNQ; *bsten* CD, *bston no* GQ, *bstono* N

A bad person can be tamed (only) by a bad person,
not by a good person.
It is said that (only) the *ariṣṭa* tree
is a suitable medicine against leprosy.

प्रखला एव खलानां प्रशमायालं न जातु सत्पुरुषः ।
कुष्ठव्याधेरौषधमनुरूपमुशन्त्यरिष्टतरुम् ।। ६२ ।। LSP 114

Only very bad persons are able
to tame (other) bad persons.
a good person (is) not at all (able to do this).
The Ariṣṭa tree is declared
to be a suitable medicine against leprosy.

For the use of *ariṣṭa* (= *nimba*) cf. e. g. Ravigupta's *Siddhasāra* 12.10–11. Sa skya Paṇḍita expresses the idea with these words:

།རྩུབ་པས་རྩུབ་པ་ཐུལ་’གྱུར་གྱི། །ཞི་བས་དུལ་བར་ག་ལ་ནུས།
།ཕོལ་མིག་བསྲེག་དང་བཅད་པས་གཏོན། །ཞི་ཆོས་དེ་ཡི་དུག་ཏུ་’གྱུར།། ༡༦༢ ||

What is rough is tamed by something rough;
how could one tame it by something mild?
An abscess is removed by cautering and cutting;
something soft would be poison for it.

—63—

།ངན་གཡོ་ཅན་དག་དང་པོར་ནི། །ཡོན་ཏན་ལྡན་པའི་ཆེ་བ་འགོག
།བུད་མེད་ཀྱི་ནི་ནུ་རྒྱས་ལ། །*རྒ་བ་དང་པོར་དེ་ལ་འབབ། ༦༣ །

a *draṅ por* GNQ **c** *nu* om. Q (new line after *ni*!), *bu* GN; *brgyas la'aṅ* GNQ **d** *dga' ba* CDGNQ; *de la 'byuṅ* GNQ (this mistake is obviously caused by the preceding mistake *dga' ba* for *rga ba*).

Cunning and deceitful people first of all
impede the great(ness) of the virtuous.
The bosom of women is swelling;
(therefore) old age at first plunges down on the (bosom).

प्रथमतरमेव धूर्ताः सगुणानत्युन्नतान्प्रबाधन्ते ।
स्त्रीणां स्तनेषु लक्ष्मीरिति तेष्वादौ जरा पतति ।। ६३ ।। LSP 115

b *saguṇān*: *guṇino 'py* H

First of all cunning people torment those,
who possess virtues and have a very high position.
The beauty of women lies in their bosoms,
and for this reason old age at first plunges down on them.

rgyas la "is swelling" is a remarkably free translation of *lakṣmī*- "beauty".

—64—

།བླུན་པོ་ལྷག་པར་སྲིད་མཐོ་ཡང་། །བློ་ལྡན་དབུལ་པོས་ཟིལ་གྱིས་གནོན།
།མཁའ་ལས་ཆར་པ་འབབ་པ་ཡིས། །རྡུལ་ཕྲན་ལྡང་བ་ཞི་བར་བྱེད། ༦༤ །

a *srin* Q; *mthos kyaṅ* GNQ **b** *blo ldan lhag par pas zil gyis gnon* G, *lhag pas zil* NQ, *dbul pos zil* CD **c** *mkha' la* GNQ; *bab pa yis* CD

A fool, even if his position is extremely high,
is defeated by a poor intelligent person.
The rain which falls down from the heaven
stops the rising of dust.

अभ्युन्नतानपि जडान्मतिमानभिभवति विभवरहितो ऽपि ।
निपतदपि दिव्यमम्भः प्रशमयति समुत्पतिष्णु रजः ।। ६४ ।। LSP 120

An intelligent person, even without wealth,
defeats fools, even if they assume a high rank.
The heavenly water, even if it falls down,
stops the rising dust.

—65—

།བློ་ལྡན་རབ་ཏུ་ཉམ་ཐག་ཀྱང་། ། བརྙས་ཐབས་བསྲེས་པའི་ནོར་མི་ལེན།
*ཁྱུག་རྟ་དག་ནི་ས་སྟེངས་ཀྱི། ། མཚོ་ཆུའང་འཐུང་བར་མི་བྱེད་དོ། ༦༥ །

a *rtag tu* GNQ; **b** *'byor mi* GNQ **c** *khu rta* C, *bu rta* D; *skad sñan khu byug sa steṅ gi* GNQ **d** *skom yaṅ mtsho ru 'thuṅ mi byed* GNQ

The intelligent, even if they are in the greatest calamity,
will never accept wealth which is mixed with humiliation.
The *cātaka* birds will never drink water
which has reached the earth, not even (that of) a lake.

कृच्छ्रगता अपि न बुधाः परिभवमिश्रां श्रियं निषेवन्ते ।
न पिबन्ति भौममम्भः सरजसमिति चातका एव ॥ ६५ ॥ LSP 122

Intelligent persons, even if they are in (great) difficulties
will never enjoy wealth which is mixed with humiliation.
The *cātaka* bird will never drink water
which has reached the earth, because it contains dust.

mtsho chu'aṅ points to a reading **sarasajam* or **sarasijam* in the Sanskrit manuscript which was used by the translators.

Lines c) and d) of GNQ clearly show that they were revised by some unknown editors of the Tibetan text.

Sa skya Paṇḍita's version of this stanza runs as follows (*Subhāṣitaratnanidhi* 13):

།མཁས་པ་ཇི་ལྟར་ཐབས་བརྟུགས་ཀྱང་། ། བླུན་པོ་འཇུག་པའི་ལམ་མི་འགྲོ།
།ཆར་འདོད་བྱེའུ་སྐོམ་ན་ཡང་། ། ས་ལ་འབབ་པའི་ཆུ་མི་འཐུང་།

"However much the wise are lacking in resources,
they will not go the way which fools have taken.
Even if the martin is thirsty,
he will not drink the water that flows onto the ground." (Bosson)

—66—

།བདག་ཉིད་ཆེན་པོ་དར་བ་དང་། །རྒུད་པ་ན་ཡང་སེམས་སྙོམས་འགྱུར།
།ཉི་མའི་དཀྱིལ་འཁོར་འཆར་བ་དང་། །ནུབ་པ་ན་ཡང་འགྱུར་བ་མེད། ༦༦ ། Q163b

b *samms* N

A noble-hearted being maintains an even mind,
in (the time of) ascendence and also in that of fall.
The disk of the sun does not change
neither when it rises nor when it sets.

मह्तामेव समानं भवति मनोऽत्युच्छ्रितौ निपाते च ।
भानोरिवाविकृतं मण्डलमुदयेऽस्तगमने च ॥ ६६ ॥ LSP 124

Whether they are in a very high position
or whether they fall down
the mind of the great remains the same.
The disk of the sun does not change
neither when it rises nor when it sets.

—67—

།ཉིན་རེ་འབྲི་བའི་སྡུག་བསྔལ་ཡང་། །ཟླ་དེས་ལྟ་བུར་བཟོད་པར་ནུས།
།ཉི་མ་ལྟ་བུའི་བཙན་པོ་ཡང་། །ནུབ་འདོད་འབྲི་བར་སྤྲོ་བ་མེད། ༦༧ །

a *bsṅal dag* CD **b** *de lta bus* GNQ **d** *bri ba* CD, *bri bar* GQ, *bre bar* N

(He) who is like the tender moon is able to bear
even the sorrow of daily diminishment.
(He) who is strong like the sun may wish to sink down,
but does not rejoice in the state of diminishment.

प्रतिदिनमपचयदुःखं शक्तो मृदुरेव चन्द्र इव सोढुम् ।
तीक्ष्णोऽस्तमेति कामं न तु रविरिव खण्डनं सह्ते ॥ ६७ ॥ LSP 125

Only he who is soft is able to bear daily
the sorrow of reduction—like the moon.
He who is sharp might sink down, like the sun,
but he does not stand being cut into pieces.

In line b) the word order of the translation should have been **zla ltar des pa*. Obviously the translators wrongly took *mṛdur* as attribute of *candra*, not as the subject of the first sentence. With the present word order it became difficult for the editors of GNQ to realize that *des* stands for the adjective *des pa* "delicate", the equivalent of *mṛdur*. They wrongly regarded it as pronoun and changed *des* to *de* and *lta bur* to *lta bus* in an attempt to improve upon the grammar.

nub 'dod "wish(ing) to sink down" in line d) looks as if the translators read **astamitikāmo*. They did not recognize that *kāmaṃ* here is an adverb, which can be used as a particle of assent "well, indeed" and also as a kind of conjunction "it may be that".

—68—

།རང་ཉིད་ཉམ་ཐག་མ་བྱུང་བར། །དེ་སྲིད་མི་དག་གྲོགས་བྱེད་དོ།
།ཀླད་པར་གནམ་ལྕགས་བབ་པ་སྟེ། །སུ་ཞིག་གིས་ནི་བསྐྱབ་པར་ནུས། ༦༨ །

b *sred* Q; *mi daṅ 'grogs byed de* CD, *byedo* N **c** *glad* CD; *pa na* GNQ **d** *la ni* GNQ; *skyabs* Q

As long as he does not find himself in calamities
a man is able to make friends.
When the thunderbolt has (already) fallen
upon one's head— who is (then) able to save (him)?

तावत्सन्ति सहाया यावज्जन्तुर्न कृच्छ्रमाप्नोति ।
विनिपतति शिरसि वज्रे कं कः शक्तः परित्रातुम् ॥ ६८ ॥ LSP 127

As long as a human being is not in a difficult situation
he has friends.

When the thunderbolt has (already) fallen
upon one's head— who is (then) able to save him?

In line d) one would expect *su źig su la* (or *su ni*) for *kaṃ kaḥ*. VS 3183 (attributed to Ravigupta) reads *mṛtyau* i. o. *vajre*.

—69—

།ཡོན་ཏན་ལྡན་པ་གཞན་ཕན་པ། །མི་བྱེད་ཕལ་པས་ཁྱད་ཅི་ཡོད། C115a
།ཉི་མ་མུན་སེལ་མི་བྱེད་ན། །དེ་ནི་མུན་ལས་ཁྱད་པར་མེད། ༦༩ །

a *yon tan ldan pa mi byed pa* G, *yon tan ldan pa yon tan mi byed pa* NQ **b** *phal daṅ* CD **c** *bsal* CD **d** *mun daṅ* GNQ

If a virtuous one does not help others,
how is he then different from an ordinary being?
If the sun would not remove darkness,
then it would not be different from darkness.

गुणवानपि योऽन्यद्धितं न करोति स भिद्यते कथं विगुणात् ।
अवशिष्टः सोऽस्तमिताडुदितो ऽपि न यः प्रकाशयति ।। ६९ ।। LSP 130

If somebody, although virtuous, does not help others,
how would he then be different from a person without virtues?
[The sun] that does not emit light, although it has risen,
is not different from [that sun]
that has (already) sunk down.

—70—

།འགའ་ཞིག་འགའ་བསྒོམས་མཐུ་ཡོད་ཀྱི། །གཅིག་པུས་ཀུན་འགྲུབ་ཡོད་པ་མིན།
།རྡོ་རྗེས་ཕ་བོང་འབིགས་བྱེད་ཀྱང་། །དེ་ཉིད་ར་རུས་གཅོད་པར་བྱེད། ༧༠ །

a *źig dga'* CD; *yod kyis* C; *yod kyaṅ* GNQ **b** *cig pus* GQ, *gcig pos* CD; *thub* N, *grub* GNQ; *yod ma yin* GNQ **d** *rwa* CD

Somebody might be(come) powerful,
when united with somebody else,
he will not be able to accomplish everything alone.
Although the thunderbolt splits a piece of rock,
it can be split by a goat's horn.

कश्चित्क्वचिद्बलीयान्नैकः सर्वार्थसाधनायालम् ।
शैलं भिनत्ति वज्रं स्वयमेति भिदां विषाणेन ॥ ७० ॥ LSP 132

Somebody might be very strong in some field,
however a single person will not be able
to accomplish everything.
A thunderbolt can split a rock,
but it cracks by itself because of a horn (?).

It is not clear to me why "the thunderbolt (or the rock?) cracks by itself because of a horn". No hints in IS², DANGE or MANI. It is also not clear to me why the simple form *kva cid* 'somewhere' was translated by *'ga' bsdoms* 'united with someone.'

—71—

།འདབ་གཤོག་རྫོགས་ཀྱང་འགྲོ་འདོད་པའི། །འབད་རྩོལ་གྱིས་འཕངས་ཐག་རིང་འཕུར།
།འཕངས་པའི་ཤུགས་ཟད་མདའ་དག་ཀྱང་། །རང་ཉིད་ལྷུང་བར་བྱེད་པ་བཞིན། ༧༡ །

a *śog* GNQ; *rdzogs bya 'chi 'dod pa* GNQ **b** *'phaṅ* N

When (someone) wishes to go (to die GNQ)
although his wings are fully developed,
he will be thrown by (his) endeavour
and soar up high (into the sky).
In the same manner also an arrow will fall down by itself
when the momentum of being shot becomes exhausted.

दृढपक्षो ऽपि जिघांसुः कर्मी क्षेपात्सुदूरमपि गत्वा ।
स्वयमेव पतति सर्वो बाण इव क्षीणसंस्कारः ।। ७१ ।। LSP 134

Every *karmin* (an energetic person?) intent on killing,
will fall by himself when his merits (?) are exhausted,
however far he has gone by his invectives,
even if his (own) party is strong,
like an arrow (that is destined to kill
will fall down by itself when its *saṃskāra* is exhausted
even when its feathers are strongly fixed,
however far it has gone by its momentum.)

Both stanzas offer several probems. I can offer no convincing explanation of the Sanskrit original since the specific meaning of *karmī* is not clear to me. The structure of the stanza leaves little doubt that it is the subject of the sentence that is compared with an arrow (*bāṇa*) and that all the attributes refer to both terms by way of a *double entendre.* The Tibetan translation is of little help since it obviously interprets **karmikṣepāt* as a compound: *'bad rtsol gyis 'phaṅs* "thrown by (his) energy". While *'phaṅs* for *kṣepāt* can easily be justified, *'bad rtsol* for *karmin* is not so clear. *'bad rtsol* is attested as equivalent of *āyāsa-* in *Bodhicaryāvatāra* 9.155b, of *prayatna-* in *Aṣṭāṅgahṛdayasaṃhitā* 1.12.6, of *prayāsa-* in *Bodhisattvāvadānakalpalatā* 17.52 and of *vyavasāya* in *Bodhisattvāvadānakalpalatā* 6.129. Was *karmī* taken in its meaning "an active, determined (person)"? However, the equivalents just quoted clearly show that *'bad rtsol* designates an abstract concept, not a person, as one would expect from the formation of the compound; cf. similar verb-verb compounds like *'bab rtsol.*[8] Thus it remains doubtful what the translators actually read.

The next unclear expression in the Tibetan translation is the rendering of *jighāṃsu-* "desirous to kill". In GNQ we find *'chi 'dod pa* "wishing to die" which is not correct although there is a certain semantic relationship between "to kill" and "to die." In CD we read *'gro 'dod pa* "wishing to go" which is even less correct. One can only guess what happened, and unfortunately there are numerous possiblities:

8. For verb-verb compounds cf. my paper "A propos the term *gtsug-lag*", *Proceedings of the 7th Seminar of the International Association for Tibetan Studies*, Wien 1997, pp. 341–348.

a) *'dab gśog rdzogs bya 'chi 'dod pa'i* (GNQ) represents the original translation. This would yield the following interpretation: "A bird whose wings are fully developed throws (itself into the air) in an energetic attempt that is motivated by the wish to die and soars high." In this case the translators either read **jigamiṣu* instead of *jighāṃsu* or they mistook *jighāṃsu* for **jigamiṣu.*

b) Unfortunately *'chi* could also be a spelling variant of *mchi* "to go" in which case the translators might have read *jighāṃsu* but have chosen an unusual rendering. However, why should the translators have chosen the elegant form instead of the ordinary verb *'gro ba*, the reading of CD? In both cases *bya* for *kyaṅ* seems to be a later editorial change. First, *kyaṅ* renders (*dṛḍhapakṣo*) *'pi*, and second there is no word in the Sanskrit text representing *bya* "bird". It is not possible to read **pakṣī* instead of *karmī* since there is already an equivalent of *karmī*: *'bad rtsol.*

c) *'dab gśog rdzogs kyaṅ 'gro 'dod pa'i* (CD) represents the original translation. This would again point to **jigamiṣu.*

d) Unfortunately *'gro* could also be a mutilated form of *'groṅ* "to die" in which case the translators might have read *jighāṃsu* but have chosen an unusual rendering. However, why should the translators have chosen the elegant form instead of the ordinary verb *'chi ba*, the reading of GNQ?

The two particles *dag kyaṅ* after *mda'* seem to render *sarvo.* Cf. the usage of *api* after numerals or adjectives expressing totality. Or is *kyaṅ* a corruption of an original **kun*?

No attempt on the part of the translators can be seen to maintain the *double entendre* (*śleṣa*) of the original Sanskrit text.

—72—

།ཡོངས་སྤྱོད་བདོག་ཀྱང་འཇུངས་པ་དག ། རང་གི་ལས་ཀྱིས་སྤྱོད་དབང་མེད།
།རྒུན་གྱི་འབྲས་བུ་སྨིན་པའི་ཚེ། ཁྭ་ལ་མཆུ་ནད་འོང་ཞེས་གྲགས། ༧༢ །

a *loṅspyod* G **c** *dgun* GNQ **d** *kha* GNQ; *chu* N

Because of his own (former) deeds
the miser cannot freely enjoy enjoyments,
even if they are at hand.
It is said that the crows develop a disease of the beak
when the grapes are ripe.

प्राप्तानपि न लभन्ते भोगान्भोक्तुं स्वकर्मभिः कृपणाः ।
मुखपाकः किल भवति द्राक्षापाके बलिभुजां हि ॥ ७२ ॥ LSP 135

Because of their own (former) deeds
misers cannot enjoy enjoyments, even if they are at hand.
As it is known, the crows develop an abscess
on their beaks when the grapes are ripe.

It is difficult to decide which of the two main readings of the second half of stanza formed the basis of the Tibetan translation. The wording of the alternative is: *drākṣāprapākasamaye mukhapāko bhavati kākānām.* In line c) *tshe* seems to reflect *samaye,* however *źes grags* "thus it is heard or known" clearly points to *kila* "as it is known".

This is Sa skya Paṇḍita's version of the stanza (*Subhāṣitaratnanidhi* 92):

།ལོངས་སྤྱོད་ཡོད་ཀྱང་ལས་ངན་གྱིས། །འཇུངས་པ[ས]་སྤྱོད་པའི་རང་དབང་མེད།
།རྒྱུ་འབྲུམ་སྨིན་པ་ཟ་བའི་ཚེ། །ཁྭ་ལ་མཆུ་ནད་རྒྱུན་དུ་འབྱུང་།

"Even if objects of enjoyment are at his disposal,
the miser, on account of his bad karma,
has not the freedom to enjoy them.
When they eat the ripe grapes
crows always develop a disease of their beaks."

—73—

།ཤེས་རབ་ལྡན་པས་རྫས་བཟང་པོ། །མཐོང་ན་མོད་ལ་བྱེ་བྲག་ཕྱེད།
།ལག་པའི་ཚོད་ལ་རབ་གོམས་པས། །སྲང་ཚད་རྣམས་ནི་ཤེས་པར་བྱེད། ༧༣ । N183b

b *phye* CD

When a wise person sees something good,
he judges its quality in an instant.
He who has great experience in measuring with his hands
knows the size of the *sraṅ* weight.

सकृदपि दृष्ट्वा पुरुषं प्राज्ञास्तुलयन्ति सारफल्गुत्वम् ।
हस्ततुलयापि निपुणाः पलपरिमाणं विजानन्ति ।। ७३ ।। LSP 139

Even when they have seen a man only once,
the wise can measure both his qualities and deficiencies.
Those who are experts in weighing with their hands
only recognize the size of the *pala* weight.

puruṣaṃ "a man" has been rendered rather freely by *rdzas bzaṅ po* "a good matter", and likewise *sāraphalgutvam* "qualities and deficiencies". Nevertheless there is no reason to assume that this was not deliberately done.

—74—

།སྡིག་པས་སྦགས་པའི་རང་བཞིན་ལས། །དཀའ་བས་ཡིད་ནི་དག་འགྱུར་ཏེ།
།ངང་གིས་དྲི་མ་ཅན་གྱི་གོས། །རབ་ཏུ་འབད་པས་དཀར་པོར་འགྱུར། ༧༤ །

a *sṅags* N **b** *dag 'gyur* CD, *dga' 'gyur* GNQ

A mind which is by nature defiled by sin
becomes pure (again only) with (great) difficulties.[9]
A garment which has become dirty by itself
will become white (only) with great effort.

शुध्यति दुःखेन *मनः पापेषु तु मज्जति प्रकृत्यैव ।
स्वयमेव भवति मलिनं वासः शुक्लं प्रयत्नेन ।। ७४ ।। LSP 141

9. Cf. the philological commentary. Literally and without emendation the text means: "A mind that is defiled by sin becomes happy (again only) with (great) difficulties because of its nature."

a **manaḥ*: *malaḥ* S, *yid* "mind, heart" ĀKtib. There can be little doubt that *malaḥ* is an inferior reading which owes its existence to the adjective *malinaṃ* in line c).

A mind is purified (only) with (great) pain;
however, it immerses into sin by its very nature.
A garment gets dirty by itself,
white (only) with great effort.

Our translation of the first half of the stanza is based on the assumption that the translators fully understood the meaning of the Sanskrit text, but allowed themselves a certain freedom both with regard to single words and to the syntax. In the standard word order the translation should have run: *raṅ bźin las sdig pas sbags pa'i yid ni dka' bas dag 'gyur te.* The two sentences with the two predicates *śudhyati* and *majjati* have been combined into one sentence by transforming the first sentence into an attribute of *yid*, the equivalent of **manaḥ*. Moreover "immersed into sin" has been altered into "defiled by sin".

Sa skya Paṇḍita has used this stanza as model of stanza 175 of his *Subhāṣitaratnanidhi*:

།ངན་པ་ཇི་ལྟར་བཙོས་གྱུར་ཀྱང་། །རང་བཞིན་བཟང་པོ་འབྱུང་མི་སྲིད།
།སོལ་བ་འབད་དེ་བཀྲུས་ན་ཡང་། །ཁ་དོག་དཀར་པོ་མི་སྲིད་དོ།

"However one remedies an evil person,
he cannot possibly get a good nature.
Although one has diligently washed charcoal,
its colour cannot possibly become white."

—75—

།གཡོན་ཅན་གྲུས་པ་སྟོན་པ་ནི། །དགོས་པའི་ཆེད་ཡིན་གྲུས་པས་མིན།
།སླད་འཚོང་སྐྱེས་པ་དགའ་བྱེད་པ། །འདྲིད་པའི་ཆེད་ཡིན་དགའ་བས་མིན། ༧༥ ། D119b

a *g.yo* NQ; *sten* Q

When a cunning person behaves respectfully,
this happens (only) because he aims at something,
not out of (genuine) respect.
When a prostitute pleases a man,
this happens (only) in order to entice him,
not out of friendliness.

अस्निग्धा अपि भक्तिं धूर्ता उपदेशयन्ति फलद्धेतोः ।
वेश्या रमयन्ति जनं भावेन न चानुरज्यन्ते ।। ७५ ।। LSP 143

Even when they do not feel any affection
cunning people show devotion
when they have a (certain) purpose (in their minds).
Prostitutes please men,
but they do not really love them.

—76—

།སྐྲ་དང་མྱུ་གུ་སྒོང་སྐྱེས་མེ། །དུག་དྲེའུ་ཤིང་སྲིན་རྨ་འབུ་དང་།
།རང་བཞིན་ཁྲེལ་མེད་མི་དག་ནི། །རང་རྟེན་མ་ཕུང་མི་གཏོང་ངོ་། ༧༦ །

d *mi phuṅ* CDN(?); *gtoṅo* N

Hair, a sprout, an egg-born being, fire, poison,
a (she-)mule, a wood-worm, an insect living in wounds
and human beings who are shameless by nature
do not leave their own basis without destroying it.

रोगोऽण्डजोऽङ्कुरोऽग्निर्विषमश्वतरी घुणा व्रणकृमयः ।
प्रकृतिकृतघ्नाश्च नराः स्वाश्रयमविनाश्य नैधन्ते ।। ७६ ।। LSP 144

A disease, an egg-born being, a sprout, fire, poison,
a she-mule, wood-worms, insects living in wounds
and men who are ungrateful by nature
cannot thrive without destroying their own basis.

Instead of *rogo* the translators seem to have read **keśo* "a hair". This alteration makes little sense.

The sequence of *aṇḍajo* and *aṅkuro* is changed in Tibetan.

kṛtaghna- "ungrateful" became *khrel med* "immodest, shameless" in Tibetan. This is again not a felicitous modification of the Indian original.

The predicate *naidhante* "do not thrive, prosper" has been changed to *mi gtoṅ ṅo* "do not leave, abandon". Did the Sanskrit manusript read **nojjhanti* or was this a deliberate alteration?

In the Tibetan *Janapoṣaṇabindu* we find a similar stanza:

།རྨ་འབུ་དུག་དྲེའུ་ཤིང་སྲིན་དང་། །ས་བོན་མྱུ་གུ་*སྒོང་སྐྱེས་མེ།
།དེ་བཞིན་ངན་པའི་མི་རྣམས་ནི། །རང་རྟེན་ཕོན་འཕུང་བ་སྐྱུབ། ༧༦ །

Insects living in wounds, poison, a she-mule, wood-worms,
a seed, a sprout, an egg-born being, fire,
likewise bad people
cannot thrive without destroying their own basis.

Here the Sanskrit seems to have read **bījo* i. o. *rogo*! *de bźin* is most likely a corruption of an original *raṅ bźin* (< Skt. *prakṛti-*).

Subhāṣitaratnanidhi 136 offers a loose parallel:

།ངན་པ་རང་རྟེན་ཁྱད་པར་འཇོམས། །དམ་པ་གང་ལ་བརྟེན་པ་སྲུང་།
།སྲིན་བུ་རང་རྟེན་ཟད་ཟད་ཟ། །སེང་གེ་རང་གི་ཡུལ་འཁོར་སྲུང་།

"The bad destroy their own support in particular.
Whatever the excellent rely on, they protect.
The worm eats up his own support completely.
The lion protects his own province."

—77—

།ཡོན་ཏན་ལྡན་ལ་ཕྱུག་པོ་དཀོན། །ཕྱུག་པོ་ཕལ་ཆེར་ཡོན་ཏན་མེད།
།མེ་ཏོག་ཙ་རྒྱན་རབ་མཛེས་ཀྱང་། །ཡི་ཤིའི་མེ་ཏོག་དྲི་རབ་ཞིམ། ༧༧ ། Q164b

A rich person is rare among the virtuous,
and the rich are generally lacking virtues.
While the flower of the *karṇikāra* tree is very beautiful,
the clove plant smells very sweet.

गुणावत्सु नातिलक्ष्मीर्धनिनो ऽपि प्रायशो गुणदरिद्राः ।
अतिचारु कर्णिकारं सुरभीनि लवङ्गकुसुमानि ।। ७७ ।। LSP 145

Excessive wealth cannot be found among the virtuous,
and the rich are generally lacking virtues.
While the flower of the *karṇikāra* tree is very beautiful,
the flowers of the clove plant smell very sweet.

For *karṇikāra*- (Pterospermum acerifolium Willd.) cf. Renate SYED, *Die Flora Altindiens in Literatur und Kunst*, München 1990, pp. 189–193. Many stanzas of the classical Sanskrit literature allude the beauty of the white, yellow or golden *karṇikāra* flowers, however there is only one *locus classicus* which expressly mentions its lack of fragrance, Kālidāsa's *Kumārasaṃbhava* 3.28:

वर्णप्रकर्षे सति कर्णिकारं दुनोति निर्गन्धतया स्म चेतः ।
प्रायेण सामान्यविधौ गुणानां पराङ्मुखी विश्वसृजः प्रवृत्तिः ।।

The first half of this stanza can also be found in the first half of stanza 5 of Vararuci's *Gāthāśataka*. Its wording is slightly different:

།ཡོན་ཏན་ལྡན་ལ་ཕྱུག་པོ་དཀོན། །ཕྱུག་པོ་ལ་ཡང་ཡོན་ཏན་དཀོན།

—78—

།རང་བཞིན་མི་བརྟན་ལྷག་པར་གཡོ། །གཟུང་དཀའ་བཅོས་དཀའ་སྐྱོན་ལྡན་པའི།
།དངུལ་ཆུ་ལྟ་བུའི་སྦྱོར་བ་ཡིས། །མ་བསྡུམས་དམ་པ་གང་ལ་འགྲུབ། ༧༨ །

c *ruṅ chu* GNQ

Which good person will be successful,
who is like quicksilver because his nature is unstable,
because he is extremely fickle, difficult to hold,
difficult to prepare and full of faults (danger),
if he is not controlled by Yoga (a suitable mixture).

अतिचपलमस्थिरगुणां दुर्ग्रहमविधेयमाचितं दोषैः ।
योगेन रसमिव सतामनिबध्य मनः कुतो भूतिः ॥ ७८ ॥ LSP 146

If the mind, which is extremely fickle,
of unsteady qualities, difficult to grasp,
difficult to handle and full of faults (danger),
is not controlled by contact with the good,
as quicksilver is controlled by a recipe
(prepared) by experts,
how will it attain (supernatural) power[10]?

The Tibetan translation omits *manaḥ* "mind" which is the central term of the stanza. There is only one possible explanation for this omission: the translators read **anibadhyamānaḥ* (or *°naṃ*) i. o. *anibadhya manaḥ*. Then they made *satām ... kuto bhūtiḥ* "how can there be success for the good" the main construction. The result is still tolerable as far as the agreement of the general idea is concerned.

—79—

།མཐོ་ན་དྲེགས་པར་མི་བྱ་སྟེ། །རྒུད་ནའང་ཡིད་ཆད་མི་བྱའོ།
།ཉི་མས་སྨུན་པ་བསལ་མོད་ཀྱི། །ཉི་མ་ཤར་བ་ནུབ་པར་འགྱུར། ༧༩ །

a *mthon dregs* CD; *mi byed de* CD **b** *yi* CD **c** *gsal* CDN, *bsal ba mod kyi* G

Do not become haughty when you are in a high position,
and do not become despondent

10. Or: well-being?

when you have fallen down.
The sun dispels darkness,
however (even) the risen sun will (eventually) set.

उदये मा यात मदं व्यसनेषु *माभ्युपेत संतापम् ।
*उदयति तमो ऽपि संहृतमुदितः सवितापि यात्यस्तम् ॥ ७९ ॥ LSP 147

b **mābhyupeta*: *mābhyupaiti* (°*ta*?) S. ĀKtib. has *yid chad mi bya'o* "shall not become despondent". **c** **udayati*: *udyati* S. There can be little doubt that the locative of the active present participle is required here.

Do not become haughty when you are successful,
and do not grieve when you are in trouble.
When (the sun) rises even darkness is dispelled,
(however) even the risen sun will (eventually) set.

A very loose parallel offers *Subhāṣitaratnanidhi* 398:

།ཕོངས་ཀྱང་གདུང་བར་མི་བྱ་སྟེ། །འབྱོར་ཀྱང་དགའ་བས་དྲེགས་མི་བྱ།
།ལས་ཀྱི་འཕེན་པ་རྒྱང་རིང་བས། །སྐྱིད་སྡུག་སྣ་ཚོགས་ད་གདོད་འབྱུང་།

"Even if you become impoverished,
do not become pained,
and even if you become rich,
do not rejoice and become haughty.
Because the reach (casting) of karma is (very) long,
the various pleasant and unpleasant (retributions)
will be forthcoming (or) wait (for you right) now." (Bosson)

—80—

།ཀུ་ལའི་རི་བརྟན་རབ་ཆེ་ཡང་། །མི་གཞོལ་སྐྱོན་གྱིས་སྤྱངས་ནས་ནི།
།ཆུ་རྣམས་རྒྱ་མཚོར་འབབ་པ་ཡང་། །བདག་ཉིད་རིམ་གྱིས་གཞོལ་བ་ལྟོས། ༨༠ །

b *nas na* GNQ **d** *rin gyis* N; *ldos* Q

Having left even the very high and firm mountain
of origin because of their fault of being high
the water flows down to the ocean—
look at its nature which gradually flows down!

अतिसुमहतः स्थिरानप्युन्नतिदोषेण कुलगिरींस्त्यक्त्वा ।
सरितः प्रयान्ति सागरमनुन्नतेः पश्यत महत्त्वम् ॥ ८० ॥ LSP 148

Having left even the very high and firm mountain
of origin because of their fault of being high
the rivers flow down to the ocean—
look, how great it is not to be haughty!

The Tibetan text of line d) seems to be corrupt. *rim gyis* has no counterpart in the Sanskrit text, and *bdag ñid* renders only *tvam* of *mahattvam.* One would expect *bdag ñid che ba* or *che bdag* as equivalent of *mahattvam.* For a comprehensive list of correspondences cf. stanza 37.

—81—

།ཆོ་རིགས་ཡོན་ཏན་ལྡན་ན་ཡང་། །རང་བཞིན་མི་སྲུན་བཤེས་མི་བྱ།
།མེ་མཆེད་གྱུར་ན་མ་ལ་ཡའི། །ཙན་དན་གྱིས་ཀྱང་སྲེག་པར་བྱེད། ༨༡ །

b *bsrun* GNQ **d** *bsreg* GNQ

Even if they descend from a noble family
and possess virtues
one should not make friends with evil-natured beings.
When a fire has spread, it burns
even with the sandal-wood from the Malaya mountains.

कुलज्ञोऽयं गुणवानिति विश्वासो न क्षमः खलप्रकृतौ ।
ननु मलयचन्दनादपि समुत्थितोऽग्निर्दहत्येव ॥ ८१ ॥ LSP 149

One should not have confidence in an evil-natured being
(only) because he was born in a noble family
and has some virtues.
Does not also that fire burn which has risen
from the sandal-wood from the Malaya mountains?

For *cho rigs* cf. the correspondence *cho rigs can* ~ *abhijanaśālin* [< *Bodhisattvāvadānakalpalatā* 9.4] in LC[2], p. 611b.

For *na kṣamaḥ* VS 2859 has the variant reading *nācaret*.

By omitting *ayaṃ* and *iti* the Tibetan has changed the construction of the first line, however this could be a deliberate change. Therefore it is niether necessray to assume that the Sanskrit read **api* instead of *iti* nor to emend the Tibetan to *ldan *de źes*.

—82—

།སྨད་རིགས་གཟེངས་མཐོས་ཐོག་མར་ནི། །རྗེ་དཔོན་ཁྱད་དུ་གསོད་པར་བྱེད།
།ས་རྡུལ་གྱེན་དུ་འཐོར་བ་ཡང་། །འཐོར་བྱེད་ཉིད་ལ་ཐོག་མར་འབབ། ༨༢ ། C115b

a *dmaṅs rigs gzeṅ* GNQ

A low person who has been raised into a high rank
will at first humiliate his own lord.
The dust of the ground, too, when is has been scattered,
will at first fall on him who has scattered it.

लब्धोच्छ्रायो नीचः प्रथमतरं स्वामिनं पराभवति ।
धूलिरुदञ्चन्नादावुत्थापकमेव संवृणुते ॥ ८२ ॥ LSP 152

a *labdhocchrāyo nīcaḥ: labdhocchrayo hi nīcaḥ* H

A low person who has been raised into a high rank
will at first humiliate his own lord.
The dust which is raising upwards
will at first cover him who has raised it.

The *Lokasaṃvyavahārapravṛtti* reads *labdhocchrayo hi nīcaḥ* in line a). I find the *hi* difficult to account for. Usually it is found only in the second half of the stanza, together with the simile. Therefore I have adopted the reading of ŚP 351 and VS 414.

For the internal parallel and other external parallels cf. stanza 14.

—83—

།གང་གིས་བླུན་པོ་ཉམ་ཐག་པས། །བགྲོད་དཀའ་ཤེས་རབ་ལྡན་པས་རྒལ།
།ལྕགས་གོང་ཆུ་ནང་བྱིང་བ་དག །དེ་ཉིད་སྣོད་བྱས་སྟེང་ན་འཕྱོ། ༨༣ །

b *brgal* GNQ

Whereby the fool is troubled
thereby the wise crosses what is hard to cross.
The same ball of iron which sinks down in the water
swims on top (of the water) after it has been made a vessel.

सीदति येनैव जडः प्राज्ञस्तेनैव तरति दुर्गाणि ।
पिण्डितमयोऽप्सु मज्जति तदेव पात्रीकृतं प्लवते ॥ ८३ ॥ LSP 154

Whereby the fool becomes despondent
(thereby) the wise crosses what is hard to cross.
The iron which sinks down in the water when it forms a lump
swims on top of the water after it has been made a vessel.

—84—

།ཕྱུང་ཁྲོལ་རང་ཉམས་འཇུངས་ནོར་དང་། །དམན་པ་གསོན་པོར་གྱུར་པ་དང་།
།བྱ་རོག་ཡུན་རིང་འཚོ་བ་དག །གནོད་པར་འགྱུར་གྱི་ཕན་པ་མེད། ༨༤ །

a *krol* GQ, *grol* N **c** *'tshe* Q **d** *gyis* CD

> The well-being ('own strength') of the useless (and dangerous),
> the wealth of a miser, the revival of a low being
> and the longevity of crows do (only) harm,
> they are of no use.

स्वास्थ्यमुपघातकानां कृपणस्य धनं प्रभुत्वमज्ञस्य ।
चिरञ्जीविता बलिभुजामुपघातायैव न महिम्ने ॥ ८४ ॥ LSP 155

> The well-being of murderers,
> the wealth of a miser, the reign of an ignorant person,
> the longevity of crows—
> (all these) lead to destruction, not to greatness.

As for *phuṅ khrol* (= Skt. *anartha-*, cf. *Bodhicaryāvatāra* 8.39b and 79b) there are various forms of spelling. J (p. 356b, s. v. *'phuṅ ba*) gives the two forms *phuṅ dkrol* and *phuṅ khrol* whereas SCD and ZHD (p. 1715b and 1716a) give only the form *phuṅ krol* whereas CG (p. 522b and 523a) has both *phuṅ krol* and *phuṅ khrol*. The etymology of the word is not completely clear. There can be little doubt that it is a verbal compound. Its first part is the 'root' of the verb *'phuṅ ba* "to degenerate, to decay, to be in declining circumstancs, to wear away". Its second part seems to be the reduced form of the future stem *dkrol* of the verb *'khrol ba* "to cause to sound; to make a noise; to play", however the meaning of this verb does not suit the context. Cf. also *khrol khrol* and *khrol po* "bright, shining, sparkling, glittering, dazzling". The formative *krol, khrol* occurs also in the compound *'thab khrol* "quarrel" (Skt. *kalaha-*).

raṅ ñams "one's own condition, state, strength" (not "one's own degeneration"!) seems to be an idiosyncratic rendering of *svāsthyam* "health". The compound can be found in ZHD (p. 2647a) where it is explained as (1) *raṅ gi rgyud*, (2) *raṅ ñid ñams dmas pa* and (3) *raṅ bźin*. LC^2 (p. 1782a) quotes the equivalent *uddāmaga-* "going unbound, unrestrained" from *Rāṣṭrapālaparipṛcchā* p. 30.12 (= p. 90.27 in Ensink's edition of the Tibetan text).

It is not clear to me why *prabhutvam ajñasya* "the reign of an ignorant person" was translated as *dman pa gson par gyur pa* "the revival of a low being".

—85—

།དམ་པ་སྙིང་རྗེའི་གཟི་ལྡན་པ། །འགྲོ་བ་ཀུན་ལ་མཉེན་པར་བྱེད།
།འཇིག་རྟེན་*ཕན་ཕྱིར་*ཉི་མའི་ཟེར། །མཐོན་པོའི་གནས་ནས་ས་ལ་འབབ། ༨༥ །

a *sñiṅ brtse'i* GNQ **b** *'gro bi* C; *gñen* CD **c** *phar phyin* CDGNQ

The good person who is endowed
with the splendour of compassion

behaves with softness towards everybody.
In order to help the world the rays of the sun
fall down to the earth from their high place.

कृपयैव सर्वजन्तुषु सन्तस्तेजस्विनोऽप्यवनमन्ते ।
लोकहिताय भुवि रवेः कराः पतन्त्युच्चगतयो ऽपि ॥ ८५ ॥ LSP 158

Only out of compassion towards all beings
the good bow down, even if they are mighty.
In order to help the world the rays of the sun fall down
to the earth, although they assume a high position.

sñiṅ rje'i (Skt. *kṛpayaiva*) as attribute of *gzi ldan pa* (Skt. *tejasvino 'pi*) is not in agreement with the Sanskrit text. It is tempting to emend *sñiṅ rje'i* to *sñiṅ rjes*, however there remains a problem of word order, because the instrumental should have been placed **after**, not **before** *gzi ldan pa* to allow for a correct and meaningful translation. Only for this reason I have not altered the transmitted text although it is difficult to conveive how the translators could have referred *kṛpayaiva* to *tejasvino 'pi*.

The rendering *mñen par byed* "softens" for *avanamante* "bow down" is not only unnecessarily free but spoils the parallel with *patanti* "fall down" in the second half of the stanza.

In the light of the Sanskrit text which has *lokahitāya* the emendation *'jig rten phan phyir* is inevitable.

—86—

།སྨད་རིགས་ཕལ་ཆེར་དམན་རྣམས་ལ། །ཧྲན་ཅན་བྱེད་ཀྱི་མི་མཆོག་མིན། N184a
།ཏིལ་མར་ཆུ་ནང་ཁྱབ་བྱེད་ལ། །མར་གསར་བཙུག་ན་འཁྱུག་པར་བྱེད། ༨༦ །

b *chan byed kyis* GNQ **d** *mar sar* GNQ

Low people usually despise (other) low beings
excellent people do not do this.
Sesamum oil penetrates (when poured) into water,
but when fresh butter is poured (into it) it coagulates.

प्राकृत एव प्रायो मृडुषु भृशं दीप्यते न सत्पुरुषः ।
वारिणि तैलं विकसति निष्ठ्यूतं स्त्यायते सर्पिः ॥ ८६ ॥ LSP 159

An ordinary person generally blazes with anger
against soft people, good people do not do this.
Sesamum oil spreads in water,
clarified butter spit (into water) coagulates.

The same idea is expressed in the following two Āryā stanzas (A. A. R. in MSS 186; the stanza is quoted from VS 466):

अगुणकणो गुणराशिर्द्वयमिह्न दैवात्खलमुखे पतितम् ।
प्रसरति तैलमिवैकः सलिले घृतवज्जडत्वमेत्यन्यः ॥

"Fate has placed two things in the mouth of the wicked:
a particle of badness and a heap of goodness.
The former spreads like a drop of oil in water
and the latter shrinks like ghee (in the water)."

The other stanza is found in CNTT 408 (= CR 3.37):

तनुरुपकारः साधुषु विकसति परमप्सु तैलबिन्दुरिव ।
अधमेषु तु मह्वानपि सुमह्वानपि संकुचति यथा घृतं तुह्विने ॥

"A small favour done to good people
spreads excessively like a drop of oil in water.
But even a great (favour) annoys and shrinks
like ghee in the snow, when done to very low people."

Sternbach, following his manuscripts, wrongly inserts *bādhate* before *mahān api*. This violates both the metre and meaning of the second half of the stanza. Therefore we have deleted it.

—87—

།སྐྱེ་བོ་དམ་པ་རབ་ཁྲོས་ཀྱང་། །ཐབས་ཀྱིས་*མཉེན་འགྱུར་དམུ་རྒོད་མིན།
།ཆབ་རོམ་སྲ་ཡང་གཞུ་བ་ཡི། །ཐབས་ཡོད་རྩ་འཇམ་མ་ཡིན་ནོ། ༨༧ །

b *gñen* CDGNQ; *gyur* GNQ **c** *bźu* GN, *bźu ba yin* CD **d** *rtswa* CD, *'jams* GN, *yino* N

A good person, even if he has become very angry,
will become mellow by a suitable means,
but not a wild and unmanageable being.
There is a means to melt even the hard ice,
but not (to melt) the soft grass.

अतिकुपिता अपि सुजना योगेन मृदूभवन्ति न क्लीबाः ।
हेम्नः कठिनस्यापि द्रवणोपायोऽस्ति न तृणानाम् ।। ८७ ।। LSP 160

Good persons, even if they are extremely angry,
will become mellow by a suitable means,
but not weak-minded and low persons.
There is a means to melt even the hard gold
but not (to melt) grass.

dmu rgod usually renders Skr. *khaṭuṅka-*, cf. *Mahāvyutpatti* 2450 or *Prasādapratibhodbhava* 103, the meaning of which is given as "unruly, unmanageable" in BHSD. This looks like an attempt at rendering the not so common word *klība-* i. o. of the variant reading *nīcāḥ* which can be found in VS 249.

chab rom "ice, frozen water" seems to indicate that the translators interpreted *hemnaḥ* as **himasya*!

This is Sa skya paṇḍita's version of this stanza (*Subhāṣitaratnanidhi* 106):

།དམ་པ་ཁྲོས་ཀྱང་བཏུད་ན་ཞི། །དམན་ལ་བཏུད་ན་ལྷག་པར་རེངས།
།གསེར་དངུལ་སྲ་ཡང་བཞུ་ནུས་ཀྱི། ཁྱི་ལུད་བཞུ་ན་དྲི་ངན་འབྱུང་།

"Although the excellent are angry,
when one has paid reverence to them, they are calmed.

Although gold and silver are hard, they can be melted.
If one (tries to) melt dog excrement
a foul odor issues forth." (Bosson)

It is noteworthy that Sa skya Paṇḍita has the correct equivalent of *hemnaḥ*! Did he have access to the original Sanskrit stanza or does this point to a corruption in the transmission of the Tibetan text?

—88—

།སྨད་རིགས་དག་ནི་ཕན་བྱེད་ནའང་། །ཡ་རབས་ལ་གནོད་ཁྲོས་ཅི་སྨོས།
།གཤིན་རྗེ་འཛུམ་ནའང་འཆི་འགྱུར་ན། །རབ་ཏུ་*ཁྲོས་ན་སྨོས་ཅི་དགོས། ༨༨ །

a *dmaṅs rigs* G (*riḍ*) NQ **d** *khros ni* N

Even when they (try to) do a favour
people of low descent do harm to the noble-born,
not to speak (of what they do), when they are angry!
Even when the God of Death smiles, one will (have to) die,
not to speak (of what happens), when he is angry!

उपकुर्वन्नपि नीचः साधूनुपहन्ति किं पुनर्निघ्नन् ।
प्रद्वेषे कैव कथा हसितमपि यमस्य मारयति ।। ८८ ।। LSP 161

Even when he (tries to) help,
a low person does harm to the good—
what to say about him as an opponent!
Even the smile of the God of Death kills
—what to say about his hatred!

A loose parallel to this stanza is Sa skya Paṇḍita's *Subhāṣitaratnanidhi* 120:

།དམ་པ་རྒོལ་ཡང་ཕན་པ་སྒྲུབ། །སྐྱེ་བོ་ངན་པ་མཛའ་ཡང་གནོད།
།ལྷ་རྣམས་ཁྲོས་ཀྱང་སེམས་ཅན་སྲུང་། །གཤིན་རྗེ་འཛུམ་ཡང་པ་རོལ་གསོད།

"Even if one attacks the excellent,
they are beneficent (to their attackers).
If one befriends the wicked, they harm (one).
The gods protect the sentient creatures with their anger.
If Yama smiles, he kills others."

—89—

།དམ་པ་ཡོན་ཏན་སྟེན་བྱེད་དེ། །སྐྱེ་བོ་ངན་པ་སྐྱོན་ཉིད་སྟེན།
།ནོར་བུ་རིན་ཆེན་རང་བཞིན་ལྕི། །ཀ་ཤའི་ཤིང་བལ་རང་བཞིན་ཡང་། ༨༩ ། D120a

a *ston* CD **b** *bstan* CD **d** *ka śi'i* GNQ

Virtues reside with a good person,
while vices reside with a bad person.
A precious jewel is heavy by nature,
a tuft of Kāśa grass is light by nature.

स्वयमेव गुणा गुणिनं भजन्ति भजन्त्येव दुर्जनं दोषाः ।
गरयति को मणिरत्नं लघयति वा काशतूलानि ।। ८९ ।। LSP 162

Virtues adhere to a virtuous person,
vices, as if full of devotion, to a bad person.
Who makes a jewel heavy,
and who makes the tufts of Kāśa grass light?

The second half seems to be a rhetoric question whose expected answer is "their own nature", as implied by *svayam eva* in line a). The Tibetan translators also understood the Sanskrit text in this sense, as can be seen from their translation.

Note that *garayati*, formed in analogy to *laghayati*, is so far not attested in the dictionaries.

Only the image has been used by Sa skya Paṇḍita in stanza 103 of his *Subhāṣitaratnanidhi*:

།བླུན་པོའི་ཡོན་ཏན་ཁར་འབྱིན་ཏེ། །མཁས་པའི་ཡོན་ཏན་ཁོང་དུ་སྦེད། །སོག་མ་ཆུ་ཡི་སྟེང་ན་འཕྱོ། །ནོར་བུ་སྟེང་དུ་བཞག་ཀྱང་འབྱིང་།

"The fool lets his attainments proceed into his mouth.
The sage hides his virtues inside.
A straw floats on top of the water;
if one places a jewel on top it sinks." (Bosson)

—90—

།འགྲོ་བ་ཤིན་ཏུ་གྲངས་མེད་ཀྱང་། །སེམས་ཅན་ཡོན་ཏན་ལྡན་པ་དཀོན།
།ཡུལ་ལྗོངས་དཔག་ཏུ་མེད་མོད་ཀྱི། །རིན་པོ་ཆེ་དག་འབྱུང་བ་དཀོན། ༩༠ །

There are a great many of living beings,
but the virtuous among them are rare.
The regions (of the world) are indeed uncountable,
but the occurrence of jewels (in them) is rare.

अतिसंख्येष्वपि जन्तुषु सत्वास्ते दुर्लभा गुणा येषु ।
देशास्ते च भुवोऽल्पा येभ्यो रत्नानि जायन्ते ।। ९० ।। LSP 164

While the total of living beings is very high,
those who possess virtues are hard to find.
And (likewise) the regions in the world are few,
where jewels can be found.

—91—

།རྒྱུ་སྤུན་མང་པོ་བསྡོམས་པ་བཞིན། །སྐྱེ་བོ་ངན་བསྡོངས་གཞིག་པར་དཀའ།
།བྱིའུ་དུས་གཅིག་འཕུར་བ་ཡིས། །ཉི་མའི་འོད་ནི་ཁེབས་པར་བྱེད། ༩༡ །

a *bźi* G **b** *ṅan sdoṅs* GNQ, *ṅan pa bsdoms* C, *ṅan bsdoṅs* D **c** *cig* Q **d** *ñi ma'i ṅos* CD

Bad persons are like the threads of cloth
which are woven together lengthwise and crosswise—
they are difficult to destroy when they are joined.
Even small birds are able to obscure
the splendour of the sun when they fly up jointly.

तन्तव इव संघाताल्लघवो ऽपि नरा भवन्ति दुश्छेदाः ।
आवृण्वन्ति दिनकरं शलभा अपि युगपदुत्पतिताः ॥ ९१ ॥ LSP 166

When they unite even weak persons
will become difficult to separate, like threads.
Even moths are able to obscure the sun,
when they fly upwards simultaneously.

For *rgyu spun* cf. SCD: "the threads stretched lenghtwise and crosswise to make cloth" (p. 317a) and CG: *snam bu'i srid du btaṅ ba'i skud la rgyu zer ba daṅ 'phred skud la spun zer* "the threads of cloth running lengthwise are called *rgyu* and those running crosswise are called *spun*" (p. 179b).

—92—

།དམན་ལས་ཡོན་ཏན་ལྡན་པ་འབྱུང་། །དམ་པ་ལས་ཀྱང་ངན་པ་འབྱུང་།
།འདམ་གྱི་ནང་ནས་པད་མ་འབྱུང་། །པད་མ་ལས་ཀྱང་སྲིན་བུ་འབྱུང་། ༩༢ །

a *ldan par* C.

Something possessing virtues can arise
from something which is low
and even from something which is good
something bad can arise.
The lotus arises from the mud,
and a worm might crawl out even from a lotus.

असतो ऽपि भवति गुणवान्सद्भ्यो ऽपि परं भवन्त्यसद्वृत्ताः ।
पङ्कादुदेति कमलं कृमयः कमलादपि भवन्ति ॥ ९२ ॥ LSP 169

A virtuous one can be born even from a bad (person),
and beings with a bad conduct can be born
even from good (people).
The lotus arises from the mud,
and worms might crawl out even from a lotus.

—93—

།རྒྱལ་པོ་མི་སྲུན་གཅེས་བྱེད་*ལ། །ཡོན་ཏན་ལྡན་པའི་གོ་འཕང་མེད།
།ཁང་པ་སྦྲུལ་གདུག་ཅན་དག་ཏུ། །སྒྲོན་མ་ལེགས་པར་གསལ་མི་འགྱུར། ༩༣ །

a *bsrun* GNQ; *las* CDGNQ **b** *'phaṅs* Q **c** *dug can* G

When a king makes evil persons his favourites,
then (his realm) is not a place for the virtuous.
In a house which is full of poisonous snakes
a lamp will not shine brightly.

राज्ञि खलप्रधाने गुणा इवार्या न यान्ति परभागम् ।
साशीविषेषु वेश्मसु न साधु दीपाः प्रकाशन्ते ॥ १३ ॥ LSP 171

When a king shows a predilection for evil persons,
neither virtues nor noble people
will assume a prominent position.
In houses which are full of poisonous snakes
lamps will not shine brightly.

Sa skya Paṇḍita has used this stanza as model for *Subhāṣitaratnanidhi* 91:

།སྐྱེ་བོ་ངན་པའི་ཚོགས་ནང་དུ། །ཡོན་ཏན་ལྡན་ཡང་ག་ལ་འཁུར།
།སྦྲུལ་གདུག་གནས་པའི་ས་ཕྱོགས་སུ། །སྒྲོན་མེ་གསལ་ཡང་འོད་མི་བྱེད།

"How will even a virtuous (person) be honoured
in an assembly of bad persons?
In those places where poisonous snakes live
even a bright lamp will not emit splendour." (Bosson)

In the first line the translators seem to have tried to maintain somehow the *locativus absolutus* construction of the Sanskrit stanza. The second line was translated rather freely.

—94—

།བདག་ཉིད་ཆེན་པོ་ཉམས་པ་ལ། །ཆེན་པོ་མིན་པས་མི་བཀུར་རོ།
།ཟླ་བའི་ཤས་ཙམ་ལུས་པ་ཡང་། །དྲག་པོ་ཉིད་ཀྱིས་སྤྱི་ལ་བཀུར། [illegible] །

d *kyi* Q

They who are not great do not honour the noble-hearted
who have fallen into a difficult situation.
The moon, (however), is carried by Rudra himself
on his head, even when only one digit is left.

> विनिपतितान्मानयितुं महतो जानन्ति नाममहात्मानः ।
> शिरसा कलावशेषं हरः शशाङ्कं समुद्वहति ॥ १४ ॥ LSP 172

> Only the noble-hearted (are able to) honour great persons
> who have fallen down.
> Śiva carries the moon on his head
> (even) when (only) one of its digits is left.

In the light of the extant Sanskrit text and also of the related stanza *Prajñā-śataka* 37 which is quoted below it seems certain that an original *drag po ñid kyis* was altered into ~ ~ *ñid kyi* by way of haplography. This alteration was facilitated by the fact that *ñid kyi* could now be interpreted as "(on) his own (head)". The editors, however, overlooked that in such a case *drag po* should have been followed by the instrumental particle, like *chen po min pa* in line b).

There are many stanzas expressing a similar idea in Indian literature. I would like to adduce only two of them. The first is *Prajñāśataka* 37:

> །ཡོན་ཏན་ལྡན་པ་ཆུང་ཡང་ནི། །འཇིག་རྟེན་ཐབས་ཆེན་ཐོབ་པར་འགྱུར།
> །ཟླ་〈བའི་〉ཤས་ཙམ་ལུས་པ་ཡང་། །དྲག་པོ་ཡིས་ནི་སྤྱི་ལ་ཐོགས།

> "A virtuous person, even when he is weak ('small'),
> will attain great possibilities in the world.
> The moon is carried by Rudra himself on his head,
> even when only one digit is left."

The second half is more or less identical with *Āryākoṣa* 94cd.

The second parallel is found in Jalhaṇa's *Sūktimuktāvalī* (6.14):

> सैव परं न विनश्यति तनुरपि या श्रीर्निवेशिता सत्सु ।
> अवशिष्यते हिमांशोः सैव कला शिरसि या शम्भोः ॥

> "That good fortune, however small it may be,
> that has been transferred to the good will never perish.
> Only that digit of the moon survives
> which is (carried) on Śiva's head."

—95—

།གནོད་པ་བྱེད་ལ་ཕན་འདོགས་དང་། །དཔོན་བྱེད་*ངང་ཆེ་ཉམ་ཐག་བརྟན།
།ཕོངས་ཀྱང་སྦྱིན་གཏོང་སེམས་ཡོད་པ། །བདག་ཉིད་ཆེན་པོ་ཆེ་བའི་རྟགས། ༩༥ །

a *byed na* CD **b** *daṅ* CDGNQ; *bsten* CD, *brten* G **d** *bdag* / N

To help those who do harm (to oneself),
greatness (even) when one is a leader,
steadfastness in distress, to have a charitable mind,
even when one is in a plight—
these are the characteristics of a true ('great') great being.

अपकारिषुपकारः कृपा महत्त्वेऽप्यसंभ्रमः कृच्छ्रे ।
सति च विपत्तौ दित्सा चिह्नान्युच्चैर्महत्त्वस्य ।। ९५ ।। LSP 175

To help (even) those who have done harm (to themselves),
(to be) compassion(ate) even when one is great,
fearlessness in a difficult situation,
and the desire to give even when one is poor—
these are the characteristics of the highest magnanimity.

Although it is tempting to regard **naṅ che* as rendering of *mahattve* this would leave us with the question as to why *kṛpā* was translated as *dpon byed*. I therefore assume that *dpon byed* "acting as a leader, leadership" is a free but nevertheless suitable rendering of *mahattva* "greatness" while **ṅaṅ che* "magnanimity" is a free but suitable rendering of *kṛpā*. *ṅaṅ che* is attested once more in *Āryākoṣa* 97b, again as a rather free rendering, this time of the root *kṣam*.

Subhāṣitaratnanidhi 41c was clearly composed under the influence of *Āryākoṣa* 95d although its first three lines are completely different:

།བྱིན་ནས་སྨྲ་ཡང་མི་ལེན་པ། །དམན་པའི་བརྙས་པ་དང་དུ་ལེན།
།ཕན་པ་ཆུང་ངུའང་མི་བརྗེད་པ། །བདག་ཉིད་ཆེན་པོའི་ཆེ་རྟགས་ཡིན།

"Not taking back after having given,
readily putting up with the contempt of the vulgar,
not even forgetting a small benefit (rendered)–
these are the marks of a great individual."

Sa skya Paṇḍita's transformation is noteworthy inso far as it show how *Āryākoṣa* 95d was understood by a Tibetan reader.

Another loosely related stanza is MSS 7006 which belongs to the *Pañcatantra/Tantrākhyāyika* tradition (PT 4.6, PRE 4.6) and is also composed in the Āryā metre:

उपकर्तुमनुपकर्तुः प्रियाणि कर्तुं कृतान्यनुस्मर्तुम् ।
विनिपतितांश्चोद्धर्तुं कुलान्वितानामुचितमेतत् ॥

"To benefit those to whom one owes no benefits,
to do kindness, to be mindful of favors done,
and to raise the fallen –
this is characteristic of the noble." (F. EDGERTON's translation)

—96—

།ཡ་རབས་དག་གི་ངར་ཅན་ཚིག །ཚང་ཤུའི་ཁྲུ་བས་ཟ་འཛིལ་བཞིན།
།ངན་གཡོ་ཚིག་སྙན་རྒྱ་ཤུག་གི །འབྲས་བུ་མངར་ཡང་*འཁྲུ་བར་བྱེད། ༩༦ །

a *ṅaṅ* GQ, *daṅ* N **d** *'bru* N, *'khru* CDGQ

The energetic word of the noble-born is like
an emetic [or: purgative] (which is effective) by castor-oil.
The pleasant word of cunning people, however,
harms (like) the Badara fruit, even if it is sweet.

अम्लमपि साधुवचनं दाहविबन्धघ्नमारनालमिव ।
शठवाक्यं तु बदरवन्मधुरमपि जनं विभेदयति ॥ १६ ॥ LSP 176

The word of the good, even if it is acid,
cures obstruction by heat, like gruel made of boiled rice.
The word of evil persons, however, even if it is sweet,
destroys people, like the Badara fruit.

amla- "sour, acid" has been freely rendered as *ṅar can* "strong, vigorous". The second line poses serious difficulties, both in the Sanskrit original and its Tibetan translation. For *vibandhadhra-* cf. *vibandhahṛt-* "destroying or curing obstructions". Perhaps *dhram* is to be emended as *haram. tsaṅ śu* seems to be a *hapax legomenon.* Cf. *tsan cu* "*cañcu* grain from which oil is extracted (K. *du, ṅa,* 346)" (SCD, p. 996a); *tsam tsa* ~ *cañcā* (LC[1], p. 1892a; the word is said to occur in *Prasādapratibhodbhava* 4, however I cannot find it there). It seems as if *tsaṅ śu'i khu ba* renders *cañcutaila-* "castor-oil" which might have been regarded as a synonym of *āranāla-* (or *dāhavibandhadhra-* ?). *āranālam* is "gruel made from the fermentation of boiled rice" (Apte, p. 351b). In the light of the Sanskrit text there can be little doubt that *'khru* is to be emended to *'khu*; cf. *'khu ba* "to offend, insult"; = *druh*, cf. LC[2], p. 300b–301a.

—97—

།ཕན་བཏགས་དྲིན་བགྲང་མི་བྱེད་དང་། །དམན་ལ་དང་ཆེ་མ་བསླངས་སྟེར། C116a N184b
།བྱེ་བ་འདུམ་བྱེད་ཡོན་ཏན་ཅན། །བརྒྱ་ཡི་ནང་ན་འགའ་*འགས་ཤེས། ༩༧ །

a *bskyaṅ* N **b** *daṅ che* GNQ, *dad chen* CD **c** *bya ba* CD **d** *'gar* CDGNQ

Not to expect a favour (in return) when one has helped,
great friendliness towards low beings,
to give without having been requested,
to have the virtue to unite those who are separated—
among hundreds there are only few who master (this.)

उपकर्तुमप्रकाशं ज्ञन्तुं न्यूनेष्वयाचितं दातुम् ।
अतिसंधातुं च गुणैः शतेषु केचिद्विजानन्ति ।। ९७ ।। LSP 177

> "To render help to others without courting publicity,
> to forgive the weaknesses of inferiors,
> to give (donations) unasked for,
> and to unite people by virtuous conduct—
> only a few among a hundred know how to do."
> (A. A. R. in MSS 7007)

aprakāśam "not in public" has been translated so freely by *drin bgraṅ mi byed* "not to expect a favour (in return)" that one wonders whether the translators had a different text. Likewise the translation *dad chen* (CD) "great friendliness towards" or "great confidence in" or **ṅaṅ che* (GNQ) for *kṣantuṃ* is a rather free rendering.

In the case of *yon tan can* "a virtuous person" for *guṇaiḥ* "by virtues" not only the word but also the syntax is affected. Viewed from the Tibetan alone, *yon tan can* could also refer to the following *brgya yi naṅ na* "among hundreds of virtuous people," however it is less likely that this was intended by the translator since it presupposes a different text, e. g. **guṇavatsu śateṣu.*

bye ba (GNQ) "those who are separated" produces a better meaning than *bya ba* (CD) "deed", however neither form has a counterpart in the Sanskrit text. It has to be admitted that even *bye ba*, the perfect form of *'bye ba* "to open; to separate, i. e., to become separated" would be an incorrect and moreover ambiguous translation of **bhinna-* "separated". Incorrect, because *bye ba* basically means "open" (Skt. *apāvṛta-*, cf. LC[2] p. 1283b), and ambiguous, because it is better known by its homophone *bye ba* "ten million" (Skt. *koṭi-*). In this position one would rather expect a translation of the verbal prefix *abhi-*.

—98—

།གང་ཞིག་ཆད་པས་གཅོད་ནུས་པ། །དེ་ཉིད་ཕན་པར་བྱེད་ཀྱང་ནུས།
།ཉི་མས་སྐེམས་བྱེད་ཆར་ཉིད་ཀྱང་། །འབེབས་པར་བྱེད་ཀྱི་ཟླ་བས་མིན། ༩༨ །

a *nus śiṅ* GNQ **d** *byed kyis* Q

Only he who is able to punish
is also able to do a favour.

It is only the sun which dries up
and causes the rain to fall down—not the moon.

यो निग्रहस्य शक्तः स एव शक्नोत्यनुग्रहं कर्तुम् ।
उच्छोषयति ददाति च रविरेव जलानि न शशाङ्कः ।। १८ ।। LSP 186

Only he who is able to punish
is also able to do a favour.
It is only the sun which both dries water up
and bestows water—not the moon.

The play with *anugraha-* and *nigraha-* can als be found in *Prajñādaṇḍa* 55 = *Vṛddhacāṇakya* 9.9 (= CNTT 827A; = IS² 5358):

यस्मिन्रुष्टे भयं नास्ति तुष्टे नैव धनागमः ।
निग्रहानुग्रहो नास्ति स रुष्टः किं करिष्यति ।।

"He who does not arouse fear when he is angry
and who does not bestow wealth when he is pleased,
who neither knows to punish nor to be friendly—
what is the use of his being angry?"

Cf. also *Subhāṣitaratnanidhi* 200:

།གང་ཞིག་གནོད་པ་བྱེད་ནུས་པ། །དེ་ཡིས་ཕན་པར་བྱེད་པར་ནུས།
།མགོ་བོ་གཅོད་པར་ནུས་པ་ཡི། །རྒྱལ་པོས་རྒྱལ་སྲིད་སྦྱིན་པར་ནུས།

"Whoever is able to harm
can also perform usefulness.
A king who can cut off heads
is (also) able to give (his nation) a (just) government." (Bosson)

Perhaps the last line means only: "is (also) able to present (to somebody) a (whole) kingdom".

—99—

།དོན་ཉིད་མི་མཐོང་བྱིས་*པ་བཞིན་*། །མཁས་པ་དེས་ཀྱང་ཅི་ཞིག་བྱ།
།ལོང་བ་གཉིས་ཏེ་དམུས་ལོང་དང་། །རིག་པ་མེད་པའི་ལོང་བ་འོ། ༩༩ ། Q165b

a *don gñis* CD; *byis pas min* CDGNQ

What is the use of that (kind of) intelligent person
who like an (innocent) child does not see the thing itself?
There are two (kinds of) blind (people):
those who are blind by birth
and those who are blind because they lack knowledge.

बाल इव यो न पश्यति तत्त्वं किं तेन पण्डितेनापि ।
द्वावप्येतावन्धौ यो व्यक्षो योऽप्रसन्नाक्षः ।। ९९ ।। LSP 187

d *yo vyakṣo*: *vyakṣo yaś* H

What is the use of a person, even if he is a scholar,
who like an (innocent) child does not see the truth?
There are two (kinds of) blind people:
he has no sight at all and he who has no 'clear' sight.

The first line of the Tibetan translation is unintelligible without the emendation **byis pa bźin*. Without the Sanskrit text at hand, however, it would have been impossible to suggest this alteration.

The fourth line has an interesting variant reading in VS 2891: *'dhyakṣa-* i. o. *vyakṣa-* on which PETERSON remarks in his notes: *uttarārdham asphuṭam* (p. 623). First it has to be stated that this variant can be explained by paleography because in some of the older scripts of Northern India *dha* and *va* are very similar. Second, it seems as if the reading *(a)dhyakṣa-* is what the Tibetan translators had in their manuscript in which they, in a most ingenuous way, interpreted as *a* + *dhī* + *akṣa(n)*, "someone who is lacking the eye of wisdom", *rig pa med pa'i loṅ ba*. *aprasannākṣa-* would then refer to a person whose eyes are 'not clear', i. e., obscured, by some kind of physical defect. If *adhyakṣa-* were the original reading (at least it represents the *lectio* or *interpretatio difficilior* and moreover a nice linguistic pun) then this would point to the Buddhist background, because **dhyakṣa-* "the eye of mind" would be only a synonym of the well-known Buddhist term *prajñācakṣus-*, cf. BHSD s. v. *cakṣus.*

—100—

།བསྟན་བཙོས་བརྩོན་བྱས་ཕན་མེད་ན། །དོན་མེད་བརྩོན་པ་བྱས་ཞེས་བྱ།
།སྦྱོར་བ་མེད་པར་ནད་ཞི་ན། །བཅུད་ཀྱིས་ལེན་སོགས་དོན་མེད་དོ། ༡༠༠ །

a *brtsom* G **b** *brtsom* G, *bya źes bya* CD **c** *naṅ źi* N **d** *kyi* Q, *medo* N

If the exertions in he field of science bear no fruit
this is a useless exertion—thus it is said.
If a disease can be healed without the application (of a drug)
then the *rasāyana* and other elixirs are useless.

शास्त्रेष्वभियोगं फलादृते व्यसनमाहुरभियुक्ताः ।
शमयति विनोपयोगान्न रसायनसङ्घो रोगान् ॥ १०० ॥ LSP 188

Exertion in the field of science without a (tangible) result
is (mere) toil—thus say the diligent (the learned).
Without (proper) application
(even) a combination of drugs will not heal diseases.

The second half of the stanza has been translated somewhat freely.

—101—

།སླ་བ་དམའ་ཞིང་བག་འཁྲུམས་མིན། །བཙན་ཚིག་མ་ཡིན་རན་ན་མཛེས།
།རན་པར་འཇལ་བའི་སྲང་མདའ་ནི། །མཐོ་བ་མ་ཡིན་དམའ་བའང་མིན། ༡༠༡ །

a *smra ba smra źiṅ* CD **b** *me* (?) *yin* C

One's speech (should be) low, (but) not timid
and (also) not (too) strict; it shines if it is appropriate.
A correct measuring scale
is neither (too) low nor (too) high.

नम्रे वदन्ति दैन्यं स्तब्धे मानमिति मध्यमः श्रेयान् ।
प्रामाण्यमुपैति तुला विनोन्नतिं चावनमनं च ॥ १०१ ॥ LSP 193

If somebody is humble, they call it timidity;
if somebody is firm, they call it arrogance—
the middle one is the best.
A scale becomes a standard
when it indicates neither (too) low nor (too) high.

It seems as if the translators read *namre vadati* which they interpreted a *locativus absolutus.* In the second line they seem to have read *mā na* i. o. *mānaṃ* which they interpreted as two negations: *... min ... ma yin*!

—102—

།རང་བཞིན་མི་སྲུན་པ་ལ་ཆེར་ནི། །མ་བསྡིགས་པན་པ་མི་བྱེད་དོ།
།སྣོད་འཚོང་མ་ཡི་རྡོག་པ་ཡིས། །མྱ་ངན་འཚང་བསྣུན་མེ་ཏོག་ལྟར། ༡༠༢ ། D120b

a *bsrun* GNQ **b** *byede* N, *byed de* CD **c** *'tshaṅ mi* CD, *pa yi* Q

Persons with an evil nature
generally do not create something useful
unless they are threatened—
as in the case of the flowers of the (A)śoka (tree) (?)
that has fully been kicked by the footstep of a courtesan.

प्रायः खलप्रकृतयो नापरिभूता हिताय कल्पन्ते ।
पुष्पत्यधिकमशोको गणिकाचरणाभिघातेन ॥ १०२ ॥ LSP 194

Persons with an evil nature generally do not create
something useful unless they are humiliated.
The Aśoka begins to blossom fully
(only) when it has been kicked by the feet of a courtesan.

The second half of the Tibetan stanza may be a free rendering. It is not necessary to assume that for some strange reason the translators read *puṣpam iva* instead of *puṣpaty*.

Instead of *mya ṅan* one expects *mya ṅan med* or its metrical contraction *myaṅ med*!

'tshaṅ "enlarged, complete, made full" (alternative spelling: *tshaṅ*) seems to represent *adhikam*.

—103—

།ངན་པ་ལས་ཀྱང་ལེགས་པ་གང་། །མཐོང་ན་དེ་ནི་དེ་ལས་བླང་།
།ཡོན་ཏན་ལྡན་པའི་རིན་ཆེན་ཡང་། །ངན་ལ་ནམ་ཡང་འབྱུང་བ་མེད། ༡༠༣ །

a *legs kyaṅ* CD **b** *blaṅs* CD

If one sees something good,
(arising) even from a bad (person),
then one should take it from him.
Even the jewel of a virtuous (person)
will never arise in a bad (person). [?]

यद्यत्र साधु पश्येदसतोऽपि समाददीत तत्तस्मात् ।
यत्र क्वचनापि कलौ रत्नानि गुणाश्च जायन्ते ॥ १०३ ॥ LSP 198

The good thing which one might see in somebody
that one should take from him, even if he is a bad person.
In the Kali age (only) here and there
jewels and virtues arise.

The second half of the Tibetan translation is utterly wrong. A correct translation of line c) would run: *yon tan* ***dag dan*** *rin chen yan*. It is difficult to explain how *guṇāś* could be interpreted as attribute of *ratnāni*! It is more likely that the Tibetan text was not correctly transmitted.

In line d) *kalau* "in the Kali age" was translated as *ṅan la* "in a bad (person)", i. e., as if it were *khale*! The meaning of the word *kali-* was obviously unknown to the Tibetan translators: in stanza 12c it was translated wrongly by *dus na*, as if it were *kāle*, and in stanza 121c it was translated by *groṅ na* "in a village, hamlet".

The negation *med* in d) goes perhaps back to a wrong analysis of *kva canâpi* as *kva ca nâpi*!

—104—

།འཇིག་རྟེན་རྗེས་སུ་འགྲོ་འདོད་པས། །འཚོ་ཆོས་ཐམས་ཅད་ཤེས་པར་བྱ།
།མཁའ་འགྲོ་མ་ཡི་དམ་ཚིག་དག །མི་ཤེས་གནད་རྣམས་ཤེས་པ་མེད། ༡༠༤ །

a *rjesu* N

He who wishes to follow the (conduct of the) world
has to know thoroughly all the laws of life.
He who does not know the sacred vows of the Ḍākinīs
will not be able to find out their weak spots.

लोकमनुगन्तुकामैर्विज्ञेयाः सर्व एव वृत्तान्ताः ।
मर्माणि शाकिनीनां नासमयज्ञो विजानाति ॥ १०४ ॥ LSP 200

He who wishes to follow the (conduct of the) world
has to know thoroughly all (kinds of) topics.
Only he is able to find out the weak spots of the Śākinīs
who knows all (kinds of their) conventions and customs.

It seems as if the *śākinīs* of the Sanskrit text were deliberately replaced by the *ḍākinīs* in the Buddhist context (*mkha' 'gro ma yi*).

—105—

།འགྲོ་བའི་ནང་ན་འདི་གཉིས་བདེ། །འདི་གཉིས་རག་ལས་མེད་པ་སྟེ།
།འདོད་པ་ཐམས་ཅད་སྤྱངས་པ་དང་། །འདོད་དགུ་ཕུན་སུམ་ཚོགས་པ་འོ། ༡༠༥ །

c *spaṅs pa ste* GNQ

These two in the world are happy,
these two are (completely) independent:
he who has abandoned all kinds of desire
and he who is fully endowed with all the objects of his desires.

द्वावेव जगति सुखिनौ द्वावेव ⟨च⟩ मानमवह्हितं वह्हतः ।
उपरतसर्वेच्छो वा यो वा संपन्नसर्वेप्सः ॥ १०५ ॥ LSP 206

Only those two in the world are happy,
only those two are held in great esteem and attention:
he who has abandoned all kinds of desire
and he who enjoys the complete fulfilment of all his wishes.

The second line has been translated rather freely. Did the translators read something like **mānavirahitam*—whatever this might have meant to them?

ŚĀHA's text *avahitaṃ* is metrically defective. With the insertion of *ca* after *dvāv eva* the defect is cured. Another, less felicitous, possibility would be *hi* while *tu* is not suitable in this context. For the idea expressed in this stanza cf. also *Prajñādaṇḍa* 24:

पुंसामुन्नतिचित्तानां सुखं तेषामिदं द्वयम् ।
सर्वसङ्गनिवृत्तिर्वा विभूतिर्वा सुविस्तरा ॥

"There are two kinds of happiness for men with a lofty mind:
the ceasing of all kind of attachment or excessive abundance (of enjoyable things)."

There are two sources for this stanza: Jalhaṇa's *Sūktimuktāvalī* 7.5 and IS² 4093 (quoted from the unpublished *Subhāṣitārṇava*, fol. 63)

—106—

།ཆེ་བདག་བསྐལ་བསྒྲུབས་སྤྱོད་པ་ཡང་། །ངན་པས་ཐང་ཅིག་ཆུད་གསོན་བྱེད།
།ཆུ་ཡིས་རིམ་བསྒྲུབས་ལོ་ཏོག་ཀྱང་། །སྐད་ཅིག་གིས་ནི་མེས་སྲེག་བྱེད། ༡༠༦ །

a *bsgrub* CD; *pa med* N **d** *skad cig gi* G

Even the good conduct of the great-hearted
that has been acquired in the course of a (whole) aeon,
is spoiled in an instant by a bad person.
Even the harvest which has gradually been grown by water
is consumed by fire in an instant.

कल्पार्जितमपि सुचरितमेकपदे हन्ति दुर्जनो महताम् ।
वर्धयति सस्यमम्भः क्रमेण दहति क्षणेन शिखी ।। १०६ ।। LSP 213

The good conduct of the great,
that has been acquired in the course of a (whole) aeon,
is spoiled in an instant by a bad person.
Water makes the grain grow little by little,
fire consumes it in an instant.

Instead of *spyod pa yaṅ* (CDGNQ) one expects rather *spyod pa bzaṅ* for *sucaritam* "**good** conduct".

—107—

།སྐྱེ་བོ་བླུན་ཁྲོད་གཡོན་ཅན་*གྱིས། །གོ་འཕང་མཆོག་ཐོབ་ཆེ་བདག་མིན།
།རབ་རིབ་སྟུག་པོར་སྐར་མ་ལྟར། །ཉི་མ་ནམ་ཡང་གསལ་མི་འགྱུར། ༡༠༧ །

a *gyi* CDGNQ **d** *bsal* N

(In) an assemblage of dull people the cunning
attain a high position,

not (in an assemblage of) noble-hearted people.
The sun will never shine as bright (in full daylight)
as do the stars in dense darkness.

जडजनमध्ये चपलाः परभागं यान्ति जातु न महत्सु ।
घनतिमिर एव तारा न पुरः पूष्णो विराजन्ते ॥ १०७ ॥ LSP 214

Only among the dull people
the ill-mannered attain a high position,
by no means among the great.
Only in the deepest darkness the stars shine,
but not in the presence of the sun.

In line b) it is not clear whether *che bdag* refers to *skye bo blun khrod* or to *g.yon can.* The translation of the second half looks as if the translators had *iva* instead of *eva* and **punaḥ* instead of *puraḥ* which they understood in the sense of *jātu.* This mistake made them assume that *pūṣṇo* was a nominative (plural), not a genitive. The result is a different interpretation.

—108—

།རང་བཞིན་རྣམ་དག་བསོད་ནམས་ལྡན། །བཙུན་མོའི་འཁོར་ནའང་སེམས་ཞི་ཡི།
།དགོན་པ་ཞི་བའི་ནགས་དག་གི། །སྟག་དག་ཞི་བ་མ་ཡིན་ནོ། ༡༠༨ །

While the virtuous who are pure by nature
remain calm in their minds even in the harem of a king,
tigers who live in forests with peaceful hermitages
are not peaceful.

प्रकृतिविशुद्धं चेतः शाम्यत्यन्तःपुरेऽपि पुण्यवताम् ।
व्याघ्राणां नोपशमं विदधति शान्तान्यरण्यानि ॥ १०८ ॥ LSP 215

The mind of virtuous people which is pure by nature
remains calm even in the harem of a king.
But even peaceful forests
are not able to pacify the tigers.

The construction of the stanza has slightly been altered in the Tibetan translation.

A loose parallel can be found in *Subhāṣitaratnanidhi* 108:

།སྡིག་སྤྱོད་ནགས་ན་གནས་ཀྱང་ཉམས། །དམ་པ་གྲོང་ན་གནས་ཀྱང་དུལ།
།ནགས་ཀྱི་གཅན་གཟན་ཁྲོ་བ་དང་། །རྟ་མཆོག་གྲོང་གནས་དུལ་བར་མཐོང་།

"Even if evil-doers live in a forest, they go to ruin;
the excellent, even if they live in a city, are gentle.
See (how) the carnivorous animal of the forest is ferocious,
and the city-dwelling, excellent horse is tame!" (Bosson)

—109—

།མི་སྲུན་འདྲིས་བྱས་འཕུང་འགྱུར་ཞེས། །མི་དག་ཟེར་བ་དེ་རེ་བདེན།
།སྦྲུལ་གདུག་དང་ནི་རྩེ་བའི་མི། །བདེ་ལེགས་ཞིག་ཏུ་ག་ལ་འགྱུར། ༡༠༩ । N185a

a *bsrun* GNQ; *phuṅ* CD **c** *ba'i dus* CD

They who place confidence in very bad persons
will perish—how true is this saying of men!
How will a man who (starts to) play with poisonous snakes,
attain happiness and well-being?

नश्यन्ति कृतप्रणयाः प्रखलेष्विति सत्यमाह लोकोऽयम् ।
*क्षेमं न यान्ति जन्तोः कस्यचिदाशीविषक्रीडाः ।। १०९ ।। LSP 216

c **ksemaṃ na*: *kṣemeṇa* H

They who place confidence in very bad persons
will perish—this has rightly been stated by men.
It will increase neither happiness nor well-being
of anybody, if he (starts to) play with poisonous snakes.

The Sanskrit text as printed by Śāha can hardly be correct, because it literally means: "If some human being plays with poisonous snakes, this will go on safely (or peacefully)." Only an interrogative particle like *kim* which would turn the sentence into a rhetorical question (or the replacement of *cid* by *api* or *tu* which would have a similar effect) or a negation which reverts the meaning of the translation given above will make the sentence meaningful. Therefore I suggest reading *kṣemaṃ na.* A loose parallel can be found in *Subhāṣitaratnanidhi* 165:

།གལ་ཏེ་རིག་པ་ཡོད་ན་ཡང་། །སྐྱེ་བོ་རང་བཞིན་ངན་པ་སྤང་།
།དུག་སྦྲུལ་ནོར་བུས་མགོ་བརྒྱན་ཡང་། །མཁས་པ་སུ་ཞིག་པང་དུ་ལེན།

"Even if he has talent,
a creature with a bad character will be rejected.
Although a poisonous snake has his head adorned with a jewel,
what prudent person would take it to his bosom." (Bosson)

Sa skya Paṇḍita's stanza, however, is based not on *Āryākoṣa* 109 but on *Gāthāśataka* 55:

།ཇི་ལྟར་རིག་པས་བརྒྱན་གྱུར་ཀྱང་། །སྐྱེ་བོ་ངན་པ་ཡོངས་སུ་སྤང་།
།སྦྲུལ་གདུག་ནོར་བུས་བརྒྱན་གྱུར་ཀྱང་། །ཅི་སྟེ་འཇིགས་པ་མི་སྐྱེད་དམ།

"A bad person is to be avoided completely,
however much he is adorned with knowledge.
Does not a poisonous snake arouse fear,
even if it is adorned with a jewel?"

This is nothing but the very famous stanza

दुर्जनः परिहर्तव्यो विद्ययालंकृतो ऽपि सन् ।
मणिना भूषितः सर्पः किमसौ न भयंकरः ॥

which belongs to the genuine *Cāṇakya Nīti Text Tradition* (No. 466) and which has also been incorporated into the stanzas attributed to Bhartṛhari (No. 27 in Kosambi's edition) and the *Hitopadeśa.*

—110—

།རང་བཞིན་ཤིན་ཏུ་མ་དག་པའི། །སྐྱེ་བོ་ངན་པའི་སྡོམ་པ་ཡང་།
།ངུར་པ་ངུར་སྨྲིག་གོས་བགོས་པས། །རི་དྭགས་འདྲིས་ནས་གསོད་པ་བཞིན། ༡༡༠ །

a Read *sin tu ma dag *pas?* **c** *smig gos* G **d** *ri dags* GN; *'dis* Q

Even the discipline of bad people,
whose nature is extremely impure,
is (as dangerous) as the killing of hunters
who get the confidence of the deer
by wearing an ochre robe.

विनयो ऽपि दुर्जनानां परमतिशयितुं न भावशुद्धतया ।
काषायेणापि मृगान्व्याधा विश्वास्य निघ्नन्ति ॥ ११० ॥ LSP 217

Even the modesty of bad people aims at defeating others;
it does not indicate the purity of their hearts.
Hunters use even the ochre robe of monks
to get the confidence of the deer before they kill it.

param atiśayitum was either left out deliberately by the translators or they did not fully understand its meaning. Note that *ati* has survived in the form of the adverb *śin tu* which now refers to *śuddha-* in *bhāvaśuddhatayā*. For a deliberate change speaks the fact that the meaning has not been spoiled by the reduction.

—111—

།བློ་ལྡན་ཀུན་ཏུ་ཐོག་མར་ནི། །འདུལ་བའི་ཆེད་དུ་*སྦུངས་བསྐྱེད་དེ། C116b
།གསེར་ནི་སྦྱང་བ་མ་བྱས་པར། །ལས་སུ་རུང་བར་མི་འགྱུར་རོ། ༡༡༡ །

a *kun du* CD **b** *phyed du* Q; *sbruṅs* GN(?)Q, *spuṅs* CD **d** *ruṅ ba mi 'gyuro* N

In the beginning wise people everywhere
develop energy in order to tame.
Gold will not become manageable
unless it has been cleansed (by heating).

आदौ सर्वत्र शठाः संनतये तेज एव शंसन्ति ।
भवति सुवर्णमयो वा संतापेनैव कर्मण्यम् ॥ १११ ॥ LSP 218

Evil persons (?) declare that in every respect
in the beginning nothing but force (heat)
is the suitable means to bend (something).
Both gold and iron become manageable
only after they have been subjected to great heat.

It is not clear whether the translators had a different reading in the first line—**budhāḥ* i.o. *śaṭhāḥ*—or whether they deliberately decided to change the term because they found the meaning of the Sanskrit original strange. Or is *blo ldan* a corruption of *g.yo ldan*?

For *sbuṅs bskyed de* ~ *teja eva śaṃsanti* cf. Mvy 7531 (= S 7575) *ūrjā* = *sbuṅs skyes pa'am pag* (DNL, *bag* C, *sag* Q) *rtsa skyes pa.* In my opinion the correct reading of the alternative translation should rather be *bag rtsa ⟨ma⟩ skyes pa* "fear**less**ness". For *sbuṅs med* "lack of energy" cf. Nāgārjuna's *Ratnāvalī* 5.16a (wrongly printed as *spuṅs med* in my edition; corrected by Lambert SCHMITHAUSEN, in StII 1987, p. 4), and *sbuṅs med* is perhaps also the correct reading in Āryadeva's *Catuḥśataka* VI.3b where CDNQ read *spuṅs med* and Karen Lang in her edition emends as *dpuṅ med*.

As for *bskyed de* one feels tempted to emend it to **bstod de* which would be closer to *śaṃsanti*.

—112—

།སློང་བ་བྱིན་པས་ཕྱུག་པོ་ནི། །ཆོས་དང་གྲགས་འབྱུང་སློང་བ་མིན།
།དེ་བཞིན་ཕྱུག་ལ་བཀུར་སྟི་འབྱུང་། །སློང་ལ་མིན་པས་སློང་བ་*བཀུར། ༡༡༢ །

a *sloṅ la* CDNQ **c** *phyugs* CD **d** *kun* CDGNQ

Because he has given to a beggar, the wealthy person
obtains both the dharma and fame, not the beggar.
Likewise the wealthy person is respected, not the beggar—
therefore the beggar should be honoured.

धनमर्थिने प्रयच्छति धनवान्धर्मं यशश्च धनिनेऽर्थी ।
मानं तथापि धनवान्प्रयाति नार्थीति गुरुरर्थी ॥ ११२ ॥ LSP 221

The wealthy (person) gives to the beggar wealth,
but the beggar gives both rightfulness and fame
to the wealthy person.
Nevertheless the wealthy person is held in high esteem,
not the beggar—therefore the beggar is the worthy person.

In the first half of the Tibetan translation the construction has been abbreviated and simplified.

In line c) *tathāpi* has been translated as if it were *tathaiva.*

sloṅ ba kun "all the beggars" can now be identified as a fault of transmission: the original translation must have been *sloṅ ba *bkur* "(although this is so) the beggar should (in fact) be honoured", cf. *bkur sti* in line c). We can even reconstruct the genesis of the fault: first the initial *b-* of *bkur* was lost by way of haplography and then the remaining defective form **kur* was changed into the more common noun *kun,* despite the fact that the construction now became unintelligible.

—113—

།ངན་གཡོ་ཚིག་སྙན་སྨྲ་བ་དག །སྤྱོད་པ་སྤུ་གྲི་བཞིན་དུ་བྱེད།
།ལག་འགྲོ་ལ་སོགས་བྱ་བ་གཞན། །སྒྲ་སྙན་རྨ་བྱའང་བྱ་བ་གཞན། ༡༡༣ །

c *log* GNQ **d** *bya ba bźin* CD

Cunning people speak sweet words,
but their behaviour is like a (sharp) knife.
(Towards) snakes and other (beings they) act in one way,
and (with) the(ir) sweet voice the peacocks act in another way.

स्रवति मधु वाक्छठानां व्यवहाराः क्षुरमतीत्य वर्तन्ते ।
भुजगादिषु क्रियान्या वाशितमन्यन्मयूरस्य ॥ ११३ ॥ LSP 222

The word of cunning people flows sweetly,
but their behaviour is sharper than a knife.
The actions of the peacocks against snakes
are different from their crying.

madhu can be interpreted either as a separate adverb or as first part of a compound. I prefer the first possibility. The translation of the second half of the Tibetan text is based on the knowledge of the Sanskrit stanza. The Tibetan text alone would rather suggest the following translation: "Snakes and other (animals) act in one way, and the peacock with his sweet voice in another." Did the Tibetan translators understand the Sanskrit text in the following way: "In snakes and other beings one way of action is found, another one is the crying of the peacocks"?

It is again tempting to emend *rma bya'aṅ* as **rma bya'i* because then there would be a very close agreement with the Sanskrit original and moreover the Sanskrit text does not contain *api*, the equivalent of *(y)aṅ*.

—114—

།བློན་པོ་བློ་ལྡན་གསལ་བ་ཡི། །བླ་འོག་གི་ནི་དོན་མི་ཉམས།
།མིག་ལྡན་ལམ་དུ་ཞུགས་པ་ནི། །གོམ་པ་ཆུད་ཟོས་མི་འགྱུར་རོ། ༡༡༤ །

a *blun po* CD; *ba yis* CDGN **d** *goms* N; *'gyuro* GN

When the minister is intelligent and bright,
then all the matters concerning
above and below will not be spoilt.
When someone who has eyes enters a way
his steps will not be wasted.

मन्त्रिणि विशुद्धबुद्धौ राज्ञः प्रभुशक्तिरविहता भवति ।
पथि चक्षुषो विशुद्धे स्खलन्ति न पदानि गन्तृणाम् ॥ ११४ ॥ LSP 219

When the minister has a pure mind
then the king's ability to rule will remain unimpeded.
When the eye-sight is clear
the feet of a person do not stumble.

The first half of the stanza, in particular line b), has been translated somewhat freely.

—115—

།དབང་ཕྱུག་ཡོན་ཏན་མ་དད་གང་། །བླུན་ནམ་འོན་ཏེ་བརྙས་ལས་འགྱུར།
།མུ་ཏིག་མི་ཤེས་ལོང་བ་ཡིས། །གཅེས་པར་མ་བརྩིས་ཅི་ཞིག་འགྱུར། ༡༡༥ །

b *'oṅ te* GN, *'oṅ ste* Q; *brñas las* G **d** *rtsis* GNQ

When a ruler has no faith in qualities, this happens
either because of stupidity or because of contempt.
How is it possible that a blind person.
who does not know pearls did not rate them as valuable?

ज्ञाड्यमिदं नावज्ञा यदीश्वरा गुणिषु न प्रसीदन्ति ।
मुक्ताफलेषु विदुषः प्रोषितनयनस्य का गुरुता ॥ ११५ ॥ LSP 220

It is (simply) ignorance, not contempt
when rulers are not friendly towards those
who possess virtues.
What kind of weight (importance)
will a knowledgeable person give to pearls,
when he has lost his eyesight?
[Or: What is the authority of a blind person
with regard to pearls even if he is knowledgeable?]

In the first line the translators seem to have read **sâvajñā* i. o. *nâvajñā*. This, of course, spoiled the meaning of the first half of the stanza. What the translators read in the second half of the stanza and how they understood it is even more enigmatic. They translate **muktāphale 'suviduṣah* (or **muktāphaleṣv aviduṣaḥ*), and *kā gurutā* has practically been rendered twice by *ma brtsis* "(did) not appreciate" and *ci źig 'gyur* "how will it be possible that".

—116—

།རྒྱལ་པོའི་བྱིན་དང་བློན་པོའི་མཐུས། །ཐབས་ཀྱིས་འགྲུབ་པར་འགྱུར་བ་ནི། D121a
།*ཆང་བ*དམ་པོར་བསྡམས་པའི་མཐུས། །རལ་གྲིའི་གཟས་པ་ཆད་པར་འགྱུར། ༡༡༦ །

b *thams* (?) C; *thabs kyis 'grub par 'grub par 'gyur pa ni* G **c** *chad pa dam por* CD, *chad par dam pos* GNQ **d** *gris* GNQ

It is by the magnificence of the king
and the might of the minister
that (they) will become successful with their means—[11]
it is by the force of a tightly held grip
that the blow of a sword will cut.

11. Or: that their means (*thabs *ni*) will become successful.

सिद्धिं व्रजन्त्युपायाः प्रभविष्णोर्मन्त्रिणश्च सामर्थ्यात् ।
घातश्छिनत्ति दृढमपि मुष्टेः खड्गस्य बन्धेन ॥ ११६ ॥ LSP 223

The contrivances of a ruler and a minister
become successful when[12] they have the same objective.
The blow of a sword hits severely
when it is hold with a tight grip.

The construction of the first half of the Tibetan stanza would agree much better with the Sanskrit original if we emend *thabs kyis* as *thabs ni.* The replacement of a genitive or instrumental particle by the topical particle *ni* (and vice versa) is one of the most common phenomena in the transmission of canonial texts.

For *chaṅ ba* ~ *muṣṭi-* cf. Mvy 2835 (S 2831): *riktamuṣṭiḥ* = *chaṅs* (Q, *chaṅ ba* DCNL) *stoṅ pa.* The reading *chad pa* (CDNQ) owes its existence to the form *chad par 'gyur* in line d).

bandhena "by a grip" has been translated freely by *mthus* "by the power, by the force" because the meaning of *bandha-* is already contained in the noun *chaṅ ba* which is derived from *'chaṅ ba* "to hold".

For *gzas pa* cf. SCD, p. 1103b: "... 2. to brandish, = *brdeg par brtsams pa* and Mvy 8413 (S 8472): *udguraṇam* = *gzas pa.* It is noteworthy that *ghāta-* "blow" has been translated in a very specific, but nevertheless very appropriate manner.

—117—

།གཞུང་ལུགས་རྣམས་ལ་བྱང་བྱས་ཀྱང་། །ཉམས་སུ་ལེན་པར་མི་བྱེད་ན།
།ལག་པ་ན་ནི་སྒྲོན་ཡོད་ཀྱང་། །ལོང་བས་ལམ་ནི་མི་མཐོང་བཞིན། ༡༡༧ །

b *ñamsu* N **c** *lag pa la ni* G

If somebody has been made an expert in the scriptures
but does not apply (his knowledge)

12. Or: because.

then this is like (the case of) the blind man
who does not see the way
although he holds a lamp in his hand.

शास्त्रेषु कृतजया अपि दैवोपहताः स्खलन्ति कर्तव्ये ।
पश्यति न मार्गमन्धः करसंस्थितेनापि दीपेन ॥ ११७ ॥ LSP 224

Even they who have been successful in the field of science
will fail in their tasks when they are struck by fate.
A blind man does not see the way,
even when he holds a lamp in his hand.

The second line has been translated completely freely, perhaps for lack of space. It would indeed have been very difficult to press the meaning of *daivopahatāḥ skhalanti kartavye* into the seven syllables of one line. For the meaning of *ñams su len pa* cf. Mvy 1802 (= S 1797) where it translates *āsthitikriyā-* "acting with perseverance, persistence". In the same meaning it is also used in *Subhāṣitaratnanidhi* 273c "to take to heart" (Bosson).

The same verse can also be found as stanza 169 of the *Prajñādaṇḍa* with only minor variants: *dag la* i. o. *rnams la* in line a), *lag na sgron ma yod kyaṅ ni* in line c), and *mi mthoṅ 'gyur* i. o. *mi mthoṅ bźin* in line d). It is obvious that the Tibetan version of *Prajñādaṇḍa* 169 does not represent an independent translation but must have been taken from *Āryākoṣa* 117, or it is a revision—perhaps by the editors of the canon?—of this stanza.

IS^2 3505 quotes a stanza which can be found in two editions of the *Hitopadeśa* (HS 1.163 and HJ 181) which expresses a similar idea:

न स्वल्पमप्यध्यवसायभीरोः करोति विज्ञाननिधिर्गुणं हि ।
अन्धस्य किं हस्ततलस्थितो ऽपि प्रकाशयत्यर्थमिह प्रदीपः ॥

"A whole store-house of knowledge
does not create the smallest advantage
if one is too fearful to apply it earnestly.
Does the lamp which is hold by the hand of blind person
illuminate anything for him?"

—118—

།ཀུན་ལ་ཕྱོགས་སུ་མ་ལྷུང་ཞིང་། །ལྷག་པར་བྱམས་སྡང་མི་བྱའོ།
།རོ་གཅིག་ཟས་ཀྱི་སྤྱོད་པ་ནི། །ནད་མི་འགྱུར་ཞེས་སྨྲ་བ་ཡིན། ༡༡༨།

a *phyogsu* N **c** *zas kyis* GNQ

One shall not be partial to anybody
nor show excessive love or hatred.
It is said that one will not fall ill,
if one eats food of one taste only.

अत्यन्तपक्षपातः सर्वत्र न भूतये न च द्वेषः ।
एकरसाभ्यवहारं भिषजो न बलाय कथयन्ति ॥ ११८ ॥ LSP 226

Nowhere do excessive partiality
or hatred anything good.
The doctors say that it does not increase one's strength
if one sticks to food of one taste only.

Did the translators understand *na bhūtaye* as if it were *mā bhūt*? How else can we explain *mi bya'o* "should not be done"? *byams* "love" seems to have been added by the translators as a complement of *sdaṅ* "hatred".

The rendering of (*bhiṣajo*) *na balāya* "does not increase (one's) strength" by *nad mi 'gyur* "will not become a disease" is strange and moreover it spoils the sense of the stanza. Or did the original translation read *nad *du 'gyur*?

There is no direct equivalent of *bhiṣajo*.

—119—

།ཀུན་ཏུ་དབུས་ན་གནས་པ་ནི། །མཁས་པ་རྣམས་ཀྱིས་བསྔགས་པ་ཡིན།
།ཉི་མ་འཆར་ཚེ་ཆེ་བ་སྟེ། །ནམ་མཁའི་དཀྱིལ་ཕྱིན་རན་པར་འགྱུར། ༡༡༩ །

a *kun du* CD **b** *bsdams pa* C **d** *namkha'i* GNQ

To assume a middle position with regard to everything,
this is what the wise praise.
The sun is great when it has risen,
assuming its right size in the centre of the sky.

माध्यस्थ्यमेव सर्वत्र सिद्धये पण्डिताः प्रशंसन्ति ।
सवितुः प्रभातिमहती भवति नभोमध्यगतस्यैव ॥ ११९ ॥ LSP 227

The wise say that only a middle position
leads to success.
The splendour of the sun becomes extremely bright
only when the sun has reached the middle position in the sky.

In line c) the translators seem to have read **prabhāte* (instead of *prabhāti*) which they translated as *'char tshe* "at the time of rising". Thereby the meaning of the second half of the stanza was completely spoilt.

—120—

།བུད་མེད་ཆེ་བདག་ཉིད་ཀྱང་ཡང་། །རྒྱལ་པོའི་འབྱོར་པ་སྨད་འཚོང་བཞིན།
།འཁོར་ཡུག་གནས་པའི་ས་ཉིད་ཀྱང་། །གདེངས་ཅན་ཆ་ཤས་གཡོ་བར་བྱེད། ༡༢༠ །

a *spaṅ* CDGNQ **c** *khor* GNQ

Women, even if they are great-natured, are light,
the wealth of a king is like a courtesan.
Even the earth which rests
on the Cakravāla mountain range
is made to tremble by the parts of the snake (Śeṣa).

स्त्रीलघुतया महत्यपि तिष्ठति नो बन्धकीव नृपलक्ष्मीः ।
शेषफणाचक्रवालस्थितापि धरणी चलत्येव ॥ १२० ॥ LSP 228

Like a courtesan the good fortune of a king,
even if it is great, does not stay, because women are fickle.
(Even) the earth shakes although it rests
on the Cakravāla-like hood of the snake Śeṣa.

strīlaghutayā was translated as if it were *strī laghvī*.

Does *cha śas* point to a variant reading *kalā* for *phaṇa* or was this a deliberate change because the literal translation *gdeṅs* (*ka*) would have been too close to *gdeṅs can* "'the hooded one', a snake"; here = Śeṣa?

—121—

།*ད་ལྟར་འགྲོར་པ་འགས་རྙེད་ལྟར། །མཁས་*པའི་ཡོན་ཏན་མཁས་པས་ཤེས།
།གྲོང་ན་སྐྱོན་ཅན་ལམ་ལོག་སྤྱོད། །རྩྭ་བཞིན་དུ་ནི་རབ་ཏུ་མང་། ༡༢༡ ། Q166b

a *de ltar* CDGNQ; read *rñed dka'* instead of *'gas rñed*? **b** *mkhas pa* CDQ(?); *mkhas pas* G; *mkhas pa'i* GN **d** *rtsa* GQ; *bźin tu* N

In the same way as good fortune is nowadays
difficult to obtain [so are] the wise, (good) qualities
and those who appreciate qualities.
Sinful people, however, who walk the wrong way
are as frequent as grass in a (certain) region.

संपद् इव दुष्प्रापाः संप्रति गुणिनो गुणा गुणज्ञाश्च ।
दोषास्तु दुर्जनैः सह विपद् इव कलौ तृणप्रचुराः ॥ १२१ ॥ LSP 232

Virtuous persons, virtues and those
who appreciate virtues
are now as difficult to obtain as good fortune.
Faults, however, together with bad persons
are—like bad luck in this Kali age—as frequent as straw.

The stanza has been translated very freely. I suspect that in the first half an originally correct translation became corrupted in the course of transmission. I translate according to my restoration.

The second half is marred by two gross mistakes: *vipada* "bad luck" was translated as **vipatha-* "a wrong path", *lam log*, and *kalau* "in the (present) Kali age" as if it were **kule* "in a community", *groṅ na*. For *kula-* = *groṅ* cf. Mvy 8445 (S 8508) and 8459 (S 8521).

—122—

།ལེགས་པ་མ་མཐོང་བདག་ཉིད་ཆེའི། །ཡོན་ཏན་ཡོད་ཀྱང་ཡིད་མི་ཆེས།
།རྒྱ་མཚོའི་ཆུ་ནི་རྒྱ་ཆེ་ཞེས། །ཁྲོན་པའི་རུས་སྦལ་སུས་ཡིད་ཆེས། ༡༢༢ །

a *leg pa* C; *cha'i* C, *che* G **c** *cha źes* D **d** *rus sbral* G

They who did not see what is good do not believe
in the virtues of a noble-hearted person, even if they exist.
Which turtle living in a well would believe
that the water of the ocean is vast?

प्रतिपद्यन्ते महतां न सतोऽपि गुणानदृष्टकल्याणाः ।
श्रद्दधति केनपृथुतामुदन्वतः कूपमण्डूकाः ॥ १२२ ॥ LSP 234

They who did not behold good fortune
do not believe in the virtues of the great even if they exist.
Why should the frogs in a well
believe in the vastness of the ocean?

The translation of *kena* by *sus*, although formally correct, is not felicitous. Here it is definitely meant as an interrogative adverb ("how"), whereas the translation creates the impression as if it were a interrogative pronoun referring to *kūpamaṇḍūkāḥ* which is, of course, not the case in the Sanskrit original. Nevertheless this change of construction did **not** spoil the meaning of the second half of the stanza.

—123—

།སྒྲུབ་པ་སྣ་ཚོགས་སྒྲོ་ནས་ནི། །ལ་*ལར་ངན་དགོས་ཆེ་བདག་མིན། N185b
།མཁར་བ་ལས་ནི་བྱས་པ་ཡི། །མེ་ལོང་སྟེན་གྱི་གསེར་གྱི་མིན། ༡༢༣ །

a *tshod* G **b** *la la* CDGNQ **c** *'khar* C, *'khor* D **d** *ston gyi* D

Because the tasks to be done are so different
for some of them a low one is needed, not a great one.
The mirror which is made of bell-metal is used,
not the one made of gold.

कार्यगतेर्वैचित्र्यान्नीचो ऽपि क्वचिदलं न जातु महान्।
कांस्येनैवादर्शः क्रियते राज्ञामपि न हेम्ना ॥ १२३ ॥ LSP 233

Because of the heterogeneity of requirements
sometimes even a low person is suited better
(for a task) than a great person.
Even the mirror of a king is made of bell-metal,
not of gold.

In line b) both meaning and construction are improved if we read *la lar* "in some (cases)" for *la la*, in accordance with the locative of the Sanskrit text.

—124—

།དམ་པ་གཞན་གྱིས་ཕྱེ་ན་ཡང་། །རང་གི་ཡོན་ཏན་གྱིས་འདུམ་བྱེད།
།མི་སྲུན་ལྕགས་གྱོང་འདྲ་བ་ནི། །འབྱེད་པར་ནུས་ཀྱི་འདུམ་མི་ནུས། ༡༢༤ །

c *bsrun* GNQ; *byoṅ* (?) C **d** *nus kyis* CD

By his own qualities a good person brings together
even (what) has been separated by others.
A bad person, who is like hard iron (or: a lump of iron),
is only able to split, not to unite.

म*ध्विव भिन्नमपि परं साधुः स्वगुणेन संदधात्येव ।
प्रखलास्तु मुद्गरा इव भेदे पटवो न संधाने ।। १२४ ।। LSP 237

Like honey a good person by his qualities unites others,
even if they have been separated.
Bad persons, however, are like hammers
skilled in splitting, not in uniting.

madhv eva (thus Śāha's edition) is metrically not possible since the second syllable has to be short. I suspect that it is a reading or printing mistake for *madhv iva* and emend accordingly. The Tibetan has no equivalent of either form.

In line a) of the Tibetan translation the instrumental *gźan gyis* is not in accordance with the accusative *paraṃ* in the Sanskrit text. Both construction and meaning would be improved by the emendation *gźan *ni*. For a similar case cf. 116b. With the emendation *gźan ni* one would have to translate: "A good person unites (or: reconciles) himself with another (person), even if they have been separated (before)." In its present form the first half of the stanza can also be translated in the following manner: "The good one, even if he has been separated (from a friend?) by someone unites himself (again with that person) because of his own virtues."

lcags gyoṅ "hard iron" or *lcags *goṅ* "a ball, a lump of iron" is a rather free translation of *mudgara-* "hammer, mallet".

—125—

།བདག་ཉིད་ངན་པ་མ་རིག་པ། །རིག་པའི་ལམ་ལའང་རྨོངས་པ་སྐྱེ།
།སྒྲོན་མས་ཕྱུང་བའི་སྣང་བ་ལ། །མཁའ་ལ་རྒྱུ་བ་ལོག་པར་རྒྱུ། ༡༢༥ །

a *ṅan pa'i ma* GNQ

A bad-natured person, devoid of knowledge,
will become confused even on the path of knowledge.
When a bright splendour is emitted by a lamp
the birds will revert their course.

जनयति संमोहपदं विद्यापि दुरात्मनामविद्येव ।
उल्का प्रकाशयन्त्यप्यालोकान्धान्खगान्कुरुते ॥ १२५ ॥ LSP 238

Even the knowledge of evil-minded persons
creates an occasion for confusion, as if it were ignorance.
A meteor, although it emits light,
makes the birds blind by its brightness.

The first half of the stanza has been translated very freely into Tibetan, but the general idea can still be recognized.

—126—

།ཇི་ལྟར་ཉོངས་སྐྱོན་མེད་པའི་ཚིག །དྲག་པོའི་སྐྱོན་གྱིས་འགྱུར་བ་ལྟར། C117a
།གནོད་བྱེད་དེ་ལྟར་མ་ཡིན་ཏེ། །སྲེག་པའི་གནོད་འགྱུར་ཆུ་སྐྱར་མིན། ༡༢༦ །

c *de lta* GNQ **d** *sreg par* G; *gyur* N

The word of him who is free of faults and errors
can be altered (into something bad) by severe mistakes;
(that of him) who does harm cannot.
Harm arises for a partridge, not for a heron.

हिंस्रा अपि न तथान्तं यान्ति यथानागसो ऽपि वाग्दोषैः ।
मौखर्येण बकादपि तित्तिरिरेवापदमुपैति ॥ १२६ ॥ LSP 240

Mischievous beings do not find such a (bad) end
as do innocent persons on account of their verbal faults.
Because of its talkativeness
the partridge suffers greater mischief than even the heron
[which kills other beings, but always remains mute.]

The Tibetan has handled the Sanskrit text rather freely: *antaṃ yānti* "find a bad end" became *'gyur* "is changed, altered"; *vāgdoṣaiḥ* became *tshig drag po'i skyon gyis* "by severe mistakes"[13]; *anāgaso 'pi* "(even) of innocent people", here nominative singular, was interpreted as a genitive singular, referring to *vāgdoṣaiḥ*; *maukharyeṇa* "because of talkativeness, garrulity" was not translated at all. Thus the main idea was lost, and I doubt whether a Tibetan can arrive at a meaningful interpretation of the stanza.

A similar idea is expressed in stanza 692 of Vallabhadeva's *Subhāṣitāvalī*:

कटु रटति निकटवर्ती वाचातष्टिट्टिभः पटुर्यत्र ।
अपसरणमेव शरणं मौनं वा तत्र हंसस्य ॥

"Where the garrulous *ṭiṭṭibha* (*parra facana*) stands nearby,
shrilling loudly, there the only protection for a *haṃsa*
(*anas casarca*) is either to run away or to keep silent."

The stanza is taken from Sundarapāṇḍya's *Nītidviṣaṣṭikā*, No. 118 which reads *yatas tasmāt* i. o. *paṭur yatra*, *yuktaṃ* i. o. *śaraṇaṃ* and *rāja°* i. o. *tatra*. Since Sundarapāṇḍya has borrowed several stanzas from the *Āryākoṣa*, it is very likely that he composed this stanza under the influence of *Āryākoṣa* 126.

—127—

།བདག་ཉིད་ཆེན་པོའི་འབྱོར་པ་གང་། །དེ་ལས་རིམ་གྱིས་རྒུད་པ་འབྱུང་།
།ཉི་མས་ཡུན་རིང་བསྐྱངས་ནས་ནི། །དུས་ཀྱི་མཐའ་མར་འགྲོ་སྲེག་བྱེད། ༡༢༧ །

a *chen po* N **c** *riṅs* GN **d** *tha mar* GNQ; *bsreg* N

From that which is the good fortune of the noble-hearted
gradually arises (also) destruction.
After having protected the world for a long time
the suns burn it at the end of an aeon.

यत एवार्था महतां भवन्ति तस्मात्क्रमेण विपदोऽपि ।
चिरमनुपाल्य युगान्ते दहन्ति पूषण एव जगत् ॥ १२७ ॥ LSP 241

13. Is *drag po'i* the corruption of another word meaning "speech"?

The same thing which is the origin of the wealth
of the great is also the reason of their gradual decay.
After having protected the world for a long time
the suns scorch it up at the end of an aeon.

Line d) *pūṣāṇa*: Śāha rightly remarks: "*etat tv aśuddhaṃ vyākaraṇadṛṣṭyā* (Pā.A.Sū. 6.4.12)".

—128—

།འབྱོར་པ་རང་བཞིན་མི་བརྟན་པའང་། །སེམས་ཅན་ཆེ་ལ་བརྟན་པར་འགྱུར།
།དངུལ་ཆུས་བྱེར་བ་སྦྱོར་བ་ཡིས། །ཕན་ཚུན་འབྱེད་སྡུད་ཅིས་མི་ནུས། ༡༢༨ །

a *brten* G **b** *brten* G **c** *chus* CDGNQ, read *chu*? **d** *bsdu* CD, *bsdud* N

Although it is fickle by nature
good fortune becomes stable for noble hearted beings.
Is it not possible to separate and to unite
the volatile quicksilver by an (appropriate) mixture?

प्रकृतिचपलापि लक्ष्मीः स्थिरतामापद्यते महासत्त्वैः ।
योगैः पतन्नपि रसो न बध्यते पारदीयः किम् ।। १२८ ।। LSP 242

Although it is fickle by nature
good fortune becomes stable by noble-hearted beings.
Is not the essence of quicksilver, even when it falls down,
fixed by (appropriate) mixtures?

There is a very loose parallel in *Subhāṣitaratnanidhi* 128:

།དམ་པ་དབྱེ་དཀའ་འདུམ་ན་སླ། །དམན་པ་དབྱེ་སླ་འདུམ་ན་དཀའ།
།ལྗོན་ཤིང་དང་ནི་སོལ་བ་ཡི། །བཅད་དང་སྦྱོར་བའི་ཁྱད་པར་ལྟོས།

"To separate the excellent is difficult,
but, if one reconciles them, it is easy.
To separate the base is easy,
but, if one reconciles them, it is difficult.
Look at the difference in cutting and joining a tree or charcoal."
(Bosson)

—129—

།ངན་གཡོའི་འཇམ་ཚིག་རྣོན་པོ་ཡིས། །ཇི་ལྟར་སྙིང་ལ་གདུང་བྱེད་པ། D121b
།དེ་ལྟར་རལ་གྲི་རྣོན་པོ་དང་། །རླུང་ཆུ་དེ་བཞིན་མེས་མི་བྱེད། ༡༢༩ །

Neither a sharp sword nor wind
nor water nor fire torment the heart that much
as does the sweet word of a cunning person
which is (in fact) sharp.

तापयति हृदयमधिकं मधुरशठस्तीक्ष्णसामवचनो ऽपि ।
तेजयति यथा खड्गं शीतमपि पयस्तथा नाग्निः ॥ १२९ ॥ LSP 244

That wicked person torments the heart very much,
who is sweet, but who lets even his conciliatory words
sound sharp.
Not even fire sharpens a sword so well
as does cold water.

The first half of the Sanskrit stanza is not fully clear to me. What is the function of the *api* in line b)?

In the second half the Tibetan translates the following Sanskrit text: (*tejayati*) *yathā* ***khaḍgaḥ vātaś ca*** *payas tathā nāgniḥ*. It is also possible that *rluṅ chu* is the corruption of an original *graṅ chu* "cold water". Then it would not be necessary to presuppose a different Sanskrit text at all. The only mistake of the translators would then have been to take *khaḍgaṃ* as the nominative of a neuter noun.

In Sundarapāṇḍya's *Nītidviṣaṣṭikā* 13 we find the same idea expressed in different words:

न तथा रिपुर्न शस्त्रं न विषं न हि दारुणो महाव्याधिः ।
उद्वेजयति पुरुषं यथा हि कटुकाक्षरा वाणी ॥

"Neither an enemy nor a sharp weapon
nor poison nor a deadly disease
afflicts a person as much
as does harsh speech."

—130—

།ཉམས་པར་གྱུར་ན་སེམས་ཅན་དག །སྤྱོད་པ་ལོག་པར་བྱེད་པར་འགྱུར།
།རྨི་ལམ་ན་ནི་འོད་མེད་པའི། །ཉི་མ་མཐོང་ན་འཆི་བར་འགྱུར། ༡༣༠ །

After they have been met upon a difficult situation,
the behaviour of living beings becomes perverted.
When one sees in a dream a sun without rays
one is going to die.

विपरीताः सत्त्वानां भवन्ति चेष्टा विनाश आपन्ने ।
स्वप्ने ऽपि ना मुमूर्षुः पश्यति सवितारममयूखम् ॥ १३० ॥ LSP 245

Perverted are the actions of living beings,
when the time of destruction has come over them:
even in his dream a man who is at the eve of death
beholds the sun without rays.

Despite the very rare occurrence of the nominative *nā* (cf. Wackernagel, AIG III, § 119, p. 212–2) it seems preferable to me to read *nā mumūrṣuḥ* i. o. *nâmumūrṣuḥ* (Śāha). Otherwise one would have to assume a very clumsy double negation: *na* + *amumūrṣuḥ*, probably used to express a strong affirmation: "Everybody who is going to die ..." For the content cf. *Bṛhadāraṇyakopaniśad* 5.5.2:

तद्यत्तत्सत्यमसौ स आदित्यः । य एष एतस्मिन्मण्डले पुरुषो यश्चायं दक्षिणेऽक्षन्पुरुष-
स्तावेतावन्योन्यस्मिन्प्रतिष्ठितौ । रश्मिभिरेषोऽस्मिन् प्रतिष्ठितः प्राणैरयममुष्मिन् । स
यदोत्क्रमिष्यन्भवति शुद्धम् एवैतन्मण्डलं पश्यति । नैनमेते रश्मयः प्रत्यायन्ति ।

(Cf. *Eighteen principal Upaniṣads.* Vol I. Ed. LIMAYE/VADEKAR, Poona 1958, p. 259.)

—131—

།གཞན་ལ་གནོད་པས་ཡིད་གདུངས་ལྟར། །རང་ལ་གནོད་པས་དེ་ལྟ་མིན།
།རང་ལ་གནོད་ན་མི་གཡོ་བའི། །ས་ནི་གཞན་ལ་གནོད་པས་གཡོ། ༡༣༡ །

a *gduṅ* GNQ

The heart is not so much tormented
by the damage done to oneself
as it is by the damage done to others.
Unmoved, when damage has occurred to herself,
the earth quakes when others are harmed.

स्वविपदि तथा महान्तो न यान्ति खेदं यथा परापत्सु ।
आत्मोपहतिष्वचला प्रचलति धरणी परव्यसने ।। १३१ ।। LSP 246

Great beings are not so much annoyed
about their own misfortune
as they are about the calamities of others.
Unmoved when she is damaged herself
the earth quakes when others are in calamities.

—132—

།མཁས་པས་འདི་ནི་གཉེན་སྡུག་ཅེའམ། །དབང་ཕྱུག་ཤེས་རབ་བག་མི་དབབ།
།རླུང་གིས་མེ་ཡང་སྤོར་མོད་ཀྱི། །སྒྲོན་མ་འབར་བའང་གསོད་པར་བྱེད། ༡༣༢ །

a *gdug* CD **c** *gtoṅ/gtod med* C, *gtor mod* D; *kyis* N **d** *bsod* Q

A wise person should not become careless in his wisdom
with regard to a ruler, thinking 'He is a dear friend'.
The wind is able to raise a fire,
but it extinguishes even a burning lamp.

बन्धुरयं सुहृदिति विश्वासो नेश्वरे क्षमो विदुषः ।
मित्रमपि वायुरग्नेर्दीपशिखामुत्थितो हन्ति ॥ १३२ ॥ LSP 247

A wise person should not place
(too much) confidence in a lord,
thinking 'He is a relative, he is a friend'.
Although the wind is a friend of the fire,
when it has risen, it extinguishes the flame of a lamp.

The origin and interpretation of *śes rab* is difficult since it seems to have no equivalent in the Sanskrit original, and its syntactical relationship is unclear. *Subhāṣitaratnanidhi* 113 is clearly modelled upon this stanza:

།ཆེ་ལ་གནོད་བྱེད་གྲོགས་སུ་འགྱུར། །དམན་ལ་གནོད་བྱེད་གནོད་བྱེད་འགྱུར།
།ནགས་མེ་རླུང་གིས་སྤོར་མོད་ཀྱི། །དེ་ཡིས་སྒྲོན་མ་ཆུང་ངུའང་གསོད

"The great can become friend to those
who have done them harm,
(but) the base become harmful to those
who have done them mischief.
While the wind, to be sure, inflames the forest fire,
it extinguishes the small lamp." (Bosson)

A simpler version of the same idea is expressed in the following stanza:

वनानि दहतो वह्नेः सखा भवति मारुतः ।
स एव दीपनाशाय कुतः क्षीणेषु सौहृदम् ॥

"The wind becomes the friend
of the fire which devours the forests,
the same wind extinguishes a lamp—
how could there be friendship with the low."

The stanza occurs in *Prajñādaṇḍa* 41 from where it was taken to *Gāthāśataka* 20. The other Indian sources seem to be younger than the *Prajñādaṇḍa*: No. 728 (spurious) of the stanzas attributes to Bhartṛhari, stanza No. 3.57 of the *Pañcatantra* (textus simplicior) and anthologies of Śārṅgadhara, Vallabhadeva and the *Subhāṣitārṇava*; cf. CNTT No. 1911.

—133—

།གཏུམ་པོ་འདིས་ནི་ཕན་བཏགས་ཞེའམ། །འཕངས་ཞེས་སུ་ཡི་ངོར་མི་བལྟ།
།མེ་མཆེད་གྱུར་ན་སྦྱིན་སྲེག་མཁན། །ཡོ་བྱད་བཅས་ཏེ་འཚིག་པར་འགྱུར། ༡༣༣ | Q167a

b *'phaṅ* CD **c** *ched* N; *bsreg* GQ **d** *byed* C, *tshig* CD

A fierce person never considers
'This one has done me a favour, he has saved me.'
When a fire has spread, it will burn
the priest together with his utensils.

उपकृतमनेन सुहृदयमित्यसतामस्ति न क्वचिदपेक्षा ।
होत्रा सह स्वमाश्रयमुद्वृत्तो निर्दहति वह्निः ॥ १३३ ॥ LSP 248

'He has done me a favour, he is my friend'—
bad persons never take this into consideration.
The fire rises and burns up
its own basis together with the priest.

gtum po "fierce" is a rather unusual translation of *asatām*, likewise *su yi ṅor* "in the presence of who(soever)" of *kva cid*.

'phaṅs (*'phaṅ* CD) can hardly be explained as equivalent of *suhṛd ayam*. It is also very unlikely that the translators had the variant reading *sutarām* in their manuscript because this is found only in BÖHTLINGK's edition of the stanza (IS² 1283) which is based on his manuscript of the *Śārṅgadharapaddhati*. The printed text, however, also reads *suhṛd ayam*. Nevertheless STERNBACH decided in favour of *sutarām* in his presentation of the stanza in MSS 7038.

yo byad can "together with (his) utensils" seems to be a free rendering of *svam āśrayam* "its own basis". It cannot be connected with the text which was adopted by STERNBACH, *hotuḥ svahastam āśrita(ḥ)*, which in its combination of a *genitivus possessivus* and *sva°* is rather poor Sanskrit.

—134—

།སྲོག་ལ་བབ་ཀྱང་བློ་ལྡན་ཉིད། །ངང་གཙང་ཡོན་ཏན་འདོར་མི་བྱེད།
།དུང་ནི་མེ་ཡིས་བསྲེགས་ན་ཡང་། །རང་བཞིན་དཀར་བ་མི་འདོར་རོ། ༡༣༤ །

b *daṅ gtsaṅ* G **c** *sregs* N, *bsrags* Q

Even when his life is endangered,
only a wise person, who is pure by nature,

does not abandon virtue.
Even after a conch shell has been burnt by fire
it does not abandon its characteristic whiteness.

The Sanskrit original of this stanza is missing in the *Lokasaṃvyavahārapravṛtti*, but it can be found as stanza 243 of Vallabhadeva's *Subhāṣitāvalī*:

अनित्यावस्थो ऽपि बुधः स्वगुणं न जहाति जातिशुद्धतया।
न श्वेतभावमुज्झति शङ्खः शिखिभुक्तमुक्तो ऽपि॥ १३४॥

References: VS 243 and SSR 30.144 attributed to Ravigupta; SR 48.142 attributed to *Pañcatantra* (4,7b), but following Ravigupta's text. Also Pts 4.110, Ptsk 4.76.

Variant readings: **a** *antyāvasthāgato 'pi* Pts, *antyāvastho mahān* Ptsk; **b** *mahān svaguṇāñ jahāti na śuddhatayā* Pts; *svāmiguṇān na jahāti tu śuddhatuyā* Ptsk; **d** *°yukti°* Ptsk.

Because of his genuine purity a wise person
does not abandon his own virtues, not even in the face of death.
A conch shell does not abandon its whiteness,
even after it has been swallowed by fire and then released.

It should be noted that the Tibetan translation confirms the text of Vallabhadeva, not the variant readings quoted from the *Pañcatantra* recensions which have been adopted by STERNBACH in his *Mahāsubhāṣitasaṃgraha* No. 1671. In the English translation given there *śikhi°* is translated as "peacock", not as "fire"! I think, the interpretation of the Tibetan translation is correct which is, by the way, also the interpretation of BÖHTLINGK in IS[2] No. 355. Cf. also IS[2] No. 6794:

सन्तो न यान्ति वैवर्ण्यमापत्सु पतिता अपि ।
दग्धो ऽपि वह्निना शङ्खः शुभत्वं नैव मुञ्चति ॥

"The good never lose their caste (colour),
even when they have fallen into misfortune.
Although burnt by fire,
the conch shell does not abandon its whiteness."

Cf. also the loose parallel in *Subhāṣitaratnanidhi* 51:

།དམ་པ་སྲོག་ལ་བབ་ན་ཡང་། །རང་བཞིན་བཟང་པོ་ག་ལ་འདོར།
།ས་ལེ་སྦྲམ་ནི་བསྲེག་བཅད་ཀྱང་། །དེ་ཡི་ཁ་དོག་ཉམས་མི་འགྱུར།

"Even if the excellent are in mortal danger,
how can they abandon their natural goodness?
Even though one burns and chops gold dust,
its color will not spoil" (BOSSON)

—135—

།ཁྲེལ་མེད་བྱ་བ་བྱ་བ་མིན། །*དཔྱོད་པས་ནམ་ཡང་ཚིམ་པ་མེད།
།སྨྱ་ངམ་ལམ་དུ་ཞུགས་པ་དག །ཆུ་གཙང་མི་གཙང་སུ་ཞིག་རྟོག ༡༣༥ །

b *sbyoṅ bas* Q, *spyod pas* CDGNQ **c** *mya ṅan* G **d** *rtogs* N

The impertinent will never become content
by scrutinizing what shall be done and what not.
Those who have entered a path (leading) through a desert
will never reflect on whether the water is clean or unclean.

कार्याकार्ये तुलयति सर्वस्तृप्तो न जातु तृष्णार्तः ।
स्वादु शुचि वाथ जलमिति मरुपथिकः को विचारयति ॥ १३५ ॥ LSP 249

Everyone who is satiated scrutinizes
whether something should be done or not—
not he who is suffering from thirst.
Would a person who traverses a desert deliberate
whether the water (which he finds there)
is sweet or clean?

The Tibetan translators erroneously construed the first half of the stanza as one sentence, interpreting *tulayati* in the sense of **tulayan* or (*kāryāka-rya*)*tulanayā*. *svādu śuci vā* "sweet or clean" has been rendered freely by *gtsaṅ mi gtsaṅ* "clean or unclean". Or did the Sanskrit manuscript read **śucy aśuci vā*?

—136—

།ངང་གིས་རབ་བསྒྲིམས་བྱ་བ་*ལ། །དེ་ལས་ལྷག་པར་ལ་བཟླར་མེད།
།བདེ་བར་ཤིང་རྩེར་འཛེགས་པས་ཀྱང་། །དེ་ལས་བརྩལ་ན་ལྷུང་བར་འགྱུར ། ༡༣༦ །

a *las* CDGNQ **b** *da las* D **c** *'dzeg* Q **d** *rtsal* GNQ; *ltuṅ* (?) CN

He who takes the greatest pains in achieving an aim
has no chance to go beyond (that aim).
Even he who has comfortably climbed to the top of a tree
will fall down, if he strives beyond that top.

अभ्यधिकतयात्मानं कुर्वन्नत्युच्छ्रितं न शक्नोति ।
तरुमस्तकमधिरूढः सुखमपि नास्ते न चोत्पतति ॥ १३६ ॥ LSP 250

If one tries to place oneself too high,
one will not be able to do this.
He who has climbed to the top of a tree
does not stay there comfortably nor can he go further.

The Tibetan translation is very free in the first half and in line d). The main idea is not very faithfully represented. In line a) one might be tempted to read *byas pa* instead of *bya ba*. And is *lhag par la* in line b) an ellipsis for *lhag par {mtho ba'i sa} la*?

This stanza seems to have influenced *Subhāṣitaratnanidhi* 314 and 315:

།རིགས་པས་རྙེད་པའི་ཟ་ནོར་བླང་། །མི་འོས་གཞན་ལ་རློམ་སེམས་སྤང་།
།ཤིང་ཐོག་ཤིང་རྩེ་ལས་བླང་གི། །དེ་ལས་ཐལ་ནས་ས་ལ་ལྷུང་།

"One should accept food and possessions
that have been acquired rightfully.
One should abandon covetousness
for the other unrightful (things).
One gathers fruits (MH; 'food' Bosson) from the top of a tree,
but when one steps beyond that, one falls to the ground."
(Bosson)

།མཁས་པས་སྒྲིམ་པ་མི་བྱེད་པ། །དེ་ཡི་བར་ལ་ཉེས་པ་འབྱུང་།
།བློ་དང་ལྡན་པས་རབ་སྒྲིམས་ན། །ཉེས་པ་འབྱུང་བའི་གོ་སྐབས་དཀའ།

"Harm arises in that interval
when the wise are not applying mindfulness.

If the sensible ones exert themselves well,
it is difficult for harm to have an opportunity to arise."
(Bosson)

—137—

།ཕལ་ཆེར་འགྲོ་མང་ཕ་རོལ་ལས། །སྐྱོན་འབྱུང་སྨྲ་རིགས་རང་ལས་མིན། N186a
།བུད་ཤིང་དང་ནི་མེ་གཉིས་ལ། །བརྟེན་ནས་མེས་ནི་སྲེག་པར་འགྱུར། ༡༣༧ །

b *byuṅ* GNQ **d** *bsreg* N

Generally the majority of people regard it as appropriate
to mention the faults that happen from others,
not from themselves.
(However), fire can burn (only) when it is based
both on fire-wood and fire.

प्रायः परमेव जडाः स्वापदि हेतुं वदन्ति नात्मानम् ।
दाह्यं दहनं चोभयमपि निश्रित्योद्भवति दाहः ॥ १३७ ॥ LSP 251

Generally a dull person makes someone else responsible
for his own misfortune, not himself.
A fire, however, arises only when it is based
both on something which burns
and something which can be burnt.

If the Tibetan text is correct, the translators seem to have read **janāḥ* i. o. *jaḍāḥ* in line a), *'gro maṅ*. In all the other places where *jaḍa-* occurs in the *Āryākoṣa* it is translated by *blun po*, cf. 25d, 30a, 40a, 64a, 83a, 107a.

Vallabhadeva's *Subhāṣitāvalī*, No. 2858, contains a loose parallel which can also be found in the *Lokasaṃvyavahārapravṛtti*, No. 123:

शिक्षयति लोक एव प्रायः कुसृतिर्जनं सुशीलमपि ।
इन्धनमेव प्रथयति हविर्भुजो दाहसामर्थ्यम् ॥

"Generally the world teaches even a person
of high moral standards the wrong ways of action.
It is the fire-wood which enhances
the ability of the fire to burn."

—138—

།ཐོས་པ་མང་བས་ང་རྒྱལ་དང་། །ཕྱུག་ཁེངས་གཟུགས་མཛེས་རྒྱགས་པ་དང་།
།རྒྱ་མཚོ་ལ་ནི་བུལ་ཏོག་རྒྱུ། །གཤིན་རྗེའི་རྩེད་མོ་ཕྱིན་ཅི་ལོག ༡༣༨ །

c *na bi/u la rtog* C **d** *rtse* Q

The arrogance caused by great learning,
the haughtiness of the wealthy, the pride of the beautiful,
and the salty water in the ocean—
they are the perverted games of the god of death!

अभिमानः श्रुतमहतां धनिनां गर्वो मदः सुरूपाणाम् ।
क्षारजलता च जलधेः कृतान्तखलदुर्विलसितानि ॥ १३८ ॥ LSP 252

The arrogance of those who possess great learning,
the pride of the wealthy, the madness of the beautiful,
and the saltiness of the water of the ocean—
these are the bad jokes of that rascal Death!

—139—

།བཀྲེན་པ་འདི་བས་བདག་འབྱོར་བས། །བདག་ལ་མི་ཕོད་དེ་མི་བསམ།
།མི་གཡོ་*རི་ཆེན་རྩེ་མོ་ཡང་། །ཅི་ག་རྡོ་རྗེས་མི་འབིགས་སམ། ༡༣༩ །

a *'byor pas* GN **c** *rin chen* CDGNQ

'Since I am wealthier than that indigent person
he cannot defeat me'—thus one should not think.
Why would the thunderbolt not pierce
even the peak of a great, immovable mountain?

पृथुरहमयं कृशीयानगम्यो नास्याहमित्यनास्थैषा ।
किमचलशिरो ऽतिमहदपि वज्रमणीयो न दारयति ॥ १३९ ॥ LSP 253

c *'timahad api*: *hi mahad iti* H; I have selected those variant readings which are in agreement with ĀKtib.

'I am mighty, he is very weak,
(therefore) he is not able to defeat me'—
this is a wrong attitude.
Would the very small thunderbolt omit the opportunity
of splitting the peak of a mountain only because it is big?

Note the usage of *ci ga* (= *ci* or *cis*) for Skt. *kim*.

—140—

།ནོར་གྱི་བདག་པོ་སྲུང་མཁས་ཀྱང་། །ནད་(?)བྱེད་ཤིན་ཏུ་བསྲུང་བར་དཀའ།
།ཉ་དག་རྒྱ་མཚོའི་ཆུ་འཐུང་ཡང་། །འཐུང་དོ་བར་ནི་མཐོང་བ་མེད། ༡༤༠ ། C117b

a *nor gyi* (?) C; *bsruṅ* GNQ **b** *nad* C, read *noṅ*? *byad* D **c** *rgya mtsho* G **d** read *'thuṅ ba'i bar du*? *mṅon pa med* GNQ

Treasurers, even when the guardians are skilled,
are very difficult to guard against evil-doing.
Although the fishes drink the water of the ocean,
they cannot be seen while they are drinking.

धनमधिकृता हरन्तः कुशलैरपि रक्षिभिर्दुरारक्ष्याः ।
प्रज्ञायन्ते मत्स्याः सरःसु न पयः पिबन्तो ऽपि ॥ १४० ॥ LSP 257

Treasurers who take the money away
are difficult to be detected even by the most skilled watchmen.
The fishes are not recognized in the ponds,
although they drink its water.

nor gyi bdag po seems to render *dhanam adhikṛtāḥ*, as if it were **dhanādhikārāḥ*, *dhanam*, however, is the object of *harantaḥ*.

naṅ byed is certainly not the Tibetan translation of *antaḥkaraṇa-* "inner organ" as one might think when reading the Tibetan only (cf. LC[1], p. 1338, and LC[2], p. 1044, s. v. *naṅ gi byed pa*), since it renders *harantaḥ* "those who are taking". It is difficult to find out what the Tibetan translators originally translated and what they intended by their translation. If *naṅ* goes back to an original *noṅ ba* or *noṅ(s) pa* the chain of association could have been "taking away > robbing > robber > criminal". Or does it go back to *nod pa* "to keep, take, obtain, receive", a synonym of *len pa* "to take"? Or is *naṅ* a simple metathesis of an original **ṅan* with *ṅan byed* meaning "evil-doer?" *ṅan byed* is attested in LC[2] as rendering of *kukṛta-* and *duṣkṛta-*.

'thuṅ ṅo bar ni is also difficult to understand and moreover it has no equivalent in the Sanskrit original, because all the words of the second half of the stanza already have their Tibetan counterparts. Either it belongs to the interpretation of *prajñāyante* "are recognized" by *mthoṅ ba med* [CD] "cannot be seen" (or *mṅon pa med* [GNQ] "are not visible") or it repeats what has already been expressed by *chu 'thuṅ yaṅ* "although they drink (its) water". In the latter case I would expect something like *'thuṅ ba'i bar du* (or *na*) "while they are drinking".

—141—

|སྦྱིན་པས་ཕྱུག་པོ་ཉིད་རྙེད་ནས། |ཕོངས་ལ་སྦྱིན་པར་མི་བྱེད་པའི།
|ཁྲེལ་མེད་གང་ཡིན་དེ་ལ་ནི། |གྲོགས་པས་ལྷག་པར་ཕྱིས་མི་སྟེར ། ༡༤༡ །

a *rñede* D **b** *phoṅs pa* G **d** *phyir* CD

To that shameless person
who does not give to the needy

after having obtained wealth by the donations (of others)
later on not much will be given, out of anger (about him).

दानादेव विभूतिं प्राप्य पुनर्यो ददाति नार्थिभ्यः ।
एष कृतघ्न इति न तं रुषेव भूयो भजन्त्यर्थाः ॥ १४१ ॥ LSP 262

If someone, having obtained wealth
only because of the charity (of others)
does not (readily) give to supplicants,
then material goods will never come to him again,
as if they were angry about his ingratitude.

kṛtaghna- "ungrateful" has been translated rather freely by *khrel med* "shameless" and the whole construction has been simplified, thereby spoiling the nice figure of speech *Utprekṣā* of the original stanza.

It seems as if the topic of this stanza is the appraisal of *dāna* "charity", the first of the six moral perfections, *pāramitā*.

—142—

།ཇི་སྲིད་དམ་པ་མི་བརྩོན་པ། ། དེ་སྲིད་ཉེས་པ་སྟོབས་ལྡན་འགྱུར།
།བརྩོན་པས་ཉོན་མོངས་སྡར་མ་ལ། ། བློ་ལྡན་སྐྲག་པར་མི་བྱ་སྟེ། ༡༤༢ །

As long as a good person does not show *energy*
(his moral) faults will become strong(er and stronger).
By (the application of) *energy* the wise one should
not be terrified with regard to cowardly defilements.

This stanza cannot be found in the *Lokasaṃvyavahārapravṛtti*. It seems as if its topic is the appraisal of *vīrya* "energy", the fourth of the six moral perfections, *pāramitā*.

The translation of the second half of the stanza is uncertain.

—143—

།ཉོན་མོངས་བག་ཆགས་དྲི་མ་ནི། །ཤེས་རབ་མེས་བསྲེག་ཏིང་འཛིན་ཆུས།
།རྡོ་ཐལ་རྡོ་བསྲེགས་ཆུས་གཏོར་ན། །དུམ་བུ་བརྒྱར་འགྱེས་བཞིན་དུ་བྱ། ༡༨༣ । D122a

a *d[r]i* D **b** *bsregs* GN, *sreg* CD **c** *bsrags* Q, *bsregs* CDN **d** *du 'gya* C

One should (first) burn the dirt
"propensity towards defilements" with the fire "wisdom"
and (then) sprinkle it with the water "meditation"
so that it will split into one hundred pieces
like chalk which is (first) burnt into stone.
[Or: and then sprinkle it with water
so that it will split into one hundred pieces.]

This stanza cannot be found in the *Lokasaṃvyavahārapravṛtti*. It seems as if its topic is the appraisal of *dhyāna* "meditation" and *prajñā* "wisdom", the fifth and sixth of the six moral perfections, *pāramitā*.

Meaning and construction of the third line are uncertain.

—144—

།བདག་ཉིད་ཆེན་པོས་བསྟེན་པའི་ལམ། །གཞན་དག་གོམས་པར་བྱེད་པ་ཡིས།
།ཅི་ནས་འདི་ལ་དགའ་ལྟའི་ཕྱིར། །འདི་ནི་བསམས་ནས་སྨྲས་པ་ཡིན། ༢༨༨ । Q167b

d *goms* CD

The path which is followed by the magnanimous ones
is also practised by others.
(I) have first reflected upon it and then spoken about it
so that one may somehow rejoice in it.

अपि नाम कश्चिदेतद्विलोकयन्काव्यं परिचयेनापि ।
पदवीं भजेत महतामिति यत्नोऽयं प्रलापे ऽपि ॥ १४४ ॥ LSP 266

'May it be that (at least) somebody glances
through this poetry and then,
having become familiar (with its content),
follows the path of the great!'
Thinking this, I have taken the trouble
(to compose) this prate.

—145—

།དེ་ལྟར་འགྲོ་བ་ཉེས་པ་སྣ་ཚོགས་མེས། །དགེ་ལེགས་ས་བོན་སྨྱུ་གུ་བསྐྱེད་བསྲེགས་པས།
།ཇི་སྲིད་སྲིད་གསུམ་ཟ་ཡོད་འཆི་བདག་ནི། །གནམ་ལྕགས་འབབ་ལ་གྲགས་པའི་ཚོགས་སྐྱེད་ཤོག
། ༡༤༥ །

d *'babs* CD, *'bab pa* G; *bskyed* N

May (this) therefore produce abundant fame and glory
as long as the God of Death
who is able to swallow the Three Worlds
lets his club fall down on human beings
because they have burnt with the fire of manifold vices
the seed which had been produced by good deeds.

इति जगति विचित्रदोषवह्निहतशुभबीजगुणाङ्कुरप्रसूतौ ।
उपचिनुत यशांसि नैति यावत्त्रिभुवनघस्मरमृत्युवज्रपातः ।। १४५ ।। LSP 267

Therefore one should accumulate fame in this world,
in which the fire of manifold vices
has destroyed the seeds of goodness
from which the sprouts of virtues come forth,
as long as the God of Death,
who is eager to devour the Three Worlds,
lets not fall down his thunderbolt(-like club).

A literal translation of the compound in the first half of the stanza would run: "in which the coming forth of the sprouts of virtues from the seeds of goodness has been destroyed by the fire of manifold vices". In the Tibetan *guṇa-* was omitted which spoils the *Rūpaka* of the Sanskrit original.

The Tibetan translators omitted the negation *na*; had they written *mi 'bab* i. o. *'bab la* the Tibetan would almost fully agree with the Sanskrit.

—Colophon—

།ཚིགས་སུ་བཅད་པའི་མཛོད་ཅེས་བྱ་བ། །སློབ་དཔོན་ཉི་*མས་སྦས་པས་མཛད་པ་རྫོགས་སོ།།
།།ཟ་ཧོར་གྱི་མཁན་པོ་ཛྙཱ་ན་ཤཱན་ཏི་དང་། བོད་ཀྱི་ལོ་ཙ་བ་དཔལ་གྱི་ལྷུན་པོའི་སྡེས་བསྒྱུར་ཅིང་ཞུས་ཏེ་
གཏན་ལ་ཕབ་པའོ།། G253b N186b

tshigsu N; *ñi ma* CDGNQ; *śāṃ ti* GN, *śā ti* Q; *lo tstsha ba* GNQ; *bsgyur źiṅ* G; *phab pa* CD

The *Āryākoṣa*, composed by the teacher Ravigupta, is completed.

It was translated, corrected and edited by abbot Jñānaśānti from Za hor and the Tibetan translator Dpal gyi lhun po'i sde.

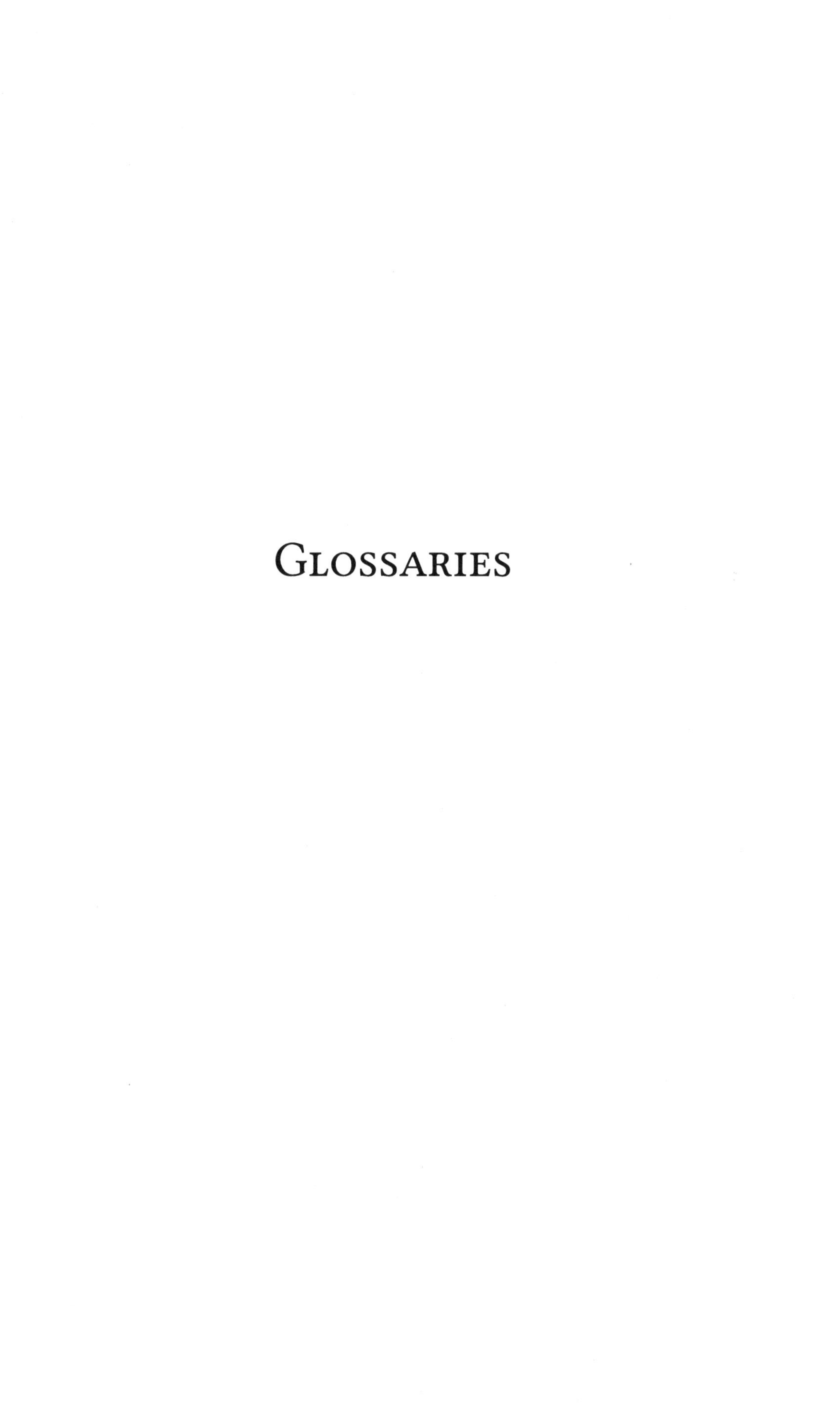

Glossaries

Sanskrit-English-Tibetan

A

akaraṇīya- adj. *not to be done* 60b (tib. *mi byed*)

akasmāt adv. *accidentally, suddenly* 2a (tib. *glo bur*)

akārya- nt. *what should not be done* 135a (tib. *bya ba min*)

akṣara- nt. *letter* 34c (tib. *yi ge*)

akṣi- nt. *eye* 51c (tib. *mig*)

aguru- m./nt. *the Aloe wood* 48c (tib. *a ka ru*)

agni- m. *fire* 29b, 33b, 48d, 53d, 76a, 81d, 129d, 132c (tib. *me*)

agniśikhā- f. *flame* 13c (tib. *me lce*)

agra- nt. *foremost point, uppermost part, tip; prominent position* 14a (tib. *n. e.*), 46d (tib. *mtho*)

aṅkura- m. *sprout, shoot* 76a, 145b (tib. *myu gu*)

acala- adj. *not moving, immovable* 131c (tib. *mi g.yo ba'i*); m. *mountain* 139c (tib. *mi g.yo *ri*)

ajña- m. *ignorant person* 34b, 38a (tib. *blun po*); 84b (tib. *dman pa*)

aṇīyas- (comp. of *aṇu-*) *very small* 139dtib. *n. e.*)

aṇu- adj. *fine, minute, small* 13a (tib. *chuṅ*)

aṇḍaja- m. *an egg-born being* 76a (tib. *sgoṅ skyes*)

ati- adv. *beyond, over, excessively, exceedingly* 7a, 77c, 80a, 87a (tib. *rab*); 12a, 78a, 136b (tib. *lhag par*); 14a (tib. *drags*); 15c (ativṛddhi; tib. *thaṅ skyed* perhaps for misread skt. *atidṛḍhi*); 17a (atyucchritān; tib. *'phaṅ mtho*); 22a, 119c, 139c (tib. *n. e.*); 29a, 44c, 90a (tib. *śin tu*); 53d (atyupacitā; tib. *spor*); 63b (atyunnatān; tib. *che ba*); 66b ('tyucchritau; tib. *dar ba ... na*); 77a (na ati°; contextually tib. *dkon pa*); 97c (atisaṃdhātuṃ i. o. abhi°?; tib. *bye ba 'dum byed*)

ati-√i (2, *atyeti*) *to pass by; surpass* 113b (atītya; contextually tib. *bźin du*)

ati-√śī (2, *atiśete*) *to surpass, excel* 110b (atiśayituṃ; only tib. *śin tu* referring to *ma dag pa'i*, skt. *°śuddhatayā*)

atyanta- adj. *excessive, very great* 118a (tib. *lhag par*)

atyartha- adj. *excessive, exceeding* 41b (tib. *lhag par*)

atyartham adv. *excessively, exceedingly* 61b (tib. *lhag par*)

atha adv. *now; then* 135c (tib. *n. e.*)

adṛṣṭa- adj. *unseen; not experienced* 122b (tib. *ma mthoṅ*)

adhikam adv. *exceedingly, too much* 8c (tib. *lhag par*); 29d (tib. *śin tu*); 102c, 129a (tib. *n. e.*)

adhikṛta- ppp. of adhi-√kṛ *ruled, administered* 140a (tib. *bdag po*)

adhirūḍha- ppp. of adhi-√ruh *ascended, mounted* 136c (tib. *'dzegs pas*)

adhi-√sthā (1, *adhitiṣṭhati*) *to stand upon; inhabit, abide* 46a (adhitiṣṭhaṃl; tib. *rñed na*)

anāgas- m. *innocent person* 126b (tib. *noṅs skyon med*)

anārabhya- adj. *improper to be commenced, what should not be undertaken* 37b (tib. **mi brtsam*)

anārya- m. *ignorant person, unrespectable man* 35b (tib. *n. e.*); 50a (tib. *phal pa*); 61b (tib. *ṅan pa*)

anāsthā- f. *want of consideration, wrong attitude* 139b (tib. *mi bsam*)

anipuṇa- m. *unskilled man* 55b (tib. *mi mkhas pa*)

a-ni-√bandh (9, *anibadhnāti*) *not to bind on, not join, not control* 78d (anibadhya; tib. *ma bsdams*)

aniśam adv. *incessantly, always* 61b (tib. *n. e.*)

aniścaya- adj. *not certain, uncertain* 32b (tib. *ma ṅes te*)

anukta- adj. *unuttered, unsaid, untold* 27b (tib. *mi smra*)

anu-√gam (1, *anugacchati*) *to go after, follow* 104a (anugantukāmair; tib. *rjes su 'gro 'dod pas*)

anugraha- m. *favour, kindness* 98b (anugrahaṃ kartum; tib. *phan par byed*)

anucita- adj. *improper, inappropriate* 21a (tib. *mi rigs*)

anudātta- adj. *not raised, not elevated;* m. *low-pitched tone* 16b (freely tib. *ṅan*)

anunnati- f. *no rising; lack of haughtiness* 80d (tib. *gźol ba*)

anu-√pā (caus. *anupālayati*) *to preserve, keep, cherish* 127c (anupālya; tib. *bskyaṅs nas*)

anupāya- m. *inappropriate means* 45a (tib. *thabs daṅ bral ba*)

anurakta- ppp. of anu-√rañj *fond of, attached* 47a (contextually tib. *'khor na*)

anu-√rañj (4, *anurajyati*) *to be attached, devoted* 75d (°ānurajyante; contextually tib. *'drid pa'i ched yin*)

anurūpa- adj. *corresponding, fit, suitable* 15b (tib. *'os pa*); 62d (tib. *mthun pa*)

anta- m. *end; death, destruction* 126a (antaṃ yānti; freely tib. *'gyur ba*); 127c (tib. *mtha ma*)

antaḥpura- nt. *the king's harem* 108b (tib. *btsun mo'i 'khor*)

antyāvastha- adj. *being in a state just before death, in the face of death* 134a (tib. *srog la bab*)

andha- adj. *blind* 99c (tib. *loṅ ba*); 125d (contextually tib. *log pa*); m. *blind man* 117c (tib. *loṅ ba*)

anya- pron. adj. *other* 4d, 40c, 69a, 113c, 113d (tib. *gźan*)

anvita- adj. *followed by, possessed of* *1a (tib. *ldan*)

ap- f. *water* 83c (tib. *chu*)

apakārin- m. *one who is doing harm* 95a (tib. *gnod pa byed pa*)

apakṛta- ppp. of apa-√kṛ *done wrongly, offensively or wickedly committed* 5a (tib. *'tshe ba*); *injury, offence* 61c (tib. *gnod pa*)

apakṛti- f. *wrong doing, offence* 41a (tib. *mi mthun byas pa*)

apacaya- m. *diminution, decay, decrease* 67a (tib. *'bri ba*)

apa-√rañj (4, *aparajyate*) *to become unfavourable, become disinterested in* 44d (aparajyante; tib. *yoṅs su spoṅ bar byed*)

aparibhūta- adj. *not humiliated* 102b (tib. *ma bsdigs*)

apasṛti- f. *retreat* 19a (tib. *n. e.*)

api adv. *and, also, even, moreover, surely* 4a, 12c, 13a, 13b, 13c, 17a, 26c, 27b, 29a, 30a, 41c, 46c, 49b, 57d, 58c, 64a, 80a, 87c, 96d, 103c, 106a, 110a, 124a, 132c, 134d, 139c, 140d (tib. *yaṅ*); 5d, 7b, 13d, 17b, 17d, 22a, 22c, 23d, 24c, 27c, 27d, 28c, 29c, 32c, 34d, 36c, 39c, 41a, 44a, 44c, 45c, 47d, 50b, 51a, 51b, 53d, 56b, 57a, 58a, 59a, 59c, 60c, 61a, 64b, 64c, 69a, 69d, 73c, 75a, 77b, 79d, 85b, 85d, 91b, 91d, 92a, 95b, 96a, 110c, 116c, 123b, 125c, 125b, 126b, 126c, 127b, 128c, 129b, 137d, 144b, 144d (tib. *n. e.*); 24b, 26a, 28d, 36a, 45b, 54c, 65a, 71a, 72a, 81c, 87a, 90a, 92b, 92d, 99b, 103b, 117a, 117d, 120a, 122b, 134a, 136d, 140b (tib. *kyaṅ*); 32b (tib. *gcig tu*); 38b, 47a, 88a, 88d, 108b, 125b, 128a (tib. *'aṅ*); 52d (tib. *tsam*); 73a (sakṛd api; tib. *mod la*); 79c (tib. *mod kyi*); 99c (tib. *te*); 123d (tib. *gyi*); 129d (tib. *de bźin*); 130c (tib. *ni*)

api nāma *may it be that, I wish that* 144a (tib. *n. e.*)

apa-√i (2, *apaiti*) *to go away, withdraw; run away, escape* 21c (apāsya; tib. *spoṅ bar byed*)

apuṣpa- adj. *not flowering* 27d (tib. *me tog med*)

apekṣā- f. *consideration, regard* 133b (tib. *blta*)

aprakāśam adv. *not in public, without publicity* 97a (very freely tib. *drin bgraṅ mi byed*)

aprasannākṣa- adj. *with no clear sight, mentally obscured* 99d (tib. *rig pa med pa'i loṅ ba* renders as if skt. **a + dhī + akṣa(n)*)

aphala- adj. *fruitless* 27c (tib. *'bras bu med*)

abhi-√krudh (4, *abhikrudhyati*) *to be angry with, get angry* 55c (abhikrudhyati; freely tib. *sñegs*)

abhighāta- m. *striking; kicking* 102d (tib. *bsnun*)

abhijāta- ppp. of abhi-√jan *well-born, noble* 17d (tib. *rigs ldan*)

abhijña- adj. *knowing, skilful, proficient* 30b (tib. *śes rig*)

abhidroha- m. *injuring* 50b (tib. **'tshe*)

abhiniveśin- adj. *intent upon, devoted to* 40a (asthānābhiniveśī; tib. *thub chod*)

abhi-√bhū (1, *abhibhavati*) *to overcome, overpower, predominate, surpass* 17b (abhibhavati; tib. *zil gyis gnon*); 64b (abhibhavati; tib. *zil gyis gnon*)

abhimāna- m. *arrogance, haughtiness* 138a (tib. *ṅa rgyal*)

abhiyukta- ppp. of abhi-√yuj *applied, intend on, dilligent, versed in* 100b (tib. *n. e.*)

abhiyoga- m. *application; effort, exertion* 100a (tib. *brtson byas*)

abhi-√laṣ (1, *abhilaṣati*) *to desire, wish for* 8c (abhilaṣati; tib. *mṅon par 'dod*)

abhi-vi-√añj (7, pass. *abhivyajyate*) *to be manifested, become manifest* 48b (abhivyajyate; tib. *lhag par ... gsal*)

abhyadhikatā- f. *surpluss, excess* 136a (tib. *rab bsgrims*)

abhyavahāra- m. *taking food* 118c (tib. *zas kyi spyod pa*)

abhi-ud-√dhṛ (1, *abhyuddharati*) *to take out, draw (as water)* 43d (abhyuddharanti; tib. *'thuṅ bar byed*)

abhyunnata- ppp. of abhi-ud-√nam *raised, elevated* 64a (tib. *lhag par srid mtho*)

abhi-upa-√i (2, *abhyupaiti*) *to go near, approach; enter a state or condition* 79b (mābhyupaita; tib. *mi bya'o*)

amayūkha- adj. *without rays* 130d (tib. *'od med pa'i*)

amahātman- m. *one who is not noble-hearted* 94b (tib. *chen po min pa*)

amitra- m. *enemy, adversary* 33b (tib. *mi mdza' ba*)

ambu- nt. *water* 39c (tib. *char*)?

ambhas- nt. *water* 40c, 106c (tib. *chu*); 64c (tib. *char pa*); 65c (ambhaḥ sarajasam; tib. *mtsho chu* as if the translators read *ambhaḥ *sarasajam*)

amla- adj. *sour, acid* 96a (freely tib. *ṅar can*)

ayas- nt. *iron, metal* 83c (tib. *lcags*); 111c (tib. *n. e.*)

ayācita- adj. *not asked for, unsolicited* 97b (tib. *ma bslaṅs*)

araṇya- nt. *forest* 108d (tib. *nags*)

ariṣṭa- m. *the Ariṣṭa tree* 62d (tib. *a ri ta*)

arka- m. *sun* 36c (tib. *ñi ma*)

arjita- ppp. of √arj *acquired, gained, earned* 106a (tib. *bsgrubs*)

arta- ppp. of ā-√ṛ *afflicted, pained* 135b (tṛṣṇārtaḥ; tib. *chog pa* renders as if **tṛṣṇāḍhyaḥ*)

artha- m. *aim, purpose; use; thing, object, affair* 70b (sarvārtha°; tib. *kun*); 127a (tib. *'byor pa*)

arthin- m. *beggar* 112a, 112d[1] (tib. *sloṅ*); 112b, 112d[2] (tib. *sloṅ ba*); 141b (tib. *phoṅs*)

alaṃkṛti- f. *ornament, decoration* 24d (tib. *rgyan*)

alam adv. *enough, sufficient, adequate; able, capable* 28a (nālam; tib. *mi chog ste*); 36c (na ... alam; tib. *mi nus so*); 38a (nālaṃ; tib. *mi nus*); 70b (na ... alam; tib. *yod pa min*); 123b (tib. *dgos*)

alpa-	adj. *small, minute, little* 41a (tib. *cuṅ zad*); 90c (tib. *dpag tu med mod kyi ... dkon*)
alpabala-	m. *one of little strength* 43b (tib. *phal pa*)
avajñā-	f. *contempt* 115a (tib. *brñas*)
ava-√nam	(1, *avanamate*) *to bow down, make a bow* 85b (avanamante; tib. *mñen par byed*)
avanamana-	nt. *bowing down; lowness* 101d (tib. *dma' ba*)
avaśeṣa-	nt. *remainder* 94c (tib. *lus pa*)
avahita-	ppp. of ava-√dhā *placed into, confined within, attentive* 105b (mānam avahitaṃ vahataḥ; tib. *rag las med pa*?)
avikārin-	adj. *unchangeable, invariable* 61a (tib. *g.yo med*)
avikṛta-	adj. *unchanged, not deformed* 66c (tib. *'gyur ba med*)
avidyā-	f. *ignorance* 125b (tib. *ma rig pa*)
avidheya-	adj. *difficult to handle* 78b (tib. *bcos dka'*)
a-vi-√naś	(4, *avinaśyati*; caus. *avināśayati*) *not to destroy, not ruin* 76d (avināśya; tib. *ma phuṅ*)
avirāgin-	adj. *not indifferent, affectionate; not without reddishness* 52a (tib. **skyo ba med*)
aviśiṣṭa-	adj. *not distinct, not different* 69c (tib. *khyad par med*)
aviśuddha-	adj. *impure* 114c (tib. *n. e.*)
avihita-	adj. *uneffected, unimpeded* 114b (tib. *mi ñams*)
aśuci-	adj. *impure, foul* 14d (tib. *rdzas*)
aśoka-	m. *the Aśoka tree* 102c (tib. *mya ṅan 'tshaṅ*)
aśvatarī-	f. *she-mule* 76b (tib. *dre'u*)
√as	(2, *asti*) *to be* 48d, 60b, 133b (asti; tib. *n. e.*); 68a (santi; tib. *byed do*); 87d ('sti na; tib. *ma yin no*); 95c (sati; tib. *yod pa*); 122b (sato; tib. *yod*); 136d (nāste na cotpatati; freely tib. *rtsal na lhuṅ bar 'gyur*)
asaṃśliṣṭa-	adj. *not connected with, uninfluenced* 23d (tib. *gos pa med*)
asadvṛtta-	nt. *bad conduct* 92b (tib. *ṅan pa*)
asant-	m. pl. *bad people* 23d (tib. *skyon*); 39b (tib. *n. e.*); 92a (tib. *dman*); 103b (tib. *ṅan pa*); 133b (strangely tib. *gtum po*)
asamayajña-	adj. *not knowing the conventions and customs* 104d (tib. *dam tshig dag mi śes*)
asamartha-	adj. *unable to, incapable* 50d (tib. *mi nus*)
asaṃbhrama-	adj. *composed, cool, fearless* 95b (freely tib. *bsten*)
asādhu-	m. *wicked man, bad person* 13b (tib. *ṅan pa*)
asita-	adj. *dark-coloured, black* 31c (tib. *nag po*)
asta-	nt. *setting (of the sun), sunset* 79d (yāty astam; tib. *nub par 'gyur*)

astagamana- nt. *setting (of the sun)* 66d (tib. *nub pa*)

astamita- adj. *set (as the sun)* 19b (tib. *nub pa*)?; 69c (tib. *mun*)

astam-√i (2, *astameti*) *to set (as the sun)* 67c (tib. *nub*)

asthāna- nt. *not a fit place, inappropriate place* 40a (asthānābhiniveśī; tib. *thub chod*)

asthi- nt. *bone* 60c (contextually tib. *śa*)

asthira- adj. *unsteady* 78a (tib. *mi brtan*)

asnigdha- adj. *not smooth; harsh, without affection* 75a (tib. *gus pas min*)

√ah (only perf. 3rd sg. and pl.) *to say, consider* 100b (āhur; tib. *śes bya*); 109b (āha; tib. *zer ba*)

ahi- m. *snake* 39c (tib. *sbrul*)

Ā

ākāra- m. *form, figure, appearance* 32a (tib. not transmitted)

ākṛti- f. *form, figure, shape, appearance* 12b (tib. *raṅ bźin*)

ā-√kram (1, *ākrāmati*) *to step, go near to; attack, invade* 42b (ākramya; peculiarly tib. *thibs non*)

ā-√gam (1, *āgacchati*; caus. *āgamayati*) *to cause to come near, obtain information about, ascertain* 7a (āgamayaty; is tib. *sbed* 'to hide, conceal' a corruption of *sdud* 'to collect, gather'?)

āgas- m. *transgression, offence, injury, sin* 51a (tib. *skyon*)

ācita- ppp. of ā-√ci *accumulated, heaped, filled with* 78b (tib. *ldan pa'i*)

ātapa- m. *heat, sunshine* 29c (tib. *ñi ma*); 29d (contextually tib. *sprin me*)

ātura- adj. *suffering, sick* 60a (freely tib. *groṅ ba*)

ātman- m. *self*; adj. *own* 51b, 137b (tib. *raṅ*); 131c (tib. *raṅ la*); 136a (tib. *ṅaṅ*)

ādarśa- m. *mirror* 18c, 123c (tib. *me loṅ*)

-ādi *beginning with, et cetera, and so on* 6a (tib. **stsogs*); 113c (tib. *la sogs*)

ādau adv. *in the beginning, at first* 63d (tib. *daṅ po⟨r⟩*); 82c, 111a (tib. *thog mar*)

√āp (5, *āpnoti*) *to reach, overtake; obtain, gain, come to* 68b (na ... āpnoti; tib. *ma byuṅ bar*)

ā-√pad (4, *āpadyate*) *to come; enter, get into any state* 128b (sthiratām āpadyate; tib. *brtan par 'gyur*)

āpad- f. *misfortune, calamity, distress* 48a (tib. *rgud*); 126d (tib. *gnod*); 131b (tib. *gnod pa*); 137b (tib. *skyon*)

āpanna- ppp. of ā-√pad *got into (any state); gained, obtained* 130b (vināśa āpanne; tib. *ñams par gyur na*)

āyāta- ppp. of ā-√yā *come, arrived, attained* 5b (na tṛptim āyātaḥ; tib. *ṅoms pa med*)

āyus- nt. *life* 20a (tib. *tshe*)

āranāla- nt. *sour gruel made from the fermentation of boiled rice* 96b (tib. *tsaṅ śu'i khu?*)

ā-√rabh (1, *ārabhate*) *to undertake, commence, begin* 37b (nārabhate; tib. *rtsom mi byed*)

ārūḍha- ppp. of ā-√ruh *ascended, elevated on high* 46d (tib. *'dug pas*)

ārya- adj. *honourable, respectable, noble* 93b (tib. *n. e.*)

āloka- m. *light, lustre, splendour* 33c, 125d (tib. *snaṅ ba*)

āvṛta- ppp. of ā-√vṛ *covered, concealed; enclosed, surrounded; filled with* 29b (tib. *g.yogs*)

ā-√vṛ (5, *āvṛṇoti*) *to cover, hide, conceal* 91c (āvṛṇvanti; tib. *khebs par byed*)

āśin- adj. *eating, consuming* 58c (tib. *za*)

āśīviṣa- m. *poisonous snake* 109d (tib. *sbrul gdug*)

āśraya- m. *basis; asylum, shelter* 76d (tib. *rten*); 133c (svam āśrayam; freely tib. *yo byad bcas*)

I

√i (2, *eti*) *to go; attain (a certain state)* 23b (pararūpam eti; freely tib. *dri yi rjes su 'braṅ*); 41b (vikāram ... eti; tib. *khro*); 70d (eti bhidāṃ; tib. *gcod par byed*)

icchā- f. *wish, desire, inclination* 105c (tib. *'dod pa*)

iti *thus, with these words* 16b, 63d, 101b, 135c, 139b, 145c (tib. *n. e.*); 32b (tib. not transmitted); 65d (tib. *'aṅ*); 81a (tib. *yaṅ*); 109b, 133b (tib. *źes*); 132a (tib. *ce*); 141c (tib. *ni*); 144d (contextually tib. *bsgoms nas*); 145a (tib. *de ltar*)

idam- pron. *this (here)* 2b, 139a, 144d ('yam; tib. *'di*); 7c (anayoḥ; tib. *'di gñis*); 23a ('yaṃ; tib. *ni*); 25d (iyaṃ; tib. *'di*); 31a (asmād; in tib. expressed with the abl. ptcl.); 32a ('yaṃ; tib. not transmitted); 32b, 81a, 133a ('yaṃ; tib. *n. e.*); 32b (asmād; tib. not transmitted); 109b ('yam; tib. *de*); 115a (idaṃ; tib. *n. e.*); 132a (ayaṃ; tib. *'di ni*); 133a (anena; tib. *'dis*); 139b (asya; tib. *n. e.*);

indu- m. *moon* 40d, 49c (tib. *zla ba*)

indradhanus- nt. *Indra's bow, rainbow* 24c (tib. *dbaṅ po'i gźu*)

iva adv. *like, in the same manner as; as it were, as if* 2d* (tib. *ji bźin*); 7b (tib. *mtshuṅs*); 15d, 23c, 71d, 91a, 120b (tib. *bźin*); 23a, 121d (tib. *bźin du*); 52c (tib. *'dra*); 53d (tib. *n. e.*; see note to verse 53); 67b (tib. *lta bur*); 67d, 78c (tib. *lta bu'i*); 89b, 93b, 125b, 141d (tib. *n. e.*); 99a (tib. **bźin*); 121a (tib. *ltar*); 124c (tib. *'dra ba*)

Ī

īpsā- f. *desire, wish* 105d (tib. *'dod*)

īśvara- m. *supreme soul; master, lord, ruler* 115b, 132b (tib. *dbaṅ phyug*)

U

ucita- ppp. of √uc *delightful, agreeable; proper, suitable* 16b (tib. *rigs*)

ucca- adj. *high, lofty;* 85d (tib. *mthon po'i*); m. *elevated person* 16a (tib. *mchog*)

uccais adv. *aloft, high, above; much* 46a (tib. *mchog*); 95d (tib. *che ba'i*)

ud-√śuṣ (4, *ucchuṣyati*; caus. *ucchoṣayati*) *to cause to dry up* 98c (tib. *skems byed*)

ucchrāya- m. *rising, elevation; height, high rank* 20c (tib. *go 'phaṅ*); 82a (tib. *gzeṅs mthos*)

ucchrita- ppp. of ud-√śri *raised, elevated up* 17a (atyucchritān; tib. *'phaṅ mtho*); 66b ('tyucchritau; tib. *dar ba ... na*); 136b (atyucchritaṃ; tib. *lhag par*)

ucchvāsa- m. *breathing out; breath* 43c (tib. *dbugs rṅub pa*)

√ujjh (6, *ujjhati*) *to leave, abandon; avoid, escape* 13a (ujjhaty; tib. *spoṅ*); 22b (ujjhanti jātu na; tib. *'dor mi srid*); 134c (na ... ujjhati; tib. *mi 'dor ro*)

ud-√kṝ (6, *utkirati*) *to dig up; carve, engrave* 34d (utkirati; tib. *zos pa'i rjes*)

utkṣipta- ppp. of ud-√kṣip *thrown upwards, tossed, raised* 14d (tib. *gtor na*)

utthāpaka- m. *one who raises something upwards* 82d (tib. *'thor byed*)

utthita- ppp. of ud-√sthā *raised, elevated, high* 132d (tib. *spor mod*)

ud-√pat (1, *utpatati*) *to arise, rise* 136d (nāste na cotpatati; freely tib. *rtsal na lhuṅ bar 'gyur*)

utpatita- ppp. of ud-√pat *risen, ascended* 91d (tib. *'phur ba*)

uda- nt. *water* 36d (tib. *chu*)

udaka- nt. *water* 4c (tib. *chu*)

ud-√añc (1, *udañcati*) *to elevate, raise upwards* 82c (udañcann; tib. *gyen du 'thor ba*)

udanvat- m. *sea, ocean* 36d (tib. *mtsho*); 122d (tib. *rgya mtsho'i chu*)

udaya- m. *going up, rising, rise (of the sun); success, prosperity* 66d (tib. *'char ba*); 79a (tib. *mtho*)

udātta- ppp. of ud-ā-√dā *lifted up, upraised, lofty;* m. *the accute accent, high-pitched tone* 16a (tib. *mchog*)

udita- ppp. of ud-√i *risen, ascended* 69d (tib. *n. e.*); 79d (tib. *śar ba*)

ud-√i (2, *udeti*) *to go up, rise* 16a (udayati; tib. **skye ba*); 18d (udeti; tib. *'byuṅ la*); 54b (udeti; tib. *'khruṅ*); 79c (udayati; contextually tib. *ñi ma*); 92c (udeti; tib. *'byuṅ*)

ud-√bhū (1, *udbhavati*) *to come up to, rise, come forth, arise, spring from* 31b (udbhavati ... na; tib. *mi 'byuṅ*); 137d (udbhavati dāhaḥ; tib. *sreg par 'gyur*)

udyukta- ppp. of ud-√yuj *undertaking; zealously active, intent upon* 9a (tib. *brtson*)

udvṛtta- ppp. of ud-√vṛt *burst open; excited* 133d (tib. *mched gyur na*)

unnata- ppp. of ud-√nam *bent upwards, elevated* 63b (atyunnatān; tib. *che ba*)

unnati- f. *rising, height; prosperity* 80b (tib. *mi gźol*); 101d (tib. *mtho ba*)

ud-√nam (1, *unnamati*) *to raise up, lift up* 41d (unnamati; tib. *'thul bar byed*)

upakāra- m. *help, assistance, benefit; use, advantage* 6d (tib. *phan par byed*); 54a (tib. *phan byed*); 95a (tib. *phan 'dogs*)

upa-√kṛ (8, *upakaroti*) *to assist, help, favour* 88a (upakurvann; tib. *phan byed na*); 97a (upakartum; tib. *phan btags*)

upakṛta- ppp. of upa-√kṛ *helped, assisted, benefited* 5a (tib. *phan 'dogs*); 133a (tib. *phan btags*)

upaghāta- m. *stroke, hurt, injury, harm* 24a (tib. *gnod*); 58d (tib. *'tshe ba*); 84d (upaghātāya; tib. *gnod par 'gyur gyi*)

upaghātaka- m. *injury, damage; murderer* 84a (tib. *phuṅ khrol*)

upaghātin- adj. *hurting, injuring* 12a (tib. *gnod*)

upa-√ci (5, *upacinoti*) *to heap up, collect, accumulate* 145c (upacinuta; tib. *tshogs skyed śog*)

upacita- ppp. of upa-√ci *heaped up, increased* 53d (atyupacitā; tib. *spor*)

upatapta- ppp. of upa-√tap *heated, hot; distressed, afflicted* 8b (tib. *rab gtses na*); 60d (kṣudupataptaḥ; tib. *ltogs*)

upa-√diś (6, *upadiśati*) *to point out, indicate, explain; exhibit* 30c (upadiśati; tib. *ston par byed*); 75b (upadeśayanti; tib. *ston pa*)

upa-√yā (2, *upayāti*) *to arrive at, reach, obtain; get into any state or condition* 26d (upayāti; tib. *snaṅ*)

upayoga- m. *employment, use, application* 100c (tib. *sbyor ba*)

uparata- ppp. of upa-√ram *ceased, stopped, indifferent* 105c (tib. *spaṅs pa*)

upari adv. *above, upon, on* 42d (tib. *steṅ na*)

upala- m. *rock, stone* 26c (tib. *sbram*)

upaśama- m. *tranquility of mind, calmness, patience* 108c (tib. *źi ba*)

upahata- ppp. of upa-√han *hit, hurt, damaged, afflicted, pained* 6c (tib. *gnod*); 117b (daivopahatāḥ skhalanti kartavya; tib. *ñams su len par mi byed na* renders another text)

upahati- f. *hurt, damage, injure* 131c (°opahatiṣv; tib. *gnod na*)

upa-√han (2, *upahanti*) *to beat, hit, do harm* 88b (upahanti; tib. *gnod*)

upāya- m. *means, expedient* 87d, 116a (tib. *thabs*)

upa-√i (2, *upaiti*) *to come near to, reach obtain, enter into any state* 26b (param upaiti mahimānam; tib. *śin tu skyed kyaṅ 'byuṅ*); 101c (prāmāṇyam upaiti; tib. *ran par 'jal ba'i*); 126d (āpadam upaiti; tib. *gnod 'gyur*)

upta- ppp. of √vap *scattered, sown, planted* 54a (tib. *btab*)

ubhaya- adj. *both, of both kinds* 137c (tib. *gñis*)

ulkā- f. *meteor* 125c (tib. *sgron ma*)

Ū

ūṣara- nt. *saline soil, barren ground* 54b (tib. *tsha sgo*)

Ṛ

ṛju- adj. *straight; upright, honest* 28c (tib. *draṅ ba*); 45c (tib. *draṅ*)

ṛjutā- f. *straightness; sincerity, honesty* 28a (tib. *draṅ ba*)

ṛte adv. *with the exclusion of, excepting, without* 24b (tib. *spaṅs*); 100b (tib. *med*)

E

eka- num./adj. *one; single, sole, only* 57a (tib. *gcig*); 70b (tib. *gcig pu*); 106b (ekapade; tib. *thaṅ cig*); 118c (ekarasa°; tib. *ro gcig*)

ekānta- m. *exclusiveness, absoluteness, necessity* 31b (tib. *ṅes*)

etad- pron. *this (here)* 31a, 141c (eṣa; tib. *n. e.*); 99c (etāv; tib. *n. e.*); 139b (eṣā; tib. *de*); 144a (etad; tib. *'di la*)

√edh (1, *edhate*) *to prosper, increase; thrive, become happy* 76d (naidhante; freely tib. *mi gtoṅ ṅo?*)

eva ind. *just, only* 2b, 11d, 44d, 82d, 83d, 98b, 105a, 105b, 120d (tib. *ñid*); 3c, 8a, 11a, 15b, 18a, 28a, 28b, 30d, 33a, 35a, 37d, 41d, 42a, 42c, 43c, 56c, 62a, 74b, 74c, 81d, 83a, 83b, 85a, 89a, 104b, 107c, 111b, 119a, 124a, 126d, 127a, 127d, 137a, 141a (tib. *n. e.*); 10b, 84d (tib. *gyi*); 10d (tib. *bźin* perhaps for misread skt. *iva*?); 21d, 71c?(tib. *kyaṅ*); 22d (tib. *ṅes par*); 32d (in tib. expressed by means of a rhetoric question *cis mi 'gyur*); 33c (tib. *kho nas*); 35c, 66a, 66c, 67b (tib. *yaṅ*); 40b (tib. *de lta*); 48a (tib. *'aṅ*); 63a, 65d, 123c (tib. *ni*); 86a, 98d (tib. *kyi*); 111d (in Tibetan double negative expressing emphasis)

AU

auṣadha- nt. *medicine* 62c (tib. *sman*)

K

kajjala- nt. *lampblack* 31c (freely tib. *dud pa*)

kaṭhina- adj. *hard, firm; inflexible* 87c (tib. *sra*)

√kath (10, *kathayati*) *to tell* 118d (kathayanti; tib. *smra ba yin*)

katham interr. adv. *how?, in what manner?* 69b (tib. *ci*)

katham api indef. pron. *somehow, by some means or other* 34c (tib. *n. e.*)

kathā- f. *condersation, talk* 88c (kaiva kathā; tib. *smos ci dgos*)

kamala- m./nt. *lotus, lotus-flower* 92c, 92d (tib. *padma*)

kamalinī- f. *the lotus plant* 61c (tib. *pad ma*)

kara- m. *hand; ray of light* 13c, 117d (tib. *lag pa*); 85d (tib. *zer*)

karṇikāra- nt. *the Karṇikāra tree (Pterospermum acerifolium)* 77c (literally tib. *rna rgyan*)

kartavya- nt. *that which ought to be done, duty, task* 117b (daivopahatāḥ skhalanti kartavya; tib. *ñams su len par mi byed na* renders another text)

karmaṇya- adj. *fit for any work; manageable* 111c (tib. *ma byas par ... mi 'gyur ro* for skt. *bhavati ... karmaṇyam*)

karman- nt. *action, deed; consequences of one's deeds* 72b (tib. *las*)

karmin- m. *doer, performer of an action* 71b (contextually tib. *'bad rtsol*)

kalaṅka- m. *stain, spot; defamation* 47d, 49d, 51d (tib. *ra ri*)

kalā- f. *small part; digit of one sixteenth of the moon's diameter* 94c (tib. *śas tsam*)

kali- m. *name of the last and worst of the four ages, the Kali age* 12c (tib. *dus na* translates skt. **kāle* i. o. *kalau*!); 103c (tib. *ṅan la* wrongly as if skt. **khale*); 121d (kalau; tib. *groṅ na* renders as if it were **kule*!)

kalpa- m. *great period of time, aeon* 106a (tib. *bskal*)

kalpana- nt. *forming, making, performing* 15b (tib. *dpyad*)

kalyāṇa- nt. *good fortune, happiness, prosperity* 122b (tib. *legs pa*)

kāṃsya- nt. *white-copper, bell-metal, brass* 123c (tib. *mkhar ba*)

kākatāliya- nt. *coincidence (as in the fable of the crow and the palm-fruit)* 34b (tib. *bya rog ta lar*)

kāma- m. *wish, desire* 104a (°kāmair; tib. *'dod pas*)

kāmam adv. *well, indeed, surely* 67c (literally tib. *'dod*)

kāminī- f. *young woman* 30c (tib. *'dod ldan*)

kārya- nt. *work to be done, duty, affair* 27b, 45b (tib. *don*); 123a (kāryagati-; tib. *sgrub pa*); 135a (tib. *bya ba*)

kāvya- nt. *poetry* 144b (tib. *n. e.*)

kāśa- m. *the Kāśa grass (Saccharum spontaneum)* 89d (tib. *ka śa*)

kāṣāya- nt. *brown-red cloth; ochre robe* 110c (tib. *ṅur smrig gos*)

kāṣṭha- nt. *wood, timber* 34d, 42c (tib. *śiṅ*)

kim- interr. pron. *who?, what?* 4d (ko; tib. *su yis*); 25d (kaṃ; tib. *cis*); 31d, 60d (kiṃ; tib. *cis*); 40c, 135d (ko; tib. *su źig*); 60b (kiṃ nāma; tib. *cis*); 61c (kim; contextually tib. *ma byas par*); 68d[1] (kaṃ; tib. *n. e.*); 68d[2] (kaḥ; tib. *su źig gis*); 88c (kaiva kathā; tib. *smos ci dgos*); 89c (ko; tib. *n. e.*); 99b (kiṃ with instrumental case; tib. *ci źig bya*); 115d (kā gurutā; rendered twice in tib. *ma brtsis* and *ci źig 'gyur*); 122c (kena; tib. *sus*); 128d (na ... kim; tib. *cis mi nus*); 139c (tib. *ci ga*)

kim api indef. pron. *whosoever, whatsoever* 1d (ke 'pi; tib. *gaṅ źig*)

kiṃ cit indef. pron. *whosoever, whatsoever* 27a, 27b (kaś cit; tib. *kha cig*); 70a (kaś cit; tib. *'ga' źig*); 97d (ke cid; tib. *'ga' gas*); 109d (kasya cid; tib. *ga la*); 144a (kaś cid; tib. *ci nas*)?

kiṃ tu conj. *but, however, nevertheless* 7c (tib. *'on kyaṅ*)

kiṃ punar *how much more? how much less?* 88b (kiṃ punar; tib. *ci smos*)

kila ptcl. *indeed, verily, as it is known* 72c (tib. *źes grags*)

kuṇapa- nt. *dead body, corpse* 21d (tib. *ro*)

kutas interr. pron. *whence? how?, in what manner?* 78d (tib. *gaṅ la*)

kupita- ppp. of √kup *excited, agitated, angry* 87a (atikupitā; tib. *rab khros*)

kuruvinda- m. *ruby* 3c (tib. *kur byin da*)

kulagiri- m. *chief mountain-range* 80b (tib. *ku la'i ri*)

kulaja- m. *one born in a noble family* 81a (tib. *cho rigs*)

kulīna- m. *man of noble family, noble person* 10b (tib. *stod rigs*) adj. *belonging to a noble family* 25b (tib. *rigs ldan*)

kulocchrita- adj. *of noble family, of high rank* 17b (tib. *rigs ldan*)

kuśala- adj. *skilful, clever* 140b (tib. *n. e.*); m. *skilful person* 26d (tib. *bzo bo mkhas pa*)

kuṣṭha- nt. *leprosy* 62c (tib. *mdze*)

kusuma- nt. *flower, blossom* 77d (tib. *me tog*)

√kusumay (10, denom., *kusumayati*) *to make blossom, furnish with flowers* 11d (kusumayati; tib. *kha ... 'bu*)

kūpa- m. *well, spring* 43d, 122d (tib. *khron pa*)

√kṛ (8, *karoti*) *to do, make* 9c (chidraṃ karoti; tib. *phug pa yi bu ga*); 27a (na karoti; contextually tib. *lhur len te*); 69b (na karoti; tib. *mi byed*); 98b (anugrahaṃ kartum; tib. *phan par byed*); 123d (kriyate; tib. *byas pa yi*), 125d (kurute; contextually tib. *rgyu*); 136b (kurvann; tib. *bya ba*)

kṛcchra- m./nt. *difficulty, trouble, hardship* 65a (kṛcchragatā; tib. *rab tu ñam thag*); 68b, 95b (tib. *ñam thag*)

kṛtaghna- adj. *ungrateful* 76c, 141c (tib. *khrel med*)

kṛtajaya- m. *one who is successful* 117a (tib. *byaṅ byas)*

kṛtapraṇaya- m. *one who places confidence in s. o. else* 109a (tib. *'dris byas)*

kṛtānta- m. *name of the God of Death, Yama* 138d (tib. *gśin rje)*

kṛtya- fpp. of √kṛ *right, proper to be done* 6b (tib. *rigs)*

kṛpaṇa- m. *poor man; miser* 72b (tib. *'juṅs pa*); 84b (tib. *'juṅs)*

kṛpā- f. *pity, tenderness, compassion* 85a (tib. *sñiṅ rje*); 95b (tib. *dpon byed* translates as if **kriyā* interpreted as 'the activity of a ruler, leader')

kṛmi- m. *worm, insect* 76b (tib. *'bu*); 92c (tib. *srin bu)*

√kḷp (1, *kalpate*) *to prepare, arrange; produce, cause, effect, create* 14b (hitāya kalpate; tib. *phan btags*);; (caus. *kalpayati*) *to make, arrange, bring about* 44b (kalpayanti; tib. *bskyed*); 102b (na ... kalpante; tib. *mi byed do)*

kevalam adv. *only, merely, solely* 14c (tib. *thog mar)*

keśa- m. *hair* 15d (tib. *skra)*

kauṭilya- nt. *crookedness; falsehood, dishonesty* 28b (tib. *gya gyu)*

kauśala- nt. *welfare; sklifulness, cleverness, experience* 6b (tib. *'phan mkhas)*

krameṇa adv. *gradually, little by little* 106d (tib. *rim*); 127b (tib. *rim gyis)*

kraśīyas- (compar. of *kṛśa-*) *extremely lean* 139a (contextually tib. *bkren pa)*

kriyā- f. *doing, action, work* 113c (tib. *bya ba)*

krīḍā- f. *play* 109d (tib. *rtse ba)*

klība- m. *eunuch; coward, weak-minded person* 87b (tib. *dmu rgod)*

kva interr. pron. *where?* 25a[1] (tib. *gaṅ źig*); 25a[2], 25b (twice) (tib. *gaṅ)*

kva cana indef. adv. *somewhere* 103c (tib. *nam yaṅ ... med* wrongly interprets **kva ca nāpi)*

kva cit indef. adv. *somewhere* 70a (tib. *'ga'*); 123b (tib. *la la⟨r⟩*); 133b (strangely tib. *su yi ṅor)*

kṣaṇika- adj. *momentary, transient* 53a (tib. *gñug thuṅ)*

kṣaṇena adv. *in a moment, in an instant* 106d (tib. *skad cig)*

kṣata- ppp. of √kṣaṇ *wounded, destroyed* 145b (tib. *bsregs pas)*

√kṣam (1, *kṣamate*) *to be patient, bear, endure* 13d (na kṣamate; tib. *'dzem par byed*); 97b (kṣantuṃ; freely tib. *dad chen?)*

kṣama- adj. *adequate, fit, appropriate, proper* 81b (na kṣamaḥ; tib. *mi bya*); 132b (na ... kṣamo; tib. *mi dbab)*

kṣaya- m. *loss, waste; wane, diminution; wearing away; waining (of the moon)* 19b (tib. *bri*); 47c (tib. *'grib pa)*

kṣāra- adj. *caustic, saline* 138c (tib. *bul tog)*

√kṣi (5, *kṣiṇoti;* caus. *kṣapayati*) *to destroy, ruin, make disappear* 36c (kṣapayitum; tib. *skems par)*

kṣīṇa- adj. *diminished, wasted, worn away, exhausted* 71d (tib. *zad)*

kṣīra- nt. *milk, thickened milk* 4c (tib. *'o ma*)

kṣīrī- f. *Kṣīrī plant* 27d (tib. *star ka*)

kṣudh- f. *hunger* 60d (kṣudupataptaḥ; tib. *ltogs*)

kṣura- m. *razor, knife* 113b (tib. *spu gri*)

kṣepa- m. *throw, cast; insult, invective, abuse* 71b (tib. *'phaṅs*)

kṣema- m./nt. *safety, peace; happiness, well-being* 109c (tib. *bde legs*)

KH

kha- nt. *cavern; vacuity, empty space, sky* 59c (tib. *mkha'*)

khaga- m. *bird* 125d (tib. *mkha' la rgyu ba*)

khaṇḍana- nt. *breaking, dividing, reducing to pieces* 67d (tib. *'bri bar*)

khaḍga- m. *sword* 50c (tib. *sta re*); 116d, 129c (tib. *ral gri*)

khala- adj. *mischievous* 102a (tib. *mi srun*); 138d (tib. *n. e.*); m. *mischievous man* 5b, 6b, 20c, 21b, 54b, 59b, 81b, 93a (tib. *mi srun*); 7d (tib. *smad rigs*); 9b, 10b, 17a (tib. *ṅan pa*); 15d, 62a (tib. *mi srun pa*)

khalajana- m. *mischievous person* 11a (tib. *skye bo ṅan pa*); 23a (tib. *phal pa*); 25a (tib. *mi srun*)

kheda- m. *lassitude, depression; pain, affliction, distress* 131a (skt. *na yānti khedaṃ*; tib. yid gduṅs ... min)

G

gaṇikā- f. *courtezan* 102d (tib. *smad 'tshoṅ ma*)

gata- ppp. of √gam *gone, departed, past, disappeared* 20d (tib. *'das pa*); 65a (kṛcchragatā; tib. *rab tu ñam thag*); 85d (tib. *gnas nas*); 119d (tib. *phyin*)

gati- f. *going; manner of doing, procedure* 123a (kāryagati-; tib. *sgrub pa*)

gantṛ- m. *one who is walking* 114d (tib. *źugs pa*)

gandha- m. *smell, odour* 48c (tib. *dri źim*)

√gam (1, *gacchati*) *to go* 37a (paryantaṃ ... gacchati; tib. *mthar phyin pa*); 71b (gatvā; tib. *'phur*)

gamita- ppp. of √gam *caused to go, sent, brought* 14b (tib. *n. e.*)

gamya- adj. *approachable, attainable; vulnerable* 139b (tib. *phod*)?

√gar (10, *garayati* only here!) *to make heavy* 89c (garayati; tib. *lci*)?

garva- m. *pride* 138b (tib. *kheṅs*)

guṇa- m. *quality; degree; virtue* 1a*, 2a, 28a, 33a, 38b, 44a, 57b, 77b, 89a, 90b, 121b, 122b, 124b, 134b (tib. *yon tan*); 21a, 57d?(tib. *n. e.*); 78a (tib. *raṅ bźin*); 93b, 103d (tib. *yon tan ldan pa'i*); 97c (tib. *yon tan can*); *thread, string* 24c (tib. *rgyud*)

guṇajña- m. *one who knows virtues, one who appreciates virtues* 121b (tib. *mkhas pas śes*)

guṇavat- adj. *virtuous* 81a (tib. *yon tan ldan*); 92a (tib. *yon tan ldan pa*); m. *one who is endowed with (good) qualities, virtuous man* 18a, 19c, 69a (tib. *yon tan ldan pa*); 35b (tib. *skye bo yon tan ldan pa*); 42a (tib. *yon tan can*); 77a (tib. *yon tan ldan*)

guṇin- m. *virtuous person* 89a (tib. *dam pa*); 115b (tib. *yon tan*); 121b[1] (freely tib. *mkhas pa*)

guru- m. *venerable person* 112d (tib. **bkur*)

gurutā- f. *weight, heaviness* 115d (kā gurutā; rendered twice in tib. *ma brtsis* and *ci źig 'gyur*)

gṛdhra- m. *vulture* 2c (tib. *bya rgod*)

√gras (1, *grasati, -te*) *to swallow, devour; consume* 5c (grasate; tib. *snaṅ ba min*)

√grah (9, *gṛhṇāti*) *to take, seize* 40d (jighṛkṣati; tib. *dzin*)

grīṣma- m. *the hot season, summer* 29c (tib. *so ga*)

GH

ghaṭṭana- nt. *pushing, touching, rubbing, striking together* 6a (tib. *gcod*)

ghana- adj. *compact, dense, thick* 107c (tib. *stug po*)

ghasmara adj. *voracious, desirious of, eager for* 145d (tib. *za phod*)

ghāta- m. *strike, blow* 116c (tib. *gzas pa*)

ghuṇa- m. *woodworm* 34d (tib. *sriṅ bu*); 76b (tib. *srin*)

C

ca conj. *and* 1b, 137c (tib. *śiṅ*); 19c (tib. *kyaṅ*); 20c, 25b, 90c, 97c, 101d[1], 118b, 121b, 136d (tib. *n. e.*); 28b (tib. *ste*); 66b, 66d, 76c, 112b, 116b (tib. *daṅ*); 95c, 98c (tib. *kyaṅ*); 101d[2] (tib. *'aṅ*)

√cakās (2, *cakāsti*) *to shine, be bright* 17c (cakāsati; tib. *gzi mi 'byin*)

cakra- nt. *wheel; fraudulent device* (here: *spider's web*) 59c (tib. *rgya*)

cakravāla- m. *the Cakravāla range of mountains* 120c (tib. *'khor yug*)

cakṣus- nt. *eye* 114c (tib. *mig ldan*)

candana- m./nt. *sandal (wood)* 21c, 81c (tib. *tsan dan*)

candra- m. *moon* 67b (tib. *zla*)

capala- adj. *moving to and fro, unsteady, wavering* 78a (aticapalam; tib. *lhag par g.yo*); m. *ill-mannered person* 107a (tib. *g.yon can*); 128a (tib. *mi brtan pa*)

caraṇa- nt. *foot* 102d (tib. *rdog pa*)

carita- nt. *acting, doing; behaviour, acts, deeds* 8a (tib. *spyod*); 30b (is tib. *skyes bu* only a later corruption of original *spyod pa* as in NQ?)

√cal (1, *calati*) *to move on, proceed; go astray, move away, sway* 52d (na ... calati; tib. *'gyur ba med*); 120d (calaty; tib. *g.yo bar byed*)

cātaka- f. *the cātaka bird* 65d (tib. *khu⟨g⟩ rta*)

cāru- adj. *agreeable, pleasing, lovely* 77c (aticāru; tib. *rab mdzes*)

citta- nt. *thinking, reflecting; mind* 56a (tib. *sems*)

cira- adj. *long, lasting a long time* 44a, 84c (tib. *yun riṅ*)

ciram adv. *for a long time* 127c (tib. *yun riṅ*)

cihna- nt. *mark, sign, characteristic* 95d (tib. *rtags*)

cetas- nt. *consciousness, mind* 108a (tib. *sems*)

ceṣṭā- f. *action, activity, effort* 130b (tib. *spyod pa*)

CH

√chid (7, *chinatti*) *to cut, chop, split* 50d (chettum; tib. *gcod*); 116c (chinatti; tib. *chad par 'gyur*)

chidra- nt. *hole, slit, cleft, opening* 9c (tib. *bu ga*)

J

jagat- nt. *the world, the people of this world* 5a, 127d (tib. *'gro*); 15a, 50b, 105a, 145a (tib. *'gro ba*)

jaḍa- m. *fool, idiot* 30a, 40b, 64a, 83a (tib. *blun po*); 107a (tib. *blun*); 137a (tib. *'gro maṅ* renders **janāḥ*)

jaḍatā- f. *stupidity* 25c (tib. *raṅ bźin blun po*)

√jan (4, *jāyate*) *to be born, arise* 90d, 103d (jāyante; tib. *'byuṅ ba*); (caus. *janayati*) *to generate, beget, produce, create* 15a (janayati; tib. *'byuṅ 'gyur*); 31d (na janayanti; tib. *mi 'byuṅ*); 125a (janayati; tib. *skye*)

jana- m. *being; people* 3b, 8a, 51b, 107a (tib. *skye bo*); 75c (tib. *skyes pa*); 96d (tib. *n. e.*)

jantu- m. *creature, living being* 28b, 38c (tib. *skye bo*); 68b (tib. *raṅ ñid*); 85a, 90a (tib. *'gro ba*); 109c (tib. *mi*)

jarā- f. *old age* 63d (tib. **rga ba*)

jala- nt. *water* 43d, 135c (tib. *chu*); 98d (tib. *char*)

jalatā- f. *the state of water* 138c (tib. *chu*)

jaladhi- m. *ocean* 42c (tib. *chu bo*); 138c (tib. *rgya mtsho*)

jāḍya-	nt. *ignorance, stupidity* 115a (tib. *blun*)
jāti-	f. *birth, production; rank, caste, lineage; kind, genus, species* 3d (tib. *rigs*); 134b (tib. *ṅaṅ*)
jātu	→ na jātu
jighāṃsu-	adj. *desirous of killing* 71a (incorrectly tib. *'gro 'dod pa'i*)
jīvitā-	f. *state of life, duration of life* 84c (tib. *'tsho ba*)
√jñā	(9, *jānāti*) *to know; understand* 4d, 11b (jānāti; tib. *śes*); 94b (jānanti; tib. *n. e.*)
jyotsnā-	f. *moonlight* 16c (tib. *zla zer*)
jvāla-	m. (jvālā f.) *flame* 20b (tib. *me lce*)

Ḍ

ḍākiṇī-	f. *female imp feeding on flesh* 104c (tib. *mkha' 'gro ma*)

T

tattva-	nt. *true state, truth, fact* 46b (tib. *de la* perhaps free for skt. *tattveṣu* or did the translators read **tat teṣu*?); 99b (tib. *don ñid*)
tathā	adv. *thus, in that way* 9b (tib. *de bźin*); 48c, 49b, 131a (tib. *de lta*); 49d (tib. *n. e.*); 126a, 129d (tib. *de ltar*)
tathāpi	conj. *even thus, nevertheless* 112c (tib. *de bźin* renders **tathaiva*)
tad-	pron. *he, she, it; that* 1d (tebhyaḥ; tib. *de la*); 6b, 6d, 34b (tat; tib. *de*); 34b (tasya; tib. *n. e.*); 56a (tal; tib. *n. e.*); 61d (tāṃ; tib. *n. e.*); 63d (teṣv; tib. *de la*); 69b (sa; tib. *n. e.*); 69c (so; tib. *de*); 83b (tena; tib. *n. e.*); 83d (tad eva; tib. *de ñid*); 90b, 90c (te; tib. *n. e.*); 98b (sa eva; tib. *de ñid*); 99b (tena; tib. *des*); 103b[1] (tat; tib. *de ni*); 103b[2], 127b (tasmāt; tib. *de las*); 141c (taṃ; tib. *de la*)
tadanu	adv. *after that, afterwards* 9d (tib. *n. e.*)
tanu-	adj. *thin, little, minute* 49b (tib. *phra*); f. *body* 28d (tib. *lus*)
tantu-	m. *thread, cord, string* 9d (tib. *skud pa*); 91a (tib. *rgyu spun*)
√tap	(1, *tapati;* caus. *tāpayati*) *to cause pain, trouble, torment* 25d (na tāpayati; tib. *mi gduṅ*); 53c (tāpayati; tib. *gcod byed*); 129a (tāpayati; tib. *gduṅ byed pa*)
tamas-	nt. *darkness* 5c, 16d, 33c, 33d, 38d, 79c (tib. *mun pa*)
taru-	m. *tree* 62d, 136c (tib. *śiṅ*)
tāpita-	ppp. of caus. from √tap *heated; pained, tormented, distressed* 8d (tib. *rab gduṅs na*)

tāra- m. *star* 107c (tib. *skar ma*)

tāvat adv. *to that extent, that long* 68a (tib. *de srid*)

√tij (1, *tejate*; caus. *tejayati*) *to make sharp, sharpen* 50c (tejayati, tib. *bdar bar byed*); 129c (tejayati ... na; contextually tib. *mi byed*)

tittiri- m. *partridge* 126d (tib. *sreg pa*)

timira- nt. *darkness* 107c (tib. *rab rib*)

tīkṣṇa- adj. *sharp; hot; pungent; harsh* 12a ('titīkṣṇāḥ; tib. *lhag par gdug pa*); 29a (atitīkṣṇo; tib. *śin tu gtum*); 67c (tib. *btsan po*); 129b (tib. *rnon po*)

tu advers. ptcl. 13b, 13d (tib. *ni*); 15c (tib. *gyi*); 23c, 27d, 29b, 54b, 74b, 96c, 121c, 124c (tib. *n. e.*); 55b, 55d (tib. *kyi*); 67d (tib. *yaṅ*)?

√tul (10, *tulayati*) *to weigh, measure* 73b (tulayanti; tib. *phyed*); 135a (tulayati; tib. **dpyod pas*)

tulā- m. *weight; measure; scale* 73c (tib. *tshod*); 101c (tib. *sraṅ mda'*)

tuṣa- m. *chaff* 29b (tib. *phub*)

tūla- nt. *tuft of grass* 89d (tib. *śiṅ bal*)

tṛṇa- nt. *grass* 29b, 121d (tib. *rtswa*); 33b (tib. *phub*); 42c (tib. *rtswa*); 87d (tib. *rtsa*)

tṛpta- ppp. of √tṛp *satiated* 135b (tib. *n. e.*)

tṛpti- f. *satisfaction, contentment* 5b (na tṛptim āyātaḥ; tib. *ṅoms pa med*)

tṛṣita- ppp. of √tṛṣ *thirsty, thirsting* 44c (atitṛṣitā; tib. *śin tu skom pas*)

tṛṣṇā- f. *thirst* 135b (tṛṣṇārtaḥ; tib. *chog pa* renders as if **tṛṣṇāḍhyaḥ*)

√tṝ (1, *tarati*) *to cross over, get through* 83b (tarati; tib. *rgal*)

tejas- nt. *glow; splendour; energy, power* 111b (tib. *sbuṅs*?)

tejasvin- adj. *brilliant, powerful, energetic* 85b (tib. *gzi ldan pa*)

taila- nt. *sesamum oil* 54c, 86c (tib. *til mar*)

√tyaj (1, *tyajati*) *to leave, abandon, quit* 80b (tyaktvā; tib. *spaṅs nas*)

tribhuvana- nt. *the three worlds* 145d (tib. *srid gsum*)

D

daridra- adj. *poor, needy; deprived of* 50b (tib. *phoṅs pa*); 77b (guṇadaridrāḥ; tib. *yon tan med*)

daśadiś- f. *the ten directions* 18a (tib. *phyogs bcu*)

√dah (1, *dahati*) *to burn, consume by fire, scorch* 61d (dahati; tib. *skems par byed*); 81d (dahaty; tib. *sreg par byed*); 106d (dahati; tib. *sreg byed*); 127d (dahanti; tib. *sreg byed*)

dahana- nt. *fire; something that burns* 137c (tib. *me*)

√dā (3, *dadāti*) *to give, bestow, impart* 59b (dattvā; tib. *btags*); 97b (dātum; tib. *ster*); 98c (dadāti; tib. *'bebs par byed*); 141b (dadāti na; tib. *sbyin par mi byed pa'i*)

dāna- nt. *act of giving; donation, gift* 141a (tib. *sbyin pa*)

dāruṇa- adj. *harsh, hard; sharp, severe, cruel* 12b (tib. *rstub pa*); 32a (tib. not transmitted)

dāha- m. *burning; heat; fire* 96b (dāhavibandhadhram; tib. *za 'jil?*); 137d (udbhavati dāhaḥ; tib. *sreg par 'gyur*)

dāhya- nt. *something that can be burnt* 137c (tib. *bud śiṅ*)

ditsā- f. *desire of giving* 95c (tib. *sbyin gtoṅ sems*)

dinakara- m. *sun* 8d (tib. *ñi ma*); 91c (tib. *ñi ma'i 'od*)

divya- adj. *divine, heavenly, celestial* 64c (tib. *mkha' las*)

√dīp (4, *dīpyate*) *to blaze, shine* 86b (bhṛśaṃ dīpyate; contextually tib. *rṅan can byed*)

dīpa- m. *lamp, lantern* 31d (tib. *mar me*); 93d, 132d (tib. *sgron ma*); 117d (tib. *sgron*)

duḥkha- nt. *uneasiness, pain, trouble* 67a (tib. *sdug bsṅal*); 74a (tib. *dka' ba*)

duḥsādhya- adj. *difficult to be conquered, hard to be defeated* 36b (tib. *gdul bar dka'*)

durātman- m. *evil-hearted being* 60b (tib. *raṅ bźin ṅan pa*); 125b (tib. *bdag ñid ṅan pa*)

durābdha- adj. *difficult to be undertaken; difficult to be caught* 140b (tib. *bsruṅ bar dka'*)

durupacāra- adj. *difficult to attend* 53b (tib. *mgu dka'*)

durga- nt. *place difficult to pass; difficulty* 83b (tib. *bgrod dka'*)

durgandhi- adj. *ill-smelling, stinking* 60c (tib. *dri mi źim pa*)

durgraha- adj. *difficult to grasp* 78b (tib. *gzuṅ dka'*)

durjana- m. *bad man, villain, scoundrel* 58b, 106b (tib. *ṅan pa*); 89b, 110a (tib. *skye bo ṅan pa*); 121c (tib. *skyon can*)

durlabha- adj. *difficult to be obtained, scarce* 90b (tib. *dkon*)

durvilāsa- nt. *bad joke, naughty trick* 138d (tib. *rtsed mo phyin ci log*)

duṣprāpa- adj. *hard to obtain* 121a (freely tib. *'gas rñed*)

duścheda- adj. *difficult to separate* 91b (tib. *gźig par dka'*)?

dūram adv. *far, far from* 14d (tib. *gyen du*)

dūre adv. *far, far away, at a distance* 51a (tib. *thag riṅ*)

dṛḍha- adj. *fixed, firm, strong* 71a (tib. *rdzogs*)

dṛḍham adv. *firmly, strongly; severely* 116c (tib. *dam por*)

√dṛś (1, *paśyati*) *to see* 10a (dṛṣtvā; tib. *mthoṅ*); 46c (paśyati; tib. *mthoṅ*); 49a (dṛśyante; tib. *bsal* misspelled for **gsal*); 51c (na paśyati; tib. *mi mthoṅ*); 73a (dṛṣṭvā; tib. *mthoṅ na*); 80d (paśyata; tib. *ltos*); 99a (na paśyati; tib. *mi mthoṅ*); 103a (paśyed; tib. *mthoṅ na*); 117c (paśyati na; tib. *mi mthoṅ*), 130d (paśyati; tib. *mthoṅ na*)

√dṝ (9, *dṛṇāti*; caus. *dārayati*) *to split, to tear asunder, divide by splitting* 37c (dārayati; tib. *'joms byed*); 139d (na dārayati; tib. *mi 'bigs sam*)

deśa- m. *region, place, country* 90c (tib. *yul ljoṅs*)

dainya- nt. *timidity* 101a (tib. *bag 'khums*)

daiva- nt. *divine power, destiny* 117b (daivopahatāḥ skhalanti kartavya; tib. *ñams su len par mi byed na* renders another text)

daivāt adv. *by chance, accidentaly* 34c (tib. *stes dbaṅ*)

doṣa- m. *fault; moral fault* 1b*, 2a, 4a*, 7b, 28b, 33b, 38b, 49b, 57b, 59a, 78b, 80b, 89b (tib. *skyon*); 121c (tib. *n. e.*); 145a (tib. *ñes pa*)

dyāvāpṛthivī- f. du. *heaven and earth* 24d (tib. *sa daṅ nam mkha'*)

dyuti- f. *splendour, brightness, lustre* 3d (is tib. *spa ba* a corruption of *spra ba* as a free rendering of skt. *dyutiṃ labhate*?)

dravaṇa- nt. *melting* 87d (tib. *gźu ba*)

drākṣā- f. *vine, grape* 72d (tib. *rgun*)

√druh (4, *druhyati*) *to hurt, seek to harm, be hostile* 55d (druhyati; tib. *gsod*)

dva num. *two* 99c, 105a, 105b (tib. *gñis*)

dveṣa- m. *hatred* 118b (tib. *sdaṅ*)

DH

dhana- nt. *wealth, riches, property* 84b, 140a (tib. *nor*); 112a (tib. *n. e.*)

dhanavat- m. *wealthy person* 112b (tib. *n. e.*); 112c (tib. *phyug*)

dhanin- m. *rich man, wealthy person* 77b, 112b (tib. *phyug po*); 138b (tib. *phyug*)

dharaṇī- f. *earth* 120d, 131d (tib. *sa*)

dharma- m. *rightfulness* 112b (tib. *chos*)

dhātṛ- m. *creator* 25d (tib. *byed pa*)

dhārā- f. *sharp edge, blade* 50c (tib. *rnon po*)

dhīmat- m. *intelligent person, wise man* 43b (tib. *blo daṅ ldan pa*)

dhur- f. *yoke; front, place of honour* 42b (dhuraṃ puraḥ prakarṣanti; contextually tib. *brñas thabs sna tshogs byed*)

dhūrta- m. *rogue, cheat, deceiver* 63a (tib. *ṅan g.yo can*); 75b (tib. *g.yon can*)

dhūli- f. *dust* 82c (tib. *sa rdul*)

dhṛta- ppp. of √dhṛ *held, supported, possessed, worn* 22d (tib. *thogs*)

N

na neg. ptcl. *not* 5b, 18c, 20d, 21b, 52d, 67d, 72a, 84d, 104d, 136b, 140d (tib. *med*); 6b (tib. *ma yin*); 6d, 14b, 17c, 25d, 28a, 31a, 31d, 36c, 37b, 37d, 38a, 45b, 45d, 47b, 51c, 57d, 58d, 60d, 65a, 65c, 69b, 69d, 76d, 81b, 93d, 94b, 99a, 102b, 107d, 114d, 118d, 122b, 124d, 128d, 129d, 132b, 134b, 134c, 139b, 139d, 141c (tib. *mi*); 10b, 29b, 33b, 43b, 48b, 48c, 49d, 51b, 54b, 54d, 56d, 70b, 75d, 86b, 87b, 98d, 123d, 131b, 137b (tib. *min*); 13d (na kṣamate; tib. *'dzem par byed*); 15c, 42d, 68b, 87d, 108c, 110b, 115b, 118b^{2}, 126a (tib. *ma*); 27a, 109c, 136d^{1}, 136d^{2}, 145c (tib. *n. e.*); 28b (tib. *min no*); 31b (tib. *med de*); 77a (na ati°; contextually tib. *dkon pa*); 93b (na yānti; tib. *min*); 100d (tib. *med do*); 112d (tib. *min pas*); 115a (tib. *'on te* freely or for misread skt. **sa°*); 118b^{1} (na bhūtaye; tib. *mi bya'o* as if it was read skt. *mā bhūt*); 133b (na kva cid; strangely tib. *su yi ṅor*)

na jātu *not at all, by no means, never* 19d (tib. *nam du'aṅ ... mi*); 22b (jātu na; tib. *mi srid*); 33d (naiva jātu; tib. *min*); 62b, 123b (tib. *min*); 107b (jātu na; tib. *min*); 135b (tib. *nam yaṅ ... med*)

nakha- m./nt. *finger-, toenail* 15d (tib. *sen*)

nanu interr. ptcl. *not? is it not?; certainly, surely* 22d, 81c (tib. *n. e.*)

nabhas- nt. *sky* 119d (tib. *nam mkha'*)

namas- nt. *bow, obeisance, salutation, homage* 1d (tib. *phyag 'tshal lo*)

namra adj. *submissive; humble* 101a (tib. *dma'*)

nayana- nt. *eye* 13d, 38c (tib. *mig*); 115d (proṣitanayana-; tib. *loṅ ba*)

nara- m. *man, male, person* 76c (tib. *mi dag*); 91b (tib. *skye bo*)

√naś (4, *naśyati*) *to perish, disappear* 109a (naśyanti; tib. *'phuṅ 'gyur*)

nāma ind. *indeed* (enforcing the preceding word) 60b (kiṃ nāma; tib. *cis*)

nigraha- m. *confinement; punishment* 98a (tib. *chad pas gcod*)

ni-√han (2, *nihanti*) *to strike down, assail; kill, destroy* 88b (nighnan; tib. *khros*)

√nind (1, *nindati*) *to blame, censure, despise* 11a (ninditum; tib. *smad par*)

nindā- f. *blame, censure, reproach* 39a (tib. *smad*)

ni-√pat (1, *nipatati*) *to fly down, rush upon, fall upon, attack* 2c (nipatanti; tib. *'bab*); 16c (nipatati; tib. *'bab par byed*); 37c (nipatati; tib. *babs*); 55a (nipatanti; tib. *'joms*); 64c (nipatad; tib. *'bab pa yis*)

nipāta- m. *falling down; decay destruction, ruin* 66b (tib. *rgud pa*)

nipuṇa- adj. *clever, skilful,capable of* 73c (tib. *rab goms pa*)

ni-√bandh (9, *nibadhnāti*) *to bind on; enchain, fetter* 35d (nibadhyante; tib. *sruṅ bar 'gyur*)

niyukta- ppp. of ni-√yuj *bound on, chained; fastened, attached; used, employed* 45a (tib. *byed pa na*)

ni-√rūp (10, *nirūpayati*) *to perform; perceive, notice; investigate, examine* 51d (nirūpayati; tib. *rtog par byed*)

nirguṇa- adj. *having no (good) qualities, not virtuous* 47a (tib. *yon tan med*)

nir-√dah (1, *nirdahati*) *to burn up* 133d (nirdahati; tib. *'tshig par 'gyur*)

ni-√vṛt (1, *nivartate*) *to turn back; return* 20d (na ... nivartante; tib. *zlog med*)

niśchidra- adj. *having no holes; immaculate, having no weak points* 52b (freely tib. *sel med*)

ni-√śri (1, *niśrayati*) *to lean on, rely on* 137d (niśritya; tib. *brten nas*)

niṣikta- ppp. of ni-√śic *sprinkled, infused* 36d (tib. *bźag pa*)

niṣiddhi- f. *warding off, keeping back, removal* 33d (tib. *sel 'gyur*)

ni-√sev (1, *niṣevate*) *to stay in, abide; frequent, follow, enjoy* 65b (na ... niṣevante; tib. *mi len*)

niṣṭhyūta- ppp. of ni-√ṣṭhīv *spit out, emitted, sent forth* 86d (tib. *bcug*)

nistriṃśa- adj. *merciless, cruel;* m. *sword* 12d (tib. *spyi rtol can*)

ni-√han (2, *nihanti*) *to kill, destroy* 110d (nighnanti; tib. *gsod pa*)

nīca- adj. *low, not high; inferior;* m. *low, base, mean being* 7b, 14b, 26a, 82a, 88a (tib. *smad rigs*); 16b, 123b (tib. *ṅan*); 53c (tib. *ṅan pa*)

nṛ- m. *man, person* 130c (tib. *n. e.*)

nṛpa- m. *king* 120b (tib. *rgyal po*)

no neg. ptcl. *not* 13b, 49b (tib. *min*); 40b (tib. *ma*)

nyūna- m. *inferior being* 97b (tib. *dman*)

P

pakṣa- m. *wing, feather; side, part, party* 71a (tib. *'dab gśog*)

pakṣapāta- m. *partiality* 118a (tib. *phyogs su ... lhuṅ*)

paṅka- m./nt. *mud, mire* 92c (tib. *'dam*)

√pac (1, *pacati*) *to cook, bake, roast; burn* 29d (tib. *sreg*)

pañjara- nt. *cage* 35d (tib. *gzeb*)

paṭu- adj. *sharp, pungent, harsh, keen; smart, clever, skilful* 51b (tib. *gcam bu*); 124d (tib. *nus*)?

paṇḍita- m. *learned man, scholar* 99b, 119b (tib. *mkhas pa*)

√pat (1, *patati*) *to fall down, descend; fall, get into* 2b*, 63d (patati; tib. *'bab*); 37d (na ... patati; tib. *'babs par mi byed do*); 71c (patati; tib. *ltuṅ bar byed pa*); 85d (patanty; tib. *'bab*); 128c (patann; tib. *byer ba*)

patita- ppp. of √pat *fallen, descended* 48d (contextually tib. *bsregs na*)

pathika- m. *traveller* 135d (tib. *lam du źugs pa*)

pathin-	m. *way, path, road* 114c (tib. *lam*)
pada-	nt. *step; place, station; rank* 21b (tib. *gźi*); 46a (tib. *go 'phaṅ*); 106b (ekapade; tib. *thaṅ cig*); 114d (tib. *gom pa*); 125a (tib. *n. e.*)
padavī-	f. *road, path, way* 144c (tib. *lam*)
payas-	nt. *water* 129d, 140d (tib. *chu*)
para-	adj. *the other* 6a, 7b, 23b, 24a, 50a, 58b, 124a, 131b, 131d (tib. *gźan*); 9a, 10a, 51a, 58d, 137a (tib. *pha rol*); 110b (tib. *n. e.*)
parabhāga-	m. *excellence, supremacy; prosperity* 15b (tib. *thag bcad pa* as if rendering skt. *parabhāga-* in the sense of *paramārtha*); 93b, 107b (tib. *go 'phaṅ*)
param	adv. *in a high degree, excessively, greatly* 26b (tib. *śin tu*); 92b (tib. *n. e.*)?
parā-√bhū	(1, *parābhavati*) *to overcome, conquer; hurt, injure, humiliate* 82b (parābhavati; tib. *khyad du gsod par byed*)
parigṛhīta-	ppp. of pari-√grah *seized, grasped; accepted, adopted* 26a (tib. *yoṅs bzuṅ*)?
paricaya-	m. *acquaintance, familiarity with, contact* 30a (tib. *'go na*); 44a (tib. *'dris pa*); 144b (tib. *goms par byed pa yis*)
pariciti-	f. *acquaintance, familiarity* 53c (tib. *mdza' bśes*)
pari-√trai	(2, *paritrāti*) *to rescue, save, protect* 68d (paritrātum; tib. *bskyab par*)
paribhava-	m. *insult, injury, humiliation* 65b (tib. *brñas thabs*)
parimāna-	nt. *measuring; measure, weight* 73d (tib. *tshad*)
pariśuddha-	ppp. of pari-√śudh *cleaned, purified, pure* 58a (strangely tib. *tshul 'chos pa* 'full of hypocrisy')
paryanta-	m. *circuit; limit, border; end* 37a (tib. *mtha'*)
parvata-	m. *mountain* 46d (tib. *ri*)
pala-	nt. *a particular weight* 73d (tib. *sraṅ*)
pavana-	m. *wind, breeze* 41c, 58c (tib. *rluṅ*)
√pā I	(2, *pāti*) *to watch, keep, preserve, protect* 1c (pānti; tib. *skyoṅ ba*); 7d (pātuṃ; tib. *sbed*); 28d (pāti; tib. *sruṅ*)
√pā II	(1, *pibati*) *to drink* 44d (pibanta; tib. *'thuṅ na*); 65c (na pibanti; tib. *'thuṅ bar mi byed do*); 140d (pibanto; tib. *'thuṅ*)
pāka-	m. *ripening, ripeness; abcess, ulcer* 72c (tib. *nad*); 72d (tib. *smin pa*)
pāta-	m. *fall, downfall* 145d (tib. *'bab la*)
pātrī-√kṛ	(8, *pātrīkaroti*) *to make anything a recepient or vessel* 83d (pātrīkṛtaṃ; tib. *snod byas*)
pāpa-	nt. *evil, misfortune; sin, vice, crime* 13a, 74b (tib. *sdig pa*)
pāradīya-	adj. *with the character of quicksilver* 128d (raso ... pāradīyaḥ; tib. *dṅul chu*)

pi-√dhā (3, *pidadhāti, pidhatte*) *to shut, close; stitch, sew together* 9d (pidhatte; tib. **dgod par byed*)

piṇḍita- ppp. of √piṇḍ *rolled into a ball, formed into a lump* 83c (tib. *goṅ*)

pīḍā- f. *pain, suffering, harm, injury* 10a (tib. *gtses*)

puṇyavat- m. *righteous man, virtuos being* 108b (tib. *bsod nams ldan*)

punar adv. *again, once more* 141b (tib. *n. e.*)

puras adv. *in front of, before, in the presence of* 17d (tib. *mdun du*); 42b (dhuraṃ puraḥ prakarṣanti; contextually tib. *brñas thabs sna tshogs byed*); 107d (na puraḥ; freely tib. *nam yaṅ ... mi?*)

puruṣa- m. *man, human being* 55d (tib. *mi*); 73a (freely tib. *rdzas bzaṅ po*)

√puṣp (1, denom., *puṣpati*) *to blossom* 27c (puṣpaty; tib. *n. e.*)?; 102c (puṣpaty; tib. *me tog ltar* renders as if **puṣpam iva*)

pūrṇa- ppp. of √pṝ *filled, full; complete* 49c (tib. *ña ba*)

pūṣan- m. *sun* 19b, 107d, 127d (tib. *ñi ma*)

pṛthu- adj. *broad, wide; great, mighty* 139a (contextually tib. *'byor ba*)

pṛthutā- f. *vastness* 122c (tib. *rgya che*)

pra-√kāś (1, *prakāśate*) *to become visible, shine* 93d (na ... prakāśante; tib. *gsal mi gyur*); (caus. *prakāśayati*) *to make visible, illuminate, irradiate; reveal* 5d (prakāśayati; tib. *gsal bar byed*); 69d (na ... prakāśayati; tib. *mun sel mi byed na*); 125c (prakāśayanty; tib. *phyuṅ ba'i*)

prakāśa- m. *clearness, brightness, light* 38d (tib. *snaṅ ba*)

prakṛti- f. *nature, natural form, character; by nature* 2d* (tib. *ṅaṅ gis*); 22b, 76c, 81b, 102a, 108a, 128a (tib. *raṅ bźin*); 53b (tib. *khoṅ*); 74b (tib. *raṅ bźin las*)

pra-√kṛṣ (1, *prakarṣati*) *to draw forth; drag along* 42b (dhuraṃ puraḥ prakarṣanti; contextually tib. *brñas thabs sna tshogs byed*)

prakhala- m. *very bad person, great scoundrel, villain* 42a, 124c (tib. *mi srun*); 62a (tib. *mi bsrun pa*); 109b (tib. *mi srun*)

pra-√cal (1, *pracalati*) *to be set in motion, quake* 131d (pracalati; tib. *g.yo*)

pracura- adj. *much, many, abundant; frequent* 121d (tib. *rab tu maṅ*)

pra-√jñā (9, *prajānāti*) *to know, understand* 140c (prajñāyante ... na; tib. *mthoṅ ba med*)

pratanu- adj. *very thin, delicate, minute, small* 56b (tib. *'phran tshegs*)

pratidinam adv. *daily, every day* 67a (tib. *ñin re*)

prati-√pad (4, *pratipadyate*) *to regard, acknoledge; believe* 122a (pratipadyante ... na; tib. *yid mi ches*)

pratibimba- nt. *reflection, reflected image* 18d (tib. *gzug brñan*)

prathamataram adv. *first of all* 63a (tib. *daṅ por*); 82b (tib. *thog mar*)

pradveṣa- m. *dislike, repugnance, aversion, hatred* 88c (tib. *rab tu *khros*)

pradhāna- nt. *chief thing or person, most important part* 93a (°pradhāne; tib. *gces byed las*)

pra-√bādh (1, *prabādhate*) *to press forward, urge, promote; torment, injure, annoy* 59b (prabādhante; tib. *'tshe[r] ba⟨r⟩ byed*); 61b (prabādhate; tib. *'tshe bar byed*); 63b (prabādhante; tib. *'gog*)

prabhaviṣṇu- m. *king* 116b (tib. *rgyal po'i byin*)

prabhā- f. *light, splendour* 119c (freely tib. *'char tshe*)

prabhutva- nt. *lordship, reign, might* 84b (tib. *gson par gyur pa*)

prabhuśakti- f. *ability to rule* 114b (freely tib. *bla 'og gi ni don*)

pra-√mṛj (2, *pramārṣṭi*) *to wipe,wipe off* 57c (pramārṣṭuṃ; tib. *reg par* translates *pramārṣṭum*)?

prayatnena adv. *with great effort* 74d (tib. *rab tu 'bad pas*)

pra-√yam (1, *prayacchati*) *to bestow, present, give* 112a (prayacchati; tib. *byin pas*)

pra-√yā (2, *prayāti*) *to go forth, advance towards* 80c (prayānti; tib. *'bab pa*); 112d (prayāti; tib. *'byuṅ*)

prayojana- nt. *occasion, object, purpose* 34a (tib. *don*)

pralāpa- m. *talk, discourse; prattling* 144d (tib. *smras pa yin*)

pra-√śaṃs (1, *praśaṃsati*) *to proclaim, declare, praise* 119b (praśaṃsanti; tib. *bsṅags pa yin*)

pra-√śam (4, *praśāmyati*; caus. *praśamayati*) *to appease, calm, terminate* 64d (praśamayati; tib. *źi bar byed*)

praśama- m. *calmness, tranquillity, quiet, rest* 62b (tib. *'dul 'gyur*)

pra-√sad (1, *prasīdati*) *to become satisfied; be gracious, be friendly* 115b (na prasīdanti; tib. *ma dad*)

prasūti- f. *procreation, bringing forth* 145b (tib. *bskyed*)

prākṛta- m. *low being, vulgar man* 86a (tib. *smad rigs*)

prājña- m. *wise man* 73b (tib. *śes rab ldan pa*); 83b (tib. *śes rab*)

prāñc adv. *before* 48d (tib. *n. e.*)

pra-√āp (5, *prāpnoti*) *to get, aquire* 141b (prāpya; tib. *rñed nas*)

prāpta- ppp. of pra-√āp *attained to, reached, obtained* 72a (tib. *bdog pa*)

prāmānya- nt. *authoritativeness, standard* 101c (tib. *ran par*)

prāyas adv. *mostly, commonly, generally* 10c, 12c, 35b, 40b, 46b, 77b, 86a, 102a, 137a (tib. *phal cher*); 23b (tib. *n. e.*); 47b (freely tib. *kha cig*)?

prīta- ppp. of √prī *pleased, delighted, satisfied* 10b (prītaḥ ... bhavati; tib. *dga' bar 'gyur*)

pra-√īr (2, *prerte*; caus. *prerayati*) *to set in motion, urge, stimulate, instigate* 50a (prerayati; tib. *rtsol*)

pra-√ūrṇu	(2, *prorṇoti*) *to cover, veil, envelop* 57b (prorṇute; tib. *'tshub par byed*)
proṣita-	ppp. of pra-√vas *absent, effaced, deceased* 115d (proṣitanayana-; tib. *loṅ ba*)
√plu	(1, *plavate*) *to float, swim* 42d, 83d (plavate; tib. *'phyo*)

PH

phaṇa-	m. *hood of a serpent* 120c (freely tib. *cha śas*)
√phal	(1, *phalati*) *to bear fruit, ripen* 27d (phalaty; tib. *'bras bu*)
phala-	m. *shield* 28d (tib. *phub*); nt. *fruit; result, fulfillment* 75b (tib. *dgos pa*); 100b (tib. *don*)

B

baka-	m. *heron* 126c (tib. *chu skyar*)
badara-	m. *the Badara tree* (*a kind of jujube tree*) 96c (tib. *rgya śug*)
√bandh	(9, *badhnāti*) *to bind, tie, fix; catch* 56c (badhnāti; freely tib. *'dzin byed*); 128d (na badhyate; tib. *sdud ... mi nus*)
bandha-	m. *binding; grip; capture, arrest, imprisonment* 35d (tib. *spyil bu*); 116d (bandhena; tib. *bsdams pa'i mthus*)
bandhakī-	f. *harlot, courtezan* 120b (tib. *smad 'tshoṅ*)
bandhu-	m. *relative* 132a (tib. *gñen*)
bala-	nt. *power, stength* 118d (bhiṣajo na balāya; strangely tib. *nad mi 'gyur*)
balibhuj-	m. *crow* 72d (tib. *khwa*); 84c (tib. *bya rog*)
balīyaṃs-	adj. (comp. of *balin*) *more powerful, stronger, mightier* 70a (tib. *mthu yod*)
bahu-	adj. *much, many, numerous* 57d (tib. *maṅ po*)
bāṇa-	m. *arrow* 71d (tib. *mda'*)
bāla-	adj. *young, not full-grown; newly risen* 29d (contextually tib. *mi gsal*); m. *child, boy* 40c (tib. *byis pa*); 99a (tib. *byis *pa*)
bindu-	m. *drop* 36d (tib. *thigs*); 54c (tib. *thigs pa*)
bimba-	m./nt. *disk, sphere; reflected image* 40d (tib. *gzugs brñan*)
bīja-	nt. *seed, grain* 145b (tib. *sa bon*)
buddhi-	f. *intellect, mind* 114a (tib. *blo ldan*)
budha-	m. *learned man, wise man* 55a, 65a (tib. *blo ldan*); 134a (tib. *blo ldan ñid*)

BH

bhakti- f. *attachment, devotion, fondness* 75a (tib. *gus pa*); 89b (tib. *n. e.*)

bhaṅgin- adj. *fragile, transient, perishable* 53b (strangely tib. *khrel med*)

√bhaj (1, *bhajati*) *to divide, allot; share, partake, possess* 89b (bhajanti; tib. *sten byed de*); 141d (na ... bhajanty; tib. *mi ster*); 144c (bhajeta; tib. *bsten pa'i*)

bhaya- nt. *fear, dread; danger, distress* 31b (tib. *'jigs pa*); 32b (tib. *'jigs*)

bhāja- adj. *sharing, participating in, enjoying; forming a part of* 47c (tib. *n. e.*)

bhājanatā- f. *the being a vessel for* 39a (tib. *snod*)

bhānu- m. *brightness, lustre; sun* 66c (tib. *ñi ma*)

bhāva- m. *becoming; state, disposition of mind; love, affection* 75d (tib. *dga' ba*); 110b, 134c (tib. *raṅ bźin*)

√bhid (7, *bhinatti*) *to break, split* 70c (bhinatti; tib. *'bigs byed*); (pass. *bhidyate*) *to be split; be distinguished, differ from* 69b (bhidyate; tib. *khyad ... yod*)

bhidā- f. *splitting, bursting, destruction* 70d (eti bhidāṃ; tib. *gcod par byed*)

bhinna- ppp. of √bhid *split, broken; divided, separated* 124a (tib. *phye na*)

bhiṣaj- m. *phyisian, doctor* 118d (tib. *n. e.*)

bhukta- ppp. of √bhuj *eaten; consumed* 134d (tib. *bsregs na*)

√bhuj (7, *bhunakti*) *to enjoy; make use of* 72b (bhoktuṃ; tib. *spyod*)

bhujaga- m. *snake, serpent* 58c, 113c (tib. *lag 'gro*)

bhuvana- nt. *the world* 1c (skt. *sa*); 5c (tib. *sa steṅs*)

√bhū (1, *bhavati*) *to become* 10b (prītaḥ ... bhavati; tib. *dga' bar gyur*); 30b (bhavanty; tib. *'gyur*); 32c, 39d (bhavati; tib. *'gyur*); 36a (bhavati; tib. *n. e.*); 38d (bhavataḥ; tib. *n. e.*); 40b (bhavati; tib. *byed*); 66b, 74c (bhavati; tib. *'gyur*); 72c (bhavati; tib. *'oṅ*); 91b (bhavanti; tib. *n. e.*); 92a (bhavati; tib. *'byuṅ*); 92b (bhavanty; tib. *'byuṅ*); 92d (bhavanti; tib. *'byuṅ*); 111c (bhavati; tib. *mi 'gyur ro* with second negative *ma byas par* for skt. *karmaṇyam*); 114b (avihatā bhavati; tib. *mi ñams*); 119d (tib. *ran par 'gyur*); 127b (bhavanti; tib. *'byuṅ*); 130b (bhavanti; tib. *byed par 'gyur*)

bhū- f. *earth, ground, soil* 85c (tib. *sa*); 90c (tib. *n. e.*)

bhūti- f. *existence, thriving; might, superhuman power* 78d (tib. *'grub*); 118b (na bhūtaye; tib. *mi bya'o* as if it was read skt. *mā bhūt*)

bhūmi- f. *soil, ground* 54b (tib. *sa*)

bhūyas adv. *more, most, exceedingly; once more, again* 20d (tib. *phyir*); 141d (tib. *lhag par*)

bhṛśam adv. *strongly, violently, excessively, very much* 8b (tib. *lhag par*); 86b (bhṛśaṃ dīpyate; contextually tib. *rṅan can byed*)

bheda- m. *breaking, splitting; separation, division, disuniting* 9a (tib. *'byed*); 38b (tib. *n. e.*); 52b (tib. *dbye*); 124d (tib. *'byed par*)

bhoga- m. *enjoyment; pleasure, delight* 72b (tib. *loṅs spyod*)

bhauma- adj. *relating to the earth, earthly* 65c (tib. *sa steṅs kyi*)

M

√majj (6, *majjati*) *to sink, submerge* 74b (majjati; freely tib. *sbags pa'i*); 83c (majjati; tib. *byiṅ ba*)

maṇi- m. *jewel, gem, pearl* 17d, 89c (tib. *nor bu*)

maṇḍala- nt. *disk (of the sun), globe, orb* 66d (tib. *dkyil 'khor*)

maṇḍūka- m. *frog* 122d (tib. *rus sbal*)

matimat- adj. *intelligent (person)* 64b (tib. *blo ldan*)

matsya- m. *fish* 140c (tib. *ña*)

mad- pron. *I* 139a (aham; tib. *bdag*); 139b (aham; tib. *bdag la*)

√mad (4, *mādyati*; caus. *madayati*) *to gladden, exhilarate, intoxicate* 56b (madayanti; strangely tib. *drod mi thub*; cf. notes)

mada- m. *hilarity, excitement, intoxication* 30d, 138b (tib. *rgyags pa*); 79a (tib. *dregs pa*)

madhu adv. *sweetly* 113a (tib. *sñan*)

madhura- adj. *sweet, pleasant* 96d (tib. *mṅar*); 129b (tib. *n. e.*)

madhya- adj. *middle* 119d (tib. *dkyil*)

madhyama- adj. *middle, moderate; mediocre* 101b (tib. *ran*)

madhye adv. *in the middle, within, among* 107a (tib. *khrod*)

√man (4, *manyate*; caus. *mānayati*) *to honour, esteem, value highly* 94a (mānayituṃ ... na; tib. *mi bkur ro*)

manas- nt. *mind, heart* 60a (tib. *yid*); 66b (tib. *sems*); 74a* (tib. *yid*); 78d (tib. *n. e.*)

mantrin- m. *king's counsellor, minister* 114a, 116b (tib. *blon po*)

mayūra- m. *peacock* 113d (tib. *rma bya*)

maru- m. *sandy waste, desert* 135d (tib. *mya ṅam*)

marman- nt. *mortal spot, vulnerable point, weak or sensitive part of the body* 6a, 104c (tib. *gnad*)

malaya- m. *the Malaya mountain-range* 81c (tib. *ma la ya*)

malina- adj. *dirty, filthy, impure* 74c (tib. *dri ma can*)

√malinay (10, denom., *malinayati*) *to make dirty, defile* 14c (malinayati; contextually tib. *'bab par gyur*)

maśaka- m. *mosquito, gnat, fly* 56c, 59d (tib. *sbraṅ bu*)

mastaka- m./nt. *head; top, summit* 136c (tib. *rtse*)

mahattva- nt. *greatness, success* 25a (tib. *che bdag*); 80d (tib. *bdag ñid*); 95b (tib. *che; daṅ che* goes back to **ṅaṅ che* equivalent to *bdag che* but not attested); 95d (tib. *bdag ñid chen po*)

mahant- adj. *great* 119c (atimahatī; tib. *che ba*); 120a (tib. *che bdag ñid*); 139c (tib. *chen*); m. *great, noble man* 12c, 66a, 94b, 127a, 144c (tib. *bdag ñid chen po*); 48a, 49a, 122a (tib. *bdag ñid che*); 106b, 107b, 123b (tib. *che bdag*); 131a (tib. *n. e.*); 138a (tib. *maṅ ba*)

mahātman- m. *great soul, noble-hearted being* 26b (tib. *bdag ñid chen po*)

mahābhairava- adj. *extremely frightening;* m. *name of Śiva* 32c (tib. *'jigs byed chen po*)

mahārgha- adj. *high-priced, precious, valuable* 52a (tib. *rin chen*)

mahāśani- m. *great thunderbolt* 37d (tib. *thog*)

mahāsattva- m. *noble-hearted being* 36b, 128b (tib. *sems can che*)

mahiman- m. *greatness* 26b (is tib. *skyed* a corruption of *che*?); 84d (tib. *phan pa*)

mahīyas adj. *greater, mightier* 13b (tib. *che*)

maheśvara- m. *great lord; name of Śiva* 22c (tib. *dbaṅ phyug*)

mā prohib. ptcl. *not, that not, lest* 79a, 79b (tib. *mi*)

māṇikya- nt. *ruby* 26d, 52c (tib. *nor bu*)

mātaṅga- m. *elephant* 56d (tib. *ma taṅ ka yi glaṅ po*)

mādhyastha- nt. *middle position; impartiality* 119a (tib. *dbus na gnas pa*)

māna- m. *self-conceit, arrogance, pride* 101b (tib. ... *min* ... *ma yin* renders as if skt. *mā na* interpreted as two negations); 105b (mānaṃ avahitaṃ vahataḥ; strangely tib. *rag las med pa*?); 112c (tib. *bkur sti*)

mārga- m. *track, road, path* 117c (tib. *lam*)

mitra- m. *friend* 132c (tib. *n. e.*)

miśra- adj. *mixed, mingled* 65b (tib. *bsres pa'i*)

mukta- ppp. of √muc *set free, released* 134d (tib. *n. e.*)

muktāphala- nt. *pearl* 39d, 115c (tib. *mu tig*)

mukha- nt. *mouth* 39c (tib. *kha*); 72c (tib. *mchu*)

√muc (6, *muñcati*) *to loose, release; leave, quit, give up* 58d (na muñcanti; tib. *mi gtoṅ ṅo*)

mudgara- m. *hammer* 124c (tib. *lcags gyoṅ* 'hard iron' perhaps better read *lcags goṅ* 'lump of iron')

mumūrṣu- m. *one who is about to die* 130c (tib. *'chi bar 'gyur*)

muṣita- ppp. of √muṣ *bereft of, deprived of* 38c (muṣitanayanasya; tib. *mig ni loṅ ba la*)

muṣṭi- m./f. *clenched hand, fist* 116d (tib. **chaṅ ba*)

√muh (4, *muhyati*) *to err, be mistaken* 46b (muhyati; tib. *rmoṅs par 'gyur*)

mūla- nt. *root; basis, foundation* 55a (contextually tib. *srog*)

√mṛ (1, *marati;* caus. *mārayati*) *to cause to die, kill* 28c (mārayati; tib. *gsod par byed*); 88d (mārayati; tib. *'chi 'gyur na*)

mṛga- m. *forest animal; deer* 110c (tib. *ri dwags*)

mṛgendra- m. *lion* 55d (tib. *seṅ ge*)

mṛta- ppp. of √mṛ *dead, deceased, torpid* 21d (tib. *rul pa*)

mṛtyu- m. *the God of Death, Yama* 145d (tib. *'chi bdag*)

mṛdu- adj. *soft, delicate, tender, mild* 29b (tib. *n. e.*); 41c (tib. *phra* translated as an attribute of skt. *rajas* and not of *pavana*); 52b (tib. *dbye* **dka'* translates skt. *mṛdur bhede* as if separated **mṛ durbhede*); 67b (tib. *des*) m. *one who is soft, tender person* 86b (tib. *dman*)

mṛdū-√bhū (1, *mṛdūbhavati*) *to become soft, become mellow* 87b (mṛdūbhavanti; tib. **mñen 'gyur*)

maukharya- nt. *talkativeness, garrulity* 126c (tib. *n. e.*)

Y

yataḥ adv. *whence, wherefrom, for which reason* 127a (tib. *gaṅ*)

yatna- m. *effort, exertion, attempt* 7a (atiyatnād; tib. *rab bsgrims te*); 144d (tib. *n. e.*)

yatra adv. *where* 37c (tib. *gaṅ du*); 103a, 103c (tib. *n. e.*)

yathā adv. *how, in what manner* 9b, 131b (tib. *ltar*); 48d, 49a (tib. *n. e.*); 49d, 126b, 129c (tib. *ji ltar*)

yathābhyāsam adv. *according to practice, through habituation* 2b (tib. *goms pa*)

yad- rel. pron. *who; which* 1d (ye; tib. *gaṅ ... la*); 6b (yat; tib. *n. e.*); 6c (yat; tib. *'di ltar*); 34a, 103a, 115b (yat; tib. *gaṅ*); 56b (yad; tib. *gaṅ dag*); 61d (yat; tib. *n. e.*); 69a, 99a, 99d (twice), 105d (yo; tib. *n. e.*); 69d (yaḥ; tib. *n. e.*); 83a (yena; tib. *gaṅ gis*); 90b (yeṣu; tib. *n. e.*); 90d (yebhyo; tib. *n. e.*); 98a (yo; tib. *gaṅ źig*); 141b (yo; tib. *gaṅ yin*)

yama- m. *Yama, the Lord of Death* 88d (tib. *gśin rje*)

yaśas- nt. *honour, glory, fame, renown* $18b^1$, $18b^2$, 145c (tib. *grags pa*); 112b (tib. *grags*)

√yā (2, *yāti*) *to go, proceed; go to any state, become* 35b (vināśaṃ ... yānti; tib. *ñams*); 45d (na yānti; tib. *phog mi 'gyur*); 79a (mā yāta; tib. *mi bya ste*); 79d (yāty astam; tib. *nub par 'gyur*); 93b (na yānti; tib. *min*); 107b (yānti; tib. *thob*); 109c (na yānti; tib. *źig tu ... 'gyur*); 126b (na ... yānti; tib. *ma yin te*); 131b (na yānti khedaṃ; tib. *yid gduṅs ... min*)

yāvat adv. *to which extent* 68b (tib. *n. e.*); 145c (tib. *ji srid*)

yuktyā adv. *properly, suitably, fitly, justly* 15a (tib. *rigs*)

yuga- nt. *age of the world, long period of years* 127c (tib. *dus*)

yugapad adv. *together, at the same time, simultaneously* 91d (tib. *dus gcig*)

√yuj (7, *yunakti*; pass. *yujyate*) *to be made ready for or prepared for; be fit or proper for* 12d (yujyante; tib. *bkur* renders skt. *pūjyante*!)

yoga- m. *yoking, joining; union, contact; means, remedy, cure* 23d (in tib. expressed with the instr. ptcl.); 78c (tib. *sbyor ba*); 87b (tib. *thabs*); 128c (tib. *sbyor ba*)

yogyatā- f. *suitableness, fitness, propriety, ability* 35a (tib. *mkho ba*)

yauvana- nt. *youth* 20a, 30d (tib. *laṅ tsho*)

R

rakta- ppp. of √rañj *coloured; reddened, red* 26c (contextually tib. *tshon gyis bsgyur na*)

rakṣin- m. *guard, watchman* 140b (tib. *sruṅ mkhas*)

rajas- nt. *impurity, dirt; dust* 13d, 41d, 57b (tib. *rdul*); 14d (tib. *rdzas*); 64d (tib. *rdul phran*)

ratna- nt. *gem, jewel* 3c, 89c, 103d (tib. *rin chen*); 42d, 90d (tib. *rin po che*)

√ram (1, *ramate*; caus. *ramayati*) *to gladden, please* 24b (ramayati; tib. *dga' bar byed*); 75c (ramayanti; tib. *dga' byed pa*)

ramaṇīya- adj. *pleasant, delightful, charming* 18d (tib. *dga' ba*)

raya- m. *stream, current* 20b (tib. *rgyun*)

ravi- m. *sun* 67d, 85c, 98d (tib. *ñi ma*)

ravikara- m. *sunbeam* 23c (tib. *ñi zer*)

rasa- m. *juice; taste; mercury, quicksilver* 78c (tib. *dṅul chu*); 118c (ekarasa°; tib. *ro gcig*); 128c (raso ... pāradīyaḥ; tib. *dṅul chu*)

rasāyana m. *drug* 100d (tib. *bcud kyis len*)?

rahita- ppp. of √rah *left; deserted, free from, deprived of* 24c (tib. *'bral ba*); 64b (vibhavarahito; tib. *dbul po*)

rāgitā- f. *fondness, desire, longing* 21a (tib. *źen pa*)

√rāj (1, *rājati*) *to be illustrious, be resplendent, shine* 15c (na rājati; tib. *bzaṅ po ma yin te*)

rājan- m. *king, sovereign* 93a (tib. *rgyal po*); 114b, 123d (tib. *n. e.*)

ripu- m. *deceiver, cheat, rogue; enemy, adversary* 18b, 36a (tib. *dgra*)

√rudh (7, *ruṇāddhi, runddhe*) *to obstruct, cheek, restrain, suppress* 18b (rundhānam; tib. *'tshub*)

ruṣā- f. *anger, wrath* 141d (tib. *khros pa*)

rūkṣa- adj. *rough, dry; harsh, coarse, unkind* 53b (tib. *rtsub pa*)

rūpa- nt. *form, shape, figure; nature, character* 23b (pararūpam eti; freely tib. *dri yi rjes su 'braṅ*); 32d (tib. *gzugs*)

roga- m. *disease, sickness* 76a (i. o. *rogo* tib. *spu* seems to render **keśo*)

L

√lakṣ	(1, *lakṣate*) *to perceive, observe* 49c (lakṣyata; tib. *mṅon*)
lakṣman-	nt. *mark, sign, characteristic spot* 57c (tib. *bkra śis*)
lakṣmī-	f. *mark, (good) sign; beauty, loveliness, charm; wealth, riches* 63c (freely tib. *rgyas la*); 77a (tib. *phyug po*); 120b, 128a (tib. *'byor pa*)
lakṣya-	nt. *aim, mark, goal* 45c (tib. *'bem*)
√lagh	(10, *laghayati*) *to make light* 89d (laghayati; tib. *yaṅ*)
laghu-	adj. *light; insignificant, casual* 53a (tib. *yaṅ ba*); 91b (tib. *ṅan*); m. *insignificant person* 49b* (tib. *phal*); 124a* (tib. *n. e.*)
laghutā-	f. *lightness; fickleness* 120a (tib. *n. e.*)
laghutva-	nt. *lightness, weakness* 56a (tib. *yaṅ ba*)
laghusattva-	m. *person of weak character* 41b (tib. *yaṅ ba'i sems can*)
labdha-	ppp. of √labh *taken, sized; reached, gained* 82a (tib. *n. e.*)
√labh	(1, *labhate*) *to take, seize; obtain, receive, get* 3d (is tib. *spa ba* a corruption of *spra ba* as a free rendering of skt. *dyutiṃ labhate*?); 21b (na sthitiṃ ... labhate; tib. *gnas pa med*); 72a (na labhante; tib. *dbaṅ med*)
lalita-	nt. *sport, dalliance; coquettishness* 30d (tib. *'jo ba sgeg pa*)
lavaṅga-	m. *the clove tree* 77d (tib. *li śi*)
√lih	(2, *leḍhi*) *to lick* 60d (na leḍhi; contextually tib. *mi len*)
√lī	(4, *līyate*) *to cling, adhere to, settle on* 21d (līyante; freely tib. *za bas*)
lūtā-	f. *spider* 59d (tib. *ba*)
lūtātantu-	m. *spider's web, cobweb* 56d (tib. *ba rgya*)
loka-	m. *the world; human beings, men* 2b, 8d, 85c, 104a (tib. *'jig rten*); 46b, 109b (tib. *mi dag*); 59b (tib. *mi*)
loṣṭha-	m./nt. (mostly *loṣṭa-*) *lump of earth, clay* 55c (tib. *rdo*)
lohamaya-	adj. *made of iron or copper* 10d (tib. *lcags las byas pa'i*)

V

vakra-	adj. *crooked, curved, bent* 22d (vakra ... śaśī; tib. *zla ba tshes pa*); 28d (tib. *'khyogs te*)
√vac	(2, *vakti*) *to speak, say, tell* 7d (vaktum; tib. *smra*); 27a (vakti; tib. *smra ba*)
vacana-	nt. *speaking, utterance; sound, voice* 35c, 96a (tib. *tshig*)
vajra-	m./nt. *thunderbolt* 68c, 145d (tib. *gnam lcags*); 70c (tib. *rdo rje*); 139d (tib. *rdo rje*)
-vat	suffix *as, like* 96c (badaravan; tib. *rgya śug gi 'bras bu*)

√vad (1, *vadati*) *to speak, say, tell* 101a (vadanti; tib. *smra ba*); 137b (vadanti; tib. *smra*)

vana- nt. *forest, wood, grove* 11d (tib. *nags tshal*)

vapus- nt. *body* 31a (tib. *lus can*)

varam adv. *preferably, rather, better* 29a (skt. *[b]dam*)

√vaś (2, *vaṣṭi*) *to desire, wish; affirm, maintain, declare for* 62d (uśanty; tib. *ston no*)

vasanta- m. *spring* 11d (tib. *dpyid ñin*)

vastu- nt. *thing, object* 39b (does tib. *char* render a misread or miswritten skt. **varṣaḥ* for *vastu*?)

√vah (1, *vahati*) *to carry, bear* 47d (vahati; tib. *brten*); 105b (vahataḥ; tib. *n. e.*)

vahni- m. *the conveyor of oblations, i. e. fire* 133d, 145a (tib. *me*)

vā conj. *or; and* 37a (tib. *'am*); 37b, 37d (tib. *yaṅ na*); 89d, 105d, 111c, 135c (tib. *n. e.*); 105c (tib. *daṅ*)

√vā (2, *vāti*) *to blow (as the wind)* 41c (vāti; tib. *bdas pa*)

vākya- nt. *saying, statement, words* 96c (tib. *tshig*)

vāgdoṣa- m. *speking badly, verbal fault* 126b (freely tib. *drag po'i skyon*)

vāc- f. *speech, talk* 113a (tib. *tshig*)

vācyamāna- pres. pass. part. of caus. from √vac *to be made public* 57a (tib. *bskyed pa na*)?

vāyu- m. *wind* 23a, 132c (tib. *rluṅ*)

vāri- nt. *water* 86c (tib. *chu*)

vāśita- nt. *cry, scream* 113d (tib. *sgra sñan*)

vāsa- m. *garment, clothes* 74d (tib. *gos*)

vi-√kas (1, *vikasati*) *to expand; spread out, extend* 54d (vikasati; tib. *sñoms*); 86c (vikasati; tib. *khyab byed*)

vikāra- m. *change of form; perturbation, agitation* 41b (vikāram ... eti; tib. *khro*)

viguṇa- adj. *without virtues, deficient, imperfect* 69b (tib. *phal pa*)

vighana- adj. *cloudless* 29c (tib. *sprin med*)

vi-√car (1, *vicarati*; caus. *vicārayati*) *to ponder, reflect, deliberate* 135d (vicārayati; tib. *rtog*)

vicitra- adj. *various, versatile* 145a (tib. *sna tshogs*)

vijāti- adj. *belonging to another class, not genuine* 17c (tib. *bcos ma*)

vi-√jñā (9, *vijānāti*) *to distinguish, discern, recognize* 73d (vijānanti; tib. *śes par byed*); 97d (vijānanti; tib. *śes*); 104b (vijñeyāḥ; tib. *śes par bya*), 104d (na ... vijānāti; tib. *śes pa med*)

vijñāna- nt. *intelligence, knowledge, proficiency* 24b (tib. *rnam śes*)

vidagdha- ppp. of vi-√dah *burnt up; clever, shrewd* 30b (tib. *gsal ba'i*)

vidyā- f. *knowledge* 125b (tib. *rig pa*)

vi-√dhā (3, *vidadhāti*) *to distribute, apportion, bestow* 108d (nopaśamaṃ vidadhati; tib. *źi ba ma yin no*)

vidvāṃs- m. *wise, learned man* 40b, 132b (tib. *mkhas pa*); 115c (tib. *mi śes* renders skt. **aviduṣaḥ* i. o. *viduṣaḥ*)

vinaya- m. *discipline; decency, modesty* 110a (tib. *sdom pa*)

vinā ind. *without, except* 100c (tib. *med par*); 101d (tib. *ma yin*)

vināśa- m. *destruction, decay, death* 35a (vināśaṃ ... yānti; tib. *ñams*); 130b (vināśa āpanne; tib. *ñams par gyur na*)

vi-ni-√pat (1, *vinipatati*) *to fall down, fall upon* 68c (vinipatati; tib. *bab pa ste*)

vinipatita- ppp. of vi-ni-√pat *fallen down* 94a (tib. *ñams pa*)

vinipāta- m. *falling down; fall, ruin; failure* 19c (tib. *rgud gyur*)

vi-ni-√han (2, *vinihanti*) *to strike down, kill, destroy* 59d (vinighnanti; tib. *bzuṅ źiṅ gsod par byed*)

vipad- f. *misfortune, adversity, calamity* 121d (tib. *lam log* renders erroneously skt. *vipatha-* 'wrong path'); 127b (tib. *rgud pa*); 131a (tib. *gnod pa*)

vipatti- f. *misfortune* 25b (tib. *rgud pa*); 95c (tib. *phoṅs*)

viparīta- ppp. of vi-pari-√i *turned round, reversed, opposite* 45d, 130a (tib. *log par*)

vibandhadhra- adj. *curing by means of destruction* 96b (should we read *dāhavibandhahara-* or *dāhavibandhaghna-* rendered with tib. *za 'jil* or is the Tibetan word the equivalent of skt. *āranāla-*? cf. *āranāla-*)

vibhava- m. *power, greatness; wealth, money, property* 56b (tib. *'byor pa*); 64b (vibhavarahito; tib. *dbul po*)

vi-√bhid (7, *vibhinatti;* caus. *vibhedayati*) *to cause to split, divide, alienate* 96d (vibhedayati; tib. **'khu bar byed*)

vibhūti- f. *wealth, riches* 141a (tib. *phyug po ñid*)?

vimukta- ppp. of vi-√muc *released, freed of* 1b (tib. *spaṅs*)

viyoga- m. *disjunction, separation* 25c (is tib. *'byor pa* a corruption of original *sbyor pa*?)

vi-√rac (10, *viracayati*) *to construct, form, make; build, erect* 59c (viracayya; tib. *btsugs nas*)

virata- ppp. of vi-√ram *stopped, ceased; desisted from* 24a (tib. *spaṅs pa*)

virasa- adj. *juiceless, sapless; disagreeable* 60c (tib. *rul*)

vi-√rāj (1, *virājati, -te*) *to be illustrious, shine forth, glitter* 107d (na virājante; tib. *gsal mi 'gyur*)

virūpa- m. *one of ugly form, ugly person* 18c (freely tib. *g.ya' daṅ ldan pa*)

vi-√lok (1. *vilokate*; caus. *vilokayati*) *to look at, consider* 144b (vilokayan; tib. *lta'i phyir*)

vivara-	nt. *hole, chasm, vacuity* 16d (tib. *phug*)
vi-√vic	(7, *vivinakti*) *to divide, separate; distinguish* 4c (*vivektum; tib. *'byed pa*); 38a (nālaṃ ... vivektum; tib. *'byed mi nus*)
viśuddha-	ppp. of vi-√śudh *completely cleansed or purified, pure* 3d (tib. *bzaṅ po*); 108a (tib. *rnam dag*), 114a (tib. *gsal ba*)
viśeṣa-	m. *distinction, difference; specialty, peculiarity; quality* 3b (tib. *yon tan*)
viśeṣaṇa-	nt. *distinction, discrimination, distinguishing mark* 7c (tib. *khyad*)
vi-√śvas	(2, *viśvasiti;* caus. *viśvāsayati*) *to cause to trust, inspire confidence* 110d (viśvāsya; tib. *'dris nas*)
viśvāsa-	m. *confidence, trust, faith* 81b (viśvāso na kṣamaḥ; tib. *bśes mi bya*); 132b (tib. *bag*)
viṣa-	nt. *poison* 6d, 39c, 60a, 76b (tib. *dug*)
viṣama-	adj. *uneven, rugged, rough* 46c (freely tib. *gśoṅ*)
viṣaya-	m. *object of the sences* 60a (tib. *yul*)
viṣāṇa-	nt. *horn, tusk* 70d (tib. *rwa ru*)
√vṛt	(1, *vartate*) *to turn round; take place, occur* 113b (vartante; tib. *byed*)
vṛttānta-	m. *occurrence; course, manner, way; news, tidings* 104b (tib. *'tsho chos*)
vṛtti-	f. *rolling; mode of life, conduct* 58a (tib. *'tsho ba*)
vṛddhi-	f. *growth, increase* 15c (tib. *thaṅ skyed* perhaps for misread skt. *ati-dṛḍhi*); 19d (tib. *che ba ñid*); 47c (tib. *skye*)
√vṛdh	(1, *vardhate;* caus. *vardhayati*) *to cause to increase, make grow* 106c (vardhayati; tib. *bsgrubs*)
veśman-	nt. *house, dwelling* 93c (tib. *khaṅ pa*)
veśyā-	f. *prostitute, harlot* 75c (tib. *smad 'tshoṅ*)
vaicitrya-	nt. *variety, manifoldness, diversity* 123a (tib. *sna tshogs*)
vaimukhya-	m. *aversion, repugnance to* 44b (tib. *skyo ba*)
vyakṣa-	adj. *blind* 99d (tib. *dmus loṅ*, see note in text)
√vyath	(1, *vyathate*) *to tremble, waver; be agitated, be disturbed in mind* 58b (vyathate; tib. *'tshe bar byed*)
vi-abhi-√car	(1, *vyabhicarati*) *to come to naught, fail; go beyond, transgress* 19d (na ... vyabhicaranti; tib. *mi ñams*)
vyavahāra-	m. *conduct, behaviour* 113b (tib. *spyod pa*)
vyasana-	nt. *calamity, misfortune, trouble* 43a (tib. *rgud pa*); 79b (tib. *rgud*); 100b (tib. *brtson pa byas*); 131d (tib. *gnod pa*)
vyāghra-	m. *tiger* 108c (tib. *stag*)
vyādha-	m. *hunter* 110d (tib. *rṅon pa*)
vyādhi-	m. *disease, sickness, plague* 62c (tib. *nad*)
vyāmiśra-	adj. *mixed together, blended, mingled* 4a (tib. *'dres na*)

√vraj (1, *vrajati*) *to go, walk; go to any state, attain to* 33b (vrajanty; tib. *'gro ba'i* as if reading *vrajanto*); 39b (vrajati; incorrecty tib. *'gro ba*); 116a (siddhiṃ vrajanty; tib. *'grub par 'gyur ba*)

vraṇa- m. *wound, sore, ulcer* 76b (tib. *rma*)

Ś

√śaṃs (1, *śaṃsati*) *to praise* 111b (śaṃsanti; freely tib. *bskyed de*)

√śak (5, *śaknoti*) *to be able, be capable of* 43b (śaknuvanti; tib. *nus*); 57d (na śaknuvanti; tib. *mi bzod pa'i*)?; 98b (śaknoty; tib. *nus*); 136b (na śaknoti; freely tib. *bzlar med*)

śakta- ppp. of √śak *able, competent for, capable of* 67b, 68d (tib. *nus*); 98a (tib. *nus pa*)

śakti- f. *power, ability, strength* 48b, 50b (tib. *mthu*)

śaṭha- adj. *false, deceitful; malignant, wicked* 8a (tib. *g.yo*); m. *evil person, cheat, rogue* 22a (tib. *ṅan pa*); 96c, 113a, 129b (tib. *ṅan g.yo*); 111a (tib. *blo ldan* renders **buddhāḥ* i. o. *śaṭhāḥ*)

śaṅkha- m. *conch-shell* 134d (tib. *duṅ*)

śata- nt. *hundred* 17b (śatahato; freely rendered as tib. *rgud pas*); 57b (tib. *brgya ldan*); 97d (tib. *brgya*)

śatru- m. *enemy* 55b (tib. *dgra*)

√śam (4, *śāmyati*) *to become quite, be calm* 108b (śāmyaty; tib. *źi*); (caus. *śamayati*) *to appease, pacify, calm* 100c (śamayati; tib. *źi na*)

śama- m. *tranquility, calmness; pacification, extinction* 33a (tib. *'jil*)

śara- m. *arrow* 28c, 45c (tib. *mda'*); *Śara grass* 27c (tib. *'dam bu'i me tog*)

śarabha- m. *the Śarabha deer* 43c (tib. *śa ra bha*)

śalabha- m. *grass-hopper; moth* 91d (tib. *bye'u*)

śaśāṅka- m. *moon* 8c, 19b, 94d, 98d (tib. *zla ba*); 47d (tib. *zla dkyil*)

śaśin- m. *moon* 22d (vakra ... śaśī; tib. *zla ba tshes pa*); 51d, 57c (tib. *zla ba*)

śastra- nt. *weapon* 10d (tib. *mtshon cha*)

śākha- f. *limb (of the body)* 55b (tib. *yan lag*)

śāṭhya- nt. *wickedness, deceit, guile* 29b (tib. *ṅan g.yo*)

śānta- ppp. of √śam *appeased, pacified, calm, peaceful* 31a (tib. *źi ba*); 108d (tib. *źi ba'i*)

śāstra- nt. *order, precept; teaching, science* 100a (tib. *bstan bcos*); 117a (tib. *gźuṅ lugs*)

śikhara- m./nt. *point, peak, top* 46d (tib. *rtse*)

śikhā- f. *pointed flame* 31d (tib. *rtse mo*); 52c (freely tib. *'bar*); 53d (contextually tib. *mkha' la*); 132d (contextually tib. *'bar ba*)

śikhin- m. *fire* 20b (tib. *rtse*), 106d, 134d (tib. *me*)

śiras- nt. *head* 14c (tib. *mgo*); 22b (tib. *spyi bo*); 68c (tib. *klad pa*); 94c (tib. *spyi*), 139c (tib. *rtse*)

śilā- f. *stone* 50d (tib. *bdar rdo*)

śiva- m. *happiness, welfare; emancipation, mental peace* 32d² (tib. *źi ba*); *name of the god Śiva* 32d¹ (tib. *źi ba*)

śiśira- m./nt. *cold, coolness; the cool season* 11c (tib. *dgun*)

śiśu- m. *child; young moon* 49d (tib. *tshes*)

śīta- adj. *cold, cool, chilly* 129d (tib. *rluṅ chu* may be a corruption of *graṅ chu* for skt. *śītam ... payas*)

śuka- m. *parrot* 35c (tib. *ne tso*)

śukti- f. *oyster-shell* 39d (tib. *ña phyis*)

śukla- adj. *bright, light; white* 31c (tib. *dkar ba*); 74d (tib. *dkar po*)

śuci- adj. *clear, clean, pure* 135c (svādu śuci vā; tib. *gtsaṅ mi gtsaṅ* renders *śucy aśuci vā)

śucin- adj. *clear, clean, pure* 21b (tib. *rigs pa*)

śuddhatā- f. *purity, faultlessness* 110b (na ... °śuddhatayā; tib. *ma dag pa'i*); 134b (tib. *gtsaṅ*)

√śudh (4, *śudhyati*) *to be cleared, be cleansed, be purified* 74a (śudhyati, tib. *dag 'gyur te*)

śubha- nt. *good fortune, auspiciousness; goodness* 145b (tib. *dge legs*)

√śuṣ (4, *śuṣyati*; caus. *śoṣayati*) *to make dry, dry up, parch* 11c (śoṣayati; tib. *skems par byed*)

śeṣa- m. *the Śeṣa serpent* 120c (tib. *gdeṅs can*)

śaila- m. *rock* 70c (tib. *pha boṅ*)

śmaśāna- nt. *cemetery* 2d* (tib. *dur khrod*)

śrad-√dhā (3, *śraddadhāti*) *to have faith, believe* 122c (na ... śraddadhati; tib. *yid mi ches*)

śrī- f. *light, splendour; beauty; wealth, riches, fortune* 30a (tib. *dpal*); 65b (tib. *nor*)

śruta- nt. *anything heard; knowledge* 138a (tib. *thos pa*)

śreyaṃs- adj. (comp. of *śreyas*) *more excellent, superior; best* 101b (tib. *mdzes*)

śvan- m. *dog* 55c, 60d (tib. *khyi*)

śveta- adj. *white* 134c (tib. *dkar ba*)

S

sam-√yam (1, *saṃyacchati*) *to hold together; suppress, control, restrain, curb* 43a (saṃyantuṃ ... śaknuvanti; tib. *bslaṅ bar nus*)

sam-√vṛ (5, *saṃvṛṇoti*) *to cover up, enclose* 82d (saṃvṛṇute; tib. *'bab*)

saṃśrita- ppp. of sam-√śri *united with, clinging to, adhering to* 36b (tib. *bsten*)

saṃskāra- m. *putting together; accomplishment, making well, merit* 71d (tib. *'phaṅs pa'i śugs*)

saṃsthita- ppp. of sam-√sthā *placed, standing* 117d (tib. *yod*)

saṃhṛta- ppp. of sam-√hṛ *drawn together; interrupted, dispelled* 79c (tib. *bsal mod*)

sakṛt adv. *at once; once, formerly* 73a (sakṛd api; tib. *mod la*)

saguṇa- adj. *having good qualities, furnished with virtues, virtuous* 63b (tib. *yon tan ldan pa*)

saṃkhya- adj. *numbering, amounting* 90a (atisaṃkhyeṣv; tib. *śin tu graṅs med*)

saṃgati- f. *coming together; association, intercourse* 52d (tib. *n. e.*)

saṃgraha- m. *collecting; combination* 100d (freely tib. *sogs*)

saṃghāta- m. *close union, combination, multitude* 91a (tib. *bsdoṅs*)

sajjana- m. *good man, virtuous man* 7b, 9b, 11b, 61a (tib. *skye bo dam pa*)

sat- nt. *good, reality, truth* 52c, 78c (tib. *dam pa*)

satkāra- m. *kind treatment, well-treatment, honour, favour* 14a (atisatkārair; tib. *bstod drags*)

satkṛta- ppp. of sat-√kṛ *done well; honoured* 22a (atisatkṛtā; tib. *bstod*)

sattva- m. *living being, creature* 44b, 90b, 130a (tib. *sems can*)

satpuruṣa- m. *good or wise man, noble being* 5b (tib. *skyes mchog*); 62b (tib. *skye bo dam pa*); 86b (tib. *mi mchog*)

satya- nt. *truth, reality* 109b (tib. *bden*)

√sad (1, *sīdati*) *to sit upon; sink into despondency, despair* 83a (sīdati; tib. *ñams thag pas*)

sadā adv. *always* 1d (skt. *rtag tu*); 5d, 61d (tib. *rtag tu*)

sadṛśa- adj. *same, equal* 25c (tib. *'dra*)

sant- m. pl. *being; good or wise man* 23c (tib. *skyes bu dam pa*); 23d (tib. *rtag tu* renders skt. *sadā* i. o. *sad°*); 39b (does tib. *rtag tu* render a misread or miswritten skt. **sadā* in *sadasatoḥ*?); 45b, 47b, 54b, 85b, 92b (tib. *dam pa*); nt. *the good, reality, truth* 52c (tib. *dam pa*)

saṃtāpa- m. *great heat; affliction, pain, sorrow* 79b (tib. *yid chad*); 111d (contextually tib. *sbyaṅ ba*)

sam-√dhā (3, *saṃdadhāti*) *to put together, join, unite* 97c (atisaṃdhātuṃ; tib. *bye ba 'dum byed*); 124b (saṃdadhāty; tib. *'dum byed*)

saṃdhāna-	nt. *act of placing together, uniting; fixing on (an arrow)* 45d (tib. *'geṅs pa*); 124d (tib. *'dum*)
saṃdhi-	m. *junction, connection, combination, union* 9b (tib. *sdum*)
saṃnati-	f. *bending down, subjection* 111b (tib. *'dul ba*)
sapadi	adv. *at the same instant, on the spot, at once, immediately* 9d (tib. *rim gyis* in an antonymously translated sentence)
sama-	adj. *even; same* 38d (tib. *mtshuṅs*); 39b (contextually tib. *ro gcig*); 46c (freely tib. *thaṅ*)
samantāt	adv. *wholly, completely, in every respect* 1c (tib. *kun*)
samaya-	m. *time, season* 11c (tib. *dus*)
samara-	m. *hostile encounter, war, battle* 10c (tib. *g.yul ṅo*)
sam-ā-√dā	(3, *samādadīta*) *to take away, accept, receive* 103b (tib. *blaṅ*)
samāna-	adj. *same, identical* 66a (samānaṃ bhavati; tib. *sñoms 'gyur*)
sam-ā-√śri	(1, *samāśrayati, -te*) *to seek refuge with, lean on, resort to, adhere to* 16d (samāśrayate; tib. *brten pa*)
samāśrita-	ppp. of sam-ā-√śri *come together, assembled; resting or dependent on* 47b (tib. *'khor ba*); 58b (strangely tib. *glags rñed*)
samīpe	adv. *in the vicinity, near, close at hand* 51b (tib. *n. e.*)
samutthita-	ppp. of sam-ud-√sthā *risen up together, grown upwards* 81d (tib. *mched gyur na*)
samutpatiṣṇu-	adj. *desirous of raising up* 64d (tib. *ldaṅ ba*)
sam-ud-√vah	(1, *samudvahati*) *to lift up, raise, bear* 94d (samudvahati; tib. *bkur*)
saṃpad-	f. *success, accomplishment; good fortune* 48b (tib. *n. e.*); 121a (tib. *'byor pa*)
saṃpanna-	ppp. of sam-√pad *accomplished, effected, complete* 105d (tib. *phun sum tshogs pa*)
saṃparka-	m. *mixing together, association, contact* 23b (tib. *n. e.*)
saṃprati	adv. *now, at this moment, at present* 121b (tib. *da ltar*)?
saṃmoha-	m. *confusion, bewilderment, ignorance* 125a (tib. *rmoṅs pa*)
saraghā-	f. *bee* 21c (tib. *n. e.*)?
sarajasa-	adj. *dusty, dirty* 65d (sarajasam; tib. *mtsho chu* as if the translators read **sarasajam*)
saras-	nt. *lake, pond* 2d* (tib. *mtsho*); 140d (tib. *rgya mtsho*)
sarit-	f. *river, stream* 80c (tib. *chu*)
sarpis-	nt. *clarified butter* 86d (tib. *mar gsar*)
sarva-	adj. *all* 1a*, 70b, 85a (tib. *kun*); 71c (tib. *dag*)?; 104b, 105c (tib. *thams cad*); 105d (tib. *dgu*); 135b (tib. *n. e.*)

sarvatra adv. *everywhere* 1a* (tib. *rnam pa thams cad du*); 111a, 119a (tib. *kun tu*); 118b (tib. *kun la*)

salila- nt. *water* 33a, 44c, 54d (tib. *chu*)

salilanidhi- m. *ocean* 19a (tib. *rgya mtsho*)

savitṛ- m. *sun* 5d, 79d, 119c, 130d (tib. *ñi ma*)

sasya- nt. *corn, grain, crop* 106c (tib. *lo tog*)

√sah (1, *sahate*) *to suffer, endure, bear* 67b (soḍhum; tib. *bzod par*); 67d (na ... sahate; tib. *spro ba med*)

saha adv. (used also as prefix) *together with, along with* 47c (tib. *lhan cig*); 121c, 133c (tib. *n. e.*)

sahabhū- adj. *innate, natural* 22b (tib. *ldan cig skyes pa*)

sahāya- m. *companion, assistant, helper, friend* 68a (tib. *grogs*)

sāgara- m. *ocean* 80c (tib. *rgya mtsho*)

√sādh (1, *sādhati*; caus. *sādhayati*) *to bring to an end, complete, accomplish, effect* 27b (sādhayati; tib. *sgrub*); 34a (sādhayati; tib. *'grub ... yin pa*); 45b (na sādhayanti; tib. *mi 'grub*)

sādhana- nt. *accomplishment, performance* 70b (tib. *'grub*)

sādhu- adj. *good, excellent, perfect* 39c (tib. *n. e.*); 93d (tib. *legs par*); nt. *good thing or act* 103a (tib. *legs pa*); m. *good, virtuous man, holy man, saint* 8b (tib. *des pa*); 11b (tib. *legs*); 13b, 124b (tib. *dam pa*); 25b (tib. *des*); 59a (tib. *ṅan pa* translates its opposite!); 88b, 96a (tib. *ya rabs*)

sāphalya- nt. *fruitfulness, profitableness, result, success* 3b (*yāti ... sāphalyam; tib. *'char bar byed*)

sāmarthya- nt. *ability, capacity for; efficacy, power* 6c (tib. *nus*); 116b (tib. *mthu*)

sāmavacana- nt. *conciliatory speech* 129b (tib. *'jam tshig*)

sāraphalgutva- nt. *qualities and deficiencies, goodness and badness* 73b (freely tib. *bye brag*)

sāśīviṣa- adj. *full of poisonous snakes* 93c (tib. *sbrul gdug can*)

sikatā- f. *sand* 54d (tib. *bye ma*)

siddhi- f. *accomplishment, success* 116a (siddhiṃ vrajanty; tib. *'grub par 'gyur ba*); 119b (tib. *n. e.*)

sukham- adv. *happily, comfortably* 136d (tib. *bde bar*)

sukhin- adj. *happy* 105a (tib. *bde*)

sucarita- nt. *good conduct, virtuous actions* 106a (i. o. tib. *spyod pa yaṅ* one expects rather *spyod pa bzaṅ*)

sujana- m. *good, virtuous person* 7d (tib. *skyes mchog*); 87a (tib. *skye bo dam pa*)

sudūram adv. *very far away* 41d (tib. *śin tu thag riṅ*); 71b (tib. *thag riṅ*)

subodha- adj. *easy to be understood, easy to comprehend* 38b (tib. *rtogs par sla ba*)

sumahat- adj. *very great, huge* 80a (atisumahataḥ; tib. *rab che*)

surabhin- adj. *sweet-smelling, scented, fragrant* 77d (tib. *dri rab źim*)

suruc- adj. *shining brightly* 17d (freely rendered with tib. *nor bu*)

surūpa- m. (surūpā- f.) *beautiful man (woman)* 138b (tib. *gzugs mdzes*)

suvarṇa- nt. *gold* 111c (tib. *gser*)

suśīla- m. *moral person* 24b (tib. *khrims ldan*)

susādhya- adj. *easy to be kept in order, obedient* 36a (tib. *gdul bar sla ba'i*)

suhṛd- m. *friend* 132a (tib. *sdug*); 133a (very freely tib. *'phaṅs*?)

sūcī- f. *needle* 9c (tib. *khab*)

√skhal (1, *skhalati*) *to stumble* 114d (skhalanti na; tib. *chud zos mi 'gyur ro*); 117b (daivopahatāḥ skhalanti kartavya; tib. *ñams su len par mi byed na* renders another text)

stana- m. *female breast* 63c (tib. *nu*)

stabdha- ppp. of √stambh *firmly fixed, supported; stiff, unbendable* 12b (tib. *kheṅs*); 101b (tib. *btsan*)

√stu (2, *stauti*) *to praise, extol* 11b (stotum; tib. *bsṅags*)

stuti- f. *praise, eulogy* 39a (tib. *stod*)

√styai (1, *styāyate*) *to stiffen, grow dense, coagulate* 86d (styāyate; tib. *'khyag par byed*)

strī- f. *woman, lady* 63c, 120a (tib. *bud med*)

sthalī f. *soil, ground; place* 16c (tib. *than*)

√sthā (1, *tiṣṭhati*) *to stand, rest* 120b (tiṣṭhati no; freely tib. *spaṅ*)

sthita- ppp. of √sthā *standing, situated, placed* 120d (tib. *gnas pa'i*)

sthiti- f. *staying, abiding, stay, residence* 21b (na sthitiṃ ... labhate; tib. *gnas pa med*)

sthira- adj. *firm, hard, solid* 80a (tib. *brtan*)

sthiratā- f. *hardness; stability, permanence* 128b (tib. *brtan pa*)

stheyas- (compar. of *sthira-*) *firmer, stronger; constant, lasting* 52b (tib. *brtan pa*)?

√spṛś (6, *spṛśati*) *to touch, feel with the hand* 13c (spṛśati; tib. *reg par byed*)

sphaṭika- m. *crystal, quartz* 26c (tib. *śel*)

sphuṭa- adj. *open; distinct, clear* 35c (tib. *gsal*)

√sphur (6, *sphurati*) *to tremble; flash, glitter; become displayed or expanded* 10c (sphuranti; tib. **spa pa*); 18b (sphurati; skt. *grags pa*); 40d (sphurad°; tib. *n. e.*)

√smṛ (1, *smarati*) *to remember, recollect* 8b (smaranti; tib. *dran par 'gyur*)

sravaṇa- nt. *sstreaming, flowing, outflow* 51c (contextually tib. *skyon*)

sravantī- f. *flowing water, river* 20b (tib. *chu*)

√sru (1, *sravati*) *to flow* 113a (contextually tib. *smra ba*)

sva- pron. *own* 72b, 124b (tib. *raṅ gi*); 76d (tib. *raṅ*); 131a (tib. *raṅ la*); 133c (svam āśrayam; freely tib. *yo byad bcas*); 134b, 137b (tib. *n. e.*)

svapna- m. *sleep; dream* 130c (tib. *rmi lam*)

svabhāva- m. *own condition, natural state, disposition* 53a (tib. *raṅ bźin*)

svayam adv. *by one's self, alone* 50d (tib. *raṅ*); 70d (tib. *de ñid*); 71c (tib. *raṅ ñid*); 74c (tib. *ṅaṅ gis*); 89a (tib. *n. e.*)

svalpa- adj. *very small, little* 52d (tib. *'phran tshegs*); 54c (tib. *chuṅ *ṅu*)

svādu- adj. *sweet* 135c (svādu śuci vā; tib. *gtsaṅ mi gtsaṅ* renders as if *śucy aśuci vā)

svāmin- m. *owner, master, lord* 82b (tib. *rje dpon*)

svāsthya- nt. *self-dependence, health, well-being* 84a (tib. *raṅ ñams*)

H

haṃsa- m. *goose, swan* 2c, 4d (tib. *ṅaṅ pa*)

hata- ppp. of √han *struck, beaten, defeated* 17b (śatahato; freely rendered as tib. *rgud pas*)

√han (2, *hanti*) *to strike, hit; destroy, ruin* 106b (hanti; tib. *chud gson byed*); 132d (hanti; tib. *gsod par byed*)

hara- m. *'Seizer' name of Śiva* 94d (tib. *drag po*)

hasita- nt. *laughing, laughter* 88d (tib. *'dzum*)

hasta- nt. *hand* 73c (tib. *lag pa*)

√hā (3, *jahāti*) *to leave, abandon* 47b (na ... jahati; tib. *spoṅ mi byed*); 134b (na jahāti; tib. *'dor mi byed*)

hi adv. *for, because* 5c, 48a, 56c (tib. *n. e.*); 72d (tib. *n. e.*)?

hiṃsra- m. *savage being* 126a (tib. *gnod byed*)

hiṃsratā- f. *savageness, destructiveness* 12b (tib. *'tshe*)

hita- (ppp. of √dhā) nt. *benefit, advantage, profit, welfare* 14b (hitāya kalpate; tib. *phan btags*); 69a, 102b (tib. *phan pa*); 85c (tib. **phan*)

hima- m. *cold, frost* 61d (tib. *ba mo*)

√hṛ (1, *harati*) *to take away, carry off* 140a (harantaḥ; strangely tib. *naṅ byed*, see notes)

hṛdaya- nt. *heart* 129a (tib. *sñin*)

hetu- m. *cause, reason* 41a (tib. *rgyu*); 75b (tib. *ched*); 137b (tib. *'byuṅ*)

heman- nt. *gold* 87c (tib. *chab rom* 'ice, frozen water' as if **himasya* interpreted); 123d (tib. *gser*)

hotṛ- m. *sacrificer, priest* 133c (tib. *sbyin sreg mkhan*)

Tibetan-English-Sanskrit

KA

ka śa *Kāsa grass* 89d (skt. *kāsa*)

ku la'i ri *chief mountain-range* 80a (skt. *kulagiri*)

kun *all, every, each; whole* 1b (skt. **sarva*); 1c (skt. *samantāt*); 70b (skt. *sarvārtha*); 85b (kun la; skt. *sarva-*); 118a (kun la; skt. *sarvatra*)

kun tu *everywhere* 3a (skt. **prāyaḥ*); 111a, 119a (skt. *sarvatra*)

kur byin da (transliteration of skt. *kuruvinda*) *ruby* 3d (skt. *kuruvinda*)

kyaṅ (sandhi form of *yaṅ*) 14a, 24b, 26b, 28d, 36a, 45b, 54c, 65a, 71a, 72a, 81d, 87a, 90a, 92b, 92d, 99b, 103a, 117a, 117c, 120a, 120c, 122b, 134a, 136c, 140a (skt. *api*); 19c, 46c, 70c, 98b, 106c (skt. n. e.); 21c (skt. *eva*); 95c, 98c (skt. *ca*)
→ 'on kyaṅ
→ dag kyaṅ

klad pa *head* 68c (skt. *śiras*)

dka' ba *(to be) difficult* 36b (skt. *duḥ-*); 52b (dbye dka'; translation of wrongly separated skt. *mṛdur bhede!*); 53b, 78b[1], 83b, 140b (skt. *dur-*); 78b[2] (skt. *a-*); 91b (skt. *duś-*); *pains, exertion, hardship, suffering* 74b (skt. *duḥkha*)

dkar po *white* 74d (skt. *śukla*)

dkar ba *white* 31c (skt. *śukla*)

dkon pa *rare, scarce* 90b (skt. *durlabha*); 90d (skt. *alpa*)

dkyil *middle; sphere* 119d (skt. *madhya*)
→ zla dkyil

dkyil 'khor *circle, disk* 66c (skt. *maṇḍala*)

bkur → 'khur ba

bkur sti *honour, respect, reverence* 112c (skt. *māna*)

bkra śis *happiness* 57b (free for skt. *lakṣman*)?

bkren pa *poor, indigent* 139a (skt. *kraśīyas*)

skad → rgya gar skad du, bod skad du

skad cig *(for a) moment* 106d (skt. *kṣaṇena*)

skar ma *star* 107c (skt. *tārā*)

skud pa *thread, yarn* 9d (skt. *tantu*)

skems pa *to make dry, dry up* 11c (skems par byed; skt. *śoṣayati*); 36d (skems par; skt. *kṣapayitum*); 61d (skems par byed; free for skt. *dahati*); 98c (skems byed; skt. *ucchoṣayati*)

skom pa *to thirst, be thirsty* 44c (śin tu skom pas; skt. *atitṛṣitā*)

skyar	→ chu skyar
skye ba	*to be born; become; arise* 16a (bskyed pa; skt. *udayati*); 47d (skye; skt. -*vṛddhi*-); 125b (skye; skt. *janayati*)
skye bo	*human being, man* 3b, 8a, 51a, 107a (skt. *jana*); 28b, 38c (skt. *jantu*); 35a (skt. n. e.) → mi srun skye bo
skye bo ṅan pa	*evil being, bad person* 11a (skt. *khalajana*); 89b, 110b (skt. *durjana*); 91b (skt. *laghavo ... narā*)
skye bo dam pa	*noble being* 7a, 9b, 11b, 61a (skt. *sajjana*); 62b (skt. *satpuruṣa*); 87a (skt. *sujana*)
skyed	*growth, increase; producing* 26b (skt. *mahiman;* is *skyed* a corruption of *che*?)
skyed pa	*to generate, produce, develop, grow* 15c (thaṅ skyed; did the translators read skt. *atidṛdhi* i. o. *ativṛddhi*?); 16b (skyed; skt. n. e.); 44b (bskyed; skt. *kalpayanti*); 57c (bskyed pa; free for skt. *vācyamānaṃ*); 111b (bskyed de; skt. *śaṃsanti*); 145b (bskyed; skt. -*prasūtau*); 145d (tshogs skyed śog; skt. *upacinuta*) → me drod skye⟨d⟩ pa
skyes	→ sgoṅ skyes, lhan cig skyes pa
skyes mchog	*good being* 5b (skt. *satpuruṣa*); 7d (skt. *sujana*)
skyes pa	*human being* 75c (skt. *jana*)
skyes bu	*human being* 30b (is *skyes bu* a corruption of an original *spyod pa* for skt. *carita*?)
skyes bu dam pa	*noble person* 23c (skt. *sat*)
skyo ba	*weariness* 44b (skt. *vaimukhya*); 52a (*skyo ba med; skt. *avirāgin*)
skyoṅ ba	*to guard, keep, protect* 1c (skyoṅ ba; skt. *pānti*); 127c (bskyaṅs nas; skt. *anupālya*)
skyon	*fault, defect* 1b (skt. **doṣa*); 2a, 4a, 7b, 28b, 33b, 38b, 49a, 57c, 59b, 78b, 80b, 89b, 126b (skt. *doṣa*); 23d (skt. *asat*); 51b (skt. *āgas*); 51c (contextually for skt. *sravaṇa*); 137b (skt. *āpad*)
skyon can	*sinful* 121c (skt. *durjana*)
skyon med pa	*sinless, free of faults* 126a (noṅs skyon med pa; skt. *anāgas*)
skyob pa	*to protect, defend, save* 68d (bskyab par; skt. *paritrātum*)
skra	*hair* 15d (skt. *keśa*)
skrag pa	*to be terrified, frightened by* 142d (skrag par mi bya ste; skt. not transmitted)
bskal pa	*kalpa, fabulous period of time* 106a (skt. *kalpa*)
bskyaṅs	→ skyoṅ ba
bskyab	→ skyob pa
bskyed	→ skyed pa

KHA

kha	*face, mouth* 11d (kha … 'bu; skt. *kusumayati*); 39c (skt. *mukha*); 39d (skt. n. e.)
kha cig	*some* 27a, 27b (skt. *kaś cit*); 47a (free for skt. *prāyaḥ*)
khaṅ pa	*house* 93c (skt. *veśma*)
khab	*needle* 9c (skt. *sūcī*)
khu ba	→ tsaṅ śu'i khu ba
khug rta	*swallow, Cātaka bird* 65c (khu⟨g⟩ rta; skt. *cātaka*)
kheṅs pa	*proud, haughty* 12b (skt. *stabdha*); *pride* 138b (skt. *garva*)
khebs	→ 'kheb pa
kho na	*just, exactly, the very* 33c (skt. *eva*)
khoṅ	*the inside, heart* 53b (skt. *prakṛti*)
khwa	*crow* 72d (skt. *balibhuj*)
khyad	*difference, distinction* 7c (skt. *viśeṣaṇa*); 69b (khyad … yod; skt. *bhidyate*)
khyad du gsod pa	*to despise, humiliate* 82b (khyad du gsod par byed; skt. *parābhavati*)
khyad par	*difference, dissimilarity* 69d (skt. *viśiṣṭa*)
khyab pa	*to fill, penetrate* 86c (khyab byed; skt. *vikasati*)
khyi	*dog* 21c (skt. ?); 55d, 60d (skt. *śvan*)
khrims ldan pa	*lawful person* 24a (skt. *suśīla*)
khrel med	*shameless, insolent, impertinent* 53b (skt. *bhaṅgin*; most probably a corruption); 76c, 141c (skt. *kṛtaghna*); 135a (skt. n. e.)
khro ba	*(to be) angry* 41b (khro; skt. *vikāram … eti*)
khrod	→ dur khrod
khrod (pa)	*crowd, assemblage, mulitude* 107a (skt. *-madhye*)
khron pa	*well, spring* 43d, 122d (skt. *kūpa*)
khrol	→ phuṅ khrol
khros	→ 'khro ba, rab tu 'khro ba
mkhan po	*clerical teacher, abbot* 145+ → sbyin sreg mkhan
mkha'	*heaven, sky* 53d (contextually for skt. *-śikhā*); 59c (skt. *kha*); 64c (skt. *divya*) → nam mkha'
mkha' 'gro ma	*the Ḍākinīs* 104c (skt. *ḍākinī*)
mkha' la rgyu (ba)	*bird* 125d (skt. *khaga*)
mkhar ba	*bronze, bell-metal* 123c (skt. *kāṃsya*)

mkhas pa *learned man, wise* 40b, 132a (skt. *vidvāṃs*); 99b, 119b (skt. *paṇḍita*); 121b[1] (free for skt. *guṇin*); 121b[2] (mkhas pas śes; free for skt. *guṇajña*) → 'phan mkhas, mi mkhas pa, bzo bo mkhas pa; sruṅ mkhas pa

mkho ba *(to be) necessary, desirable* 35b (skt. *yogyatā*)

'khu ba *to offend, insult, harm* 96d (*'khu bar byed; skt. *vibhedayati*)

'khums pa → bag 'khums pa

'khur ba (I) *to honour* 12d (bkur; skt. **pūjyante* i. o. skt. *yujyante*!); 94b (mi bkur ro; skt. *mānayituṃ* ... *jānanti na*); 112d (*bkur; skt. *gurur*)

'khur ba (II) *to carry, convey* 94d (bkur; skt. *samudvahati*)

'kheb pa *to cover, spread over* 91d (khebs par byed; skt. *āvṛṇvanti*)

'khor *circle; retinue, attendants* 47a (free for skt. *anurakta*) → dkyil 'khor, btsun mo'i 'khor

'khor ba *to turn round; gather, come together* 47b ('khor ba; free for skt. *samāśritaṃ*)

'khor yug *the Cakravāla mountain range* 120c (skt. *cakravāla*)

'khyag(s) pa *to coagulate, congeal* 86d ('khyag par byed; skt. *styāyate*)

'khyog pa *to be crooked* 28d ('khyogs te; skt. *vakro*)

'khyogs → 'khyog pa

'khruṅ ba *to shoot, sprout, grow* 54b ('khruṅ; skt. *udeti*)

'khro ba *to be angry, get angry* 55c (khros nas; skt. n. e.); 55d (khros nas; skt. *abhikrudhyati*); 88b (khros; skt. *nighnan*); 141d (khros nas; skt. *ruṣā*)

GA

ga → so ga

ga la *whither?, how?* 109d (skt. *kasya cid*)

gaṅ *who, who?, which, which?* 1c (gaṅ ... la; skt. *ye*); 25a, 25b (twice) (gaṅ; skt. *kva*); 34a, 103a, 115a (gaṅ; skt. *yat*); 56a (gaṅ dag gis; skt. *yad*); 83a (gaṅ gis; skt. *yena*); 103c (skt. *api*); 127a (gaṅ; skt. *yataḥ*); 141c (gaṅ; skt. *yo*)

gaṅ du *where, where?* 37c (skt. *yatra*)

gaṅ źig *who, whoever, whosoever; whatever, whatsoever* 1a (skt. *ke 'pi*); 25a (skt. *kva*); 98a (skt. *yo*)

gaṅ la *whither?* 78d (skt. *kutaḥ*)

gus pa *respect, reverence* 75a (skt. *bhakti*); 75b (gus pa min; skt. *asnigdha*)

go 'phaṅ *degree; rank, dignity, high position* 14a (skt. **agraṃ*); 20d (skt. *ucchrāya*); 46a (skt. *pada*); 93b (skt. *parabhāga*); 107b (go 'phaṅ mchog; skt. *parabhāga*)

goṅ short for *goṅ po*

goṅ po *lump, mass, heap* 83c (skt. *piṇḍita*)

gom pa *pace, step* 114d (skt. *pada*)

goms pa *practice* 2b (skt. *abhyāsa*)
⟶ rab tu goms pa

goms par byed pa *to accustom one's self to, practise* 144b (goms par byed pa yis; skt. *paricayena*)

gos *garment, dress* 74c (skt. *vāsa*)
⟶ bgo ba, ṅur smrig gos

gya gyu *crookedness* 28b (skt. *kauṭilya*)

gyu ⟶ gya gyu

gyur ⟶ 'gyur ba

gyen du *upwards* 14c (skt. *dūram*); 82c (gyen du 'thor ba; skt. *udañcann*)

gyoṅ po ⟶ lcags gyoṅ

grags ⟶ 'grag(s) pa

grags pa *fame, glory* 18a, 18b, 112b, 145d (skt. *yaśas*); 72d (źes grags; skt. *kila*)

graṅs med pa *innumerable* 90a (skt. *saṃkhya*)

gri ⟶ spu gri, ral gri

grogs (po) *friend, companion* 68b (skt. *sahāya*)

groṅ *village, hamlet* 121c (groṅ na renders wrongly skt. *kalau* as if *kule*)

groṅ ba *stiff, dead* 60a (skt. *ātura*)

glags *opportunity, occasion, possibility* 58b (glags rñed; peculiar rendering of skt. *samāśrita*)

glaṅ po *elephant* 56d (ma taṅ ka yi glaṅ po; skt. *mātaṅga*)

glo bur *suddenly, accidentally* 2a (skt. *akasmāt*)

dga' ba *to rejoice, be glad* 10b (dga' bar 'gyur; skt. *prītaḥ ... bhavati*); 18d (dga' ba med; skt. *na ... ramaṇīyam*); 24b (dga' bar byed; skt. *ramayati*); 75c (dga' byed pa; skt. *ramayanti*); 75d (dga' ba min; free for skt. *na ... anurajyante*); 144c (dga'; skt. n. e.)

dge legs *good fortune, prosperity* 145b (skt. *śubha*)

dgu *many* 105d (skt. *sarva*)

dgun *winter* 11c (skt. *śiśira*)

dgod pa *to sew, stitch* 9d* (dgog par byed; skt. *pidhatte*)

dgon pa *solitary place, hermitage* 108c (skt. n. e.)

dgos pa *(to be) necessary* 123b (dgos; skt. *alaṃ*); *necessity, want, purpose* 75b (skt. *phala*)
⟶ smos ci dgos

dgra *enemy* 18b, 36a (skt. *ripu*); 55a (skt. *śatru*)

bgo ba *to put on (clothes), wear* 23d (gos pa; skt. *asaṃśliṣṭāḥ*); 110c (bgos nas; skt. n. e.)

bgos ⟶ bgo ba

bgraṅ ba *to number, count, calculate* 97a (drin bgraṅ mi byed; very free for skt. *aprakāśam*?)

bgrod pa *to walk, wander; get through* 83b (bgrod dka'; skt. *durgāṇi*)

mgu ba *to rejoice, be glad, pleased* 53b (mgu dka'; skt. *durupacara*)

mgo (bo) *head* 14d (skt. *śiras*)

'ga' *some, a few, several* 70a (free for skt. *kva cit*); 97d ('ga' 'gas; skt. *ke cid*); 121a ('gas rñed; free for skt. *duṣprāpāḥ*)

'ga' źig *some, someone* 70a (skt. *kaś cit*)

'geṅs pa *to fill* 45c ('gens pa; skt. *saṃdhānāt*)

'go ba *to be infected, be touched* 30a ('go na; skt. *paricayāj*)

'gog pa *to take away, snatch* 63b ('gog; skt. *prabādhante*)

'gyur ba *to become* 19b ('gyur; skt. n. e.); 24d (rgyan du 'gyur; skt. *alaṃkṛtaye*); 30b ('gyur; skt. *bhavanty*); 32d, 39d, 74d ('gyur; skt. *bhavati*); 39c, 115b ('gyur; skt. n. e.); 52d ('gyur ba med; skt. *na ... calati*); 66d ('gyur ba med; skt. *avikṛtaṃ*); 87b (*mñen 'gyur; skt. *mṛdūbhavanti*); 111d ('gyur ro; skt. *bhavati*); 126b ('gyur ba; free for skt. *antaṃ yānti*); 126d ('gyur; skt. *upaiti*); 128b ('gyur; skt. *āpadyate*); 142b ('gyur; skt. not transmitted)
(auxiliary verb) 8b (dran par 'gyur); 10b (dga' bar 'gyur); 14d ('bab par 'gyur); 15b ('byuṅ 'gyur); 19c (rgud gyur); 33d (sel 'gyur min); 35d (sruṅ bar 'gyur); 45d (phog mi 'gyur); 46b (rmoṅs par 'gyur); 62a ('dul 'gyur); 66b (sñoms 'gyur); 74b (dga' 'gyur te); 79d (nub par 'gyur); 81c (mched gyur na); 84b (gson por gyur pa); 84d (gnod par 'gyur); 88c ('chi 'gyur na); 93d (gsal mi gyur); 107d (gsal mi 'gyur); 109a ('phuṅ 'gyur); 114d (chud zos mi 'gyur ro); 116b ('grub par 'gyur ba); 116d (chad par 'gyur); 119d (ran par 'gyur); 130a (ñams par gyur na); 130b (byed par 'gyur); 130d ('chi bar 'gyur); 133c (mched gyur na); 133d ('tshig par 'gyur); 136d (lhuṅ bar gyur); 137d (sreg par 'gyur)
⟶ ci źig 'gyur, gcig tu 'gyur ba, 'jam dpal gźon nur gyur pa

'gye ba *to be divided, separate; disperse* 143d ('gyes; skt. not transmitted)

'gyes ⟶ 'gye ba

'grag(s) pa *to sound, become heard* 18b (grags pa; skt. *sphurati*)

'grib pa *to grow less, decrease, be diminished* 47d ('grib pa; skt. *-kṣaya-*)

'grub pa *to be made ready, be finished, accomplished* 34a ('grub ... yin pa; skt. *sādhayati*); 45b (mi 'grub; skt. *na sādhayanti*); 70b ('grub; skt. *sādhanāya*); 78d ('grub; skt. *bhūtiḥ*); 116b ('grub par 'gyur ba; skt. *siddhiṃ vrajanty*)

'gro ⟶ lag 'gro

'gro ba — *to walk, go, move* 33b ('gro ba; is skt. *vrajanty* understood as **vrajanto* or is it corrupted in the Ms?), 71a ('gro 'dod pa'i; incorrect for skt. *jighāṃsuḥ*); *a being, living creature, world, all beings* 3a ('gro ba mi srun; skt. **khala*); 5a (skt. **jagat*); 39a (skt. *vrajati* !); 15a, 50b, 105a, 127d, 145a (skt. *jagat*); 85b, 90a (skt. *jantu*); 137a (did the translators read skt. *jana* i.o. *jaḍa*?)
→ mkha' 'gro ma, rjes su 'gro ba

rga ba — *old age* 63d* (skt. *jarā*)

rgal ba — *to step, pass; cross* 83b (rgal; skt. *tarati*)

rgud — short for *rgud pa*

rgud pa — *to decline; get weak, frail* 17b (rgud pas; free for skt. *śatahato*); 19c (rgud gyur; skt. *vinipātāś*); 66b (rgud pa na; skt. *nipāte*); 79b (rgud na; skt. *vyasaneṣu*); *trouble, calamity, misery, sorrow* 25b (skt. *vipatti*); 43a (skt. *vyasana*); 48a (skt. *āpad*); 127b (skt. *vipad*)

rgun — *vine, grape* 72c (skt. *drākṣā*)

rgod — → bya rgod, dmu rgod

rgya — *(spider's) web* 59c (skt. *cakra*)

rgya gar skad du — *in Sanskrit* 0

rgya che ba — *great, large, copious* 122c (skt. *pṛthutā*)

rgya mtsho — *sea, ocean* 19a (skt. *salilanidhi*); 80c (skt. *sāgara*); 122c (skt. *udanvat*); 138c (skt. *jaladhi*); 140c (skt. *saras*)

rgya śug — *species of jujube, Badara* 96c (skt. *badara*)

rgyags pa — *arrogance, pride; madness* 30c, 138b (skt. *mada*)

rgyan — *ornament, decoration* 24d (rgyan du 'gyur; skt. *alaṃkṛtaye*)
→ me tog rna rgyan

rgyal — → ṅa rgyal

rgyal po — *king* 93a (skt. *rājan*); 116a (rgyal po'i byin; skt. *prabhaviṣṇu*); 120b (skt. *nṛpa*)

rgyas pa — *to increase, augment* 63c (rgyas la; free for skt. *lakṣmī*)

rgyu — *cause, reason* 41a (skt. *hetu*)

rgyu spun — *warp and woof* 91a (skt. *tantu*)

rgyu ba — *to go, walk, move, wander* 125d (rgyu; free for skt. *kurute*)
→ mkha' la rgyu (ba)

rgyud — *string, cord* 24c (skt. *guṇa*)

rgyun — *flow, current, torrent* 20b (skt. *raya*)

sgeg pa — *coquettishness* 30d ('jo ba sgeg pa; skt. *lalita*)

sgo — *door, gate*
→ tsha sgo

sgo nas *by means of* 35b (expresses the skt. instrumental case); 123a (expresses the skt. ablative case)

sgoṅ skyes *egg-born being* 76a (skt. *aṇḍaja*)

sgom pa *to fancy, imagine; contemplate, consider* 144d (bsgoms nas; skt. *iti*)

sgyur ba *to transform, change* 26d (*tshon gyis bsgyur*; free for skt. *rakta*); 145+ (bsgyur)

sgra *Stimme, Klang* 113d (sgra sñan; skt. *vāśita*)

sgrim pa *to endeavour* 7a (rab bsgrims te; skt. *atiyatnād*)

sgrub pa *to complete, finish, perform, achieve* 27b (sgrub; skt. *sādhayati*); 106a (bsgrubs; skt. *arjitam*); 106c (bsgrubs; skt. *vardhayati*); *task, accomplishment* 123a (skt. *kārya*)

sgron ma *lamp, lantern* 93d, 117c, 132d (skt. *dīpa*); 125c (skt. *ulkā*)

brgya *hundred* 57d, 97d (skt. *śata*); 143d (skt. not transmitted)

bsgoms → sgom pa

bsgrims → sgrim pa, rab tu sgrim pa

bsgrubs → sgrub pa

ṄA

ṅa rgyal *arrogance* 138a (skt. *abhimāna*)

ṅaṅ *nature, essentiality* 2c (skt. **prakṛti*); 74c (ṅaṅ gis; skt. *svayam*); 134b (skt. *jāti*); 136a (skt. *ātman*)

ṅaṅ pa *goose* 2d, 4d (skt. *haṃsa*)

ṅan → mya ṅan

ṅan pa *evil, mean, wicked (being)* 9a, 10a, 17a (skt. *khala*); 13b (skt. *asādhu*); 16b[1], 53c, 123b (skt. *nīca*); 16b[2] (skt. *anudātta*); 22a (skt. *śaṭha*); 58a, 106b (skt. *durjana*); 59a (strangely for skt. *sādhu*); 60b (skt. *dur-*); 61b (skt. *anārya*); 92b (skt. *asadvṛtta*); 103a (skt. *asat*); 103d (wrongly for skt. *kali*)
→ skye bo ṅan pa, bdag ñid ṅan pa, gźuṅ ṅan

ṅan g.yo (can) *cunning (person)* 29b (skt. *śāṭhya*); 63a (skt. *dhūrta*); 96c, 113a, 129a (skt. *śaṭha*)

ṅar can *strong, vigorous* 96a (free for skt. *amla*)

ṅur smrig gos *ochre robe* 110c (skt. *kāṣāya*)

ṅes pa *(to be) certain, true, sure* 31b (ṅes med de; skt. *nāyam ekāntaḥ*); 32b (ma ṅes te; skt. *aniścayo*)

ṅes par *really, certainly* 22c (skt. *eva*)

ṅo *face, countenance, look* 133b (su yi ṅor; unusual for skt. *kva cid*)
→ g.yul ṅo

ṅom pa *to satisfy one's self, be contented* 5b (ṅoms pa med; skt. *na tṛptim āyātaḥ*)

ṅoms → ṅom pa

dṅul chu *quicksilver, mercury* 78c (skt. *rasa*); 128c (skt. *raso ... pāradīyaḥ*)

mṅar ba *sweet* 96d (skt. *madhura*)

mṅon pa *conspicuous, visible; evident* 49d (mṅon; skt. *lakṣyata*)

mṅon par (renders skt. *abhi-*)

mṅon par 'dod pa *to long for* 8d (mṅon par 'dod; skt. *abhilaṣati*)

rṅan can *jeering, disdain* 86b (rṅan can byed; free for skt. *bhṛśaṃ dīpyate*)

rṅubs → dbugs rṅubs pa

rṅon pa *hunter* 110c (skt. *vyādha*)

sṅag pa *to praise, commend, extol* 11b (bsṅags; skt. *stotum*); 119b (bsṅags pa yin; skt. *praśaṃsanti*)

bsṅags → sṅag pa

bsṅal → sdug bsṅal

CA

cad → thams cad

can (possessive particle) → skyon can, ṅan g.yo (can), ṅar can, rṅan can, dri ma can, gdeṅs can, spyi rtol can, sbrul gdug can, yon tan can, g.yon can, lus can, sems can, sems can che ba

ci *what?, how?, why?* 69b (skt. *kathaṃ*)
→ phyin ci log, smos ci dgos

ci ga *what?, why?* 139d (skt. *kim*)

ci nas *out of which or what? by which?* 144c (skt. *kaś cid*)

ci smos *what to say (about) ... not to mention* 88b (skt. *kiṃ punar*)

ci źig 'gyur *how is it possible that ...?* 115d (skt. *kā gurutā* rendered twice?)

ci źig bya *what is the use of ...?* 99b (skt. *kim* with instrumental case)

cig → skad cig, kha cig, thaṅ (g)cig, lhan cig skyes pa

cis *by what?, whereby?* 25d (skt. *kaṃ*); 31d, 60d, 128d (skt. *kiṃ*); 32d (skt. n. e.); 60b (skt. *kiṃ nāma*)

cuṅ zad *little, some* 41a (skt. *alpa*)

ce short for *ce na*

ce na (after words literally quoted) *'if one says so'* 132a (skt. *iti*)

ces bya ba *so called, named* 0 (twice); 145+

gcam bu *artificial, not natural; keen* 51a (free for skt. *paṭu*)?

gcig *one* 57c (skt. *eka*)
→ thaṅ (g)cig, ro gcig

gcig tu *at once, wholly, altogether* 32b (skt. *api*)?
→ dus gcig (tu)

gcig tu 'gyur ba *to be turned into one uniform state; attain* 109d (źig tu ... 'gyur; skt. *yānti*)

gcig pu *alone, single* 70b (skt. *eka*)

gces (pa) *dear, beloved; excellent, precious, valuable* 93a (skt. *pradhāna*); 115d (gces par ma brtsis; skt. *kā gurutā*)?

gcod pa *to cut, cut off; suppress, torment* 6a (gcod; skt. *ghaṭṭana-*); 50c (gcod mi nus; skt. *asamarthā ... chettum*); 53c (gcod byed; skt. *tāpayati*); 70d (gcod par byed; skt. *eti bhidāṃ*); 98a (chad pas gcod; skt. *nigrahasya*)

bcad → thag gcod pa

bcas pa *having, possessing, connected with* 133d (skt. *sva-*)

bcu → phyogs bcu

bcug → 'jug pa

bcud (kyi) len *elixir* 100d (skt. *rasāyana*)?

bcos → bstan bcos

bcos pa *to cure, heal; affect, perform* 78b (bcos dka'; skt. *avidheyam*)

bcos ma *artificial* 17d (skt. *vijāti*)

lcags *iron* 10c (skt. *loha*); 83c (skt. *ayas*)
→ gnam lcags

lcags gyoṅ *hard iron* 124c (free for skt. *mudgara*; perhaps better read *lcags goṅ* 'lump of iron')

lci ba *heavy* 89c (skt. *garayati*)

lce → me lce

CHA

cha → mtshon cha

cha śas *part, portion, share* 120d (perhaps free for skt. *phaṇa*)

chags pa → bag chags

chaṅ ba *grip* 116c* (skt. *muṣṭi*)

chad → 'chad pa

chad pa *punishment* 98a (chad pas gcod; skt. *nigrahasya*)
→ yid chad pa

chab rom *ice, frozen water* 87c (wrongly for skt. *heman*)

char (pa) *rain* 39b (does *char* render a misread or miswritten skt. **varṣaḥ* in *vastu*?); 64c (skt. *ambha*); 98c (skt. *jala*)

chu *water* 4c (skt. **udaka*); 20b (skt. *sravantī*); 33a, 44c, 54d (skt. *salila*); 40c, 65d, 106c (skt. *ambhas*); 43d, 135d (skt. *jala*); 80c (skt. *sarit*); 83c (skt. *ap*); 86c (skt. *vāri*); 122c (skt. n. e.); 129d, 140c (skt. *payas*); 138c (skt. *jalatā*); 143b, 143c (skt. not transmitted)
→ dṅul chu

chu skyar *heron* 126d (skt. *baka*)

chu bo *river* 42c (skt. *jaladhi*)

chu (yi) thigs (pa) *water-drop* 36c (skt. *udabindu*)

chuṅ ṅu *little, small* 54c (chuṅ *ṅu; skt. *svalpa*)

chuṅ ba *little, small* 13a (skt. *aṇu*)

chud za ba *to consume, spend, waste* 114d (chud zos mi 'gyur ro; skt. *skhalanti na*)

chud gson pa *to consume, spend, waste* 106b (chud gson byed; skt. *hanti*)

che ba *big, great* 13b (skt. *mahīyas*); 119c (skt. *atimahat*); *greatness, superiority* 63b (skt. *atyunnata*); 95b (skt. *mahattva*); 95d (skt. *uccais*)
→ rgya che ba, bdag ñid che ba, rab tu che ba, rin po che, sems can che ba

che ba ñid *greatness* 19d (free for skt. *vṛddhi*)

che bdag (ñid) *greatness* 25a (skt. *mahattva*); 106a, 107b, 120a, 123b (skt. *mahat*)

ched du *on account of, because of, for* 32d, 111b (expresses the skt. dative case)

ched (du) yin *on account of, because of, for* 75b (skt. *hetu*); 75d (skt. n. e.)

chen po *big, great* 94a (chen po min pa; skt. *amahātman*); 97b (dad chen; free for skt. *kṣantum*?); 139c (skt. *mahat*)
→ 'jigs byed chen po, bdag ñid chen po, dbaṅ phyug chen po

cher → phal cher

ches pa → yid ches pa

cho rigs *father's lineage, descent by the father's side* 81a (skt. *kulaja*)

chog pa *to be sufficient* 28a (mi chog te; skt. *nālam*); 135b (chog pa med; as if skt. **tṛṣṇāḍhyaḥ* i. o. *tṛṣṇārtaḥ*)

chod → thub chod

chos *doctrine, precept, rightfulness; custom, manner, common usage* 104b ('tsho chos; skt. *vṛttānta*); 112b (skt. *dharma*)

mchu *lip; beak, bill* 72d (skt. *mukha*)

mched pa *to spread, gain ground* 81c (mched gyur na; skt. *samutthito*); 133c (mched gyur na; skt. *udvṛtto*)

mchog *the best, superb* 16a[1] (skt. *ucca*); 16a[2] (skt. *udātta*); 46a (skt. *uccaiḥ*); 86b (skt. *sat*); 107b (skt. *para*)

'chad pa *to be cut* 116d (chad par 'gyur; skt. *chinatti*)

'char ba *to arise, appear, shine* 3b (*char bar byed; skt. *[yā]ti sāphalyam*); 66c ('char ba; skt. *udaye*); 79d (śar ba; skt. *uditaḥ*); 119c ('char tshe; contextually for skt. *prabhā*)

'chi bdag *the God of Death* 145c (skt. *mṛtyu*)

'chi ba *to die* 88c ('chi 'gyur na; skt. *mārayati*); 130d ('chi bar 'gyur; skt. *mumūrṣuḥ*)

'chos pa → tshul 'chos (pa)

JA

ji ltar (short for *ji lta bar*) *as, in what manner* 17a (skt. n. e.); 49c, 126a, 129b (skt. *yathā*)

ji bźin *as, like* 2d (skt. **iva*)

ji srid *as long as* 142a (skt. not transmitted); 145c (skt. *yāvat*)

'jam pa *(to be) soft, smooth, tender, mild* 87d (skt. n. e.); 129a ('jam tshig; skt. *sāmavacana*)

'jam dpal gźon nur gyur pa 'Mañjuśrī who has become young', i. e. *Mañjuśrī who lives in celibacy* 0

'jal ba *to weigh* 101c ('jal ba'i; skt. *upaiti*)

'jig rten *world* 2b, 8c, 85c, 104a (skt. *loka*)

'jig pa *to destroy, cut to pieces, divide* 91b (gźig par dka'; skt. *duśchedāḥ*)

'jigs pa *danger* 31b, 32b (skt. *bhaya*)

'jigs byed chen po *very frightening; name of Śiva* 32c (skt. *mahābhairava*)

'jil ba *to expel, remove; extinguish* 33b ('jil; skt. *śamaṃ*)
→ za 'jil

'jug pa *to go, walk in, enter* 86d (bcug; skt. *niṣṭhyūtaṃ*); 114c (źugs pa; skt. *gantṝṇām*); 135c (lam du źugs pa; skt. *pathika*)

'juṅs pa *miser* 72a, 84a (skt. *kṛpaṇa*)

'jo ba *beauty, charm* 30d ('jo ba sgeg pa; skt. *lalita*)

'jog pa *to put, place* 36c (bźag pa; skt. *niṣiktam*)

'joms pa *to conquer, subdue; destroy* 37c ('joms byed; skt. *dārayati*); 55a ('joms; skt. *nipatanti*)

rje → sñiṅ rje, rdo rje, gśin rje

rje dpon *master, lord* 82b (skt. *svāmin*)

rjes *trace, track, mark* 34cd (zos pa'i rjes ... 'byuṅ ba; skt. *utkirati*)

rjes su 'gro ba *to follow* 104a (rjes su 'gro 'dod par; skt. *anugantukāmair*)

rjes su 'braṅ ba *to follow* 23b (rjes su 'braṅ; skt. *eti*)

ljoṅs → yul ljoṅs

ÑA

ña	*fish* 140c (skt. *matsya*)
ña gaṅ ba	*full moon* 49c (ña ba; skt. *pūrṇa*)
ña phyis	*oyster shell* 39d (skt. *śukti*)
ña ba	short for *ña gaṅ ba*
ñam(s)	*soul* → raṅ ñams
ñams pa	*(to be) injured, hurt; spoiled, damaged* 17c (skt. n. e.); 19d (ñams; skt. *vyabhicaranti*); 35b (ñams; skt. *vināśaṃ ... yānti*); 114b (mi ñams; skt. *avihatā bhavati*); 130a (ñams par gyur na; skt. *vināśa āpanne*); *degeneration, calamity* 94a (skt. *vinipatita*) → rab tu ñam(s) thag pa
ñam(s) thag pa	*(to be) tormented, suffering, exhausted* 68a (skt. *kṛcchra*); 83a (ñam thag pas; skt. *sīdati*); 95b (ñam thag; skt. *kṛcchre*)
ñams su len pa	*to take to heart; apply* 117b (ñams su len par mi byed na; very free for skt. *daivopahatāḥ skhalanti kartavye*)
ñi zer	*sunbeam* 23c (skt. *ravikara*)
ñi ma	*sun* 5d, 79d, 119c, 130d (skt. *savitṛ*); 8c, 91d (skt. *dinakara*); 19a, 107d, 127c (skt. *pūṣan*); 29c (skt. n. e.); 36d (skt. *arka*); 66c (skt. *bhānu*); 67c, 85c, 98c (skt. *ravi*); 69c (contextually for skt. *udito ... yaḥ*); 79c (contextually for skt. *udayati*)
Ñi ma sbas pa	*Name des Verfassers* 145+ (skt. *Ravigupta*)
ñid	*just, the very; only* 2b, 11d, 82d, 89b, 98b, 120c (skt. *eva*); 55a, 94d (skt. n. e.); 98c, 134a (skt. n. e.)?; (used to denote abstract nouns) 19d (che ba ñid); 99a (don ñid); 141a (phyug po ñid)? → de ñid, bdag ñid, bdag ñid ṅan pa, bdag ñid che ba, bdag ñid chen po, raṅ ñid
ñin re	*daily* 67a (skt. *pratidinam*)
ñes pa	*moral fault, offence, sin* 142b (skt. not transmitted); 145a (skt. *doṣa*)
ñon moṅs	*misery, trouble, pain, defilement* 142c, 143a (skt. not transmitted)
gñis	*two, both* 7c (expresses a skt. dual form); 99c, 105a, 105b (skt. *dva*); 137c (skt. *ubhaya*)
gñen	*kinsman, relative* 132a (skt. *bandhu*)
gñug	→ sñugs thuṅ ba
mñen pa	*flexible, pliable; soft* 85b (mñen par byed; skt. *avanamante*); *87b (skt. *mṛdu*)
rñed pa	*to get, obtain, acquire* 46a (rñed na; skt. *adhitiṣṭhāṃl*); 58b (rñed; skt. *-āśrito*); 121a ('gas rñed; free for skt. *duṣprāpāḥ*); 141a (rñed pas; skt. *prāpya*)

sñan pa *well-sounding, sweet* 96c (skt. n. e.); 113a (skt. *madhu*); 113d (sgra sñan; skt. *vāśita*)

sñiṅ rje *kindness, mercy, compassion* 85a (skt. *kṛpā*)

sñin *heart* 129b (skt. *hṛdaya*)

sñugs thuṅ ba *of short duration, momentary* 53a (gñug thuṅ; skt. *kṣaṇika*)

sñegs pa *to hasten, run; strive, strugle for* 55d (sñegs; skt. *abhikrudhyati*)

sñoms pa *to make even, level, equalize* 54d (sñoms; skt. *vikasati*; uncertain); 66b (sñoms 'gyur; skt. *samānaṃ bhavati*)

brñan → gzugs brñan

brñas thabs *humiliation* 42b (brñas thabs sna tshogs byed; free for skt. *dhuraṃ puraḥ prakaṣanti*); 65b (skt. *paribhava*)

brñas pa *contempt* 115b (skt. *avajñā*)

TA

ta la *the palmyra tree* 34b (bya rog ta lar; literally for skt. *kākatāliyam* 'accidentally, coincidentally')

tiṅ ṅe 'dzin *meditation, contemplation* 143b (skt. not transmitted)

tiṅ 'dzin short for *tiṅ ṅe 'dzin*

til mar *sesamum, sesamum-oil* 54c, 86c (skt. *taila*)

tog → bul tog, me tog, lo tog

gtaṅ la 'bebs pa *to put in order, arrange; edit* 145+ (gtan la phab pa'o)

gtum pa *ferocity, rage; ferocious* 29a (skt. *tīkṣṇa*)

gtum po *fierce* 133a (very unusual for skt. *asat*)

gtoṅ ba *to let, leave, abandon, renounce* 58d (mi gtoṅ ṅo; skt. *na muñcanti*); 76d (mi gtoṅ ṅo; free for skt. *naidhante*)
→ sbyin gtoṅ sems

gtor ba *to strew, scatter; cast, throw* 14c (gtor na; skt. *utkṣiptam*); 143c (gtor na; skt. not transmitted)

btags → 'dogs pa, phan 'dogs pa

btab → 'debs pa

rta → khug rta

rtag tu *always* 1d, 5d, 61d (skt. *sadā*); 23d (translates skt. *sadā* i. o. *sad-*); 39b (does *rtag tu* render a misread or miswritten skt. **sadā* in *sadasatoḥ*?)

rtags *sign, token, mark, characteristic* 95d (skt. *cihna*)

rten *hold, support; abode, residence* 76d (skt. *āśraya*)

rten pa *to keep, adhere to* 16c (brten pa; skt. *samāśrayate*); 47c (brten; skt. *vahati*); 137d (brten nas; skt. *niśritya*)

rtog pa	*to consider, examine* 51d (rtog par byed; skt. *nirūpayati*); 135d (rtog; skt. *vicārayati*)
rtogs pa	*to perceive, understand, recognize* 38a (rtogs par sla ba; skt. *subodham*)
rtol ba	→ spyi rtol can
lta ba	*to look, observe, take notice* 51b (lta; skt. n. e.); 80d (ltos; skt. *paśyata*); 133b (mi blta; skt. *na ... apekṣā*); 144c (lta'i phyir; skt. *vilokayan*)
lta bu	*like, such as* 67c, 78c (skt. *iva*)
lta bur	*like, as* 9a, 131a (skt. *yathā*); 67b, 121a (skt. *iva*); 102d (skt. n. e.)
ltar	→ ji ltar, lta bur, de ltar, 'di ltar
ltuṅ ba	*to fall, fall down* 71d (ltuṅ bar byed pa; skt. *patati*); 118a (ma lhuṅ; skt. *-pātaḥ ... na*); 136d (rtsal na lhuṅ bar gyur; not very faithful for skt. *nāste na cotpatati*)
ltogs pa	*hungry* 60d (skt. *kṣudupatapta*)
ltos	→ lta ba
sta re	*axe, hatchet* 50d (skt. *khaḍga*)
stag	*tiger* 108d (skt. *vyāghra*)
star ka	*walnut* 27d (skt. *kṣīrī*)
sti ba	→ bkur sti
stug(s) po	*thick, opaque, solid, dense* 107c (skt. *ghana*)
steṅ na	*above, on the surface* 42c (skt. *upari*); 83d (skt. n. e.)
sten pa	*to adhere, stick* 36b (bsten; skt. *saṃsṛto*); 89a (sten byed de; skt. *bhajanti*); 89b, 123d (sten; skt. n. e.); 95b (bsten; free for skt. *asaṃbhramaḥ*); 144a (bsten pa'i; skt. *bhajeta*)
ster ba	*to bestow, present, grant* 97b (ster; skt. *dātum*); 141d (mi ster; skt. *na ... bhajanty arthāḥ*)
stes dbaṅ	*power of fate* 34d (short for *stes dbaṅ gis*; skt. *daivāt*)
stobs ldan	*strong, powerful* 142b (skt. not transmitted)
stod	*upper, higher* 10b (stod rigs; skt. *kulīn*)
stod pa	*to praise, commend, load, extol, glorify* 14a (bstod drags; free for skt. *atisatkāra*); 22a (bstod; skt. *atisatkṛtā*); 39a (stod; skt. *stuti*)
ston pa	*to show; teach, explain* 30d (ston par byed; skt. *upadiśati*); 62d (ston no; skt. *uśanty*); 75a (ston pa; skt. *upadeśayanti*)
brtan pa	*firm, steadfast; lasting* 52b (skt. *stheyas*); 78a (mi brtan; skt. *asthira*); 80a (skt. *sthira*); 128a (mi brtan pa; skt. *capala*); *firmness* 128b (skt. *sthiratā*)
brten	→ rten pa
bstan bcos	*science* 100a (skt. *śāstra*)
bsten	→ sten pa
bstod	→ stod pa

THA

tha mal pa *ordinary, usual* 48b, 48d (skt. n. e.)

thag gcod pa *to decide, determine; be sure* 15b (thag bcad pa; is skt. *parabhāga* understood as if *paramārtha*?)

thag pa → ñam(s) thag pa, rab tu ñam(s) thag pa

thag riṅ (po) *distant* 41d (skt. *dūra*); 51b (skt. *dūre*); 71b (skt. *sudūram*)

thaṅ *plain, steppe* 16d (skt. *sthalī*); 46d (free for skt. *sama*)

thaṅ (g)cig *moment, a little while, instant* 106b (skt. *ekapade*)

thaṅ po *tense, tight, firm* 15c (thaṅ skyed; did the translators read skt. *atidṛḍhi* i. o. *ativṛddhi*?)

thabs *way, manner, mode; opportunity, chance* 45a (thabs daṅ bral ba; skt. *anupāya*); 87b (skt. *yoga*); 87d, 116b (skt. *upāya*)
→ brñas thabs

thams cad *whole, all* 104b, 105c (skt. *sarva*)

thal → rdo thal

thigs pa *drop* 54c (skt. *bindu*)
→ chu (yi) thigs (pa)

thibs non *magic power* 42b (free for skt. *ākramya*)

thuṅ ba → sñugs thuṅ ba

thub chod *act of rashness; inappropriate deed* 40a (*thub chod byed* for skt. *asthānābhiniveśin*)

thub pa *to be able* 56b (thub; skt. n. e.)

thog *thunderbolt, lightning* 37c (skt. *mahāśani*)

thog mar *at first, first* 14d (skt. *kevalam*); 82a (skt. *prathamataram*); 82d, 111a (skt. *ādau*)

thogs pa *to bear aloft* 22d (thogs; skt. *dhṛto*)

thob pa *to find, get, obtain* 107b (thob; skt. *yānti*)

thos pa *learning, study* 138a (skt. *śruta*)

mtha ma *limit, bound, border* 127d (skt. *anta*)

mthar phyin pa *to accomplish, fulfill* 37a (skt. *paryantaṃ ... gacchati*)

mthu *power, strength* 48b, 50a (skt. *śakti*); 70a (skt. *balīyaṃs*); 116a (skt. *sāmarthya*); 116c (mthus; expresses the skt. instrumental case)

mthun pa *to be adequate, appropriate* 41a (mi mthun byas pa; skt. *aprakṛti*); 62c (skt. *anurūpa*)

mtho ba *high, lofty, elevated* 46c (skt. *agra*); 64a (lhag par srid mtho; skt. *abhyunnata*); 79a (mtho na; skt. *udaye*); 101d (mtho ba ma yin; skt. *vinonnatiṃ*)
→ 'phaṅ mtho ba, gzeṅs mtho

mthoṅ ba *to see, behold* 10a (mthoṅ; skt. *dṛṣṭvā*); 46d (mthoṅ; skt. *paśyati*); 51c, 99a (mi mthoṅ; skt. *na paśyati*); 73b (mthoṅ na; skt. *dṛṣṭvā*); 103b (mthoṅ na; skt. *paśyed*); 117d (mi mthoṅ; skt. *paśyati na*); 122a (ma mthoṅ; skt. *adṛṣṭa-*); 130d (mthoṅ na; skt. *paśyati*); 140d (mthoṅ ba med; skt. *prajñāyante ... na*)

mthon po *high, elevated* 85d (skt. *ucca*)

'thuṅ ba *to drink* 43d ('thuṅ bar byed; skt. *abhyuddharanti*); 44c ('thuṅ na; skt. *pibanta*); 65d ('thuṅ bar mi byed do; skt. *na pibanti*); 140c ('thuṅ; skt. *pibanto*); 140d ('thuṅ *ṅo; skt. n. e.)

'thul ba *to rise, spread* 41d ('thul bar byed; skt. *unnamati*)

'thor ba *to be scattered, be dispersed* 82c (gyen du 'thor ba; skt. *udañcann*); 82d ('thor byed; skt. *utthāpakam*)

DA

da ltar *now, at present* 121a (skt. *saṃprati*)?

dag 'gyur *to become pure* 74b (skt. *śudhyati*)

dag kyaṅ 71c (skt. *sarva*? see note)

dag pa *clean, pure* 110a (skt. *śuddhatā*)
→ rnam par dag pa

dags → ri dags

daṅ por *firstly, first of all* 63a (skt. *prathamataram*); 63d (skt. *ādau*)

dad *faith* 97b (dad chen; free for skt. *kṣantum*?)

dad pa *to become faithful, believe* 115a (skt. *ma dad*; skt. *na prasīdanti*)

dam pa *(to be) good, noble* 29a ([b]dam; skt. *varam*); *noble, good person* 13a, 124a (skt. *sādhu*); 45b, 47b, 52c, 54a, 78d, 85a, 92b (skt. *sat*); 89a (skt. *guṇin*); 142a (skt. not transmitted)
→ skye bo dam pa; skyes bu dam pa

dam por *strongly, firmly* 116c (skt. *dṛḍham*)

dam tshig *vow* 104c (skt. *samaya*)

dar ba *to be diffused, spread; increase* 66a (dar ba; skt. *atyucchritau*)

dug *poison* 6c, 39c, 60a, 76b (skt. *viṣa*)

duṅ *shell* 134c (skt. *śaṅkha*)

dud pa *smoke* 31d (free for skt. *kajjala*)

dum bu *piece* 143d (skt. not transmitted)

dur khrod *cemetery, burial-ground* 2c (skt. **śmaśāna*)

dus *time* 11c (skt. *samaya*); 12c (dus na; skt. **kāle* instead of skt. *kalau*!); 48a (skt. n. e.); 127d (skt. *yuga*)

dus gcig (tu) *at one and the same time, together* 91c (skt. *yugapad*)

de *that, that one* 1d (de la; skt. *tebhyaḥ*); 6b, 6d, 34b, 103b (de; skt. *tat*); 16b (de; skt. *etat*); 46b (de la; free for skt. *tattveṣu* or did the translators read **tat teṣu*?); 63d (de la; skt. *teṣv*); 69d (skt. *so*); 98b (skt. *sa*); 99b (des; skt. *tena*); 103b, 127b (de las; skt. *tasmāt*); 109b (de; skt. *ayam*); 136b, 136d (de las; skt. n. e.); 139b (de; skt. *eṣā*); 141c (de la; skt. *taṃ*)

de ñid *this very, exactly this* 44d (skt. *eva*); 70d (skt. *svayam*); 83d (skt. *tad eva*)

de lta (bu) *so, like that, in this way* 40b (skt. *eva*); 48d, 49b, 131b (skt. *tathā*)

de ltar *so, in that manner* 126c, 129c (skt. *tathā*); 145a (skt. *iti*)

de bźin *so, thus* 9b (skt. *tathā*); 20d, 129d (skt. n. e.); 112c (renders skt. **tathaiva* i. o. *tathāpi*)

de srid *so long, to such a length of time* 68b (skt. *tāvat*); 142b (skt. not transmitted)

des pa *fine, delicate; noble, chaste* 8b, 25b (skt. *sādhu*); 67b (skt. *mṛdu*)

don *sense, meaning; idea, notion; purpose, aim; affair* 27b, 45b (skt. *kārya*); 34a (skt. *prayojana*); 99a (skt. *tattva*); 114b (bla 'og gi ... don; free for skt. *prabhuśakti*)

don med *senseless, fruitless* 100b (skt. n. e.)?; 100d (skt. n. e.)

drag po *severe; Rudra* 94d (skt. *hara*); 126b (drag po'i skyon; free for skt. *vāgdoṣa*)

drags *very, much, greatly* 14a (skt. *ati-*)

draṅ po *straight* 45d (skt. *ṛju*)

draṅ ba *straightness* 28a (skt. *ṛjutā*); 28c (skt. *ṛju*)

dran pa *to think of, remember* 8b (dran par 'gyur; skt. *smaranti*)

dri *odour, smell, scent* 23b (free for skt. *rūpa*); 48d (dri zim; skt. *gandha*); 77d (dri rab źim; skt. *surabhin*)

dri ma *dirt, impurity* 143a (skt. not transmitted)

dri ma can *dirty* 74c (skt. *malina*)

dri mi źim pa *disagreeable smell, stench* 60c (skt. *durgandhi*)

drin *kindness, favour, grace* 97a (drin bgraṅ mi byed; very free for skt. *aprakāśam*?)

dre'u *small (female) mule* 76b (skt. *aśvatarī*)

dregs pa *(to be) proud, haughty, arrogant; pride, haughtiness, arrogance* 79a (skt. *mada*)

drod *warmth, heat* 56b (drod mi thub; free for skt. *madayanti*)

gdug pa *poisonous*12a (skt. *tīkṣṇa*)
→ sbrul gdug (can)

gduṅ(s) ba *to feel pain, be pained, tormented, afflicted* 25d (mi gduṅ; skt. *na tāpayati*); 129b (gduṅ byed pa; skt. *tāpayati*); 131a (yid gduṅs ... min; skt. *na yānti khedaṃ*)

gdul → 'dul ba

gdeṅs can *snake* 120d (skt. *śeṣa*)

bdag *myself, one's self* 139a (skt. *aham*); 139b (bdag la; skt. *aham*)
→ 'chi bdag, che bdag (ñid)

bdag ñid *I myself; the thing itself, substance, essence* 80d (shortly for skt. *mahattva*)

bdag ñid ṅan pa *bad-natured person* 125a (skt. *durātman*)

bdag ñid che ba *noble-hearted being* 48a, 49a, 122a (skt. *mahat*)

bdag ñid chen po *noble-hearted being* 12c, 66a, 94a, 127a, 144a (skt. *mahat*); 26a (skt. *mahātman*); 37a (tib. *bdag ñid brtsam(s) pa* emended with *bdag ñid *chen po* for skt. *mahat*); 95d (skt. *mahattva*)

bdag po *owner* 140a (nor gyi bdag po for skt. *dhanam adhikṛta* as if read as **dhanādhikārāḥ*)

bda' ba *to drive, chase, carry away* 41c (bdas pa; skt. *vāti*)

bdar rdo *whetstone* 50c (skt. *śilā*)

bdar ba *to polish, grind, whet* 50d (bdar bar byed; skt. *tejayati*)

bdas → bda' ba

bde ba *to be happy* 105a (bde; skt. *sukhinau*)

bde bar *happily, comfortably* 136c (skt. *sukham*)

bde legs *well-being* 109d (skt. *kṣema*)

bden pa *to be true* 109b (bden; skt. *satyam*)

bdog pa *to get, take possession of; be in possession of* 72a (bdog; skt. *prāptān*)

mda' *arrow* 28c, 45d (skt. *śara*); 71c (skt. *bāṇa*)
→ sraṅ mda'

mdun du *before, in front of* 17c (skt. *puras*)

'dab gśog *flag-feather, quill-feather* 71a (skt. *pakṣa*)

'dam *mud, mire, swamp* 92c (skt. *paṅka*)

'dam bu *reed* 27c ('dam bu; skt. *śara*)

'da' ba *to pass over, go beyond; abandon, disappear* 20c ('das pa; skt. *gatā*)

'das → 'da' ba

'di *this* 2b, 132a, 139a, 144d (skt. *ayam*); 7c ('di gñis; skt. *anayoḥ*); 25c (skt. *iyaṃ*); 105a, 105b (skt. *eva*); 133a ('dis; skt. *anena*); 144c ('di la; skt. *etad*)

'di ltar *so, thus, in this manner* 6c (free for skt. *yat*)

'dug pa *to sit; stay* 46c ('dug pas; skt. *ārūḍhaḥ*)

'dum pa *to be reconciled with* 97c ('dum byed; skt. *atisaṃdhātuṃ*)?; 124b ('dum byed; skt. *saṃdadhāty*); 124d ('dum mi nus; skt. *na saṃdhāne*)

'dul ba *to tame, subdue* 36a (gdul bar sla ba'i; skt. *susādhyo*); 36b (gdul bar dka'; skt. *duḥsādhyaḥ*); 62b ('dul 'gyur; skt. *praśamāya*); 111b ('dul ba'i ched du; skt. *saṃnataye*)

'debs pa *to cast, throw* 54b (btab; skt. *uptaṃ*)

'dogs pa *to bind, fasten, tie to; fix, attach* 59b (btags; skt. *dattvā*)
→ phan 'dogs pa

'dod ldan *lustful* 30c (skt. *kāminī*)

'dod pa *to want, wish, desire* 67d ('dod; wrongly interpreted skt. *kāmam*); 71a ('dod pa'i; expresses the skt. desiderative form); 104a ('dod pas; skt. -*kāmair*); *desire, wish* 105c (skt. *icchā*); 105d (skt. *īpsā*)
→ mṅon par 'dod pa

'dor ba *to throw away, abandon; refuse, reject, despise* 22b ('dor mi srid; skt. *ujjhanti jātu na*); 134b ('dor mi byed; skt. *na jahāti*); 134d (mi 'dor ro; skt. *na ... ujjhati*)

'dra ba *similar, equal* 46d (skt. n. e.); 52c, 124c (skt. *iva*)
→ mi 'dra ba

'drid pa *to deceive, cheat; entice* 75d ('drid pa'i ched yin; contextually for skt. *anurajyante*)

'dris pa *to be accustomed to, be acquainted with* 44a ('dris pa'i; skt. *paricayād*); 109a ('dris byas; skt. *kṛtapraṇayāḥ*); 110d ('dris nas; skt. *viśvāsya*)

'dre ba *to be mixed with* 4a ('dres na; skt. *vyāmiśrān*)

'dres → 'dre ba

rdul *dust* 13c, 41c, 57c (skt. *rajas*); 82c (sa rdul; skt. *dhūli*)

rdul phran *the minutest particle* 64d (skt. *rajas*)

rdo *stone* 143c (skt. not transmitted)

rdo rje *thunderbolt* 70c (skt. *vajra*); 139d (skt. *vajra*)

rdo (ba) *stone* 55d (skt. *loṣṭha*)
→ bdar rdo

rdo thal *chalk, calcined stone* 143c (skt. not transmitted)

rdog pa *step, footstep, kick* 102c (skt. *caraṇa*)

ldaṅ ba *to rise, get up* 64d (ldaṅ ba; skt. *samutpatiṣṇu*)

ldan pa *possessed of, endowed with* 1b (ldan; skt. **anvita*); 17b, 17c, 24a, 55a, 57b, 57d, 65a, 111a, 114a (ldan; skt. n. e.); 18a (ldan pa'i; skt. -*vat*); 18c, 93b, 103c (ldan pa'i; skt. n. e.); 19c, 69a, 92a (ldan pa; skt. -*vat*); 25b (ldan; skt. -*ina*); 30c (ldan; skt. -*inī*); 35a (skt. -*vat*); 43a (ldan pas; skt. -*mat*); 63b (ldan pa'i; skt. *sa*-); 64b (ldan; skt. -*mat*); 73a, 83b (ldan pas; skt. n. e.); 77a (ldan la; skt. -*vat*); 78b (ldan pa'i; skt. *ācitaṃ*); 81a (ldan na;

	skt. -*vat*); 85a (ldan pa; skt. -*vin*); 90b (ldan pa; skt. n. e.); 108a (ldan; skt. -*vat*); 114c (ldan; expresses the skt. instrumental case); 142b (ldan; skt. not transmitted); 142d (skt. not transmitted)
sdaṅ ba	*hatred, enmnity, hostility* 118b (skt. *dveṣa*)
sdar ma	*trembling, timorous, timid* 142c (skt. not transmitted)
sdig pa	*sin, misdeed* 13a, 74a (skt. *pāpa*)
sdig(s) pa	*to menace, threaten* 102b (ma bsdigs; skt. *aparibhūtā*)
sdug bsṅal	*affliction, misery, distress* 67a (skt. *duḥkha*)
sdug pa (I)	*pretty, nice; agreeable, pleasing, dear* 132a (skt. *suhṛd*)
sdud pa	*to collect, gather* 7b* (is tib. *sbed* 'to hide, conceal' a corruption of *sdud* for skt. *āgamayati*?); 128d (sdud; skt. *badhyate*)
sdum pa	*to make agree, reconcile, unite* 9b (sdum; skt. *saṃdhau*)
sdoṅ po	*trunk, stem, stump* 21d (skt. n. e.)
sdoṅ ba	*to unite, join* 91b (bsdoṅs; skt. *saṃghātāl*)
sdom pa	*to bind, fasten; bind one's, engage* 70a (bsdoms; skt. n. e.); 78d (ma bsdams; skt. *anibadhya*); 91a (bsdoms pa; skt. n. e.); 116c (bsdams pa'i mthus; skt. *bandhena*); *obligation, engagement, duty; discipline* 110b (skt. *vinaya*)
bsdams	→ sdom pa
bsdigs	→ sdig(s) pa
bsdoṅs	→ sdoṅ ba
bsdoms	→ sdom pa

NA

nag po	*black* 31d (skt. *asita*)
nags	*forest* 108c (skt. *araṇya*)
nags tshal	*forest* 11d (skt. *vana*)
naṅ (du)	(postposition) *in, into, within* 36c, 40c, 83c, 86c (expresses the skt. locative case)
naṅ na	(postposition) *in, into, within* 97d, 105a (expresses the skt. locative case)
naṅ nas	(postposition) *out of, from* 92c (expresses the skt. ablative case)
naṅ byed	[skt. *antaḥkaraṇa*] 'inner organ' 140b (unsuitably for skt. *harantaḥ*)
nad	*disease, sickness* 62c (skt. *vyādhi*); 72d (skt. *pāka*); 100c (skt. *roga*); 118d (nad mi 'gyur; strange and incorrect for skt. *na balāya*)
nam mkha'	*heaven, sky* 24d (skt. *dyāvā*); 119d (skt. *nabhas*)

nam (du) yaṅ	(with negative particle) *never* 19d (nam du'aṅ ... mi; skt. *na jātu*); 103d (nam yaṅ ... med; wrongly interpreted skt. *kva canāpi*); 107d (nam yaṅ ... mi; skt. *na puraḥ*); 135b (nam yaṅ ... med; skt. *na jātu*)
nā ma	**nāma* (transliteration of skt. *nāma* 'named, so called') o
ni	(isolative particle; verse filler) 6b, 6c, 6d, 11c, 13b, 13c, 20a, 20b, 22c, 23a, 28d, 30a, 31a, 33c, 34b, 38a, 38c, 38d, 40c, 43d, 44b, 45b, 45c, 48c, 53d (skt. *api*); 55b, 55d (skt. *tu*); 63a, 63c, 65c, 68d, 69d, 73d, 74b, 75a, 76c, 80b, 82a, 88a, 91d, 102a, 106d, 109c, 111a, 111c, 112a, 114b, 114c, 116b, 117c, 117d, 118c, 119a, 121d, 122c, 123a, 123c, 124c, 127c, 130c, 132a, 134c, 137c, 137d, 138c, 140d, 141c, 143a, 144d, 145c
nu	short for *nu ma*
nu ma	*breast, bosom* 63c (skt. *stana*)
nub pa	*to sink, go down, set* 19a (nub pa; skt. *astamitiḥ*)?; 66d (nub pa na; skt. *astagamane*); 67d (nub; skt. *'stameti*); 79d (nub par 'gyur; skt. *yāty a-stam*)
nus pa	*to be able* 6c (nus; skt. *sāmarthyam*); 6d (mi nus; skt. *na* with the dative case); 36d (mi nus so; skt. *na ... alam*); 38b (mi nus; skt. *nālaṃ*); 43b (nus; skt. *śaknuvanti*); 50c (mi nus; skt. *asamarthā*); 67b, 68d (nus; skt. *śaktaḥ*); 98a (nus pa; skt. *śaktaḥ*); 98b (nus; skt. *śaknoty*); 124d (mi nus; free for skt. *na paṭavo*); 128d (nus; skt. n. e.)
ne tso	*parrot* 35c (skt. *śuka*)
noṅs pa	*fault, crime* 126a (noṅs skyon med pa; skt. *anāgas*)
non	→ thibs non
nor	*wealth* 65b (skt. *śrī*); 84a, 140a (skt. *dhana*)
nor bu	*jewel, gem, precious stone* 17c, 89c (skt. *maṇi*); 17d (free dor skt. *suruca*); 26d, 52c (skt. *māṇikya*)
gnad	*main point, essence* 6a, 104d (skt. *marman*)
gnam lcags	*thunderbolt, lightning* 68c, 145d (skt. *vajra*)
gnas	*place, habituation* 85d (skt. *gati*)
gnas pa	*to dwell, stay, live* 21b (gnas pa med; skt. *na sthitiṃ ... labhate*); 119a (gnas pa; skt. *-stham*); 120c (gnas pa'i; skt. *sthitā*)
gnod pa	*to hurt, do harm*); *harmful* 12a (skt. *upaghātin*); 61c (skt. *apakṛta*); 84d (gnod par 'gyur; skt. *upaghātāya*); 88b (gnod; skt. *upahanti*); 126c (gnod byed; skt. *hiṃsrā*); 131c (gnod na; skt. *-upahatiṣv*); *harm, injury* 24a (skt. *upaghāta*); 95a (gnod pa byed; skt. *apakāra*); 126d (skt. *apada*); 131a (skt. *apat*); 131b (skt. *vipad*); 131d (skt. *vyasana*)
gnon pa	→ zil gyis gnon pa
rna	→ me tog rna rgyan
rnam dag	short for *rnam par dag pa*
rnam pa thams cad du	*in every respect* 1a (skt. **sarvatra*)

rnam par dag pa	*very clean, pure* 108a (skt. *viśuddha*)
rnam śes	*discriminative knowledge, intellect* 24b (skt. *vijñāna*)
rnon po	*sharp, pointed* 50d (skt. *dhārā*); 129a (skt. *tīkṣṇa*); 129c (skt. n. e.)
sna tshogs (pa)	*diverse, various* 42b (skt. n. e.); 123a (skt. *vaicitrya*); 145a (skt. *vicitra*)
snaṅ ba	*to shine, be bright; be perceived, appear* 5c (snaṅ ba min; free for skt. *grasate*); 26d (snaṅ; skt. *upayāti*); *brightness, light* 33c, 125c (skt. *āloka*); 38d (skt. *prakāśa*)
snun pa	*to prick, stab, strike* 102d (bsnun; skt. *abhighātena*)
snod	*vessel* 39a (skt. *bhājanatā*); 83d (skt. *pātra*)
bsnun	→ snun pa

PA

pad ma	*water-lily, lotus* 61c (skt. *kamalinī*); 92c, 92d (skt. *kamala*)
dpag tu med	*immensely large, ver much* 90c (contextually for skt. *alpa*)
dpal	*glory; abundance, wealth* 30a (skt. *śrī*) → 'jam dpal gźon nur gyur pa
Dpal gyi lhun po'i sde	*name of the Tibetan translator of the present work* 145+
dpon po	*master, lord* 95b (dpon byed for skt. *kriyā* i. o. *kṛpā*?) → rje dpon, slob dpon
dpyad	→ dpyod pa
dpyid	*spring* 11d (skt. *vasanta*)
dpyod pa	*to examine, scrutinize* 15b (dpyad; skt. *kalpana*); 135b (*dpyod pas; skt. *tulayati*)
spa ba	?3d, 10d
spaṅ	→ spoṅ ba
spaṅs	→ spoṅ ba
spu	*hair* 76a (did the translators read skt. *keśa* i. o. *roga*?)
spu gri	*razor, knife* 113b (skt. *kṣura*)
spun	→ rgyu spun
spoṅ ba	*to give up, renounce; avoid, abstain from, be free from* 1b (spaṅs; skt. *vimuktāś*); 13a (spoṅ; skt. *ujjhaty*); 21d (spoṅ bar byed; skt. *apāsya*); 24a (spaṅs pa; skt. *viratah̩*); 24b (spaṅs; skt. *ṛte*); 47b (spoṅ mi byed; skt. *na … jahati*); 80b (spaṅs nas; skt. *tyaktvā*); 105c (spaṅs pa; skt. *uparata*); 120a (spaṅ; free for skt. *tiṣṭhati no*) → yoṅs su spoṅ ba
spor ba	*to lift up, raise* 53d (spor; skt. *atyupacitā*); 132c (spor mod; skt. *utthito*)
spyi (bo)	*head* 22d, 94d (skt. *śiras*)

spyi rtol can *impudent* 12d (skt. *nistriṃśa*)

spyil bu *hut* 35d (gzeb kyi spyil bu; skt. *pañjarabandha*)

spyod pa *to accomplish, perform; treat, deal with; use* 72b (spyod; skt. *bhoktuṃ*); 121c (spyod; skt. n. e.); *way of acting, conduct, behaviour* 8a (skt. *carita*); 106a (skt. *sucarita*); 113b (skt. *vyavahāra*); 118c (zas kyi spyod pa; skt. *abhyavahāra*); 130b (skt. *ceṣṭa*)
→ loṅs spyod

sprin *cloud* 29c (sprin med; skt. *vighana*)

sprin me *heat of the clouds* 29d (free for skt. *ātapa*)

spro ba *to feel an inclination for, delight in* 67d (spro ba med; free for skt. *na ... sahate*)

PHA

pha boṅ *large rock* 70c (skt. *śaila*)

pha rol *other side, opposite side, counter party* 9a, 10a, 51a, 58d, 137a (skt. *para*)

phaṅ ba *to save, spare* 133b ('phaṅs; very free for skt. *suhṛd*)

phan 'dogs pa *to be of use, help, assist* 5b (phan 'dogs; skt. *-*upakṛta-*); 14b (phan btags; skt. *hitāya kalpate*); 95a (phan 'dogs; skt. *upakāraḥ*); 97a (phan btags; skt. *upakartum*); 133a (phan btags; skt. *upakṛtam*)

phan pa *to be useful, help* 6d (phan par byed; skt. *upakārāya*); 54a (phan byed; skt. *upakāra-*); 85c (phan phyir; skt. *-hitāya*); 88a (phan byed; skt. **upakurvann*); 98b (phan par byed; skt. *anugrahaṃ kartum*); *help, assistence* 69a (phan pa mi byed; skt. *-hitaṃ na karoti*); 84d (skt. *mahiman*); 100a (skt. *phala*); 102b (skt. *hita*)

phan tshun *one another* 128d (skt. n. e.)

phab → gtaṅ la 'bebs pa

phal cher *generally, commonly, ordinarily* 10d, 12d, 35b, 40a, 46b, 86a, 102a, 137a (skt. *prāyaḥ*); 77b (skt. *prāyaśas*)

phal pa *common, usual, ordinary (people)* 23a (skt. *khalajana*); 43b (skt. *alpabala*); 49b (skt. **laghuni*); 50a (skt. *anārya*); 69b (skt. *viguṇa*)

phug → 'bugs pa

phug pa *cavern, cave* 16c (skt. *vivara*)

phuṅ → 'phuṅ ba

phuṅ khrol *ruin, destruction* 84a (skt. *upaghātaka*)

phun sum tshogs pa *perfect, complete, fully endowed with* 105d (skt. *saṃpanna*)

phub *shield* 28d (skt. *phala*)

phub (ma) *chaff* 29b, 33b (skt. *tṛṇa*)

phog → 'phog pa

phoṅs pa	*poor, needy* 95c (skt. *vipatti*); 141b (skt. *arthin*) → 'phoṅs pa
phod pa	*to be able; to come up, be nearly equal in worth* 139b (mi phod; skt. *gamyo na*); 145c (za phod; skt. *-ghasmara-*)
phyag 'tshal ba	*to make a reveration, salute, bow before someone* 0; 1d (phyag 'tshal lo; skt. *namaḥ*)
phyin ci log	*wrong, deceptive; perverse* 138d (skt. *dur-*)
phyin pa	*to come, get to; advance* 119d (phyin; skt. *-gatasya*) → mthar phyin pa
phyir (I)	*more, again* 20c (skt. *bhūyas*)
phyir (II)	(postposition) *for, for the sake of, for the purpose of* 85c* (expresses the skt. dative case); 144c (skt. n. e.)
phyis	→ ña phyis
phyug	→ dbaṅ phyug, dbaṅ phyug chen po
phyug pa	*rich, wealthy* 138b (skt. *dhanin*)
phyug po	*rich man, wealthy man* 77b (skt. *dhanin*); 112a, 112c (skt. *dhanavat*)
phyug po ñid	*wealth* 141a (skt. *vibhūti*)?
phyuṅ	→ 'byin pa
phye	→ 'byed pa
phyed	→ 'byed pa
phyogs	*side, direction; part, party* 118a (skt. *pakṣa*)
phyogs bcu	*the ten directions of the compass* 18b (skt. *daśadiś*)
phra ba	*thin, fine, minute, small* 41c (skt. *mṛdu*); 49a (skt. *tanu*)
phran	→ rdul phran
'phaṅ	→ go 'phaṅ
'phaṅ mtho ba	*to be in a high position* 17a ('phaṅ mtho; skt. *atyucchritān*)
'phaṅs	→ phaṅ ba, 'phen ba
'phan mkhas	*skill, expertness, competence* 6b (skt. *kauśala*)
'phuṅ ba	*to degenerate, decay; ruin* 76d (ma phuṅ; skt. *avināśya*); 109a ('phuṅ 'gyur; skt. *naśyanti*)
'phur ba	*to fly* 71b ('phur; skt. *gatvā*); 91c ('phur ba; skt. *utpatitāḥ*)
'phen ba	*to throw, cast, fling* 71b ('phaṅs; skt. *kṣepāt*); 71c ('phaṅs pa'i śugs; skt. *-saṃskāraḥ*)
'phog pa	*to hit, strike; meet* 45d (phog mi 'gyur; skt. *na yānti*)
'phoṅs pa	*to be poor, be deprived of* 50a (phoṅs pa; skt. *daridra*)
'phyo ba	*to swim; float, flow* 42c, 83d ('phyo; skt. *plavate*)
'phran tshegs	*little troubles or difficulties, trifles* 52d (skt. *svalpa*); 56a (skt. *pratanu*)

BA

ba *cow; spider?*59c (skt. *lūta*)
ba rgya *(spider's) web* 56c (skt. *lūtātantu*)
ba mo *hoar-frost* 61d (skt. *hima*)
bag *attention, care, caution* 132b (skt. *viśvāsa*)
bag 'khums pa *to be timid* 101a (bag 'khums; skt. *dainyaṃ*)
bag chags *passion, inclination, propensity* 143a (skt. not transmitted)
bab → 'bab pa
babs → 'bab pa
bar *intermediate space, interval* 140d (expresses the skt. participle form)
bal *wool* → śiṅ bal
bas (comparative particle; sandhi form of *pas*) 29c (expresses the skt. ablative case); 139a (skt. n. e.)
bu ga *hole* 9d (skt. *chidra*)
bud med *woman* 63c, 120a (skt. *strī*)
bud śiṅ *fire-wood* 137c (skt. *dāhya*)
bul tog *soda; saltiness* 138c (skt. *kṣāra*)
boṅ → pha boṅ
bod *Tibet* 145+
bod skad du *in Tibetan* 0
bya → ci źig bya, byed pa
bya rgod *bird of prey, vulture* 2c (skt. *gṛdhra*)
bya ba *'what shall be done', action, work, deed* 113c (skt. *kriyā*); 113d (skt. n. e.); 135a[1] (skt. *kārya*); 135a[2] (bya ba min; skt. *akārya*); 136a (skt. *kurvat*)?
bya rog *crow, raven* 34b (bya rog ta ltar; literally for skt. *kākatāliyam* 'accidentally, coincidentally'); 84c (skt. *balibhuj*)
byaṅ → 'byaṅ ba
byad → yo byad
byams pa *kindness, love, affection* 118b (skt. n. e.)
byiṅ → 'byiṅ ba
byin *splendour, magnificence; blessing, bestowing of blessings* 116a (rgyal po'i byin; skt. *prabhaviṣṇu*)?
→ sbyin pa
byis pa *child* 40d, 99a (skt. *bāla*)
byuṅ → 'byuṅ ba
bye → 'bye ba

bye brag *difference, diversity* 73b (free for skt. *sāraphalgutva*)

bye ma *sand* 54d (skt. *sikatā*)

bye'u *little bird* 91c (free for skt. *śalabha*)

byed pa *to do, make, accomplish* 10c (lcags las byas pa'i; skt. *lohamaya*); 40a (byed; skt. *bhavati*); 42b (brñas thabs ... byed; free for skt. *dhuraṃ puraḥ prakarṣanti* or perhaps misread or miswritten **apakurvanti*?); 45a (byed pa na; skt. *niyuktāḥ*); 60b (cis mi byed; skt. *kiṃ nāma ... asty akaraṇīyam*); 61c (ma byas par; contextually for skt. *kim*); 68b (byed do; skt. *santi*); 69b (mi byed; skt. *na karoti*); 79a (mi bya ste; skt. *mā yāta*); 79b (mi bya'o; skt. *mābhyupaita*); 83d (snod byas; skt. *pātrīkṛtaṃ*); 85b (mñen par byed; skt. *avanamante*); 86b (rṅan can byed; free for skt. *bhṛśaṃ dīpyate*); 93a (byed las; expresses the skt. locative absolutive); 95a (gnod pa byed; skt. *apakāra*); 95b (dpon byed for skt. *kriyā* i.o. *kṛpā*?); 100b (byas; skt. n. e.); 102b (mi byed do; skt. *na ... kalpante*); 113b (byed; skt. *vartante*); 118b (mi bya'o; did the translators read skt. *mā bhūt* i. o. *na bhūtaye*?); 123c (byas pa yi; skt. *kriyate*); 130b (byed par 'gyur; skt. *bhavanti*); 143d (bya; skt. not transmitted)
(auxiliary verb) 3b ('char par byed); 3d (spa bar byed); 6d (phan par byed); 9d (*dgod par byed); 13c ('dzem par byed); 13d (reg par byed); 16d ('bab par byed); 21d (spoṅ bar byed); 24b (dga' bar byed); 30d (ston par byed); 37b (rtsom mi byed); 37d ('babs par mi byed do); 41a (mi mthun byas pa); 43d ('thuṅ bar byed); 44d (yoṅs su spoṅ bar byed); 47b (spoṅ mi byed); 51d (rtog par byed); 53c (gcod byed); 54a (phan byed); 56c (dzin byed); 57d ('tshub par byed); 58b ('tshe bar byed); 59b (rab tu 'tshe[r] ba⟨r⟩ byed); 59d (gsod par byed); 61b ('tshe bar byed); 61d (skems par byed); 65d ('thuṅ bar mi byed do); 69c (mun sel mi byed na); 70c ('bigs byed); 70d (gcod par byed); 71d (ltuṅ bar byed pa); 73d (śes par byed); 81b (bśes mi bya); 81d (sreg par byed); 82b (khyad du gsod par byed); 82d ('thor byed); 86c (khyab byed); 86d ('khyag par byed); 88a (phan byed); 89a (sten byed de); 91d (khebs par byed); 96d (*'khu bar byed); 97a (bgraṅ mi byed); 97c ('dum byed); 98b (phan par byed); 98d ('bebs par byed); 100a (brtson byas); 104b (śes par bya); 106b (chud gson byed); 106d (sreg byed); 109a ('dris byas); 111c (sbyaṅ ba ma byas par); 117a (byaṅ byas); 117b (ñams su len par mi byed na); 120d (g.yo bar byed); 126c (gnod byed); 127d (sreg byed); 132d (gsod par byed); 134b ('dor mi byed); 141b (sbyin par mi byed pa'i); 142d (skrag par mi bya ste)
(auxiliary verb forming causatives) 5d (gsal bar byed); 11c (skems par byed); 28c (gsod par byed); 37c ('joms byed); 41d ('thul bar byed); 50d (bdar bar byed); 64d (źi bar byed); 75c (dga' byed pa); 98c (skems byed); 124b ('dum byed); 129b (gduṅ byed pa); 129d (gduṅ ... mi byed)
creator 25c (skt. *dhātṛ*)
→ goms par byed pa, 'jigs byed chen po, naṅ byed

byer → 'byer ba

brag → bye brag

bral → 'bral ba

bri → 'bri ba

bla *over, above; superior, better, preferable* 114b (bla 'og gi ... don; free for skt. *prabhuśakti*)

blaṅ → len pa

blun pa *stupidity, foolishness* 115b (skt. *jāḍya*)

blun po *stupid, foolish; fool, idiot* 25d (skt. *jaḍatā*); 30a, 40a, 64a, 83a, 107a (skt. *jaḍa*); 34a, 38a (skt. *ajña*)

blo (daṅ) ldan (pa) *intelligent person, wise man* 43a (skt. *dhīmat*); 55a, 65a, 134a (skt. *budha*); 64b (skt. *matimat*); 111a (renders skt. **budha* i. o. *śaṭha*); 114a (skt. *buddhi*); 142d (skt. not transmitted)

blon po *minister* 114a, 116a (skt. *mantrin*)

dbaṅ *might, power, potency* 72b (dbaṅ med; skt. *na labhante*)
→ stes dbaṅ

dbaṅ po *lord, ruler, the mighty One, esp. Indra* 24c (skt. *indra*)

dbaṅ phyug *lord, ruler; [a]śvara* 115a, 132b (skt. *īśvara*)

dbaṅ phyug chen po *the Great Lord Maheśvara* 22d (skt. *maheśvara*)

dbab → 'bebs pa

dbugs rṅub pa *to inhale* 43c (dbugs rṅubs pas; skt. *ucchvāsa*)

dbul po *poor* 64b (skt. *vibhavarahita*)

dbus *middle, midst, centre* 119a (skt. *mādhya*)

dbye → 'byed pa

'bad pa *exertion*
→ rab tu 'bad pa

'bad rtsol *exertion, effort* 71b (skt. *karmin*)

'bab pa *to move downward, descend, fall down; enter into* 2a*, 63d ('bab; skt. *patati*); 2d ('bab; skt. *nipatanti*); 14d ('bab par 'gyur; free for skt. *malinayati*); 16d ('bab par byed; skt. *nipatati*); 37c (babs; skt. *nipatati*); 37d ('babs par mi byed do; skt. *na ... patati*); 39b ('bab pa; skt. *patitam*); 39c (bab na; skt. n. e.); 39d (bab; skt. n. e.); 64c ('bab pa; skt. *nipatad*); 68c (bab pa ste; skt. *vinipatati*); 80c ('bab pa; skt. *prayānti*); 82d ('bab; skt. *saṃvṛnute*); 85d ('bab; skt. *patanty*); 134a (bab; skt. *-avastho*); 145d ('bab la; skt. *-pātaḥ*)

'babs → 'bab pa

'bar ba *to burn; be ignated, blaze* 52c ('bar; free for skt. *śikhā*); 132d ('bar ba; skt. *-śikhām*)

'bigs pa	*to pierce, bore; break open* 70c ('bigs byed; skt. *bhinatti*); 139d (mi 'bigs sam; skt. *na dārayati*)
'bu	*worm, insect* 76b (skt. *kṛmi*)
'bu ba	*to open, unfold, blossom* 11d (kha ... 'bu; skt. *kusumayati*)
'bugs pa	*to bore, pierce* 9c (phug pa yi bu ga; skt. *chidraṃ karoti*)
'bebs pa	*to cast down, throw down* 98d ('bebs par byed; skt. *dadāti*); 132b (mi dbab; skt. *na ... kṣamo*) → gtaṅ la 'bebs pa
'bem	*aim, goal, target* 45d (skt. *lakṣya*)
'byaṅ ba	*to be cleaned, purified; used to* 117a (byaṅ byas; skt. *kṛtajayā*)
'byiṅ ba	*to sink in, sink down* 83c (byiṅ ba; skt. *majjati*)
'byin pa	*to cause to come forth, send out; emit (light)* 125c (phyuṅ ba'i; skt. *prakāśayanty*) → gzi 'byin pa
'byuṅ ba	*to come out, emerge; arise* 15b ('byuṅ 'gyur; skt. *janayati*); 18d ('byuṅ la; skt. *udeti*); 26b ('byuṅ; skt. *upaiti*); 31b (mi 'byuṅ; skt. *na ... udbhavati*); 31d (mi 'byuṅ; skt. *na janayanti*); 32a ('byuṅ; skt. n. e.); 34cd (zos pa'i rjes ... 'byuṅ ba; skt. *utkirati*); 68a (ma byuṅ bar; skt. *na ... āpnoti*); 90d ('byuṅ ba; skt. *jāyante*); 92a ('byuṅ; skt. *bhavati*); 92b, 92d, 127b ('byuṅ; skt. *bhavanti*); 92c ('byuṅ; skt. *udeti*); 103d ('byuṅ ba; skt. *jāyante*); 112b ('byuṅ; skt. n. e.); 112c ('byuṅ; skt. *prayāti*); *coming forth, originating* 137b ('byuṅ; skt. *hetuṃ*)
'bye ba	*to open; divide, separate* 97c (bye ba; skt. n. e.)
'byed pa	*to separate, keep asunder, divide; discriminate, make a difference* 4c ('byed pa; skt. **vivektum*); 9a (pha rol 'byed; skt. *parabheda*); 38b ('byed mi nus; skt. *nālaṃ vivektum*); 52b (dbye; skt. *bheda*); 73b (phyed; skt. *tulayanti*); 124a (phye; skt. *bhinnam*); 124d ('byed par ... nus; skt. *bhede paṭavo*); 128d ('byed; skt. n. e.)
'byer ba	*to disperse in flight* 128c (byer ba; skt. *patann*)
'byor pa	*wealth, riches, treasure* 25c (skt. *(vini)yoga; is 'byor pa* a corruption of original *sbyor pa*?); 56a (skt. *vibhava*); 120b, 128a (skt. *lakṣmī*); 121a (skt. *saṃpad*); 127a (skt. *artha*); 139a (contextually for skt. *pṛthu*)
'braṅ ba	→ rjes su 'braṅ ba
'bral ba	*to be separated, parted from, deprived of* 24c ('bral ba; skt. *rahitam*); 45a (bral bar; skt. *an-*)
'bras bu	*fruit* 27c ('bras bu med; skt. *aphala*); 27d (skt. *phalaty*); 72c, 96d (skt. n. e.)
'bri ba	*to lessen, decrease; wane* 19b (bri; skt. *kṣayaḥ*); 67a ('bri ba'i; skt. *apacaya-*); 67d ('bri bar; skt. *khaṇḍanaṃ*)
sbag pa	*to soil, stain, defile, pollute* 74a (sbags pa'i; free for skt. *majjati*)

sbags → sbag pa
sbal → rus sbal
sbuṅs *energy* 111b (skt. *tejas*)?
sbed pa *to hide, conceal* 7d (sbed; skt. *pātuṃ*)
sbyaṅ → sbyoṅ ba
sbyin gtoṅ sems *thought of giving gifts, charitable mind* 95c (skt. *ditsā*)
sbyin pa *to give, bestow* 112a (byin pas; skt. *prayacchati*); 141a (sbyin pas; skt. *dānād*); 141b (*sbyin par mi byed pa'i*; skt. *dadāti na*)
sbyin sreg mkhan *priest* 133c (skt. *hotṛ*)
sbyoṅ ba *to clean, cleanse, purify* 111c (sbyaṅ ba ma byas par; contextually for skt. *saṃtāpenaiva*)
sbyor ba *adjunction, conjunction; mingling, mixture* 78c, 128c (skt. *yoga*); 100c (skt. *upayoga*)
sbraṅ bu *bee; fly* 56c, 59d (skt. *maśaka*)
sbram *largeness, bulk* 26c (free for skt. *upala*)
sbrul *serpent* 39c (skt. *ahi*)
sbrul gdug *poisonous snake* 109c (skt. *āśīviṣa*)
sbrul gdug can *full of poisonous snakes* 93c (skt. *sāśīviṣa*)

MA

ma *not* 6b, 15c, 42d, 68a, 87d, 108d, 110a, 115a, 118a (skt. *na*); 32b, 76d, 78d, 97b, 102b, 122a (skt. *a-*); 40b (skt. *no*); 61c, 111c, 115d, 126c (skt. n. e.); 101b (ma yin; read skt. *na* from *māna*; cf. *min pa*); 101d (ma yin; skt. *vinā*)
→ dri ma can
ma taṅ ka *elephant* 56d (transliteration of skt. *mātaṅga*)
ma rig pa *ignorance* 125a (skt. *avidyā*)
ma la ya *the Malaya mountain* 81c (skt. *malaya*)
maṅ po *much, many* 57a (skt. *bahu*); 91a, 137a (skt. n. e.)
→ rab tu maṅ po
maṅ ba *plenty* 138a (skt. *mahatā*)
mar *butter* 86d (mar gsar; skt. *sarpis*)
→ til mar
mar me *lantern,*
→ *lamp* 31c (skt. *dīpa*)
mi *man, human being* 45c, 68b (skt. n. e.); 46a, 59a, 109b (skt. *loka*); 55c, 86b (skt. *puruṣa*); 76c (skt. *nara*); 109c (skt. *jantu*)

mi *not* 6d, 14b, 17d, 19d, 22b, 25d, 28a, 31b, 31d, 37b*, 37d, 38b, 45b, 45d, 47b, 51c, 57a, 58d, 60d, 65d, 69b, 69c, 76d, 81b, 93d, 94b, 99a, 102b, 104d, 107d, 114d, 117d, 118b, 122b, 128d, 129d, 132b, 133b, 134d, 139b[1], 139d, 141b, 141d (skt. *na*); 14c, 41a, 50c, 60b, 78a, 97a, 102a, 114b (skt. *a-*); 19b, 32d, 56b, 111d, 117b, 135d (skt. n. e.); 21a, 27b, 139b[2] (skt. *an-*); 29d (mi gsal; free for skt. *bāla*); 65b (skt. *ni-*); 79a, 79b (skt. *mā*); 80b (mi gźol; skt. *unnati-*); 115c (skt. n. e., perhaps read skt. *aviduṣaḥ* i. o. *viduṣaḥ*); 128a (mi brtan pa; skt. *capala*); 142a, 142d (skt. not transmitted)

mi mkhas pa *unlearned, stupid; stupid person* 55b (skt. *anipuṇa*)

mi 'dra ba *unequal, unlike, different, odd* 25c ('byor pa mi 'dra; skt. *sadṛśaviyoga*; cf. *'byor ba*)

mi mdza' ba *unfriendliness, hostility* 33a (skt. *amitra*)

mi g.yo ba *unmoved*131c (skt. *acala*); 139c (mi g.yo *ri; skt. *acala*)

mi srun pa *evil, mischievous* 3a (skt. **khala*); 5a, 6a, 15d, 20d, 21a, 54b, 59a, 62a, 81b, 93a, 102a (skt. *khala*); 25a (skt. *khalajana*); 42a, 109a, 124c (skt. *prakhala*)

mi bsrun pa *evil being, bad person, vilain* 62a (skt. *prakhala*)

mig *eye* 13c, 38c (skt. *nayana*); 51c (skt. *akṣi*); 114c (skt. *cakṣus*)

min pa *to be not* [contraction of *ma yin pa*] 5c (snaṅ ba min; free for skt. *grasate*); 10b, 29b, 33b, 43b, 48b, 48d, 49d, 51b, 54b, 54d, 56d, 75d, 86b, 87b, 98d, 123d, 137b (min; skt. *na*); 13b, 49b (min; skt. *no*); 28b (min no; skt. *na*); 33d[1], 101d, 112b (min; skt. n. e.); 33d[2] (min; skt. *naiva jātu*); 62b, 123b (min; skt. *na jātu*); 75b, 135a (min; skt. *a-*); 93b (min; skt. *na yānti*); 94b (min pa; skt. *a-*); 101a (min; read skt. *mā* i. o. *māna*!); 107b (min; skt. *jātu na*); 112d (min pas; skt. *na*); 126d (contextually for the skt. comparative with the ablative case); 131b (min; skt. *na yānti khedam*)

mu tig *pearl* 39d, 115c (skt. *muktāphala*)

mun pa *darkness* 5c, 16c, 33c, 33d, 38d, 79c (skt. *tamas*); 69c (mun sel mi byed na; skt. *na ... prakāśayati*); 69d (skt. *astamita*)

me *Feuer* 29b, 33b, 48c, 53d, 76a, 81c, 129d, 132c (skt. *agni*); 106d, 134c (skt. *śikhin*); 133c, 145a (skt. *vahni*); 137c (skt. *dahana*); 137d (mes ni sreg par 'gyur; skt. *udbhavati dāhaḥ*); 143b (skt. not transmitted)
→ sprin me, mar me

me lce *flame of fire* 13d (skt. *agniśikhā*); 20b (skt. *jvāla*)

me tog *flower* 27c (me tog; skt. *puṣpaty*); 27d (me tog med; skt. *apuṣpa*); 77d (skt. *kusuma*); 102d (me tog ltar; skt. *puṣpati*)

me tog rna rgyan *flower of the Karṇikāra tree* 77c (skt. *karṇikāra*)

me loṅ *mirror* 18c (skt. *ādarśa*); 123d (skt. *ādarśa*)

med pa *to be not, have not* 5b, 18d, 20c, 21b, 52d, 67d, 72b, 84d, 104d, 136b (med; skt. *na*); 23d, 27c, 27d, 52a, 66d, 69d (med; skt. *a-*); 29c (med; skt. *vi-*);

	31b (med de; skt. *na*); 47a (med; skt. *nir-*); 52b (med; skt. *niś-*); 77b (med; skt. *-daridra*); 99d (med pa'i; skt. *a-*); 100a (med na; skt. *ṛte*); 100c (med par; skt. *vinā*); 100d (med do; skt. *na*); 103d (med; skt. *kva canâpi* analysed as *kva ca nâpi*!); 105b (med pa ste; did the translators read skt. *virahitam* i. o. *avahitaṃ*?); 130c (med pa'i; skt. *a-*); 135b (nam yaṅ ... med; skt. na jātu); 140d (skt. *na*) → khrel med, graṅs med pa, don med, dpag tu med, g.yo med
moṅs pa	ñon moṅs pa
mod pa	*to be* 73b (mod la; skt. *sakṛd api*); **(auxiliary verb)** 79c (bsal mod); 90c (mod; skt. n. e.)
mya ṅan 'tshaṅ	*the Aśoka tree* 102d (skt. *aśoka*)
mya ṅam	*desert* 135c (skt. *maru*)
myu gu	*sprout* 76a, 145b (skt. *aṅkura*)
dman pa	*low, inferior (being)* 16b[1] (skt. *nīca*); 84b (skt. *ajña*); 86a (skt. *mṛdu*); 92a (skt. *asat*); 97b (skt. *nyūna*); *inferiority* 16b[2] (skt. *anudātta*)
dma' ba	*to be low* 101a (dma'; skt. *namre*); 101d (dma' ba; skt. *avanamanaṃ*)
dmu rgod	*wild, unruly, unmanageable* 87b (skt. *klība*)
dmus loṅ	*blind by birth* 99c (skt. *vyakṣa*)
rma	*wound* 76b (skt. *vraṇa*)
rma bya	*Pfau* 113d (skt. *mayūra*)
rmi lam	*dream* 130c (skt. *svapna*)
rmoṅ ba	*to be obscured, stupefied, confused* 46b (rmoṅs par 'gyur; skt. *muhyati*)
rmoṅs	→ rmoṅ ba
rmoṅs pa	*delusion, confusion* 125b (skt. *saṃmoha*)
smad pa	*to blame, chide; abuse, defame; despise* 11a (smad par; skt. *ninditum*); 39a (smad de; skt. *nindā*)
smad 'tshoṅ ma	*prostitute, harlot* 75c (skt. *veśyā*); 102c (skt. *gaṇikā*); 120b (skt. *bandhakī*)
smad rigs	*common people* 7b, 14a, 26a, 82a, 88a (skt. *nīca*); 7d (skt. *khala*); 86a (skt. *prākṛta*)
sman	*medicine, remedy* 62c (skt. *auṣadha*)
smin pa	*ripeness, maturity* 72c (skt. *pāka*)
smos	→ ci smos, smos ci dgos
smos ci dgos	*what to say (about), how much more* 88d (skt. *kaiva kathā*)
smra ba	*to speak, talk* 7d (smra; skt. *vaktum*); 27a (smra ba; skt. *vakti*); 27b (mi smra; skt. *anukto*); 35c (smra ba; skt. n. e.); *speech* 101a (skt. *vadanti* read as *vadati*?); 113a (smra ba; contextually for skt. *sravati*); 118d (smra ba yin; skt. *kathayanti*); 137b (smra; skt. *vadanti*); 144d (smras pa yin; skt. *pralāpe*)
smras	→ smra ba
smrig	→ ṅur smrig gos

TSA

tsaṅ śu'i khu ba *castor-oil* 96b (does this render skt. *āranāla-* or rather *dāhavibandhadhra-*?)

tsan dan *sandalwood* 21d, 81d (skt. *candana*)

tsam *as much as, only, solely* 52d (skt. *api*); 94c (śas tsam; skt. *kalā*)

gtsaṅ ba *clean, pure* 14c (mi gtsaṅ; skt. *aśuci*); 134b (skt. *śuddhatā*); 135d[1] (skt. *śuci*); 135d[2] (mi gtsaṅ; free for skt. *svādu*; did the translators read **śucy aśuci vā*?)

gtses → 'tshe ba

btsan po *strong, mighty, powerful* 67c (skt. *tīkṣṇa*); 101b (skt. *stabdha*)

btsugs → 'dzugs pa

btsun mo'i 'khor *harem* 108b (skt. *antaḥpura*)

rtsa → rtswa

rtsal → rtsol ba

rtsi ba *to count* 115d (gces par ma brtsis; skt. *kā gurutā*)?

rtsub pa *rough, rude, harsh, coarse* 12b (skt. *dāruṇa*); 53b (skt. *rūkṣa*)

rtse ba *to play, sport, frolic* 109c (rtse ba'i; skt. *-krīḍāḥ*)

rtse (mo) *point, top, peak; tip* 20b (skt. *śikhin*); 31c (skt. *śikhā*); 46c (skt. *śikhara*); 136c (skt. *mastaka*); 139c (skt. *śiras*)

rtsed mo *play, amusement, diversion* 138d (skt. *vilasita*)

rtsom pa *to begin, commence; make, accomplish* 37b[1] (mi brtsam; skt. *anārabhyam*); 37b[2] (rtsom mi byed; skt. *nārabhate*)

rtsol ba *to endeavour, take pains, give diligence* 50b (rtsol; skt. *prerayati*); 136d (rtsal na lhuṅ bar gyur; not very faithful for skt. *nāste na cotpatati*) → 'bad rtsol

rtswa *grass* 29b (skt. *tuṣa*); 42c, 87d, 121d (skt. *tṛṇa*)

brtsam → rtsom pa

brtsis → rtsi ba

brtson pa *to strive, aim at, exert one's self* 9a (brtson; skt. *udyuktaḥ*); 100a (brtson byas; skt. *abhiyogaṃ*); 142a (mi brtson pa; skt. not transmitted) *exertion, effort* 100b (skt. *vyasana*); 142c (skt. not transmitted)

TSHA

tsha sgo *barren ground* 54b (skt. *ūṣara*)

tshad *measure* 73d (skt. *parimāna*)

tshal → nags tshal

tshig *word, utterance* 35c, 96a, 129a (skt. *vacana*); 96c (skt. *vākya*); 101b, 126a (skt. n. e.); 113a (skt. *vāc*)
⟶ dam tshig

tshigs su bcad pa *verse, stanza* (here esp. the one in the Āryā metre) 0, 145+

tshigs su bcad pa'i mdzod [skt. *āryākoṣa*] *'Treasury of [Āryā] verses'* (Tibetan title of the present work) 0, 145+

tshun ⟶ phan tshun

tshul 'chos (pa) *hypocrisy* 58a (strange rendering of skt. *pariśuddha*)

tshe *time; season* 20a (skt. *āyus*); 72c (skt. n. e.); 119c ('char tshe; contextually for skt. *prabhā*)

tshegs ⟶ 'phran tshegs

tshes (gcig) *day, esp. after the new moon* 49d (skt. *śiśu*)

tshes pa ⟶ zla ba tshes pa

tsho ⟶ ne tsho, laṅ tsho

tshogs *accumulation, multitude* 145d (tshogs skyed śog; skt. *upacinuta*)

tshogs pa ⟶ phun sum tshogs pa

tshod *measure, proportion* 73c (skt. *tulā*)

tshon *colour, paint* 26d (*tshon gyis bsgyur*; free for skt. *rakta*)

mtshuṅs pa *similar, like, equal* 7b (skt. *iva*); 34b (skt. n. e.); 38d (skt. *sama*)

mtsho *lake* 2d (skt. **saras*); 36c (skt. *udanvat*); 65d (rendered as if skt. **sarasaja* i. o. *sarajasa*?)
⟶ rgya mtsho

mtshon cha *weapon, arms* 10c (skt. *śastra*)

'tshaṅ ba *enlarged, complete, made full* 102d (skt. *adhikam*)

'tshal ba ⟶ phyag 'tshal ba

'tshig pa *to burn, destroy* 133d ('tshig par 'gyur; skt. *nirdahati*)

'tshub pa *to be choked, suffocated; suppressed* 18b ('tshub; skt. *rundhānam*); 57d ('tshub par byed; skt. *prorṇute*)

'tshe ba *to hurt, do harm, injure, torment* 5a ('tshe ba; skt. **-apakṛtau*); 10a (gtses; skt. *pīḍāṃ*); *harmful, envious* 12b (skt. *hiṃsratā*); 50b (*tshe; skt. *-abhidrohe*); 58b ('tshe bar byed; skt. *vyathate*); 58d ('tshe ba; skt. *upaghātaṃ*); 61b ('tshe bar byed; skt. *prabādhate*)
⟶ rab tu 'tshe ba

'tshoṅ ⟶ smad 'tshoṅ ma

'tsho ba *life; livelihood* 58a (skt. *vṛtti*); 84c (skt. *jīvitā*); 104b ('tsho chos; skt. *vṛttānta*)

DZA

Dzñā na śānti	*name of the Indian translator Jñānaśānti* 145+
mdzad pa	(resp. for *byed pa*) *to compose* 145+ (mdzad pa)
mdza' ba	→ mi mdza' ba
mdza' bśes	*friend* 53c (skt. *pariciti*)
mdze	*leprosy* 62c (skt. *kuṣṭha*)
mdzes pa	*fair, handsome, beautiful* 101b (skt. *śreyas*); 138b (skt. *su-*) → rab tu mdzes pa
mdzod pa	*store-house, treasury* 0; 145+
'dzad pa	*to be on the decline, be consumed, spent* 71c (zad; skt. *kṣīṇa*)
'dzin pa	*to take hold of, seize, grasp* 40d ('dzin; skt. *jighṛkṣatī-*)?; 56c ('dzin byed; skt. *badhnāti*)?; 59d (bzuṅ; skt. n. e.); 78b (gzuṅ dka'; skt. *durgraham*) → tiṅ ṅe 'dzin
'dzugs pa	*to raise, erect; put down, place, found* 59c (btsugs nas; skt. *viracayya*)
'dzum pa	*to smile* 88c ('dzum na; skt. *hasitam*)
'dzeg pa	*to ascend, climb* 136c ('dzegs pas; skt. *adhirūḍhaḥ*)
'dzegs	→ 'dzeg pa
'dzem pa	*to shun, avoid, shirk* 13c ('dzem par byed; skt. *na kṣamate*)
rdzas	*thing, matter, substance* 14c (skt. *rajas*); 73a (rdzas bzaṅ po; free for skt. *puruṣa*)
rdzogs pa	*(to be) perfect, complete, finished; blameless* 71a (skt. *dṛḍha*); 145+ (rdzogs so)

ŹA

źi ba	*to become quiet, calm; heal; settle* 64d (źi bar byed; skt. *praśamayati*); 100c (źi na; skt. *śamayati*); 108b (źi; skt. *śāmyaty*); 108c (źi ba'i; skt. *śāntāny*); *tranquillity, calmness, peace* 31a (skt. *śānta*), 32c, 32d (skt. *śiva*); 108d (skt. *upaśama*)
źig	→ gaṅ źig, 'ga' źig, ci źig 'gyur, ci źig bya, su źig
źig tu	→ gcig tu 'gyur ba
źim pa	*sweet-scented, fragrant* 48d (dri źim; skt. *gandha*) → dri mi źim pa, rab ru źim pa
źu ba (I)	*to correct* 145+ (źus te)
źu ba (II)	*to melt* 87c (gźu ba; skt. *dravaṇa-*)
źugs	→ 'jug pa
źus	→ źu ba (I)

źen pa	*to desire, long for* 21a (źen pa'i; skt. *rāgitayā*)
źe	short for *źe na*
źe na	(sandhi form of *ce na*) *'if one says so'* 133a (źe'am; skt. n. e.)
źes	(sandhi form of *ces*) *so, thus* 72d (źes grags; skt. *kila*); 109a, 133b (skt. *iti*); 118d, 122c (skt. n. e.)
gźan	*other; another* 4d, 40d, 69a, 113c, 113d (skt. *anya*); 6a, 7b, 23b, 24a, 50b, 58b, 124a, 131a, 131d (skt. *para*); 19b, 144b (skt. n. e.)
gźi	*residence, abode, home; place* 21b (skt. *pada*)
gźig	→ 'jig pa
gźu (I)	*bow (for shooting)* 24c (skt. *dhanu*); 45c (skt. n. e.)
gźu (II)	→ źu ba (II)
gźuṅ ṅan	[skt. *durjana, daurjanya*] *mean person* 14b (is skt. *nīca* translated twice? Cf. *smad rigs*)?
gźuṅ lugs	*sourcel, text, scripture* 117a (skt. *śāstra*)
gźon nu	*young* → 'jam dpal gźon nur gyur pa
gźol ba	*to be low* 80b (mi gźol; skt. *unnati-*); 80d (gźol ba; skt. *anunnateḥ*)
bźag	→ 'jog pa
bźin (du)	*like, as* 10d (free for skt. *eva*?); 15d, 23a, 23c, 71d, 91a, 96b, 99a*, 120b, 121d (skt. *iva*); 34d, 47d, 110d, 117d (skt. n. e.); 113b (free for skt. *atītya*); 143d (skt. not transmitted) → de bźin, raṅ bźin
bźugs pa	*to stay, exist; be contained* (*in the present work;* thus in titles) 0

ZA

Za hor	*name of a town* 145+
za 'jil	*emetic* 96b (free for skt. *dāhavibandhadhra*?)
za ba	*to eat, consume* 21c (za bas; free for skt. *līyante*); 34c (zos pa'i rjes; free for skt. *utkirati*); 58c (za; skt. *āśino*); 145c (za phod; skt. *-ghasmara-*)
zad	→ 'dzad pa
zas	*food, nourishment* 58c (skt. n. e.); 118c (zas kyi spyod pa; skt. *abhyavahāra*)
zil gyis gnon pa	*to overcome, vanquish, defeat* 17b, 64b (zil gyis gnon; skt. *abhibhavati*)
zer	→ ñi zer, zla zer, 'od zer
zer ba	*to say* 109b (zer ba; skt. *āha*)
***zel med**	*without fissures, cleavages* 52b (skt. *niśchidra-*; cf. SRN 2.23)
zos	→ chud za ba, za ba
zla	short for *zla ba*

zla dkyil *disk of the moon* 47c (skt. *śaśāṅka*)

zla ba (I) *to pass, get beyond* 136b (bzlar med; free for skt. *na śaknoti*)

zla ba (II) *moon* 8d, 19b, 94c, 98d (skt. *śaśāṅka*); 40c, 49c (skt. *indu*); 51d, 57b (skt. *śaśin*); 67b (skt. *candra*)

zla ba tshes pa *waxing moon* 22c (skt. *vakra ... śaśī*)

zla zer *ray of the moon, moonlight* 16d (skt. *jyotsnā*)

zlog pa *to cause to return* 20c (zlog med; skt. *na ... nivartante*)
→ phyir zlog pa

gzas pa *to brandish* 116d (gzas pa; free for skt. *ghāta*)

gzi *shine, brightness, splendour* 85a (gzi ldan pa; skt. *tejasvin*)

gzi 'byin pa *to give out light, shine* 17d (gzi mi 'byin; skt. *na ... cakāsati*)

gzugs *figure, form, shape; body* 32c, 138b (skt. *rūpa*)

gzugs brñan *reflected image, mirror image* 18d (skt. *pratibimba*); 40c (skt. *°bimba*)

gzeṅs mthos *high rank* 82a (skt. *ucchrāya*)

gzeb *cage* 35d (skt. *pañjara*)

bzaṅ po *good, fine* 3c (skt. *viśuddha*); 15c (bzaṅ po ma yin; skt. *na rājati*); 73a (rdzas bzaṅ po; free for skt. *puruṣa*)

bzuṅ → 'dzin pa, yoṅs su 'dzin pa

bzo bo mkhas pa *skillful craftsman* 26c (skt. *kuśala*)

bzod pa *to suffer, bear, endure* 57a (mi bzod pa'i; free for skt. *na śaknuvanti*)?; 67b (bzod par; skt. *soḍhum*)

bzlar → zla ba

'A

'aṅ (sandhi form of *yaṅ*) 38a, 47a, 88a, 88c, 108b, 125b, 128a (skt. *api*); 48a (skt. *eva*); 65d (skt. *iti*); 79b, 113d, 132d (skt. n. e.); 101d (skt. *ca*)
→ nam du yaṅ

'am (disjunctive particle) *or, else* 37a (skt. *vā*); 132a, 133a (skt. n. e.)

'o ma *milk* 4c (skt. **kṣīra*)

'og *below, underneath* 114b (bla 'og gi ... don; free for skt. *prabhuśakti*)

'oṅ ba *to come* 72d ('oṅ; skt. *bhavati*)

'od short for *'od zer*

'od zer *ray of light* 57b (zer; skt. n. e.); 85c (skt. *kara*); 91d (skt. n. e.); 130c (skt. *mayūkha*)

'on kyaṅ *but, yet, notwithstanding* 7c (skt. *kiṃ tu*)

'on te (with interrogative particle) *or if not, or else, or also* 115b (freely for skt. *na*)

'os pa *to be worthy, suitable, adequate* 15a ('os pa'i; skt. *anurūpa*)

YA

ya rabs *respectable class of people, high class people* 88b (skt. *sādhu*); 96a (skt. *sādhu*)

yaṅ (concessive particle) *even; also, too* 4a, 12a, 13a, 13b, 13c, 26c, 27b, 29a, 30a, 41c, 46d, 49a, 57b, 58c, 64a, 80a, 87c, 96d, 106a, 110b, 124a, 132c, 134c, 139c, 140c (skt. *api*); 4c, 19b, 80c, 82c, 94c (skt. n. e.); 11d, 35c, 66b, 66d, (skt. *eva*); 67a (skt. *eva*)?; 67c (skt. *tu*); 81a (skt. *iti*); 103c (skt. *ca*)
→ nam du yaṅ

yaṅ na *or* 37b (skt. *vā*)

yaṅ po *light* 89d (skt. *laghayati*)

yaṅ ba *(to be) light; careless* 41b, 53a (skt. *laghu*); 56b (skt. *laghutva*)

yan lag *member, limb* 55b (skt. *śākhā*)

yi ge *letter* 34d (skt. *akṣara*)

yid *heart* 53c (skt. n. e.); 60a (skt. *manas*); 74b (skt. **manas*); 131a (yid gduṅs ... min; skt. *na yānti khedaṃ*)

yid chad pa *to give up, despair; despondency, despair* 79b (skt. *saṃtāpa*)

yid ches pa *to believe* 122b (yid mi ches; skt. *pratipadyante ... na*); 122d (yid ches; skt. *śraddhati*)

yin pa *to be* 1c (skyoṅ ba ... yin; skt. pānti); 6b (rigs ma yin; skt. *na ... kṛtye*); 15c (bzaṅ po ma yin; skt. *na rājati*); 34a ('grub ... yin pa; skt. *sādhayati*); 40b (ma yin no; skt. *no*); 42d (ma yin no; skt. *na*); 87d (ma yin no; skt. *asti na*); 101b (ma yin; read skt. *na* from *māna*; cf. *min pa*); 101d (ma yin; skt. *vinā*); 108d (ma yin no; skt. *na ... vidadhati*); 118d (smra ba yin); 119b (bsṅags pa yin); 126c (ma yin te; skt. n. e.); 141c (yin; skt. n. e.); 144d (smras pa yin; skt. *pralāpe*)
→ ched (du) yin

yug → 'khor yug

yun riṅ *long time; longevity* 44a, 84c (skt. *cira*)

yun riṅ (por) *for a long time* 127c (skt. *ciram*)

yul *place, province; sense object* 60a (skt. *viṣaya*)

yul ljoṅs *district, region* 90c (skt. *deśa*)

yo byad *tools, implements, necessaries* 133d (yo byad bcas; free for skt. *svam ā-śrayam*)

yoṅs su 'dzin pa *to take hold of, reach, obtain* 26b (yoṅs bzuṅ; skt. *parigṛhīto*)?

yoṅs su spoṅ ba *to give up entirely, completely avoid* 44d (yoṅs su spoṅ bar byed; skt. *-āparajyante*)

yod pa *to be, be available* 7c (yod de; skt. n. e.); 69b (khyad ... yod; skt. *bhi-dyate*); 70a (yod; skt. n. e.); 70b (yod pa min; skt. *na ... alam*); 95c (yod pa; skt. *sati*); 117c (yod; skt. *saṃsthitena*); 122b (yod; skt. *sato*)

yon tan *(good) quality, virtue* 1b, 2a, 28a, 33a, 38b, 44a, 57d, 89a, 121b, 122b, 124b, 134b (skt. *guṇa*); 3b (skt. *viśeṣa*); 4a, 4b (skt. not transmitted); 115a (skt. *guṇin*)

yon tan can *virtuous* 42a (skt. *guṇavat*); 97c (skt. *guṇa*)

yon tan (daṅ) ldan (pa) *endowed with good qualities, virtuous* 4b (skt. not transmitted); 18a, 19c, 35a, 69a, 77a, 81a, 92a (skt. *guṇavat*); 63b (skt. *saguṇa*); 90b, 93b (skt. *guṇa*); 103c (wrongly interpreted for skt. *guṇa*)

yon tan med pa *one who is devoid of qualities or virtues* 47a (skt. *nirguṇa*); 77b (skt. *guṇadaridra*)

g.ya' daṅ ldan pa *covered with dark spots* 18c (very free for skt. *virūpa*)

g.yul ṅo *battle* 10d (skt. *samara*)

g.yo ba *to move, be moved, agitated* 78a (lhag par g.yo; skt. *aticapala*); 120d (g.yo bar byed; skt. *calaty*); 131d (g.yo; skt. *pracalati*); *(to be) cunning, deceitful* 8a (skt. *śaṭha*)
→ mi g.yo ba

g.yo med *free of deceit, honest* 61a (skt. *avikārin*)

g.yog pa *to cover, pour over* 29b (g.yogs min; skt. *na ... āvṛto*)

g.yogs → g.yog pa

g.yon can *cunning person* 75a (skt. *dhūrta*); 107a (skt. *capala*)

RA

ra ri *defilement, dirt; dark spot* 47c, 49d, 51d (skt. *kalaṅka*)

rag *subject, subservient, dependent* 105b (free for skt. *māna*)?

raṅ *self* 50c (skt. *svayam*); 51b, 131c, 137b (skt. *ātman*); 51c (skt. n. e.); 72b, 76d, 124b, 131b (skt. *sva-*)

raṅ ñams *one's own condition, state; strength* 84a (skt. *svāsthya*)

raṅ ñid *one's self* 68a (skt. *jantu*); 71d (skt. *svayam*)

raṅ bźin *nature, temper, disposition* 12b (skt. *ākṛti*); 22a, 76c, 81b, 102a, 108a, 128a (skt. *prakṛti*); 25d, 89d (skt. n. e.); 53a (skt. *svabhāva*); 60b (skt. *ātman*); 74a (raṅ bźin las; skt. *prakṛtyā*); 78a (skt. *guṇa*); 89c (skt. *svayam*); 110a, 134d (skt. *bhāva*)

ran pa *to be appropriate, proportionate* 101b (ran na; free for skt. *madhyamaḥ*); 119d (ran par 'gyur; skt. *bhavati*)

ran par *moderately* 101c (skt. *prāmāṇya*)

rab short for *rab tu*
→ śes rab

rab tu *very, exceedingly* 7a (rab; skt. *ati-*)

rab tu khro ba *to be very angry* 87a (rab khros; skt. *atikupitā*); 88d (rab tu *khros na; skt. *pradveṣe*)

rab tu goms pa *accustomed; experienced* 73c (skt. *nipuṇa*)

rab tu sgrim pa *to take great pains, try hard* 136a (rab bsgrims; free for skt. *abhyadhikatayā*)

rab tu che ba *very big; very high* 80a (skt. *atisumahat*)

rab tu ñam(s) thag pa *excessive pain, greatest calamity* 65a (skt. *kṛcchragata*)

rab tu gduṅ pa *to torment heavily, torture* 8c (rab gduṅs na; skt. *tāpito*)

rab tu 'bad pa *endeavour, exertion, great effort* 74d (skt. *prayatna*)

rab tu maṅ po *very frequent, plentiful* 121d (skt. *pracura*)

rab tu 'tshe ba *to hurt, torment* 8a (rab gtses na; skt. *upataptāḥ*); 59b (rab tu 'tshe[r] ba⟨r⟩ byed; skt. *prabādhante*)

rab tu mdzes pa *very beautiful* 77c (skt. *aticāru*)

rab tu źim pa *very sweet-scented* 77d (skt. *surabhin*)

rab rib *mist, dimness, glimmer; darkness* 107c (skt. *timira*)

rabs → ya rabs

ral gri *sword* 116d (skt. *khaḍga*); 129c (skt. *khaḍga*)

ri dwags *animals of chase, game* 110d (skt. *mṛga*)

ri (bo) *mountain* 46c (skt. *parvata*); 139c (mi g.yo *ri; skt. *acala*)
→ ku la'i ri

rig pa *knowledge* 99d (rig pa med pa; free for skt. *aprasanna*); 125b (skt. *vidyā*)
→ ma rig pa

rigs *family, lineage; caste, class; kind, sort* 3c (skt. *jāti*); 10b (stod rigs; skt. *kulīna*)
→ cho rigs, smad rigs

rigs ldan pa *one of good origin, noble-born one* 17b (skt. *kulocchrita*); 17c (skt. *abhijāta*); 25b (skt. *kulīna*)

rigs pa *(to be) proper, suitable, appropriate* 6b (rigs ma yin; skt. *na … kṛtye*); 15a (rigs; skt. *yuktyā*); 16b (rigs te; skt. *ucitam*); 21a (mi rigs; skt. *anucita-*); 21b (skt. *śucin*); 137b (rigs; skt. n. e.)

riṅ po → thag riṅ (po)

rin chen *jewel, precious stone* 3c, 89c, 103c (skt. *ratna*); 52a (skt. *mahārgha*)

rin po che *jewel* 42d, 90d (skt. *ratna*)

rib → rab rib

rim gyis *by turns, gradually* 9c (in antonymic expression for skt. *sapadi*); 80d (skt. n. e.); 127b (skt. *krameṇa*)

rim par *in a row; by degrees, gradually* 106c (rim; skt. *krameṇa*)

ruṅ ba *to be fit, suitable* 111d (expresses the skt. gerundive)

rul ba — *(to be) rotten, putrid; to rot, get rotten* 21c (rul ba'i; skt. *mṛta-*)?; 60c (skt. *virasa*)

rus sbal — *turtle* 122d (free for skt. *maṇḍūka*)

re — (emphatic particle) 109b (skt. n. e.)
⟶ ñin re

reg pa — *to touch* 13d (reg par byed; skt. *spṛśati*); 57a (reg par translates skt. *pramarṣṭum* i. o. skt. *pramārṣṭum*)?

ro — *dead body, corpse* 21c (skt. *kuṇapa*)

ro gcig — *of one taste* 39b (free for skt. *samaṃ*?); 118c (skt. *ekarasa*)

rog — ⟶ bya rog

rom — ⟶ chab rom

rol — ⟶ pha rol

rwa ru — *horn* 70d (skt. *viṣāṇa*)

LA

la la — *some, few* 123b (skt. *kva cid*)

lag 'gro — *serpent* 58c, 113c (skt. *bhujaga*)

lag (pa) — *hand, arm* 13d, 117c (skt. *kara*); 73c (skt. *hasta*)

laṅ tsho — *youth* 20a, 30c (skt. *yauvana*)

lam — *way, path* 114c (skt. *pathin*); 117d (skt. *mārga*); 125b (skt. n. e.); 135c (lam du źugs pa; skt. *pathika*); 144a (skt. *padavī*)
⟶ rmi lam

lam log — *wrong way* 121c (renders wrongly skt. *vipada* as if *vipatha*)

las — *act, deed, work* 72b (skt. *karman*); 111d (las su ruṅ ba; skt. *karmaṇyam*); 136a?

li śi — *clove plant* 77d (skt. *lavaṅga*)

lugs — ⟶ gźuṅ lugs

lus — *body* 28d (skt. *tanu*)

lus can — *human being* 31a (skt. *vapus*)

lus pa — *to be remaining, be left* 94c (lus pa; skt. *avaśeṣaṃ*)

legs — short for *legs pa, legs par*
⟶ dge legs, bde legs

legs pa — *good* 11b, 103a (skt. *sādhu*); 122a (skt. *kalyāṇa*)

legs par — *well, duly, properly* 93d (skt. *sādhu*)

len pa — *to receive, get, take* 4b (blaṅ; skt. not transmitted); 60d (mi len; skt. *na leḍhi*); 65b (mi len; skt. *niṣevante*); 103b (blaṅ; skt. *samādadīta*)
⟶ bcud (kyi) len, ñams su len pa, lhur len pa

lo tog *harvest, crop* 106c (skt. *sasya*)

lo tsā ba *(Tibetan) translator* 145+

log → phyin ci log, lam log

log par *in a wrong manner* 45c, 130b (skt. *viparīta*); 125d (contextually for skt. *andha*)

loṅ → me loṅ, dmus loṅ

loṅ ba *(to be) blind* 38c (skt. *muṣita*); 99c, 117d (skt. *andha*); 99d (skt. *akṣa*); 115c (skt. *proṣitanayana*)

loṅs spyod *enjoyment, fruition* 72a (skt. *bhoga*)

rluṅ *wind* 23a, 132c (skt. *vāyu*); 41c, 58c (skt. *pavana*); 53d (skt. n. e.); 129c (skt. n. e.; is *rluṅ chu* a corruption of *graṅ chu* for skt. *śītam ... payas*?)

ŚA

śa *meat* 60c (free for skt. *asthi*)

śa ra bha (transliteration of skt. *śarabhā*) *a kind of deer or mythological eight-legged animal* 43c (skt. *śarabhā*)

śar → 'char ba

śas *part; digit of the moon* 94c (śas tsam; skt. *kalā*)
→ cha śas

śiṅ *wood*34c, 42c (skt. *kāṣṭha*); 62d, 136c (skt. *taru*)
→ bud śiṅ

śiṅ bal *cotton from the cotton tree* 89d (skt. *tūla*)

śiṅ srin *wood-worm* 76b (skt. *ghuṇa*)

śin tu *very, greatly, utmost* 26b (skt. *param*); 29a, 44c, 90a, 110a (skt. *ati-*); 29d (skt. *adhikam*); 41d (skt. *su-*); 140b (skt. n. e.)

śug → rgya śug

śugs *inherent strength, power, energy* 71c ('phaṅs pa'i śugs; skt. *-saṃskāraḥ*)

śel *crystal, glass* 26c (skt. *sphaṭika*)

śes pa *to know, be proficient in, be able to* 4d, 11b (śes; skt. *jānāti*); 11a (śes; skt. n. e.); 73d (śes par byed; skt. *vijānati*); 97d (śes; skt. *vijānanti*); 100b (śes bya; skt. *āhur*); 104b (śes par bya; skt. *vijñeyāḥ*); 104d[1] (mi śes; skt. *a-...jño*); 104d[2] (śes pa med; skt. *na vijānāti*); 115c (śes; skt. *viduṣaḥ*); 121b (śes; skt. *-jñāś*)

śes rab *wisdom* 132b (skt. n. e.); 143b (skt. not transmitted)

śes rab (daṅ) ldan pa *wise person, very talented being* 73a, 83b (skt. *prājña*)

śes rig *knowledge* 30b (skt. *abhijña*)

gśin rje *God of Death* 88c (skt. *yama*); 138d (skt. *kṛtānta*)

gśog → 'dab gśog

gśoṅ *deep valley* 46d (free for skt. *viṣama*)

bśes pa *to know, be acquainted* 81b (bśes mi bya; free for skt. *viśvāso na kṣamaḥ*) → mdza' bśes

SA

sa *earth, globe, world* 1c (skt. *bhuvana*); 24d (skt. *pṛthivī*); 54a (skt. *bhūmi*); 82c (sa rdul; skt. *dhūli*); 85d (skt. *bhū*); 120c, 131d (skt. *dharaṇī*)

sa steṅs *earth, ground* 5c (skt. *bhuvana*); 65c (skt. *bhauma*)

sa bon *seed* 54a, 145b (skt. *bīja*)

su *who?* 4d (su yis; skt. *ko*); 122d (sus; skt. *kena*); 133b (su yi ṅor; unusual for skt. *kva cid*)

su źig *who?* 40d, 135d (skt. *ko*); 68d (su źig gis; skt. *kaḥ*)

seṅ ge *lion* 55c (skt. *mṛgendra*)

sen mo *finger-/toenail* 15d (skt. *nakha*)

sems *soul, mind* 56b (skt. *citta*); 66b (skt. *manas*); 108b (skt. *cetas*) → sbyin gtoṅ sems

sems can *animated being, man* 41b, 44b, 90b, 130a (skt. *sattva*)

sems can che ba *noble-hearted being* 36b, 128b (skt. *māhasattva*)

sem(s) pa *to think, consider* 14b (sems te; skt. *kalpate*); 139b (mi bsam; skt. *anāsthā*)

sel ba *to remove* 33d (sel 'gyur min; skt. *niṣiddhaye*); 69c (mun sel mi byed na; skt. *na ... prakāśayati*); 79c (bsal mod; skt. *saṃhṛtam*)

so ga *hot season, summer* 29c (skt. *grīṣma*)

sogs (short for *la sogs pa*) *et cetera, and so forth, and the like* 6a (*stsogs; skt. *ādi*); 100d (free for skt. *saṃgraha*); 113c (skt. *ādi*)

sra ba *hard, solid, compact, firm* 87c (skt. *kaṭhina*)

sraṅ *a kind of measure, about an ounce* 73d (skt. *pala*)

sraṅ mda' *lever of a pair of scales* 101c (skt. *tulā*)

srid *length, extension; domion* 64a (lhag par srid mtho; skt. *abhyunnata*) → ji srid, de srid

srid pa *to be possible* 22b (mi srid; skt. *jātu na*) → mi srid dṅos po

srid (pa) gsum *the three worlds* 145c (skt. *tribhuvana*)

srin → śiṅ srin

srin bu *insect, worm* 34c (skt. *ghuṇa*); 92d (skt. *kṛmi*)

sruṅ mkhas pa *keeper, guardian, watchman* 140a (skt. *rakṣin*)

sruṅ ba	*to protect, shelter, preserve* 28d (sruṅ; skt. *pāti*); 35d (sruṅ bar 'gyur; skt. *nibadhyante*); 140b (bsruṅ bar dka'; skt. *durārabdhāḥ*)
srun pa	→ mi srun pa
sreg pa (I)	*partridge* 126d (skt. *tittiri*)
sreg pa (II)	*to burn* 29d (sreg; skt. *pacati*); 48c (bsregs na; skt. *-(agni)patitasya*); 81d (sreg par byed; skt. *dahaty*); 106d (sreg byed; skt. *dahati*); 127d (sreg byed; skt. *dahanti*); 134c (bsregs na; skt. *-bhukta-*); 143b (bsreg; skt. not transmitted); 143c (bsregs; skt. not transmitted); 145b (bsregs pas; skt. *kṣata-*) → sbyin sreg mkhan
srog	*life* 55a (free for skt. *mūla*); 134a (srog la bab; skt. *antyāvastha*)
sla ba	*(to be) easy* 36a, 38a (skt. *su-*)
sloṅ ba (I)	*to cause to rise, help to rise* 43b (bslaṅ bar nus; skt. *saṃyantuṃ ... śaknuvanti*)
sloṅ ba (II)	*to ask, require* 97b (ma bslaṅs; skt. *ayācitaṃ*); *beggar* 112a, 112b, 112d (twice) (skt. *arthin*)
slob dpon	*teacher* 145+
gsar pa	*new, fresh* 86d (mar gsar; skt. *sarpis*)
gsal ba	*(to be) clear, distinct, bright, shine; illuminate* 5d (gsal bar byed; skt. *prakāśayati*); 29d (mi gsal; free for skt. *bāla*); 30b (gsal ba'i; skt. *vidagdha°*); 35c (skt. *sphuṭa*); 48b (lhag par ... gsal; skt. *abhivyajyate*); 49b (*gsal; skt. *dṛśyante*); 93d (gsal mi gyur; skt. *na ... prakāśante*); 107d (gsal mi 'gyur; skt. *na ... virājante*); 114a (skt. *viśuddha*)
gsum	*three* → srid (pa) gsum
gser	*gold* 111c (skt. *suvarṇa*); 123d (skt. *heman*)
gsod pa	*to kill, slay, murder* 28c (gsod par byed; skt. *mārayati*); 55c (gsod; skt. *druhyati*); 59d (gsod par byed; skt. *vinighnanti*); 110d (gsod pa; skt. *nighnanti*); 132d (gsod par byed; skt. *hanti*) → khyad du gsod pa
gson po	*to live, be alive; remain alive* 84b (gson por gyur pa; free for skt. *prabhutvam*) → chud gson pa
bsam	→ sem(s) pa
bsal	→ sel ba
bsod nams ldan pa	*one who is fortunate, virtuous* 108a (skt. *puṇyavat*)
bsrun	→ mi bsrun pa
bsregs	→ sreg pa (II)
bsres pa	*mixed up* 65b (skt. *miśra*)
bslaṅ	→ sloṅ ba
bslaṅs	→ sloṅ ba

HA

lhag par — *more, still more, far more, extremely* 8b (skt. *bhṛśam*); 8d (skt. *adhikam*); 12a, 78a (skt. *ati-*); 41b (skt. *atyartha*); 48b (skt. *abhi-*)?; 61b (skt. *atyartham*); 64a (skt. *abhi-*); 118b (skt. *atyanta*); 136b (skt. *atyucchritam*); 141d (skt. *bhūyas*)

lhan cig (tu) — (postposition) *with one another, together with* 47d (skt. *saha-*)

lhan cig skyes pa — *born together with, inborn* 22b (skt. *sahabhū*)

lhuṅ — → ltuṅ ba

lhur len pa — *to apply one's self, bestow pains, be eager* 27a (lhur len te; free for skt. *na karoti*)

A

a ka ru — (transliteration of skt. *aguros*) *Aloe wood* 48c (skt. *aguru*)

a ri ta — (transliteration of skt. *ariṣṭa*) *soapberry tree* 62d (skt. *ariṣṭa*)

ā rya koṣa — **Āryākoṣa* (transliteration of the Sanskrit title of the present work) o

Appendices

Stanzas from LSP not contained in ĀK

ज्ञात्वा यत्किंचिदपि प्राज्ञाः कृति [◡◡ ◡◡ ◡◡ ◡ — ◡ ◡◡ ◡◡ ⏓ ।
◡◡ ◡◡ ◡◡ ◡◡ ◡◡ ◡◡ ◡◡ ◡◡] ⟨अ⟩णुनापि रन्ध्रेण ॥ २ ॥

2. Knowing just a little bit
the wise ....
....
.... even by a small hole.

सत्स्वेव सतामधिकं यान्ति विशेषाः प्रसिद्धिमणवो ऽपि ।
सीधुगुण ए[◡ ◡◡ ◡◡ ◡◡ ◡◡ ◡◡ ◡◡ ◡ ◡◡ ◡◡ ⏓ ॥ ६ ॥]

6. Only among the good will the qualities of the good,
even the smallest ones, be appreciated greatly.
The qualities of rum ....
....

शशिकरशुचयो ऽपि गुणाः शठेषु दोषा भवन्ति साधूनाम् ।
कलधौतमपि रुमायां निपतितमूषीभवत्येव ॥ १२ ॥

12. Even if the virtues of good people are as pure
as the rays of the moon—for the bad they become faults.
Even gold which has fallen into a salt lake
becomes completely acid (or salty).

विदुषि कथयत्यपि हितं मनःप्रसादो ऽपि भवति न शठस्य ।
रत्नभुव एव रत्नं गर्जति जलदे समुद्भवति ॥ १७ ॥

17. Even when a wise person tells (him) something useful,
a bad person is not pleased in his heart at all.
When a cloud emits the sound of thunder
jewels come forth only from the ocean.

चूडामणिरिव गुणवान् शिरसापि धृतो नरं विभूषयति ।
कुङ्कुममुपर्यपि कृतं चन्दनमवभासयत्येव ॥ १९ ॥

19. A virtuous person, even if carried on one's head,
adorns a man like a crest-jewel.
Sandal-wood easily surpasses saffron,
even if the latter is placed high.

पुलकोद्गम इव करिणां दोषो ऽपि महात्मनां प्रियो जगतः ।
धनुष इव दुर्जनस्य तु गुणो ऽपि लोकोपघाताय ॥ २८ ॥

28. Like the bristling of the hairs of elephants
even a fault of great beings is pleasant to other people.
The virtues of bad people, however,
do (only) harm to other people, like (the string) of a bow.

व्यवहारेणैव जनो लोके [◡ ◡] गु [◡ ◡ — ◡ ◡◡ ◡◡ ◡] ।
परिभोग एव कथयति सौभाग्यगुणं विलासिन्याः ॥ ३३ ॥

33. Only by daily usage can the qualities [of the good people
be appreciated] in the world.
Only enjoying them tells us something
about the pleasant qualities of a beautiful woman.

आदावेव गुरुष्वपि विदूष्य चित्तं भवन्ति दुष्प्राज्ञाः ।
मत्स्याः किल हन्तव्या इति कैवर्ता वपन्ति शणाम् ॥ ३८ ॥

38. Already in the beginning people of low intelligence
are polluted in their hearts even towards venerable persons.
"As it is known fishes are to be killed"—
saying this the fishermen throw their nets.

साहसिकत्वं गुणा इति यल्लघवः कल्पयन्ति तद् युक्तम् ।
गुञ्जाफलेषु दृष्टा प्रवालकाशा पुलिन्द्राणाम् ॥ ४१ ॥

41. 'Rashness can be a virtue'—
this statement made by frivolous people is appropriate:
in the berries of the Guñjā plant
there is the splendour of corals for the Pulindas.

किमपीदमिन्द्रजालं स्वल्पे ऽपि यदाश्रये समाने च ।
व्यवहारा वचनानि च न मिलन्ति नृणां मुखानीव ॥ ४५ ॥

45. This is indeed some kind of jugglery
that while the basis is rather limited and uniform
the actions and the declarations of men
do not coincide as do their faces.

अनुरञ्जिता अपि गुणैर्न नमन्ति प्रकृतयो विना दण्डात् ।
अङ्गगतापि न वीणा किल मधुरमताडिता क्वणति ॥ ४६ ॥

46. Though propitiated because of his good qualities,
the people do not bow (to the king) without (fear of) punishment.
As it is known, a lute, though in the lap (of a person)
does not produce sweet sounds unless (the strings are) struck.

सङ्गतमसता महतः काञ्चनमयसेव नैति संधानम् ।
भेर्या न मिलति वीणा कल्याणप्रक्वणा सती ॥ ४७ ॥

47. If a great and a bad person meet,
they cannot form an alliance, as in the case of gold and iron.
A vīṇā does not go together with a kettle-drum
because the vīṇā produces such a fine (and characteristic) sound.

गुणवद्भिरेव गुणिनां कृतशुद्धं भवति सङ्गतमजर्यम् ।
सुचिरं प्रवाति गन्धः ककुभादिष्वेव कुसुमानाम् ॥ ४८ ॥

48. Only the alliance of the virtuous with the virtuous
remains pure and everlasting.
The fragrance of the flowers wafts
for a very long time only on the peaks [of mountains].

स्वल्पापि साधुसंपद्भोग्या महतां न पृथ्व्यपि खलश्रीः ।
सारसमेव पयस्तृषमपनयति न यादसां पत्युः ॥ ५१ ॥

51. Even the smallest welfare of the good is enjoyable for the great person,
but not the most abundant wealth of the evil.
Only the water of the pond quenches thirst,
but not (the water) of the ocean.

मतिमानपि न विराजत्यपथेन प्रस्थितो विसंवादात् ।
श्रोतुः कलापि वीणा न वितन्त्री चित्तमाक्षिपति ॥ ५५ ॥

55. Even an intelligent person does not shine
if he has set out on a wrong path on account of deception.
Even the sweet-sounding vīṇā will not captivate
the heart of the listener if it is without strings.

तज्जन्मनापि न जडः कर्तुमलं यद्बुधः क्षणात्कुरुते ।
कल्पार्जितमपि रूपं पश्यति नाश्वेव किं चक्षुः ॥ ५६ ॥

56. A dull-witted person is not able to accomplish in a lifetime
what a wise person can do in a split second.
Does the eye not perceive quite rapidly
the form which has been acquired over an eon?

मह्देव बलिन उच्चैः सर्वमभिघ्नन्ति न प्रकृतिनम्रम् ।
अशनिः प्रायो निपतति गिरिशिखरेष्वेव न तृणेषु ॥ ५७ ॥

57. The strong attack all that is great,
not that which is humble by nature.
The thunderbolt usually hits the tops
of the mountains, not the grass.

दुर्बल एव बलीयसि शक्तिं दर्शयति वाग्विषाणेन ।
कुण्ठित एव ग्रावणि टङ्को ऽधिकमुद्वमति तेजः ॥ ५८ ॥

58. Only the weak one demonstrates his strength
towards the stronger one with the sword ('horn') of his speech.
Only when it has become blunt,
the stone-cutter's chisel emits sparks at a rock.

अद्यापि यान्ति नान्तं बहवः कृतिनो ऽपि धूर्तचरितानाम् ।
वेश्यारुदितस्यार्थं वृद्धविटा अपि न जानन्ति ॥ ५९ ॥

59. Even today many very intelligent people
cannot reach the end of the conduct of cunning people.
Even old paramours do not understand
the motive behind the weeping of courtesans.

आदौ लज्जयति कृतं मध्ये परिभवति तिक्तमवसाने ।
खलसंगतस्य कथयत यदि सुस्थितमस्ति किंचिदपि ॥ ६२ ॥

62. In the beginning his activity makes us feel ashamed,
in the middle period it brings us insult,
and is all empty (useless) in the end;
say, is there anything that is stable and trustworthy
in associating with the wicked? (A.A.R. in MSS)

उपलक्षयन्ति शीलं प्रायः सब्रह्मचारिणो जगतः ।
सूक्ष्मां गतिमप्यम्भसि मत्स्यो मत्स्यस्य जानाति ॥ ६३ ॥

63. Generally the companions observe
whether people behave in accordance with the laws of morality.
It is the fish who knows even the finest movements
of another fish in the water.

उद्वेगकरी परुषा यत्किंचनकारिणी बिभेत्री च ।
भार्येव सत्यरहिता वाग्नरमचिराद्विनाशयति ॥ ६५ ॥

65. Like a wife that does not speak the truth
a speech that agitates, is harsh,
haphazard and causes fear
ruins a man within a short time.

क्रोधिनमेव क्रोधः प्रथमं ग्रसते परं च नैकान्तः ।
स्वाश्रयमवश्यमग्निर्दहति तदन्यं तु नावश्यम् ॥ ६८ ॥

68. Anger first devours just him who is angry,
but not necessarily the opponent.
Fire necessarily destroys its own basis,
but not necessarily that which is separated from it.

प्राज्ञकृतेनैव पथा व्रजञ्जनः स्वस्ति यात्यकुशलो ऽपि ।
वज्रस्यैव स महिमा यन्मणिमध्यं विशति तन्तुः ॥ ६९ ॥

69. Even if he is without skills, a man walks safely
if he follows only that path which has been laid by the intelligent.
It is only due to the power of a diamond-pin
that a thread can go through a jewel.

नावश्यमधीयानाः सर्वे फलमाप्नुवन्ति विद्यानाम् ।
उष्ट्रः कुङ्कुममनिशं वहतीति न तत्समालभते ॥ ७१ ॥

71. Not all of those who study
will necessarily attain the fruit of knowledge.
Although the camel constantly carries saffron
it never obtains it.

पापाद्विरतो ऽपि शठः प्रत्ययमासाद्य विकुरुते ऽवश्यम् ।
दग्धस्थिता चिरादपि सुधाम्बुसिक्ताग्निमुद्वमति ॥ ७६ ॥

76. Even if a bad person abstains from sinful deeds
he will inevitably do harm once he has found a reason.
Even after a long time a brick that has remained hot
emits fire when sprinkled with water.

मित्रोदये विवर्णो *दोषेकाविष्कृताभ्यधिकसारः ।
स्नेहक्षयेण निर्वृतिमभ्येति खलः प्रदीप इव ॥ ७७ ॥

b *doṣekā°*] *doṣaika°* Ed.

77. A wicked person becomes pale when a friend is successful,
his essence is made visible only through his arms,
and he becomes pleased by the loss of love,
thereby resembling a lamp
which becomes pale when the sun rises,
whose great importance is revealed only at night
and which becomes extinguished when the oil is consumed.

श्रोतरि सत्यपविघ्नाः सदसि गिरो वाग्मिनां प्रकाशन्ते ।
भुवमेव प्राप्य यवः (?) शुद्धिमुपैत्यश्मरत्नस्य ॥ ७८ ॥ (?)

78. When there are listeners then the words of speakers
shine forth in an assembly free of impediments.
Barley attains the purity of an *aśmaratna*
only when it has been placed in the earth. (?)

अहमग्रणीर्नृपसभाश्रेष्ठतमो ऽहं पुरे च सर्वत्र ।
अहमेव चास्य मित्रं नीतिचणः काव्यचुञ्चुश्च ॥ ८० ॥

80. 'I am the leader, I am the very best
in the assembly of the king and everywhere in the city.
And only I am his friend,
skilled in the fields of policy and poetry.'

इति धृष्टशब्ददुर्भगपरुषवचनचेष्टभग्नगरिमाणः ।
प्रथयन्ति स्वयमबुधाः श्रुतधनदारिद्र्यमन्तःस्थम् ॥ ८१ ॥

81. The stupid people who by such a kind of speech,
which is unfortunate, harsh, and full of arrogant words,
spoil their reputation,—they display their inner poverty
as far as their learning is concerned.

अल्पश्रुतबल एव प्रायः प्रकटयति वाग्वैभवमुच्चैः ।
सर्वत्र कुनट एव हि नाटकमधिकं विडम्बयति ॥ ८२ ॥

82. Generally only those with little strength of learning
make a great show of their command of language.
Everywhere it is the only poor actor
who overdoes his performance.

प्राकृतकर्मणि गुणिनः शक्ता इति बुद्धिमान्न संदध्यात् ।
सर्वधुरीणाः प्रबले दाम्नि महोक्षा न युज्यन्ते ॥ ८४ ॥

84. A wise person should not appoint talented people,
for an ordinary task only because they are capable (of doing it).
Strong bulls who are fit for all kinds of burdens
are not fixed with a weak rope. (?)

महतामेव महत्त्वे चित्तं रमते न नीचपरमाणोः ।
तिष्ठत्युपरि घृतमपां स्वयमेवाधो मधु व्रजति ॥ ८७ ॥

87. It is only the mind of the great that rejoices at greatness,
not that of the low and insignificant.
While ghee floats at the surface of water
honey sinks down of its own accord.

यदि जडता यदि तेजः सर्वमलं मूढ एव न प्राज्ञे ।
पाषाणमप्सु मज्जत्यभ्याहतमग्निमुद्वमति ॥ ८८ ॥

88. Whether it is dullness (or: solidity),
or it is brightness (or: heat)—
either is sufficient only to a dull person, not to a wise.
A stone sinks down in water,
but if it is struck it emits sparks.

उपघात एव केवलमुपयोगं याति दुर्जन उपान्तः ।
मुक्त्वा परस्य विशसनमन्यच्छस्त्रेण किं क्रियते ॥ ८९ ॥

89. A bad person in one's proximity
can be used only for the purpose of destruction.
What else can be done with a knife
except slashing someone else apart?

व्याख्यातुमेव केचित् कुशलाः शास्त्रं नियोक्तुमलमन्ये ।
उपमानयति करोऽन्नं रसांस्तु जिह्वैव जानाति ॥ ९० ॥

90. Some people are skilled only in explaining something,
others are able to apply a (field of) science.
The hand offers the food,
the tongue alone, however, recognizes its taste.

मोहात्प्रायो ऽप्रतरा पयसि विषीदन्ति जानुदघ्ने ऽपि ।
प्राज्ञास्तूपायबलात् सागरमपि गोष्पदीयन्ति ॥ ९१ ॥

91. Because of their stupidity dull-witted persons
usually despair of in water that reaches up only to their knees.
For the intelligent persons, however, even the ocean
becomes as shallow as the water in the footprint of an ox.

चित्तस्य तल्लघुत्वं यद्विभवाः प्रतनवो ऽपि मदयन्ति । (= ĀK 56ab)
लूतानामपि तानान्मक्षिकमशकं निधनमेति ॥ ९३ ॥

93. This is the weakness of mind
that it gets intoxicated by even the smallest possessions.
It is because of the web of the spiders
that flies and mosquitos die.

विषयगणः कापुरुषं करोति वशवर्तिनं न सत्पुरुषम् ।
बध्नाति मशकमेव हि लूतातन्तुर्न मातङ्गम् ॥ ९४ ॥ (= ĀK 56cd)

94. The sense objects govern a bad person,
not a good person.
A spider's web is able to hold only a fly,
not an elephant.

गुणवन्तमुपासीना लघवो ऽपि सभागतां व्रजन्ति सताम् ।
प्रालेयाचलमूर्धसु भवन्ति तुहिनान्यपि हिमानि ॥ ९५ ॥

95. Because they follow the virtuous,
even light-hearted persons may join the ranks of the good.
On the peaks of the Himavat mountain
even snow becomes ice.

सुजना एव व्यसने शक्तास्त्रातुं न दुर्जनभुजङ्गाः ।
तारयति लोकमम्भसि नौरेव शिला निमज्जयति ॥ ९७ ॥

97. Only good people are able to offer protection
in a calamity, not bad people who are like snakes.
Only a ship can save people while they are in the water
while a stone will drown them.

दूरे ऽपि गुणवदुदये प्रीताप्रीता भवन्ति सदसन्तः ।
उन्मिषति कमलमुदयति भानौ कुमुदानि खिद्यन्ते ॥ ९८ ॥

98. Even when it happens far away,
the good rejoice at the success of a virtuous person
while the bad are unhappy about it.
When the sun rises, the *kamala* lotus opens
while the *kumudas* become tired (and close).

दोषेषु यद्रमन्ते न गुणेषु खलास्तदप्यनाश्चर्यम् ।
परिदधति केकिपक्षान्विहाय रत्नान्यपि पुलिन्दाः ॥ ९९ ॥

99. It is not at all surprising that the wicked
rejoice in faults and not in virtues.
The wild Pulindas neglect jewels
and adorn themselves with the feathers of peacocks.

परपृष्ठमांसलुब्धा यत्किंचित्सुखमवाप्य सर्पन्ती ।
आशातिकेव खलधीर्निपतति नित्यं व्रणेष्वेव ॥ १०० ॥

100. Covetous of the flesh of someone else's back,
crawling around after having attained
some insignificant happiness,
the mind of the wicked, like a bluebottle fly,
always comes down only on wounds ('vulnerable spots').

दोषमपि गुणवति जने दृष्ट्वा गुणरागिणो न खिद्यन्ते ।
प्रीत्येव शशिनि पतितं पश्यति लोकः कलङ्कमपि ॥ १०१ ॥

101. Even when they see a fault in a virtuous person
those longing for virtues are not disappointed.
It is with pleasure that people behold the dark spots
which have fallen on the moon.

साधुष्वेवातितरामरुंतुदाः स्वां विवृण्वते वृत्तिम् ।
व्याघ्रा निघ्नन्ति मृगान्मृतमपि तु न सिंहमाददते ॥ १०५ ॥

105. Those who are able to inflict severe wounds
display their own (characteristic) behaviour only towards the good.
Tigers kill deer,
but do not even touch a dead lion.

ऋजुवक्रशिशुजरत्तासु चन्द्रमाः सर्वथा ह्रत्येव ।
सा जातु नास्त्यवस्था न यत्र सुजनः प्रियं कुरुते ॥ १०६ ॥

106. Whether it is straight or crooked, waxing or waning,
the moon is always only pleasing.
There is indeed no condition,
in which a good person is not agreeable.

कारणात एव वैरं भवतीति मृषैव भाषते लोकः ।
किं नाम तत्प्रयोजनमह्निनकुलं यत्सदा वैरि ॥ १०७ ॥

107. 'There is always a reason behind enmity'—
this popular saying is completely wrong.
Why are the snake and mongoose
always hostile to each other?

शक्ता अपि सत्पुरुषाः प्रत्यपकाराय नापकुर्वन्ति ।
निर्घातानपि सहते धरणी न दिवः प्रतिददाति ॥ १०९ ॥

109. Although they could do so,
good people never respond to an offence.
The earth tolerates even (the attacks) of hurricanes
and does not return them to the heavens.

अनपकृतावनभिज्ञः सकलजगद्व्यसनपण्डितः सततम् ।
प्रकृतिरियं काप्यसती परपीडायै खलजनस्य ॥ ११० ॥

110. He who is ignorant in not harming others
is always a great expert in creating distress for everybody.
Bad people have this kind of attitude
in order to torment others.

श्रुत्यापि यान्ति खेदं महतामधमाः कथैव का वृद्धौ ।
अभ्युदयेऽपि न दीपो राजति किमुतो च मध्याह्नम् ॥ १११ ॥

111. Mean people become annoyed
when they only hear of great beings,
and much more so in the case of their success.
Already at dawn a lamp no longer shines,
not to speak of (the time of) midday.

स्वगुणानिव परदोषान्वक्तुं न सतोऽपि शक्नुवन्ति बुधाः ।
स्वगुणानिव परदोषानसतोऽपि खलास्तु कथयन्ति ॥ ११२ ॥

112. The wise are unable to mention their own virtues
and likewise the faults of others, even if they exist.
The wicked, however, speak of their own virtues
and likewise of the faults of others, even if these do not exist.

कृत्वापि येन लज्जामुपैति साधुः परोदितेनापि ।
तदकृत्वैव खलजनः स्वयमुद्गिरतीति धिग्लघुताम् ॥ ११३ ॥

113. The good are embarrassed
if others mention their good deeds,
even if they have done them.
Even without having done them,
the wicked speak about (their good deeds) themselves—
fie upon this kind of superficiality!

व्यसनैरेवाघ्राताः शृण्वन्ति वचांसि पापमित्राणाम् ।
उद्भूतारिष्टानामपथ्यमेवाधिकं स्वदते ॥ ११६ ॥

116. Those affected by nothing but vices
listen to the words of evil friends.
Those who bear the signs of death
relish only that which is unwholesome.

लोकस्य दुःखभूयस आनन्दः पेलवो बहु व्यसनम् ।
बाल्यं जरा च सुचिरं यौवनमल्पानि तु दिनानि ॥ ११७ ॥

117. For men who are full of sorrow
joy is scarce and misfortune is abundant.
Childhood and old age last very long,
but youth only a few days.

उपचारमात्रकमलं परमार्थः कार्यिणां न सर्वत्र ।
प्रश्रय एव प्रायः सद्भावरतं क्वचित्स्त्रीणाम् ॥ ११८ ॥

118. For those industrious it is enough to be occupied,
they do not have any lofty aim in mind.
Generally (mere) courtesy is enough for women,
they rarely delight in a (genuinely) good character.

द्वयमपि दुःस्थितमेतत् प्राज्ञे दैन्यं जडेषु चोत्साहः ।
खलतिर्मूर्ध्नि न राजति मुखे ऽपि केशा न शोभन्ते ॥ ११९ ॥

119. These two are quite out of place:
the listlessness of an intelligent person
and the initiative of dull persons.
Baldness does not look resplendent on a head
and hairs do not look nice in a face.

बलवानहमिति यो मदमाश्रित्य परानुपैति न स विद्वान् ।
सवितुरपि दक्षिणायनगतस्य तेजो जडं भवति ॥ १२१ ॥

121. He who approaches others haughtily,
thinking "I am mighty," is not wise.
Even the heat of the sun becomes cool,
when it has set out for the southernly course.

शिक्षयति लोक एव प्रायः कुसृतीर्जनं सुशीलमपि ।
इन्धनमेव प्रथयति हविर्भुजो दाहसामर्थ्यम् ॥ १२३ ॥

123. The world usually teaches the wrong paths
even to people of well-founded morality.
It is only the fuel which incites
the fire's ability to burn.

स्वस्थः प्रियमनुरक्तं न जहाति जनो जनं विपत्तौ तु ।
भवति दशासौ यस्यां प्राणानपि मोक्तुमुत्सहते ॥ १२६ ॥

126. A healthy person does not abandon a beloved person,
who is dear (to him);
in a calamity, however, that situation might occur
in which he tries to throw away even his own life.

द्विषदभियुक्तावस्थामनुभवितारो विदन्ति न स्वस्थाः ।
न स्रोतसो चलाचलमनुह्यमानो विजानाति ॥ १२८ ॥

128. Only those who experience it know the condition
of being attacked by an enemy, not those living in peace.
He who has not been carried away by it
does not know the unsteadiness of a stream.

न विना नीचविमर्दादन्तःस्थैर्यं प्रकृष्टमश्नुवते ।
अग्नावेव सुवर्णं शुध्यत्कल्याणतामेति ॥ १२९ ॥

129. Without the attacks of mean people
one does not attain an excellent inner stability.
Gold attains its beauty
only after it has been purified in fire.

न विना फलनिष्पत्तेः स्वगुणानां सारतां जनो वेत्ति ।
मन्त्राणां सामर्थ्यं मनुते सर्पान्वशीकुर्वन् ॥ १३१ ॥

131. Without the ripening of the fruit
one does not see the essence of one's own qualities.
Only he who spellbinds snakes
believes in the power of Mantras.

प्रकृतेर्दुःशोधतया कुलजा अपि सन्ति केचिदतिरौद्राः ।
शीतसलिलोदितान्यपि कमलान्युष्णेन विकसन्ति ॥ १३३ ॥

133. Since (nature) is difficult to refine
even some of the noble-born are very violent.
Although they grow in cool water
the *kamala* lotuses open their blossoms (only) when it is hot.

प्राप्तविह्वीना विषयाः सुतरामुत्कण्ठयन्ति हृदयानि ।
स्वप्नक्षणादृष्टा इव दुर्लभदयितापरिष्वङ्गाः ॥ १३५ ॥

135. Objects of the senses
that are first attained and then disappear
entice the hearts (of human beings) very much;
they are like the embraces of one's beloved that are hard to get,
experienced in a dream for a split second (only).

स्वल्पेनाप्युदयेन प्रायः सर्वंकषा भवन्ति खलाः ।
उदधिर्भुवनजलैरपि न जातु सीमानमुच्चरते ॥ १३७ ॥

137. Even with the smallest success the wicked
generally become cruel to all.
Even with all the water of the earth
the ocean does not transgress its borders.

क्लीबस्य यान्ति काला व्याधस्येव सततं द्वयेनैव ।
पीडयतः परमधिकं परेण वा पीड्यमानस्य ॥ १३८ ॥

138. For the coward as for the hunter
time elapses always in a twofold manner:
either he torments his opponent excessively
or he will be tormented by his opponent.

जरयन्ति विषं गृह्णन्ति पन्नगानशनिमप्यपघ्नन्ति ।
दमयन्ति दिग्गजानपि किमसाध्यं नाम कुशलानाम् ॥ १४० ॥

140. They digest poison,
they seize snakes, they even ward off thunderbolts,
they tame even the elephants
who guard the directions of the compass—
what is there that cannot accomplished by skilful people?

तनुविभवे ऽपि हि नयवति शत्रौ प्राज्ञा भवन्त्यधिकयत्नाः ।
प्रत्यल्प एव वारिणि नावो यत्नेन वाह्यन्ते ॥ १४२ ॥

142. Even when the enemy has little wealth,
but knows the principles of policy,
the wise do not reduce their efforts.
When there is only very little amount of water,
it requires effort to set a ship in motion.

अल्पेनाप्युद्वेगं व्रजन्ति सन्तः स्वभावसुकुमाराः ।
दृष्ट्वैव सविषमन्नं स्रवतो नयने चकोरस्य ॥ १५० ॥

150. The good who are tender by nature
get excited by even a very small (reason).
Already when they behold poisoned food
the eyes of the *cakora* bird start to trickle.

प्रकृतिखलत्वादसतां दोष इव गुणो ऽपि बाधते लोकम् ।
विषकुसुमानां गन्धः सुरभिरपि मनांसि मोहयति ॥ १५१ ॥

151. Since the bad are mischievous by nature
even their virtues annoy others as if they were faults.
The fragrance of poisonous flowers
makes the mind faint, although it smells sweet.

महतां यदेव मूर्धसु तदेव नीचास्तृणाय मन्यन्ते ।
लिङ्गं प्रणमन्ति बुधाः काकः पुनरासनीकुरुते ॥ १५३ ॥

153. What the great honour on their heads,
that the mean regard as trifling as straw.
While the wise worship (Śiva's) liṅga,
the crow makes it its seat.

यदि धार्मिका यदि शठाः प्रायः संतापका मह्लीपतयः ।
दाहं प्रति न चिताग्नेराह्वनीयस्य च विशेषः ॥ १५६ ॥

156. Be they righteous, be they mischievous—
kings generally cause distress.
As far as their heat is concerned,
there is no difference between the funeral pyre
and the sacrificial fire of the householder.

नानभिभूताः प्रणतिं व्रजन्ति विजिगीषवः प्रकृतिरेषा ।
संतप्तानि हुतभुजा लोहैर्लोहानि संदधते ॥ १५७ ॥

157. Those who wish to be victorious
do not bow unless they are defeated—this is their nature.
Only after it has been made red-hot
iron unites with iron.

अर्थश्रुतबलवानपि न जहाति खलः परोपघातित्वम् ।
मणिरचितखचितकोशः किं परहिंसां त्यजति खड्गः ॥ १६३ ॥

163. Even when he possesses wealth, erudition and power
the wicked does not abstain from harming others.
Does the sword abstain from hurting others
when its sheath is made of, and studded with, jewels?

गृह्णन्त्यपास्य दोषान्प्राज्ञा गुणमेव दोषवद्भ्यो ऽपि ।
विषकुसुमेभ्यो ऽप्यलयः पिबन्ति मध्वेव न कषायम् ॥ १६५ ॥

165. Even from those who are full of faults
the wise adopt only (their) virtues, ignoring (their) faults.
Even from poisonous flowers
the bees drink only the honey and not what is astringent.

समसंहिता हिता अप्यहिताय भवन्ति भूभृतां भृत्याः ।
पथ्ये ऽपि *समं विधृते सर्पिर्मधुनी विषीभवतः ॥ १६७ ॥

167. When the servants of a king unite themselves
this will be detrimental for the kings,
even if the [servants] are useful
[when they are employed individually].
Although they are wholesome [if taken separately],
clarified butter and honey, is [taken] together, turn into poison.

विद्यामपि दुष्प्राज्ञाः प्रायः परपरिभवाय शिक्षन्ते ।
यमघण्टा किल जगतां त्रासायैवानिशं रणति ॥ १६८ ॥

168. Generally those of poor wisdom acquire even knowledge
with a view to do harm to others.
As it is known, Yama's gong sounds permanently
with the sole purpose of frightening people.

तुच्छक एवाल्पतया गहने जीर्णोदपानवद्भवति ।
अत्युत्तानो जलधिः प्रकृतिमहत्त्वादगाधो ऽपि ॥ १७० ॥

170. He who is utterly shallow
becomes [as useless] as an old well
because he is [so] limited in depth.
Although fathomless, the ocean is extremely wide (generous)
because it is great by nature.

मुनयो ऽपि न प्रसादं जनयन्ति पदे स्थितस्य शठवृत्तेः ।
पीनसशीतज्वरिणाश्चन्दनपङ्केन किं कृत्यम् ॥ १७३ ॥

173. Even Munis cannot make a wicked person friendly
that has been placed in a [high] position.
What is the use of sandal paste for those
who suffer from fever caused by catarrh or influenza?

शत्रुगुणानपि साधोः श्रुत्वा संवृण्वतो ऽपि तत्प्रीतिम् ।
स्फुरतीमन्तः कथयति सास्रो रोमाङ्कुरोद्भेदः ॥ १७४ ॥

174. The bristling of his fine body hairs, accompanied by tears,
betrays the inner pleasure of the good person,
which bursts forth despite his attempts at hiding it,
when he hears of the virtues of even an enemy.

शक्यं बहु विज्ञातुं संपादयितुं च दुष्करं क्रियया ।
यावत्पश्यति चक्षुः तावन्न स्पर्शनं स्पृशति ॥ १७८ ॥

178. While it is possible to understand much,
it is very difficult to accomplish it by a deed.
The tactile organ is not able to feel that much
as the eye is able to behold.

विभवविकलादपि जनाच्चित्तदरिद्रो ऽसुखी सदाढ्यो ऽपि ।
अन्तःखेदाद्ग्रीष्मे सुतरां करिणः प्रतप्यन्ते ॥ १७९ ॥

179. He who is poor in his heart, even if he is wealthy,
is always unhappier than even the destitute.
On account of their inner dejection (fatigue)
elephants feel even more inner pain in the summer.

लघुनि लघवः समर्था गुरुकार्ये गुरव एव कर्तुमलम् ।
हन्ति रजो ऽवश्यायस्तर्पयति घनागमः पृथिवीम् ॥ १८० ॥

180. People of minor abilities
are capable of doing [only] minor things,
while only important persons are able to do important things.
While the hoar-frost kills [only] dust,
the arrival of the clouds nourishes the [whole] earth.

व्यसनेनैव महान्तो दानमयेनाप्नुवन्ति गुणनिष्ठाम् ।
रागेणैवाभिहता व्रजन्ति सहकारतां चूताः ॥ १८१ ॥

181. Only by that kind of assiduous devotion
that consists of generosity
do the great acquire the perfection of their virtues.
Only when they are hit by redness (passion)
do the mango-trees (arrows of the god of love)
become [real] mango-trees (really effective).

किंचित्कस्यचिदिष्टं नैकं सर्वस्य जगति विश्वरुचौ ।
स्पृहयति कमलं रवये कुमुदाय तु रोचते चन्द्रः ॥ १८२ ॥

182. Something is desirable [only] for somebody,
but there is not a single thing that is desirable for everybody
in this world which has a longing for everything. (?)
The *Kamala* lotus longs for the sun,
but it is the moon that pleases the water-lily.

कुशलैः प्रसादिता अपि सन्तः कलुषाः क्षणादिरज्यन्ते ।
निर्मार्जितमपि ताम्रं पुनरपि हि मलेन संव्रियते ॥ १८३ ॥

183. Even when they have been pleased for a while by good people
the wicked become displeased [again] within a second.
Even after it has been polished
copper becomes again covered by impurities.

चिरमवकाशं लभते न मनःसु महात्मनां पराकृतम् ।
एकनिशामपि कुणपेन साकमुदधिर्न संवसति ॥ १८४ ॥

184. Harm done by others does not find room in the hearts
of the noble-minded for a long time.
The ocean does not live together
with a corpse even for a single night.

उत्प्राश्य वञ्च्यमानो ऽपि वातिकैर्नावबुध्यते लोकः ।
गीतैः प्रलोभ्य मृगयुभिरद्यापि मृगा निहन्यन्ते ॥ १८५ ॥

185. Although people have been deceived by flatterers
with loud burst of laughter, they do not recognize it.
Even nowadays the deer is killed by hunters
after it has been enticed by their songs.

अश्रुतवतश्च महतः प्रकृतिलघोः श्रुतवतश्च वरमाद्यः ।
परशुर्वनानि वृश्चति रोमेषु निशितः क्षुरो बलवान् ॥ १८९ ॥

189. If one compares a great person without learning
and a learned person that is frivolous,
then the former is to be preferred.
While the axe cuts forest trees
a knife is strong only in cutting hair.

मुक्त्वोपतापमेकं सुहृदो ऽप्यन्यत्करोति किमनार्यः ।
कुणपस्याशुचिविषमाद्गन्धो ऽन्यः कीदृशो भवति ॥ १९० ॥

190. What else can an ignoble person do even to a friend
other than tormenting?
What else can the smell of a corpse be like
than impure and disgusting?

न परस्य घातमुज्झन्ति दुर्जनाः कृच्छ्रमनुभवन्तो ऽपि ।
निर्वाति काममग्निर्न तु निजमौष्ण्यं परित्यजति ॥ १९१ ॥

191. Even when they experience hardship
bad people do not abstain from harming others.
A fire may become extinguished,
but it will never abandon its inborn heat.

व्यसनैर्जितान्तरात्मनि विनयकथाः स्थानमेव न लभन्ते ।
नीलीरक्ते वाससि कुङ्कुमरागो दुराधानः ॥ १९२ ॥

192. Instructions about modest behaviour
will never take hold in him
whose inner self is dominated by evil passions.
The yellow colour of saffron is unable
to penetrate a garment which has been dyed with a dark colour.

पीडयति परमवश्यं सर्वो ऽपि महान्हितप्रवृत्तो ऽपि ।
ह्लादयति लोकमपहृत्य तिमिरभयमेक एव शशी ॥ १९५ ॥

195. Every great person necessarily torments others,
even when he aims at their benefit. (?)
It is alone the moon who removes the fear of darkness
and thereby gladdens people.

राज्ञि प्रसादवत्यपि विश्वासो नानुजीविनां क्षमते ।
पानक्षीबाः शङ्कां जनयन्त्यभिवादयन्तो ऽपि ॥ १९६ ॥

196. Even when the king is gracious
it is not appropriate for his entourage to trust him.
Even if they greet friendly
drunkards create fear.

प्रकृतेः सुकुमारतया सन्तः परसंपदापि मोदन्ते ।
निर्मार्जनेन नखानां नयनान्यधिकं प्रसीदन्ति ॥ १९७ ॥

197. Because of their tender nature
the good are happy even about the welfare of others.
By polishing (or: removing) one's nails
the eyes become particularly friendly. (?)

मेरुमृगराजलुब्धकवराहपरपुष्टशिखिजलवृकेभ्यः ।
वाजिनराश्वावितमःकितवस्त्रीभ्यश्च शिक्षेत ॥ १९९ ॥

199. One should learn [even] from mount Meru, from lions,
hunters, boars, cuckoos, peacocks, prawns,
steeds (arrows?), men, horses, goats, darkness,
gamblers (rogues) and women!

प्रतिपादिता अपि शठा वक्रतया न स्वदृष्टिमुज्झन्ति ।
कण्टकवंशश्छिन्नो ऽपि वेणुमध्याद्दुराकर्षः ॥ २०१ ॥

201. The wicked, even when they have been taught (?),
do not abandon their own view because of their crookedness.
A thorny cane, even if it has been cut,
is difficult to drag out from a bamboo-[grove].

मृगतृष्णिका खलश्रीः श्रुतमसतां त्रिदुलवृक्षकुसुमानि ।
कृपणानां च समृद्धिः किमपेक्ष्य कृताः कृतान्तेन ॥ २०२ ॥

202. A mirage, the welfare of a wicked person,
the learning of evil people, the flowers of the ratan-tree,
the wealth of the miser—
with what in mind were they created by the God of Death?

द्वावेव निर्विभाव्यं कुर्वति परहितं स्वदुःखे ऽपि ।
यश्चातिजडो गौरिव यो वा पारं गतो बुद्धेः ॥ २०३ ॥

203. Only these two accomplish the welfare of others
without hesitation, even at the cost of their own suffering:
he who is extremely dull like an ox
or he who has reached the peak of wisdom.

नित्यं परोपकरणा लोके मूर्खाश्च शुद्धमतयश्च ।
एतावांस्तु विशेषो मोहादेको ऽपरो कृपया ॥ २०४ ॥

204. Both fools and people of pure heart
permanently work for the welfare of others.
There is, however, one great difference:
the first does it out of ignorance, the other out of compassion.

हेतोर्विनोपकारी यदि नाम शतेषु कश्चिदेकः स्यात् ।
तत्रापि निकृष्टधियां दोषविवक्षेत्यतिखलत्वम् ॥ २०५ ॥

205. If there were only one among a hundred
who helps others without an [egoistic] motive!
It is the greatest fault of the wicked-minded
that they are keen on mentioning the faults [of others].

तावद् बलिनो दोषा यावदमी साधु नाभियुज्यन्ते ।
अभियुक्तकातरेभ्यः क्लेशेभ्यो मा बिभीत बुधाः ॥ २०७ ॥

207. The faults are as long powerful
as they are not properly attacked.
O wise ones, do not be afraid of those defilements
which become powerless when attacked!

प्रज्ञाग्नौ संतप्तः क्लेशानुशयोपलः समाधिजले ।
क्षिप्तो गतश्च शतधा सुधोपल इवाम्बुनिक्षिप्तः ॥ २०८ ॥

208. When the stone «the propensity towards defilements»
has been heated in the fire of wisdom
and is then thrown into the water of meditation
it splits into hundred pieces—
like a [heated] brick which has been thrown into water.

साध्यमपि नोत्सहन्ते साधयितुं प्रतिहता असाध्येषु ।
अश्मनि विकुण्ठितो ऽसिः कदलीमपि यत्नतश्छिन्द्यात् ॥ २०९ ॥

209. Those who have failed
when they attempted something that is impossible
will not accomplish even what is possible.
The sword which has been blunted on a stone
cuts even the plantain tree [only] with great effort.

आगमशुद्धौ गुणवांश्चाप इवाकृष्यते सुखं साधुः ।
काममपर्वणि नश्यति मुसल इव खलो न चानमति ॥ २१० ॥

210. A good person, who is of pure descent
and virtuous, is easily attracted
like a (good) bow (that is of pure origin
and endowed with a string is easily bent.)
The wicked, however, perishes at the improper time
and does not bow, like a club, that breaks at the wrong place.

यत् प्रज्ञयैव साध्यं ना व्यापारो ऽस्ति तत्र शास्त्राणाम् ।
केशाकेशि रणमुखे निष्फललघवो भवन्ति शराः ॥ २११ ॥

211. When something can be accomplished only by wisdom
then there is no need to study textbooks.
In the middle of a battle when one pulls each other by the hairs
arrows become useless and unimportant.

येनैव यत्सुसाध्यं श्रेयांस्तस्यैव तत्र विनियोगः ।
भेदे शक्ताः इषवश्छेदे त्वसयो नियुज्यन्ते ॥ २१२ ॥

212. Whereby something can be accomplished easily,
exactly that is the best to be used in such a case.
Arrows are capable of splitting (piercing) something,
while swords are used to cut something.

अापदि धर्मार्थदृढैः स्वास्थ्ये सुखशीलिभिः सहासीत ।
अन्नायत्ताः प्राणाः क्रीडा फलमङ्गरागस्य ॥ २२५ ॥

225. In the time of distress stay together with those who are firm
in the fields of righteousness and acquisition,
when you are healthy, with those who are devoted to happiness.
Life depends of food,
while playfulness is the fruit of the body's passion.

स्थिरमेकमेव दैवं मित्रामित्रत्वमनियतं प्रायः ।
जीयते यैरेव जनस्तैरेवाक्षैः पुनर्जयति ॥ २२९ ॥

229. Solely one's own fate is stable;
friendship and enmity are usually not lasting.
By the same dices by which men are defeated
they become victorious again.

बालतयैव जनोऽयं वैषम्यं कुटिलतां च दर्शयति ।
परिपूर्णस्तु कलाभिर्भवति समश्चन्द्र इव सर्वः ॥ २३० ॥

230. It is only because of his stupidity (waxing state)
that this man displays harshness (unevenness) and crookedness.
Fully developed, however, in his skills (digits),
he becomes complete and even like the moon.

धूर्ता एव शठानां छन्ना उपलक्षयन्ति दुष्प्रकृतीः ।
व्यवहितभणितस्यार्थं नो बन्धक्यो विजानन्ति ॥ २३१ ॥

231. Only the rogues notice
the hidden bad nature of the wicked.
Don't the courtesans understand
the meaning of hidden speech?

दोषा एव खलानां पाटवमादधति पापचर्यासु ।
आदर्शेषु फणभृतां कोपं विषमेव दीपयति ॥ २३५ ॥

235. Only the faults create the skill
of the wicked in committing bad deeds.
It is only the poison of the snakes
which instigates their anger against in mirrors.

परदोषैरेव सतां प्रायः प्रकटीभवन्ति *चैव खलाः ।
शशमभिसमीक्ष्य लोकः सकलङ्कमुदाहरति चन्द्रम् ॥ २३६ ॥

236. Only by other faults of the good
the wicked generally become visible. (?)
When the people see the hare [in the moon]
the people call the moon spotted.

यद्यपि नश्यति दैवात् स्नेहः साधोस्तथापि सत्त्वेषु ।
घण्टाध्वनेरिवान्तश्चिरमनुबध्नाति संस्कारः ॥ २३९ ॥

239. "Even when fate cuts short
a good man's love
its impression carries on in men
like a bell's reverberation." (INGALLS)

खलमुन्नमय्य मूढा महतस्तिरयन्ति यत्नतश्चित्रम् ।
किं नाभिभूय शशिनं घनयन्ति घनास्तिमिरमेव ॥ २४३ ॥

243. It is not strange that fools, while they raise the wicked,
with great effort obscure the great.
Don't the clouds obscure the moon,
thereby increasing only darkness?

अन्ध इवाज्ञो ज्ञेयः स्फुटदृश इव संशयो न कृतबुद्धेः ।
प्रायेण रूपजातिषु तिमिरका एव विदधन्ते ॥ २५४ ॥

254. One should know that an ignorant person
is like a blind person.
A learned person has no doubts like someone
whose eyes are sharp.
Generally only someone suffering from an eye-disease (*timiraka*)
errs with regard to the [different] categories of form. (?)

शक्तिरभिभवति परबलमुद्धतमपि नयवतो वपुरतन्त्रम् ।
व्याघ्रमपि यया विध्यति दंष्ट्रा कियती वराहस्य ॥ २५५ ॥

255. [Mere] force defeats the army of opponent,
who knows the right strategy, even if it is haughty,
if its body lacks regular order (*vapur-atantram*). (?)
How strong are the fangs to the boar
by which it even pierces the tiger?

साधुजन एव कृच्छ्रे गतिः सतां भवति पाणिपादमिव ।
केशनखा इव तु खला विकार एवोपयुज्यन्ते ॥ २५६ ॥

256. The good become the shelter for the good,
who are in a plight, like hands and feet.
The wicked, however, are good only for distortion,
like hair and nails.

दण्डः प्रतापमात्रं प्रभोः प्रसिद्धौ तु मन्त्र एवालम् ।
कृशयति तपः शरीरं प्रज्ञैव मनो विशोधयति ॥ २५८ ॥

258. The only purpose of punishment
is to show the power of the lord;
for the success clever strategy alone is sufficient.
Mortification emaciates the body,
wisdom alone purifies the heart.

जिनशास्त्रेष्वपि सत्सु प्रतिपादनकौशलं न सर्वेषाम् ।
लावण्यमन्यदन्यो विज्ञानगुणः पुरन्ध्रीणाम् ॥ २५९ ॥

259. Although there are the teachings of the Victorious One,
not everybody has the skill to put them into practice.
Attractiveness [of young women] is one thing,
another is the quality of discrimination
of elderly married women.

साधुषु विनापि हेतोः स्वदोषमदिराः खलाः प्रमाद्यन्ति ।
रुधिरं किलात्र शोभन इति शबरा घ्नन्ति पाशुपतान् ॥ २६० ॥

260. Without the slightest reason the wicked,
intoxicated by their own faults,
are negligent towards the good.
'As it is known blood can here be used for decoration'—
thinking this the Śabaras kill the followers of Śiva.

तेजः क्व चित् प्रशस्तं शमस्तु सर्वत्र शस्यते तज्ज्ञैः ।
कठिनीकरोति हुतभुग्जलमेव मृदं मृदूकुरुते ॥ २६१ ॥

261. [The use of] power is recommended at some occasions,
tranquillity is recommended everywhere by the wise.
While fire hardens clay,
only water has the ability to make clay soft and flexible.

इच्छति यस्तोषयितुं न्यायानुगतैः सुभाषितैरबुधम् ।
अकृतद्वारेण बहिर्नूनमसौ सलिलमुत्किरति ॥ २६३ ॥

263. He who wishes to please an ignorant person
by sententious sayings that are full of logic
certainly pours out water in the courtyard
without having opened the door before.

सुजनो न याति विकृतिं परहितबुद्धिर्विनाशकाले ऽपि ।
छेदे ऽपि चन्दनतरुः सुरभयति मुखं कुठारस्य ॥ २६४ ॥

264. A good person, who is intent on the welfare of others,
does not change [his attitude],
even if this will cost his life.
Even when the sandal-tree is cut,
it makes the edge of the axe fragrant.

न पठ्यते साधुजनैर्न सेव्यते न चिन्त्यते संसदि वक्तुमिष्यते ।
तथाविधा नामत एव भारती दरिद्रलीलेव भृशं न रोचते ॥ २६५ ॥

265. That speech which is neither read by good people,
nor followed, nor considered to be recited in an assembly,
is regarded only a speech by name;
like the charm of poor people it does not shine much.

केनाञ्जितानि नयनानि मृगाङ्गनानां कश्चोत्पलेषु दलसंहतिमाचिनोति ।
को वा करोति रुचिराङ्गरुहान्मयूरान्को वा ददाति विनयं हि कुलोद्गतानाम् ॥ २६८ ॥

268. "Who has applied collyrium to the eyes of does?
Who makes the tails of peacocks so charming?
Who assembles, so attractively, the petals of lilies?
Who makes men of noble families possessed of modesty?" (A.A.R.)

Concordance
Lsp / ĀK

Lsp	ĀK	Lsp	ĀK	Lsp	ĀK	Lsp	ĀK	Lsp	ĀK
1	1	**31**	25	**61**	53	**91**	–	**121**	–
2	–	**32**	26	**62**	–	**92**	43	**122**	65
3	2	**33**	–	**63**	–	**93ab**	56ab	**123**	–
4	3	**34**	27	**64**	54	**94cd**	56cd	**124**	66
5	4	**35**	28	**65**	–	**95**	–	**125**	67
6	–	**36**	29	**66**	55	**96**	57	**126**	–
7	5	**37**	30	**67**	33	**97**	–	**127**	68
8	6	**38**	–	**68**	–	**98**	–	**128**	–
9	7	**39**	31	**69**	–	**99**	–	**129**	–
10	8	**40**	32	**70**	34	**100**	–	**130**	69
11	9	**41**	–	**71**	–	**101**	–	**131**	–
12	–	**42**	44	**72**	35	**102**	58	**132**	70
13	10	**43**	45	**73**	36	**103**	59	**133**	–
14	11	**44**	46	**74**	37	**104**	60	**134**	71
15	12	**45**	–	**75**	38	**105**	–	**135**	–
16	13	**46**	–	**76**	–	**106**	–	**136**	72
17	–	**47**	–	**77**	–	**107**	–	**137**	–
18	14	**48**	–	**78**	–	**108**	61	**138**	–
19	–	**49**	47	**79**	39	**109**	–	**139**	73
20	15	**50**	48	**80**	–	**110**	–	**140**	–
21	16	**51**	–	**81**	–	**111**	–	**141**	74
22	17	**52**	49	**82**	–	**112**	–	**142**	–
23	18	**53**	50	**83**	40	**113**	–	**143**	75
24	19	**54**	51	**84**	–	**114**	62	**144**	76
25	20	**55**	–	**85**	41	**115**	63	**145**	77
26	21	**56**	–	**86**	42	**116**	–	**146**	78
27	22	**57**	–	**87**	–	**117**	–	**147**	79
28	–	**58**	–	**88**	–	**118**	–	**148**	80
29	23	**59**	–	**89**	–	**119**	–	**149**	81
30	24	**60**	52	**90**	–	**120**	64	**150**	–

151	–	**175**	95	**199**	–	**223**	116	**247**	132
152	82	**176**	96	**200**	104	**224**	117	**248**	133
153	–	**177**	97	**201**	–	**225**	–	**249**	135
154	83	**178**	–	**202**	–	**226**	118	**250**	136
155	84	**179**	–	**203**	–	**227**	119	**251**	137
156	–	**180**	–	**204**	–	**228**	120	**252**	138
157	–	**181**	–	**205**	–	**229**	–	**253**	139
158	85	**182**	–	**206**	105	**230**	–	**254**	–
159	86	**183**	–	**207**	–	**231**	–	**255**	–
160	87	**184**	–	**208**	–	**232**	121	**256**	–
161	88	**185**	–	**209**	–	**233**	123	**257**	140
162	89	**186**	98	**210**	–	**234**	122	**258**	–
163	–	**187**	99	**211**	–	**235**	–	**259**	–
164	90	**188**	100	**212**	–	**236**	–	**260**	–
165	–	**189**	–	**213**	106	**237**	124	**261**	–
166	91	**190**	–	**214**	107	**238**	125	**262**	141
167	–	**191**	–	**215**	108	**239**	–	**263**	–
168	–	**192**	–	**216**	109	**240**	126	**264**	–
169	92	**193**	101	**217**	110	**241**	127	**265**	–
170	–	**194**	102	**218**	111	**242**	128	**266**	144
171	93	**195**	–	**219**	114	**243**	–	**267**	145
172	94	**196**	–	**220**	115	**244**	129	**268**	–
173	–	**197**	–	**221**	112	**245**	130		
174	–	**198**	103	**222**	113	**246**	131		

Stanzas from various collections

अकृतप्रेमैव वरं न पुनः संजातविघ्नितप्रेमा ।
उद्धृतनयनो हि यथा ताम्यत्येव न जात्यन्धः ॥ १ ॥ = 269

A 1. “Better never to have loved
than to break a love that’s grown;
as one blind is tortured less
than one whose eyes are gouged.” (D. H. H. Ingalls)

अण्वपि गुणाय महतां महदपि दोषाय दोषिणां सुकृतम् ।
तृणमपि दुग्धाय गवां दुग्धमपि विषाय सर्पाणाम् ॥ २ ॥ = 270

A 2. “Even the smallest element of the great are beneficial
whereas even a big thing associated with the impure is harmful.
Even grass contributes to the production of the (good) milk
whereas even milk is for producing poison in serpents.” (A. A. R.)

अन्त्यावस्थो ऽपि बुधः स्वगुणं न जहाति जातिशुद्धतया ।
न श्वेतभावमुज्झति शङ्खः शिखिभुक्तमुक्तो ऽपि ॥ ३ ॥ = 271

A 3. A wise man does not leave off his good qualities,
though reduced to the last extremity (of death),
because of the purity of his birth.
A conch does not abandon its whiteness
though it is released after being swallowed by fire.

अप्यात्मनो विनाशं गणयति न खलः परव्यसनहृष्टः ।
प्रायः सहस्रनाशे समरमुखे नृत्यति कबन्धः ॥ ४ ॥ = 272

A 4. “A wicked person gloating over the misfortunes of others
minds not his own destruction (downfall).
Generally, in the thick of the battle,
the headless trunk dances
though it has its head cut off.” (A. A. R.)

अविधेयो भृत्यजनः शठानि मित्राण्यदायकः स्वामी ।
विनयरहिता च भार्या मस्तकशूलानि चत्वारि ॥ ५ ॥ = 273

A 5. "These four are head-aches to a person:
a servant who is not amenable,
false friends, a parsimonious employer,
and the wife who is without good manners
[respect for the husband]." (A. A. R.)

अव्यवसायिनमलसं दैवपरं पुरुषकारविहीनम् ।
वृद्धमिव पतिं कन्या नेच्छत्यवगूहितुं लक्ष्मी ॥ ६ ॥ = 274

A 6. "Be a man irresolute, slothful,
relying on fate, and without manly courage,
then Fortune is unwilling to embrace him,
as a charming woman her aged spouse." (F. EDGERTON)

आस्वाप्यात्मविनाशं गणयति न खलः परव्यसनकष्टम् ।
प्रायः सहस्रनाशे समरमुखे नृत्यति कबन्धः ॥ ७ ॥ = 275

A 7. "A wicked person cares not for the misrey of others' troubles,
though he himself may be involved in self-destruction;
generally, when a thousand people
are killed in the thick of a battle,
the headless trunk indulges in a dance." (A.A.R.)

काकतालीययोगेन यदनात्मवति क्षणम् ।
करोति प्रणयं लक्ष्मीस्तदस्याः स्त्रीत्वचापलम् ॥ ८ ॥ = 276

A 8. "If Lakṣmī (the Goddess of prosperity) (accidentally)
gets friendly with worthless people for a short period,
as per the maxim of 'the crow and the palm fruit',
it is only due to her fickle female nature." (A. A. R.)

कुसुमस्तबकस्येव द्वयी वृत्तिर्मनस्विनः ।
मूर्ध्नि वा सर्वलोकस्य शीर्येत वन एव वा ॥ ९ ॥ = 277

A 9. "For a man of self-respect, there are but two alternatives
in life, even as for a flower
wither to be at the head of all men
or to fade away in the forest." (K. V. SHARMA)

क्वचिदपि वस्तुविशेषे दोषो ऽपि गुणेन तुल्यतामेति ।
खण्डनमेव हि मण्डनमधरमणौ भवति रमणीनाम् ॥ १० ॥ = 278

A 10. In some very special subjects
even a fault can equal a virtue:
for it is only the fissures which form an ornament
at the jewel-like lips of enjoyable women.

ख्यातिं गणयति सुजनः सुकविर्विदधाति केवलं काव्यम् ।
पुष्णाति कमलमम्भो लक्ष्म्या तु रविर्विनियोजयति ॥ ११ ॥ = 279

A 11. A good person counts (only his good) reputation,
while a good poet creates only poetry.
The water lets the water-lily grow,
however the sun deprives it of its beauty.

गहनप्रसन्नसर्वां कतिपयसूत्रामिमामनन्तमुखीम् ।
अनधीत्याक्षरमुद्रां वादसमुद्रे परिप्लवते ॥ १२ ॥ = 280

A 12. He delves into the ocean of debates
without having previously studied this mudrā of letters
which is deep, clear and all-(comprising),
which includes various sūtras and has many mouths!

गुणवानस्मि विदेशः क इव ममेत्येष दुरभिमानलवः ।
अञ्जनमक्ष्णि विराजति विन्यस्तं न पुनरधरमणौ ॥ १२ अ ॥ = 281

A 12a. "I possess virtues, every foreign country belongs to me!"
To think this is a wrong piece of haughtiness.
Collyrium shines in the eye,
but not when applied to the jewel-like lip.

गुणैः सर्वज्ञकल्पोऽपि सीदत्येको निराश्रयः ।
अनर्घमपि माणिक्यं हेमाश्रयमपेक्षते ॥ १३ ॥ = 282

A 13. Even if he equals the omniscient by his virtues
he who is without support will sit there alone.
Even the most precious ruby
requires a setting made of gold.

चित्तरत्नमसंक्लिष्टमान्तरं धनमुच्यते ।
यस्य तद्दूषितं दोषैस्तस्य सर्वा विपत्तयः ॥ १४ ॥ = 283

A 14. A jewel-like mind which is free of defilements
is called an inner wealth.
He who has spoilt it by faults
will experience all kinds of misfortune.

जगन्नेत्रश्रेणी तिमिरहरसिद्धाञ्जनसखा
मयूखा यस्यैते त्रिभुवनममोघं विदधति ।
अये कर्मालङ्घ्यं कलय किमपीदं तनुभृताम्
उलूकानामन्धंकरणकिरणः सोऽम्बरमणिः ॥ १५ ॥ = 284

A 15. The row of the eyes of the world, (i.e., sun and moon),
has as its collyrium the Siddhas who remove (inner) darkness;
its rays grant success to the three worlds.
O unsurmountable karma of men, consider this a little bit! (?)
The rays of sun, this jewel in the sky, makes the owls blind. (?)

त्यजति भयमकृतपापो मित्राणि शठं प्रमादिनं विद्या ।
ह्रीः कामिनमलसं श्रीः स्त्री क्रूरं दुर्जनं लोकः ॥ १६ ॥ = 285

A 16. The sinless abandons fear,
the friends (abandon) the wicked one,
knowledge abandons the careless one, shame leaves the lover,
welfare leaves the lazy one, the wife the cruel one,
the world leaves the bad person.

दक्षः श्रियमधिगच्छति पथ्याशी कल्यतां सुखमरोगी ।
उद्युक्तो विद्यान्तं धर्मार्थयशांसि न विनीतः ॥ १७ ॥ = 286

A 17. The clever one attains welfare, he who eats wholesome food
attains healthiness, the healthy attains happiness,
the diligent one attains the end of knowledge,
the undisciplined does not attain righteousness, wealth and fame.

दोषो गुणाय गुणिनां महदपि दोषाय दोषिणां सुकृतम् ।
तृणमपि दुग्धाय गवां दुग्धमपि विषाय सर्पाणाम् ॥ १८ ॥ = 287

A 18. A fault becomes a virtue with the virtuous,
even a great good deed becomes a fault with the wicked.
Even grass becomes milk with the cows,
and even milk becomes poison with the serpents.

न केवलं मनुष्येषु दैवं देवेष्वपि प्रभुः ।
सति मित्रे धनाध्यक्षे चर्मप्रवारणो हरः ॥ १९ ॥ = 288

A 19. Fate is the master not only of mortals,
but even of the gods.
While Kubera, the Lord of Wealth, is his friend,
Śiva is clad in a tiger´s skin.

न भवति भवति च न चिरं भवति चिरं चेद्विसंवदति ।
कोपः सत्पुरुषाणां तुल्यः स्नेहेन नीचानाम् ॥ २० ॥ = 289

A 20. It does not occur, but if it occurs it does not last long,
and even if it lasts long it is not consistent
the anger of the good resembles
the love of the low.

मातर्धर्मपरे दयां मयि कुरु श्रान्ते ऽथ वैदेशिके
द्वारालिन्दककोणके ऽथ निभृतं यातास्मि सुप्त्वा निशि ।
इत्युक्त्वा सहसा प्रचण्डगृहिणीवाक्येन निर्भर्त्सितः
स्कन्धन्यस्तपलालमुष्टिविभवः पान्थः पुनः प्रस्थितः ॥ २१ ॥ = 290

A 21. "O mother, who you are devoted to righteousness,
pity me who I am an exhausted foreigner!
After having slept secretly in a corner of the courtyard
during night I will depart [in the morning]."
Having said this the wayfarer,
scolded harshly by the furious speech of the housewife,
again sets out, his wealth consisting of handful of straw
placed on his shoulders.

मृगमदकर्पूरागुरुचन्दनगन्धाधिवासितो लशुनः ।
न त्यजति गन्धमशुभं प्रकृतिमिव सहोत्थितां नीचः ॥ २२ ॥ = 291

A 22. Garlic, anointed with the smell of musk,
camphor, aloe or sandal wood
does not abandon its impure smell
as the low one does not abandon his inborn nature.

लब्धोदयो ऽपि हि खलः प्रथमं स्वजनं तनोति परितापम् ।
उद्गच्छन्दवदहनो जन्मभुवं दारु निर्दहति ॥ २३ ॥ = 292

A 23. A bad one, even if he has attained success,
will above all cause pain for his own people.
A rising forest-fire burns the wood,
which is the place of its origin.

सहवसतामप्यसतां जलरुहजलवद्भवत्यसंश्लेषः ।
दूरे ऽपि सतां वसतां प्रीतिः कुमुदेन्दुवद्भवति ॥ २४ ॥ = 293

A 24. There is no contact with the bad, even if they are near,
as in the case of the lotus and water,
but rejoices in the good, even if they live far away,
as in the case of the night-lotus and the moon.

Sources

A1 VS 1389, MSS 95, SkV 805
A2 Dvi 104, MSS 498, Subh 276, IS 122, JS 6.13
A3 Pts 4.110, VS 243, MSS 1671
A4 JS 59.21, Pts 1.365, MSS 2139, ŚP 374
A5 VS 2850, MSS 3354, ŚP 1531
A6 PT 2.97, VS 2848, SS 3433
A7 VS 412, MSS 4971
A8 JS 417.4, VS 2675, MSS 9295, ŚP 1435
A9 CR 3.12, Bhś 34, VS 201, cf. also PD 26,
A10 VS 2863, JS 110.35
A11 VS 154
A12 Jmv, pp. 59–60
A12a VS 2877, SRh 163.142, JS 110.37
A13 VS 2683
A14 JS 110.13
A15 Śuka 1660
A16 VS 2847
A17 VS 2849
A18 VS 237
A19 VS 3111
A20 VS 236
A21 JS 96.3, VS 2416
A22 VS 415
A23 VS 395
A24 VS 399

Abbreviations

A. A. R.	A. A. RAMANATHAN of the Adyar Library and Research Centre (the translator of those stanzas in MSS for which no English translation existed)
AIG	*Altindische Grammatik*, WACKERNAGEL/DEBRUNNER 1896–1957
ĀK	Ravigupta's *Āryākoṣa*
ĀKtib	Ravigupta's *Āryākoṣa*, Tibetan version
APTE	*The Practical Sanskrit-English Dictionary*, APTE 1957
C	*Bstan 'gyur*, Co-ne edition
CNTT	*Cāṇakya-Nīti-Text-Tradition*, STERNBACH 1963–70
CR	*Cāṇakyarājanītiśāstra*, as contained in CNTT
D	*Bstan 'gyur*, Sde-dge edition
G	*Bstan 'gyur*, Dga'-ldan edition
H	Ravigupta's *Lokasaṃvyavahārapravṛtti*, HAHN 2007–08
IS^2	*Indische Sprüche*, BÖHTLINGK 1870–73
JS	Jalhaṇa's *Sūktimuktāvalī*, KRISHNAMACHARYA 1938
LC	*Tibetan-Sanskrit Dictionary*, LOKESH CHANDRA 1959–61
LC^2	*Tibetan-Sanskrit Dictionary. Supplementary volumes*, LOKESH CHANDRA 1992–94
LSP	Ravigupta's *Lokasaṃvyavahārapravṛtti*, HAHN 2007–08; other ed.: ŚĀHA 1986
MSS	*Mahāsubhāṣitasaṃgraha*, STERNBACH 1974–99
N	*Bstan 'gyur*, Snar-thaṅ edition
PD	Pseudo-Nāgārjuna's *Prajñādaṇḍa*, HAHN 2009–11
PT	*Tantrākhyāyikā*, HERTEL 1904
Pts	*Pañcatantra*, KIELHORN/BÜHLER 1881–86
Q	*Bstan 'gyur*, Beijing edition
S	Ravigupta's *Lokasaṃvyavahārapravṛtti*, ŚĀHA 1986
ŚP	*Śārṅgadharapaddhati*, PETERSON 1888
SRBh	*Subhāṣitaratnabhāṇḍāgāra*, ĀCĀRYA 1952

SRh	Kaliṅgarāya Sūrya's *Sūktiratnahāra*, Śāstrī 1938
Subh	*Subhāṣitārṇava*, as quoted in IS
VS	Vallabhadeva's *Subhāṣitāvalī*, Peterson 1886

Bibliography

Ācārya, Nārāyaṇa Rām (ed.), *Subhāṣita-Ratna-Bhāṇḍāgāra or Gems of Sanskrit poetry. Being a collection of witty, epigrammatic, instructive and descriptive verses with their sources*, Bombay, Nirṇaya Sagar Press 1952.

Apte, Vaman Shivaram, *The Practical Sanskrit-English Dictionary*, rev. and enl. ed., 3 vols., Poona: Prasad Prakashan, 1957–9.

Balk, Michael (ed.), *Prajñāvarman's Udānavargavivaraṇa. Transliteration of its Tibetan version, based on the xylographs of Chone/Derge and Peking*, 2 vols., Bonn: Indica et Tibetica 1984.

Banerji, Sures Chandra (ed.), *Saduktikarṇāmṛta of Śrīdharadāsa,* Calcutta: Mukhopadhyay, 1965.

Beresford, Brian C. et al. (ed., tr.), *Āryaśūra's Aspiration. With Commentary by Gendun Gyatso, the 2nd Dalai Lama, and A Meditation on Compassion, from a Discourse by His Holiness the 14th Dalai Lama together with a Sādhana of Avalokiteśvara with Original Tibetan Texts*, Dharamsala: Translation Bureau of the Library of Tibetan Works and Archives, 1979.

Böhtlingk, Otto von (ed., tr.), *Indische Sprüche. Sanskrit und Deutsch*, 2nd ed., 3 vols., St. Peterburg: Eggers / Riga: Kymmel / Leipzig: Voss, 1870–3.

Bosson, James E. (ed., tr.), *A treasury of aphoristic jewels. The Subhāṣītaratnanidhi of Sa Skya Paṇḍita in Tibetan and Mongolian*, Bloomington, Ind.: Indiana University publications, 1969 (Uralic and Altaic series 92).

Botto, Oscar, "L'Upadeśaśataka di Gumāni," *Rivista degli studi orientali* 27,1 (1952), 93–110.

Dange, Sadashiv Ambadas, *Encyclopaedia of Puranic beliefs and practices*, 5 vols. New Delhi: Navrang, 1986–90.

Dvivedī, Revāprasāda (ed.), *Kālidāsa granthāvalī. Complete works of Kālidāsa*, 2nd rev. ed., Varanasi: Banaras Hindu Univ., 1986.

Edgerton, Franklin (tr.), *The Panchatantra*, London: Allen & Unwin, 1965.

Ensink, Jacob (ed.), *The question of Rāṣṭrapāla*, Zwolle: Tijl, 1952.

Hahn, Michael (ed., tr.), *Jñānaśrīmitras Vṛttamālāstuti. Eine Beispielsammlung zur altindischen Metrik.* Nach dem tibetischen Tanjur zusammen mit der mongolischen Version herausgegeben, übersetzt und erläutert. Wiesbaden: Harrassowitz, 1971 (Asiatische Forschungen 33).

– *Lehrbuch der klassischen tibetischen Schriftsprache*, 7., korr. Aufl., Swisttal-Odendorf: Indica et Tibetica, 1996.

— (ed., tr.) "Ravigupta and his Nīti Stanzas", *Minami Ajia Kotengaku* (= *South Asian Classical Studies*) [Kyūshū University, Department of Indology], 2 parts, I: 2 (2007), pp. 303–355; II: 3 (2008), pp. 1–38.

— (ed., tr.) "The Tibetan Shes rab sdong bu and its Indian Sources," *Minami Ajia Kotengaku* (= *South Asian Classical Studies*) 3 parts, I: 4 (2009), pp. 1–78; II: 5 (2010), pp. 1–50; III: 6 (2011), pp. 1–71.

— (ed., tr.) "Vararuci's *Gāthāśataka*," *Minami Ajia Kotengaku* (= *South Asian Classical Studies*) 7 (2012), pp. 367–458.

HERTEL, Johannes (ed.), *Über das Tantrākhyāyika, die kasmirische Rezension des Pañcatantra. Mit dem Texte der Handschrift Decc. Coll. VIII,145*, Leipzig: Teubner, 1904 (Abhandlungen der Philologisch-Historischen Klasse der Königlich-Sächsischen Gesellschaft der Wissenschaften 22,5 / Abhandlungen der Königlich-Sächsischen Gesellschaft der Wissenschaften 50,5).

INGALLS, Daniel Henry Holmes (tr.), *An Anthology of Sanskrit Court Poetry. Vidyākara's Subhāṣitaratnakoṣa*, Cambridge, Mass.: Harvard Univ. Pr., 1965 (Harvard Oriental Series 44).

KALE, Moreshwar Ramchandra (tr.), *Ritusamhara of Kalidas*, Bombay: Vaman Yashwant & Co, 1916.

KIELHORN, Franz / BÜHLER, Georg (eds.), *Pañcatantra*, 5 vols., rev. ed., Bombay: Government Central Book Depôt, 1881–6 (Bombay Sanskrit Series 1, 3–4).

KOSAMBI, Damodar Dharmanand (ed.), *Śatakatrayādi-subhāṣitasaṅgrahaḥ. The epigrams attributed to Bhartrhari, including the Three centuries*, Bombay: Vidya Bhavan, 1948 (Singhi Jaina Granthamālā 23).

— / GOKHALE, V. V. (eds.), *The Subhāṣitaratnakoṣa composed by Vidyākara*, Cambridge, Mass.: Harvard Univ. Pr., 1957 (Harvard Oriental Series 42).

KRISHNAMACHARYA, Embar (ed.), *The Sūktimuktāvalī of Bhagadatta Jalhaṇa*, Baroda: Oriental Institute, 1938.

Limaye, Vishnu Prabhakar / Vadekar, R. D. (eds.), *Aṣṭādaśa upaniṣadaḥ / Eighteen principal Upaniṣads*, Gandhi memorial edition, Poona: Vaidika Saṃśodhana Maṇḍala, 1958.

Lindtner, Christian, "Mātṛceta's Praṇidhānasaptati", *Asiatische Studien*, 38 (1984), pp. 100–128.

Lokesh Chandra, *Bod dang legs sbyar kyi mdzod. Bhoṭa-saṃskṛtābhidhānam. Tibetan-Sanskrit Dictionary. Based on a close comparative study of Sanskrit originals and Tibetan translations of several texts*, New Delhi: International Academy of Indian Culture, 1959–61 (Bhoṭapiṭaka 1, Śatapiṭaka 3).

— *Tibetan-Sanskrit Dictionary. Supplementary volumes*, New Delhi: Aditya Prakashan, 1992–94 (Śatapiṭaka 368, 371–372, 374–375, 377–378).

Mani, Vettam, *Purāṇic encyclopaedia. A comprehensive dictionary with special reference to the epic and purāṇic literature*, 1st ed. in Engl., Delhi [etc.]: Motilal Banarsidas, 1975.

Peterson, Peter (ed.), *The Paddhati of Śārṅgadhara*, Bombay: Government Central Book Depôt, 1888 (Bombay Sanskrit and Prakrit Series 37).

— / Durgâprasâda (eds.), *The Subhâshitâvali of Vallabhadeva*, Bombay: Education Society's Pr., 1886.

Roerich, George N. (tr.), *The Blue Annals*, 2 vols., Calcutta: Asiatic Society of Bengal, 1949–53 (The Asiatic Society Monograph Series 7,1–2).

Śāha, Nīlāṃjanā (ed.), *Ācārya-Ravigupta-viracita-Lokasaṃvyavahāra-pravṛttiḥ*, Ahmedabad: Samvid S. Shah, 1986.

Śāstrī, Sāmbaśiva K. (ed.), *The Sūktiratnahāra*, Trivandrum 1938 (Trivandrum Sanskrit Series 141; Śrī Citrodayamañjarī 30).

Śāstrī, Vijayapāla (ed.), *Ācārya-Ravigupta-viracitā Lokasaṃvyavahārapravṛttiḥ. Ācārya Ravigupta dvārā racita sadācāra va Lokavyavahāra-sambandhī manohārī subhāṣita*, Balāhara: Rāṣṭrīyasaṃskṛtasthānam, 2012 (Vedayāsaparisara granthamālā 1).

Schmidt, Richard (ed.), *Die Çukasaptati. Textus simplicior*, Leipzig: Haeseler, 1893 (Abhandlungen für die Kunde des Morgenlandes 10,1).

— *Die Śukasaptati. Textus ornatior*, Stuttgart: Kohlhammer, 1899.

— *Śukasaptati. Das indische Papageienbuch*, München: Müller, 1913 (Meisterwerke orientalischer Literaturen in deutschen Originalübersetzungen 3).

STERNBACH, Ludwik (ed.), *Cāṇakya-Nīti-Text-Tradition. Six versions of Cāṇakya's collections of maxims, Cāṇakya-nīti-śākhā-sampradāyaḥ*, 5 vols., Hoshiarpur: Vishveshvaranand Vedic Research Inst., 1963–1970.

— (ed.), *Mahāsubhāṣitasaṃgraha. Being an extensive collection of wise sayings in Sanskrit*, 7 vols., Hoshiarpur: Vishveshvaranand Vedic Research Institute, 1974–1999.

SYED, Renate, *Die Flora Altindiens in Literatur und Kunst*, München: Selbstverlag, 1990

TAWNEY, Charles Henry (tr.), *Mālavikāgnimitra. A Sanskrit play*, Calcutta: Thacker, Spink and Co., 1875.

WACKERNAGEL, Jacob / DEBRUNNER, Alfred, *Altindische Grammatik*, 3 vols., Göttingen: Vandenhoeck & Ruprecht, 1896–1957.